THE

Michael Ball is J
Birkbeck College,

Fred Gray is Lecturer
University of Sussex,   the
university's adult educa.

Linda McDowell is Senior Lecturer in
Geography/Urban Studies at the Open
University.

22

THE TRANSFORMATION OF BRITAIN

Contemporary Social and Economic Change

Michael Ball, Fred Gray
and Linda McDowell

Fontana Press

First published in 1989 by Fontana Paperbacks
8 Grafton Street, London W1X 3LA

Copyright © Michael Ball, Fred Gray and Linda McDowell 1989

Set in Linotron Trump Mediaeval

Printed and bound in Great Britain by William Collins
Sons & Co. Ltd, Glasgow

Fontana Press is an imprint of Fontana Paperbacks,
part of the Collins Publishing Group

CONTENTS

LIST OF TABLES

vii

LIST OF FIGURES

ACKNOWLEDGEMENTS

The following tables and figures are reproduced with the permission of the Controller of Her Majesty's Stationery Office. *Tables: 2.1A, 3.1, 3.2, 3.4, 4.3B, 4.4, 4.5, 5.1, 6.1, 6.2, 6.3, 6.4A, 6.4B, 7.1, 7.2, 7.3, 7.4, 7.5, 7.6, 7.8, 8.1, 10.1, 10.2, 10.3, 10.4, 10.5, 10.6, 13.1, 13.2, 13.4, 13.6, 13.9; Figures: 3.1, 6.1, 6.2, 6.3, 6.4, 7.1, 7.2, 7.3, 7.4, 7.5, 7.6.*

The authors and publishers are also grateful to the following who gave permission to reproduce material contained in the tables and figures in this book. *Table 7.7*: P. Hedstron and S. Ringen 'Age and Income in contemporary society: a research note', *Journal of Social Policy*, 16, 1987; *Table 9.3*: OPCS and P.O. Goldblatt for material first published in M. Whitehead, *The Health Divide: Inequalities in Health in the 1980s*, Health Education Council, 1988; *Figure 11.1*: A. Belsey, 'The New Right, social order and civil liberties', in R. Levitas, ed., *The Ideology of the New Right*, Basil Blackwell, 1986; *Tables 14.1, 14.2, 14.3*: G. Routh, *Occupations of the People of Great Britain, 1801–1981*, Macmillan Press, 1987.

The authors and publishers would also like to thank: the Organization for Economic Cooperation and Development, Paris, for data from *OECD 1988/9 United Kingdom Economic Survey*; Cambridge University Press for permission to use material from A. Atkinson and A. Harrison, *Distribution of personal wealth in Britain*, D. Piachaud, 'Poverty in Britain 1899 to 1983', *Journal of Social Policy*, 1988, 17, 350–60, and R. Rowthorn and D. Wells, *Deindustrialization and foreign trade*; Oxford University Press for permission to use material from R. Matthews, C. Feinstein and J. Odling-Smee, *British Economic Growth, 1856–1973*, and for *World Bank Report, 1987*; Heinemann Educational Books for permission to use material from *The United Kingdom Economy*,

National Institute for Economic and Social Research; the
National Institute for Economic and Social Research for
permission to use material from 'Labour costs in manufacturing', G. Ray, *National Institute Review*, May, 1987,
71–4.

PREFACE

This book is an introductory text aimed at students and the general reader. For this reason, it uses a minimum of technical discussion and adopts a multidisciplinary approach.

One major objective has been to try to ease debate away from the narrowly political plane that dominates academic and media thinking about contemporary Britain. Assessment of the role of government, the impact of Thatcherism and any other of the wide variety of 'isms' depends on placing them in the context of broader forces in British society and the world at large. We feel such contextual features are often missing from debate. Their absence leads to views based on the idea that social change consists of a series of breaks with the past. Apart from being poor history, such perspectives leave little space for discussion of the options open to society. Ruptures posit a deterministic world in which there is no going back and only one way forward. Fortunately for democratic societies, reality is less brutal and unyielding.

We make no attempt to present our own visions of the future, nor to push a unitary analytical or political line. Facts do not speak for themselves; they have to be put into some theoretical format in order to be interpreted. In some cases the format is so commonplace that it is accepted without question. For controversial issues, however, part of the dispute may be over the ways in which information is presented. In such cases we have tried to highlight the major items of disagreement. We do not claim that our own discussion of the issues is a neutral one, but we have tried to present the information in a balanced form.

Conception of this book was the joint responsibility of all three authors, but for practical reasons we each wrote specific chapters. As a result each chapter has a named author.

A number of people generously gave of their time and advice during the preparation of this book. Specifically, we should like to thank John Allen, Fiona Atkins, Carol Gray, Lucia Hanmer, Michael Harloe, Ben Fine, Chris McDowell, and Ron Smith. None, of course, is responsible for the remaining errors. We should also like to thank John Hunt, social sciences cartographer at the Open University, for producing the figures.

1

The Transformation
of Britain?

COMMON GROUND

The usual habit of dividing recent history into distinct
decades is reinforced for the 1980s because of the
presence of one Prime Minister, Mrs Thatcher, throughout the period.

Everyone accepts that Britain in the late 1980s is not
the same as it was a decade earlier. The economy has
passed through its years of high inflation and crisis in the
1970s and early 1980s. By 1988, real growth had existed
for a number of years at levels not experienced since the
1960s. Most people had much higher standards of living
than a decade before, even if the wealthy few had gained
the most.

Not everyone has benefited from the economic transformation. Unemployment is a blackspot. Radical up-
heavals in the economy threw out of work large numbers
of manual workers in manufacturing industry. Few
employment alternatives exist for many of them. The
location, the skills and the educational requirements of
the glamorous new jobs are beyond their reach – as they
also are for many new entrants to the job market. The
low pay and poor working conditions of other new jobs
make them undesirable or impossible to accept if they
entail moving as well. Public provision has also deteriorated in key areas of health care, social security payments, housing and education, affecting both consumers

of those services and people working in them. Yet, at the same time, public expenditure in real terms has risen throughout the 1980s. By the end of 1988, balance-of-payments problems and fears of renewed inflation caused worry that the years of growth were about to end.

In parallel with economic change during the 1980s, the structure of society has altered as well. The elderly are increasing as a proportion of the population, raising anxieties about how to sustain living standards with fewer working people. Population movements put pressure on urban living space in South East England, where economic growth is concentrated. Other regions experienced the reverse side of migration – stagnation or decline. Anger at regional neglect, and the social problems associated with it, strengthened regional and local identities. Local government was one of the major political battlefields of the decade. The main union disputes of the 1980s often had a regional dimension as well, notably the long miners' strike of 1984–5. Schisms were also apparent in the inequalities experienced by ethnic minorities. The problems of Northern Ireland continued. So towards the end of the 1980s British society was in a number of key respects even more divided than a decade before. The response of government has been to centralise more power to itself.

New patterns of work had been established by the late 1980s. The long-term decline in manual jobs continued throughout the decade, while the number of non-manual jobs rose. Many of the new jobs were clerical or required a variety of acquired intellectual skills, like computer programming. The importance of women in the labour force grew. Part-time work expanded, and many people were self-employed or freelance.

Such shifts in employment patterns led to an argument that the traditional working class was disappearing. The electoral difficulties faced by the Labour Party were cited as additional evidence – as the party's core vote was shrinking. Arguments about the decline of the working

2

class had been raised before, particularly in notable debates at the end of the 1950s. Again they were associated with explanations of Labour's inability to win general elections.

What is distinct about late-1980s political debates is the idea that a new set of social beliefs dominate in Britain. Notions of collectivism are said to be on the wane, being replaced with beliefs about the efficacy of markets. Individual actions in markets are claimed to create both maximum personal satisfaction and the greatest common good. The idea of collective provision has been labelled as 'old-fashioned', while market-related individualism is 'new and exciting'. The labels are odd, because the idea of market individualism as the best motor of social change was refined during the eighteenth century by a series of innovative thinkers who were also excellent propagandists. The best-remembered one is, of course, Adam Smith (1776). The ideology of the market has a far greater acceptance than it did a decade or so ago – having governments who fervently believe in it and put a great deal effort into propaganda about it has helped considerably. Much debate about economic and social policy is now in relation to market-based arguments.

THE OPENING OF CONTENTION

A great deal of what has been said so far about Britain in the 1980s would be generally accepted as true. The narrative could be lengthened in a similar vein without too much difficulty. But controversy immediately arises over the reasons for change and their relative importance. To us it appears that discussion of the contemporary nature of British society is often coloured by particular views of the past and of the processes through which social and economic developments occur. These views often do not relate directly to the issue at hand but to broader generalisations about contemporary British society and its relation to its own past. They are not theories nor are they intended to be factually accurate; instead they are 'stylised generalisations' on which more specific analyses are based. Below we describe and comment on four common ones, highlighting that all have marked weaknesses. The four 'stylised generalisations' are simplifications, but a week's reading of the newspapers, listening to the radio and watching television would show them in abundance.

1. The radical break thesis

It is often argued that the 1980s constitute a radical break with earlier post-war decades. The origins of the rupture can be found in the political sphere, with the election of the Thatcher administrations and their subsequent implementation of New Right policies. Politicians are particularly fond of the radical break thesis. For them, 'Thatcherism' has changed the face of Britain for good or evil. But the argument is found elsewhere, as the survey in Chapter 12 shows.

One common explanation of the sharp political break is that previous post-war governments were dominated by ideologies of social consensus and equity, while the current government is not. Past Prime Ministers have added their weight to this view. Yet, although social harmony may have been more widely preached in the past, the practice of earlier post-war governments can hardly be said to have been dominated by it. Numerous examples of non-consensual politics can be found. Suez, Vietnam, persistent attempts to deal with the 'trade union problem', the 'three-day week' and the early 1970s miners' strikes, the 1979 'Winter of Discontent' were all interventions by governments that met with widespread opposition.

It could be said that the sharp break is really characterised by a government that has been prepared to stick to its strategy rather than bend at the first sign of major opposition. Yet here the evidence does not justify the claim. The Thatcher administrations have been highly pragmatic throughout the 1980s, dropping or downgrading policies which did not work and promoting those that offered greater success (see Chapter 12 for details). The wider circumstances in which government policies have existed have also been important. It is difficult to envisage the consequences of the economic policies of the first Thatcher administration if they had been implemented in 1973 prior to the first oil-price rise, but obviously they would not have been the same and the life of the government probably short.

A general problem with radical break theories is that they tend to isolate and highlight only limited aspects of society. Thatcherism emphasises governmental politics; at other times politics is combined with a wider social mood, as with the introduction of the welfare state after the Second World War or the Edwardian imperial 'twilight' prior to 1914. Broader understandings that avoid identifying an all-important rupture carry more conviction. In relation to the current situation, fundamental economic change has been taking place in Britain and elsewhere over the past twenty years. Its existence cannot be simply ascribed to government policy. Similarly, the welfare state has a much longer history than just the post-war years, and its remit has been influenced by wider forces than social moods, as social historians have pointed out (Fraser, 1973; Thane, 1982). Positing a radical break avoids having to examine those wider and complex interconnections.

Social and economic processes generally evolve more smoothly and continuously than claims of sharp ruptures with the past suggest. Current transformations of the economy cannot be understood without recognition of the previous specialised nature of the British economy. Yet, even in the economic sphere, radical breaks are posited, as with the idea that manufacturing has shifted from 'Fordist mass production' to 'neo-Fordist flexible specialisation' (see Chapter 6).

To suggest that there has been greater continuity is not to imply that there is no change nor that revolutionary ruptures cannot occur in societies. Russian society was radically changed after 1917, but that break has a qualitatively distinct status from developments in 1980s Britain. In fact, in terms of contrasting the 1980s with the 1970s, it would be just as easy and historically correct to say that the 1960s were different from the 1970s, the 1950s from the 1960s, and beyond in infinite regress. Demonstrating such shifts neither explains them nor provides a means through which to evaluate the aspects of change with the greatest importance. The radical break thesis oversimplifies processes of social transformation.

2. Golden Age ideologies

Golden Age ideologies suggest that at some time in the past 'they got it right'. Generally reference is made to idealised features of the past. The Thatcher governments have frequently praised the 'Victorian values' of family unity and self-reliance. Neil Kinnock for the Labour opposition prefers the post-1945 'caring' society that introduced the welfare state and full employment. Such views of the past, however, are usually justifications for a person's contemporary beliefs by giving them a spurious historical legitimation. Neither Victorian society nor post-war Britain was actually as Thatcher or Kinnock portrays it.

Idealised views of the past are also used to criticise developments regarded as detrimental. A time in the past might be classified as a golden age of social harmony and balance. There was such a mistaken belief about the pre-capitalist guilds amongst industrial artisanal workers well into the present century. 'Arts and crafts' movements in art and architecture are similarly mistaken. Taking another example, environmentalists may shift from a critique of the current misuse of natural resources to the erroneous idea that they were always better used in the past. One of the greatest health improvements, after all, has been a significant reduction in water and airborne pollution. Current environmental problems are extremely serious but the arguments are more convincing when conducted in terms of contemporary issues than in the context of an idealised past.

Sometimes use of a 'Golden Age' enables identification of scapegoats in the present. A current example is criticism of teachers for failing to instil in their charges adequate discipline and respect for authority. A history of teaching methods and results does not show the present in such a poor light.

3. Inexorable progress

Progress is a powerful image. It structures most people's views of modern society. Progress is seen most clearly in the increased material wealth available to all in contrast to twenty, forty or a hundred years ago. Development may exert a price, and awareness of the environmental cost is growing. But generally the benefits are regarded as outweighing the costs. Few people would wish society to return to small-scale agriculture alone or to the factories of the nineteenth century.

Progress is a classic liberal belief. In most liberal explanations it is fuelled by technological innovation and improvements in the organisation of society and its parts. In this formulation, technical and organisational changes are fundamentally unpredictable but what can be predicted is that progress is socially harmonious. Everyone benefits from growth, so only self-interested (unprepared to accept short-run costs for the greater common good) or misguided groups oppose it.

Progress, of course, can be temporarily halted or constrained. External events, such as wars and world depression, may hold back or reverse development for a number of years. Internal disharmony may also arise owing to the actions of unreasonable interest groups or because of misguided government policy. One of the objects of social science in this formulation is to point out or overcome those internal constraints. Even wars and depressions may be claimed to have a progressive role. Wars encourage invention and may help remove moribund organisational structures and states in favour of more vibrant forms. Depressions shake up expectations and work ethics, and help to 'restructure' industry.

Liberals are not the only firm believers in progress. Marxists in the traditions of the Second and Third Internationals share the belief (though many other Marxists do not). For them, progress is the development of society's productive capability, the forces of production. Unlike the liberal perspective, however, social organisations do not harmoniously develop with productive capabilities. Instead, the class nature of societies, after encouraging the development of production for a while, eventually holds back further development. Capitalism has played that role for the advanced capitalist world in this approach, and its contradictions will eventually lead to its supersession.

The belief in progress through the inevitability of rising productive capacity led traditional Marxists to give one of two potential roles to political parties. Both, not surprisingly, differ from the liberal model of good government. Conflicts over the two roles led to schisms in the socialist movement in the years prior to 1914. One role was to improve the contemporary lot of the working class through the introduction of social reforms and the encouragement of strong trade unions. This trend led to the formation of today's Western European social democrat parties (though most of them had dumped their working-class rhetoric by the mid-1970s). The other role was to speed up the decline of capitalism through the formation of small, highly motivated parties aimed at encouraging the working class to revolution and seizing

8

power in that class's name. This trend was promulgated by Lenin and led to the formation of Western Europe's communist parties. By the 1970s most communist parties had abandoned any pretence at revolution (the British party did it in the early 1950s with publication of the first *British Road to Socialism*).

The divergent uses of progress by liberals and traditional Marxists illustrates the fact that stylised generalisations are not necessarily exclusive to one theoretical or political perspective. Once placed within such perspectives, however, they can lead to opposing conclusions. The opposition may then reinforce the credibility of the initial generalisation as it is common to both viewpoints.

A problem with the idea of inexorable progress is its inherent vagueness. Vagueness exists at the global level in terms of the criteria that should be used to measure progress. Belief in steady progress also begins to pale when specific time periods are considered, as progress on any scale during the period may be scant or dimensions of social change may contradict each other. Most of the population of sub-Saharan Africa would not feel that the 1980s were a decade of progress, nor would the workers of Mexico who have seen their standard of living cut in half over the decade. Even in Britain the number of poor people has grown in the 1980s, despite the higher general standard of living. Universal progress becomes meaningless or an unsubstantiable value judgement in such time horizons.

The vagueness of the term *progress* generates bad methodological habits. Belief in inevitable progress sidesteps the need to examine most aspects of actual processes of development. If progress is not seen over a particular period, something must have stopped it. The search for the blockage can be isolated to only a few rogue phenomena – government policy and the trade unions, for instance.

Another difficulty with the liberal perspective on progress is its belief in socially harmonious development.

Evidence from real societies would suggest otherwise; but once conflict is accepted as general it becomes impossible to believe that processes of change are necessarily universally beneficial. Then, instead, a question always has to be asked: progress for whom?

4. Social conflict models

Stylised models of social conflict feature in some descriptions of contemporary Britain. The most simplistic are portrayed by the small but vocal groups on the left that classify all politically relevant groups into the 'working class' and the 'ruling class' or 'capital', with the rest of the population in some unspecified limbo. Politics is then judged on the gains it provides for the working class in their struggle to overthrow capitalism. The leaders of the working class in either the trade unions or the political parties have an unerring ability to betray the class they represent. The 1980s on this scenario have seen many working-class defeats. Paradoxically, some on the right would implicitly adopt such a crude class analysis in seeing the prime success of the 1980s as being the defeat of the organised working class in the trade unions and the Labour Party, forcing them to abandon the political road for the disciplines of the market-place.

It is not obvious that the working class ever existed in the size and form envisaged by simplistic class models. Nor is it clear that traditional trade union forms of representation are severely weakened in the late 1980s. Membership has fallen from its late-1970s peak but it is not so different from the levels of the 1950s and 1960s. Trade union organisational structures are still intact and some trade union members have been highly successful in action against their employers. A deal struck by Ford with its unions after a strike early in 1988 was being called a time-bomb later in the year, because of the unions' subtle insistence on an inflation-indexed clause

– foreseeing the course of subsequent inflation better than management.

Beyond simplistic approaches, nevertheless, class or its absence has been a recurrent theme of what has been happening in Britain over the last few decades. The issue is considered in detail in the final chapter.

Parodies of class struggle of the type described above have had the unfortunate consequence of being treated by many as the only potential forms of class analysis. Yet many more subtle Marxist positions and those of some non-Marxists would see class in complex terms and portray it as a central element in the forces generating change in contemporary Britain. Other perspectives, which reject notions of class, still emphasise the importance of plural conflicts between interest groups. To oppose harmonistic views of society does not require acceptance of crass revolutionary class struggle.

BEYOND STYLISED GENERALISATIONS

Other sweeping views of contemporary change exist. Long waves of development have been suggested, where phases of expansion alternate with periods of stagnation. In them, the world economy is currently on a down swing and therefore prone to crisis. Treating societies as if they are subject to evolutionary determinism, although less common than eighty years ago, still produces bestsellers. 'Empires', for instance, rise and, like human beings, develop rigidities in their declining years, and have to give way to stronger, younger ones. Geographical determinism alternatively may be invoked. The Atlantic was the ocean of the 1950s and 1960s, but now it is the Pacific's turn. If a country does not have a Pacific coast it loses out to economies that do. On this scenario, Western Europe is doomed.

Stylised generalisations can always be discredited because, by their nature, they have few theoretically robust premisses and facts can be produced to contradict the supposed generalisation. Their widespread use is understandable as they give such an easy introduction to complex problems and seem to provide answers. Without them, analysis may seem to degenerate into endless fact-gathering and contingent statements that offer little explanation of broader trends. Social research, however, is not faced with such a bleak choice. Particular theories can be applied to the understanding of real world events. Dispute then centres around the theory and its presentation and interpretation of the facts. Much of the literature on contemporary Britain has adopted this broad approach.

The aim of this book is to survey change in British society. Each chapter takes what we regard as important features of social and economic transformation. Under each topic we examine the available data on specific issues, and survey debates in the literature about the causes and relative importance of them. At times, the task is essentially a descriptive one such as the elaboration of population trends in Chapter 7; elsewhere the issue is primarily that of surveying and commenting on a particular theoretical debate, as with the existence and importance of deindustrialisation, a flexible workforce, and class.

We do not try to draw conclusions about the precise nature of contemporary Britain. We do not accept, however, the view that the fundamental structure of British society has been transformed in the 1980s. Changes have obviously occurred but they have to be understood in their historical context. Viewed in that light, many of the problems of British society in general and of the economy in particular take on a greater, if unfortunate, permanence.

SCOPE OF THE BOOK

Although the book covers a wide range of issues, we have deliberately limited its scope.

The book is about Britain. Northern Ireland and its problems are not dealt with because we feel they require greater historical analysis, range and depth than are possible here. An outline of the issues and debates over them needs to place Northern Ireland in the context of the whole of Irish development as well as examining its ambiguous relationship to Britain.

We have excluded a variety of topics about Britain itself. Transport, seen by many as a growing problem, is not considered. Cultural issues and the changing ways in which people spend their daily lives are largely ignored. Debates over the environment and use of the countryside are similarly undeveloped. Even in topics covered, such as politics, some changes that have been regarded as significant in the 1980s are left out. The growth and role of the middle parties stemming from the old Liberal Party and the original formation of the Social Democrat Party are barely mentioned. The reason is not that any of these topics is unimportant but that the aim of the book is to highlight those issues which we feel have been most central in recent debates, rather than to provide the definitive survey of contemporary Britain.

The rest of the book is divided into five parts. The first looks at the economy. More precisely, it considers the macroeconomy – aggregate outcomes of the economic system as a whole and some of the linkages between its constituent parts. An initial chapter highlights some of the key economic events of the 1980s, providing some broad descriptive information. This introduction is a backdrop to the debates over specific issues outlined in the following three chapters. Part 2 continues to examine aspects of the economy, adding the social dimensions of the characteristics of the workforce and population as a whole. It considers changes occurring in the work people do, and the growth of the non-working population caused by rising unemployment and demographic change. Part 3 examines three of the pillars of the welfare state: housing, health and education. All are treated in historical perspective in order to understand current developments within them and suggested areas of reform. Part 4 examines politics. The first chapter elaborates theoretical perspectives on the state and its functions, and the second describes and assesses the programmes of the three Thatcher administrations. Finally, Part 5 looks at aspects of contemporary divisions within Britain. Its first chapter examines the economic dimensions of wealth and income to see whether it is true that the rich have got richer and the poor poorer. The second chapter examines the issue of class and whether there is any point in attempts to produce stratifications of the current social structure of Britain.

TERMINOLOGY

A text on British society faces problems of the use of terminology which have to be explained at this initial stage.

Language is value-laden, and specific words often have meanings beyond their dictionary definition. The words used to describe particular racial groupings are good examples, and show the dynamic influences on terminology.

During the 1950s, black West Indians who migrated to Britain were labelled as 'non-white', 'coloured', 'brown', 'immigrant', 'negro' or 'West Indian'. Some of the terms and other worse ones are racist and pejorative. Everyone is 'non-white' in the literal sense. Widespread use of 'negro' originates in nineteenth-century pseudo-scientific research which ranked races on supposed differences in ability. Common use of 'immigrant' today to describe second- and third-generation British black people says a great deal about the continued existence of racism. During the 1970s, there was growing use of the phrase 'Afro-Caribbean' to indicate both the African and Caribbean origins of black people in Britain; 'Afro-British' has been introduced more recently. Such phraseology high-lights the changing position of black people in Britain and increasing awareness of the political implications of the terms used. On the left, the contrast of 'black' with 'white' now commonly denotes a political judgement about a basic social divide rather than skin colour itself. Not all people labelled as black would accept the twofold division, seeing themselves as British and placing no importance on race, or arguing, say, that foremost they are Asian or Muslim. In this book we have chosen primarily for simplicity to use the black/white terminol-ogy, except where greater detail is necessary.

Economy and *society* as words also present problems. Most textbooks treat society as the domain of the non-economist and the economy as a distinct region of social inquiry. More satisfying is the idea that society is the whole of a social structure and the relationships taking place within it. The economy becomes a subset of wider society. Even that definition is unsatisfactory as it still treats the economy as an identifiable, independent domain, whereas in fact there is an intermingling of economic and non-economic issues and behaviour. Gene-rally, therefore, we use *society* to mean the whole of social life including the economy. It is often necessary to distinguish certain aspects of social existence, neverthe-less, so we use in such cases the rather unfortunate economic/social distinction for want of anything better.

PART 1

The Economy

2

The Economic Record
Michael Ball

The 1980s were a period of major change in the British economy. In terms of the level of macroeconomic activity, the decade started with the worst recession since the 1930s. The collapse in national income (as measured by gross domestic product) during 1980–1, in fact, was greater than that experienced during any year of the interwar depression. Millions were added to the already high number of unemployed. Firms faced bankruptcy and thousands of plants were totally or partially closed down. As with previous recessions, the impact was uneven. Manufacturing industry took the brunt of the fall in demand, while other sectors, such as financial services, continued to prosper. The consequence was that the traditional industrial heartlands of the country fared the worst. Steel, textiles and heavy engineering in the northern cities, the 'metal-bashing' and car industries of the Midlands, and processing, consumer-durable and engineering industries in London and the other major conurbations all shed thousands of workers. So the old industrial towns and inner cities were the main locations of the new unemployed.

Those who remained in work experienced the early 1980s recession in a different way as they were partially sheltered from the worst effects of the economic crisis and some even saw improvements in their standard of living. Yet manual workers in all industries felt threatened by changes in work practices. In manufacturing industry there was also the ever-present threat of redundancy. Public-sector workers, after a brief honeymoon when previously agreed substantial rises in pay were accepted by the incoming Conservative administration, had to face a government with a declared new philosophy of running down major parts of the public sector.

The economic crisis of the early 1980s was the culmination of a long period of relative economic decline for Britain. Many other major industrial countries, especially in Europe and the Far East, had faster growth throughout the post-war years. They also seemed, at least in British eyes, to be more capable of dealing with problems of structural adjustment, the slowdown of the world economy in the 1970s and, above all, inflation. Poor growth and internal economic conflict became dubbed the 'British Disease'.

After the early 1980s the economy began to emerge from recession. In some sectors, recovery was patchy. Manufacturing output, for example, did not surpass its 1979 cyclical peak until 1988. Yet, despite the slowness of the upturn, it was sustained. This meant that Britain had during the 1980s the longest continuous period of expansion of the post-war era. For supporters of government policies, such growth signalled the end of the cycles of stop-go that had dogged economic growth and government policies since 1954. For the cynics, it showed the extent of the preceding recession and the limited concern of the Government to attempt to deal with mass unemployment by reflating earlier.

The greatest turn-rounds were in the rate of inflation, which fell dramatically from the early to the mid-1980s, and in the increased rate of growth of productivity, in the economy as a whole and in manufacturing in particular (see the data presented in Table 2.1, A to D). Britain, from always lagging behind in the international economic performance league, suddenly began to surpass major competitors. Such success can be exaggerated, however, as it tends to be measured in recent percentage changes

TABLES 2.1A–D *UK Economy, Key Indicators*

TABLE 2.1A *Changes in the Domestic Economy, 1979–88*

	1979	1981	1983	1985	1987	1988
Gross domestic product (at 1985 prices, index 1985=100)	92.8	89.7	94.7	100.0	107.5	111.6
Rate of inflation (%)[1]	13.4	11.9	4.6	6.1	4.2	4.9
Rate of increase of average earnings[2]	n.a.	13.5	8.5	8.5	7.8	8.7
Rate of unemployment[3]	4.3	8.1	10.5	10.9	10.0	8.1
Current trade balance (£bn)	−0.5	6.9	3.9	3.4	−2.9	−14.7
Export growth[4]	86.4	85.8	88.6	100.0	109.3	108.2
Import growth[4]	84.7	79.6	88.9	100.0	114.3	128.0
Real personal disposable income (1985=100)	93.2	93.5	95.8	100.0	106.5	111.6
Personal savings ratio[5]	13.0	13.1	10.7	9.7	5.6	4.1
Manufacturing output (1985=100)	105.9	91.0	93.7	100.0	106.6	114.1
Manufacturing investment (£bn)[6]	10.2	6.6	6.4	8.7	9.1	10.0
Productivity[7] (1985=100)						
Manufacturing	80.0	79.5	92.0	100.0	109.7	115.5
Whole economy	89.4	89.3	97.0	100.0	104.9	n.a.

1. Percentage increase on year earlier in retail price index.
2. Increase on year earlier, new series starting in 1980.
3. Claimant unemployed as percentage of estimated workforce.
4. Volume indices, 1985=100, all goods and services.
5. Personal savings as a percentage of personal disposable income.
6. Gross fixed investment excluding leased assets at 1985 prices.
7. Output per person employed.
Source: *Economic Trends.*

TABLE 2.1B *UK Economy Cyclical Comparisons (cyclical averages)*

	1968–73	1973–9	1979–87
	Annual rate of growth		
Gross domestic product (GDP)	3.2	1.4	1.9
Employment	0.2	0.2	–0.2
Wage rate	10.5	16.9	9.5
GDP price deflator	7.9	16.0	7.7
Unemployment as % of total workforce	2.5	3.9	9.6

Source: OECD (1988).

TABLE 2.1C *International Economic Comparisons, 1968–87 (average annual growth rates)*

	GDP at constant 1980 prices			Labour productivity		
	1968–73	1973–9	1979–87	1968–73	1973–9	1979–87
UK	3.2	1.4	1.9	3.0	1.2	2.1
W. Germany	4.9	2.3	1.5	4.1	2.9	1.5
France	6.2	2.8	1.7	5.0	2.5	1.8
Italy	4.6	2.6	2.3	4.6	1.8	1.7
USA	3.0	2.6	2.3	0.7	0.0	0.6
Canada	5.4	4.2	2.8	2.4	1.3	1.0
Japan	8.4	3.6	3.9	7.3	2.9	2.9
Average	4.3	2.7	2.4	2.9	1.4	1.4

Source: OECD (1988).

TABLE 2.1D *Relative International Labour Productivity[1] Levels, 1986*

| | Actual 1980 exchange rates | | Purchasing power parity rates[2] | |
	US $1000	Index	US $1000	Index
UK	24.8	100	21.8	100
W. Germany	34.0	137	26.1	120
France	34.0	137	28.4	130
Italy	23.9	96	27.0	124
USA	28.4	115	29.0	133
Canada	26.5	107	28.9	133
Japan	22.3	90	20.6	94

1. Labour productivity calculated by dividing GDP at constant 1980 US $ by total employment.
2. Purchasing-power parity is a controversial method that attempts to take account of differences in relative prices between countries; parities calculated at 1980 prices.
Source: OECD (1988) and own calculations.

in indicators such as productivity or national income, ignoring the levels from where proportionate comparisons start. When absolute measures of productivity and income per head are compared instead, Britain generally ranks lower than many other Western European countries.

Towards the end of the 1980s a new array of problems began to arise. Inflation was again creeping up, and, by late 1988, economic 'overheating' was generally accepted as occurring, and the question was whether the economy would slow down gently or be forced into another recession. The official government line at the time was that the difficulties were temporary and manageable through interest-rate and public-expenditure policies. Another interpretation was that the overheating had occurred because of profound structural imbalances that had long existed in the British economy, which governments in the 1980s have exacerbated rather than negated. Britain's historic problems on this scenario had not gone away.

Evidence does exist to support the structural imbalances view. Take employment first. Mass unemployment still exists, yet many employers in 1987 and 1988 were complaining of acute labour shortages, especially of skilled labour and particularly in the South East. The labour market in aggregate does not seem to be responding to increased demand in the ways the textbooks and many economists say it should do. It is not just that unemployment stubbornly remains, but also that in the workforce as a whole there are insufficient skills for the contemporary economy to achieve sustained expansion. It is generally recognised that Britain faces a training crisis both in manual and non-manual spheres. There is a pressing need to expand the skills of manual workers, including updating those already acquired to new and ever changing techniques and work practices. In addition, the general and vocational educational systems have to be able to satisfy the growing demands for 'white collar' work and the traditional and new intellectual skills associated with it. (Training is considered in detail in Part 2.)

The next obvious imbalance is in the foreign account. The deficit in trade deteriorated rapidly after 1986. In 1988, it had reached a scale previously seen only in the early 1970s oil crisis (and before that in wartime). When translated into a percentage of National Income, it is equivalent in magnitude to the much criticised US trade deficit.

A prime cause of the trade imbalance is the inflow of manufactured and semi-manufactured imports caused by buoyant home demand. For some, the inflow is an indicator of another more fundamental imbalance: an excessive rundown of domestic manufacturing industry –

deindustrialisation. Another indicator of deindustrialisation is the investment record of manufacturing firms. Improvements in manufacturing productivity in the 1980s had not occurred through major increases in fixed capital stock. Investment in manufacturing in 1988 was barely at its 1979 cyclical peak, yet overall national income was much higher. This relatively poor investment record may also indicate that the means available for sustaining the competitiveness of British manufacturing industry are weak, particularly when coupled with a poor record on research and development and the labour-supply problems mentioned earlier.

Another aspect of economic development in the 1980s has been the concentration of growth in southern England – reinforcing a trend towards greater regional inequality already apparent in the 1970s. Increased concentration of economic activity had consequences in the housing market. The house-price gap between the South and other regions has widened considerably. Labour mobility has been reduced as a result, with many people being unable to move south and join in the prosperity.

The late-1980s boom itself was fuelled by sharp increases in personal consumption facilitated by large rises in consumer credit, much of it in the form of tax-subsidised mortgage finance. In 1980, the personal sector had twice as much outstanding debt as its annual income; by early 1988 the debt–income ratio had doubled to four times annual income.

As well as buoyant personal consumption, non-housing property markets were booming with rising shop and office rents and easily available credit. Overall new orders in the construction industry rose in real terms by an incredible 22 per cent in the eighteen months up to June 1988 to one of their greatest post-war levels, by far the highest growth record of all industry. Much of the property and related construction activity has been concentrated in the South East, exacerbating regional inequalities and giving them a permanent, infrastructural fix.

Much emphasis in the press and the specialist economics literature has been on the role of government policy in producing the economic changes of the 1980s.

The Conservative government elected in 1979 declared it had radical new solutions to Britain's economic problems based on a three-pronged strategy of

(1) curbing the economic actions of the state through money-supply controls, reduced public expenditure and diminished involvement in industry;

(2) stimulating private enterprise through earnings and profit incentives, especially via a taxation policy aimed at enabling greater retention of them once earned; and

(3) restrictions on the actions of trade unions in both wage negotiations and their ability to resist changes in working practices.

During the 1980s the detailed policies of the Conservative administration changed substantially. Some of the major instruments, such as control of the broad money supply, have virtually been abandoned as unworkable or in contradiction with other aims. Such changes, like the initial measures, have generated much controversy inside and outside government circles, of which control of the money supply is one of the best examples. (A detailed assessment of Thatcherism is left until Chapter 12.)

The question generally posed of the Thatcher governments' economic policies is whether they 'worked'. Often the debate is couched in terms of current macroeconomic policy; over, for instance, contemporary exchange- and interest-rate strategies or programmes aimed at reducing the trade gap, overheating and a perceived renewed threat of inflation. In many respects, however, the economic claims for Thatcherism rest on a belief that the British economy has been fundamentally changed. This is either done in the simplistic terms of regarding government policy as the only factor affecting the economy or more sophisticatedly through claiming that government policy has transformed the economy in ways that meet the needs of Britain's role in the new world economy. Whichever position is taken, the argument about fundamental change is directed at the basic structures and processes of a complex economic system rather than just at specific macroeconomic policies, although they, of course, might be instrumental in facilitating such change.

In order to assess government policies, it is necessary to have an awareness both of their effectiveness and of the underlying problems of the economy that governments attempt to alter. Yet, with the economy, it is not possible simply to dig up the facts and apply one of a known set of remedies from the Treasury's equivalent of a medicine bag. To a great extent the diagnosis and the remedies it is suggested that a government should implement depend on the particular economic theory adopted. The range of theories is wide, and subject to considerable changes in fashion – there are, for instance, few pure Monetarists left in the late 1980s. With regard to the effectiveness of policy, some theories would suggest that there is little government can do; others argue that governments generally follow more powerful forces in the economy rather than take a leading role; while further theories give government the possibility of a more or less substantial interventionist role. Each theory, moreover, has a different interpretation of the nature of the economy and its problems.

Although there are some self-evident economic truths, differences of interpretation in economics are frequently influenced by the political opinions of the protagonists. This could occur in the theory adopted – a staunch liberal Conservative is unlikely to believe in an economic theory critical of the operations and outcomes of a market economy; whereas a socialist is unlikely to accept one that did not find the market wanting in achieving at least some major social aims. Political influences may also enter through assumptions made about the nature of the

British economy and broader society – what are some-times called the 'stylised facts' with which all researchers initially embark on their investigations. The influence of political opinions does not make all economists disguised political hacks; relatively few are. Points of logic and factual disagreement cross the boundaries of theoretical dispute. At some level, however, it has to be recognised that differences of interpretation are not about technique and fact alone, but about moral beliefs, their ordering, and fundamental views about the operation of societies. Perhaps it is more accurate to say that such non-refutable positions feed into both economics and politics rather than that politics alone structures econo-mic beliefs. All the same, it is important to be aware of the interlinkages when considering specific interpreta-tions of the economy.

One point that would be made by a number of theories, especially those critical of contemporary policy or of society more generally, is that economic analysis or policy recommendations must recognise the differential impact on people of patterns of economic change. The employed and the unemployed are a clear case of such a difference. Income and wealth distribution are similarly important. Specific social groups, moreover, whether delineated on geographic, class, gender or occupational lines, will have distinct experiences of patterns of econo-mic transformation.

The next chapter considers the interpretations of the current nature of the British economy, and puts them in the context of the broad historical evolution of the economy. In light of this analysis the following two chapters then consider a variety of issues associated with the contemporary structure of the UK economy. Before proceeding further, however, it is useful to elaborate the long-term problems of the economy that the analyses are addressing. In addition, since the mid-1970s Britain has had a characteristic in the context of the rest of Western Europe which a number of commentators have stressed gives some of the economic activity in Britain a specific international role – relatively low wages combined with low productivity.

FOUR RECURRING ECONOMIC PROBLEMS

Four issues have dogged British long-term economic performance in the post-war era: growth, trade, inflation and unemployment. Their actual and perceived significance has varied over time. Perhaps the most important is the relatively slow growth of national income per head. Britain at the same time has faced changing patterns of trade and periodic balance-of-payments problems. Britain's economy has also become increasingly orientated towards international trade, particularly after membership of the Common Market took effect from the mid-1970s. For many years Britain's traditionally large surplus of manufacturing exports slowly declined. In the 1980s, manufacturing trade moved into deficit. The overall trade balance itself also plunged into the red, leading to fears that economic expansion was once again severely constrained by balance-of-payments problems. Added to the old worries about the balance of payments, however, is a new problem – what will happen when the oil runs out? Will trade surpluses on services and property income from abroad pay for a large manufacturing deficit? Or will there be a regeneration of British industry to make up the lost export income?

The state of British manufacturing industry lies at the heart of the growth and trade debates. Between 1973 and 1982, UK manufacturing output fell by 18 per cent, whereas in the six major OECD countries it rose by an average of 15 per cent (Rowthorn and Wells, 1987). During the 1980s revival of output, labour productivity improved but the international competitiveness of British industry was still uncertain given its high relative unit labour costs and remaining weaknesses in marketing, product ranges and advanced production techniques.

Inflation became severe in Britain in the early 1970s, peaked in the mid-1970s at almost 25 per cent a year and then again in 1980 at 20 per cent a year. The Thatcher governments have emphasised the attack on inflation, although, many would argue, at severe economic cost in terms of lost jobs and output. The pattern of inflation in Britain over the past twenty years, in fact, has followed that of most other advanced capitalist countries, except that Britain's has tended to be above that of leading competitor nations. This is still the case in the late 1980s.

For many, unemployment is the contemporary scourge of the British economy. It has quadrupled since 1970, with two sharp leaps in 1975–6 and 1979–83. Many people have been unemployed for a long time with little hope of a job. Male unemployment in Britain is particularly bad – nearly twice as high in 1987 as in France, West Germany, Italy and the United States. It is difficult to make international comparisons of female unemployment rates as measured female unemployment is influenced by varying entitlement to benefits. Whoever experiences the misfortune, long-term unemployment is a sharp indicator of how unequal is the distribution of economic benefits in present-day British society.

COSTS AND PRODUCTIVITY

Low labour costs

In 1986 in a survey of sixteen countries only Ireland had marginally lower labour costs in manufacturing industry than Britain (Ray, 1987). Other leading industrial countries had much higher labour costs, as Table 2.2 shows. Labour costs consist of hourly earnings and the social charges paid by employers. They are highly sensitive to

TABLE 2.2 *International Comparisons of Manufacturing Wages, Productivity and Unit Labour Costs, 1980 and 1986[1]*

	(1) Total hourly labour costs[2]		(2) Labour productivity (output per hour)		(3) Unit labour costs[3]	
	1980	1986	1980	1986	1980	1986
United States	126	161	273	267	46	60
Japan	80	129	196	176	41	73
France	121	122	193	184	63	66
W. Germany	165	173	255	178	65	97
Italy	108	127	173	155	62	82
Belgium	176	149	207	154	85	97
Netherlands	160	156	269	205	59	76
Great Britain	100	100	100	100	100	100

1. 1986 data provisional.
2. Labour costs include the relevant social charges, i.e. employer's insurance contributions, etc.
3. Unit labour costs derived by dividing column 1 by column 2. Current exchange rates used.

Source: *National Institute Economic Review*, May 1987.

exchange-rate movements and do not accurately reflect comparative standards of living. The difference between the UK and its major world competitors, however, is so great that exchange-rate variations do not explain the scale of the difference.

The labour costs shown are for manufacturing only, but other sectors of the economy exhibit a similar comparative low wage structure. Many of the better-paid jobs in Britain are in the service sector, particularly amongst the professions and in the City – but the worst-paid jobs are also there. Internationally, apart from a few high-flyers, even professionals in Britain tend to earn less than their equivalents in other advanced countries. Office rents in the City, for example, are generally higher than in most other world cities, but lower labour costs are said to offset them for the international financial institutions locating in London.

Labour costs are one indicator of Britain's economic failure in the post-1945 era. They stem from the relatively low growth in national income, which combined with little redistribution of income has meant that most Britons have experienced slower rises in their standard of living than their counterparts in Western Europe, in industrialising Asia and in North America. In the 1950s, British living standards were among the highest in Europe, though much below those in the USA. By 1970, real income in many other European countries had overtaken those in Britain, and in the 1980s Japanese living standards followed suit.

Although relatively low standards of living for the mass of the population are an adverse product of poor economic growth, for firms they offer opportunities. Employers sensitive to labour costs should be encouraged to expand domestically or be attracted to Britain as a result of the relatively low wages. The 'cheap wage' regime, which has existed in key industries in comparison to those in major competitor nations since the nineteenth century, has had a significant impact on the pattern of economic development. It has led to specialisation in techniques and products requiring a greater labour input and also to relatively lower levels of investment in plant and machinery than in many other advanced nations. Such 'intermediate' techniques and products are highly sensitive to cost competition from countries with even lower wages. Most important, they are vulnerable to technical advances in production methods introduced abroad and to supersession by competitors producing similar but more advanced products.

The vulnerability of British manufactures to cost competition is highlighted by the fact that unit labour costs per unit of output are often greater than in countries with higher wages, because productivity in British industry is so low that lower wage costs are offset by the smaller output produced by each worker. The effect can be seen in the average data provided in Table 2.2, where British unit labour costs are the highest of the countries shown because poor productivity outweighs the lower labour costs.

Low productivity

At the end of the 1970s there was universal criticism of low productivity in British manufacturing industry. Since then there has been much comment on the increase in manufacturing productivity in the 1980s. But increases have also occurred in other countries, so by the second half of the decade the relative improvement overall was negligible. The result is that manufacturing productivity is still much lower than in most other industrial economies – sometimes less than half (Table 2.2).

The productivity paradox has fascinated commentators on the British scene (cf. Davies and Caves, 1987, and Nichols, 1986). Explanation of it seems to lie at the core of understanding the vicious circle in which relatively low productivity growth is associated with low increases in incomes, poor average rates of profit (until the 1980s) and inadequate investment. Consideration of whether the 1980s represent a break out of the vicious circle is left until Chapter 5 – where it is concluded that the evidence of a sustained transformation is weak.

One way of explaining the relatively poor historic economic performance of Britain is to pick on the inadequate behaviour of one social group – along the lines of claiming that British workers are lazy or management is incompetent. Plenty of evidence can be mustered, even if its interpretation is controversial. In the mid-1970s, for example, there was a series of influential studies claiming that the British worker was somehow productively deficient. Pratten (1976) suggests that even for products made with the same techniques British workers manage to produce far less than workers in other countries. Nichols (1986) critically evaluates Pratten's claims and questions the validity of other similar studies preferring to place the blame on the shoulders of management. Outside of a wider understanding of the nature of the British economy, however, such claims and counter-claims are primarily emotive. At best, symptoms are being confused with causes. The question has to be asked why such symptoms exist, and answering it may even lead to a reassessment of the symptoms themselves.

Adopting labour-intensive techniques with limited product innovation helps to explain high unit labour costs. Of themselves, however, high unit labour costs do not necessarily mean low profitability for employers. Labour-intensive techniques, for example, lead to lower fixed capital costs than fixed capital intensive methods, so high labour cost production could even be more profitable. British firms may even have optimised their choice of technique given the array of labour and fixed capital costs facing them in comparison, say, to their US counterparts. Many studies have pointed out the tendency for British manufacturing industry since the nineteenth century to opt for relatively labour-intensive techniques (cf. Lee, 1986; Katrak, 1973; Connell, 1979). Yet, simply discovering a combination of lower wages, poorer productivity and higher unit labour costs in Britain does not give any clues as to why the combination arose.

There is a major discussion in the economic history literature over whether British capitalists 'failed' the nation in the late nineteenth century by not adopting the most advanced production techniques of the time. One strand of the debate precisely argues the case that firms did actually adopt profit-maximising techniques. The problem was that the profit-maximising techniques kept British industry in its old ways, rather than transformed it. In economic terms the argument leads to a classic difference between individual responses (which may be optimising given the array of choices and constraints facing individual units) and global outcomes (which may be far from optimal). In this case what was the most profitable technique for the individual enterprise was not the most advantageous for economic growth in the economy as a whole.

It is impossible to assess why firms adopt specific techniques without understanding the wider context in which the decisions are made and the price of inputs formed. What is particularly missing is specification of the constraints that have faced firms during phases of British economic development, and reasons why the British economy has been such infertile territory for creating and sustaining the large-scale production of new commodities. To provide an adequate understanding of those constraints and the reasons for their existence, the economic framework of British society needs to be filled in. What is put within the framework depends on the theoretical perspective of the person undertaking the exercise. The next chapter starts with an elaboration of the major schools of thought on the British economy.

FURTHER READING

For information on the current economic situation there are a variety of sources, apart from the press and government publications. The Organisation for Economic Co-operation and Development (OECD) produces an annual economic survey of the United Kingdom in broadly non-technical language. The OECD rarely indulges in strong criticism of the contemporary Treasury line. The quarterly *National Institute Economic and Review* provides an assessment of the current state of the economy, makes forecasts from its macroeconomic model, and prints some useful articles on aspects of the economy and government policy. The National Institute also periodically revises a useful short introduction to the British economy, its structure, problems and economic policy over the last few decades (NIESR, 1982).

3

Perspectives on the British Economy
Michael Ball

In many ways the British economy typifies the impact of general trends in world economic development on a medium-sized Western European country. Britain, however, does have its own peculiarities, which can only be understood by looking at its economic history over the past two hundred years. Economic processes and developments in British society have been set in motion and successive governments have found them exceedingly difficult to change. Four major problems in the post-war era were highlighted in the previous chapter – growth, trade, inflation and unemployment – while it was noted that Britain's economy was characterised by relatively low productivity and wages in comparison to the other major economies of Western Europe. The first part of this chapter considers the variety of explanations given for these economic characteristics. The second half then considers Britain's longer-term economic history.

EXPLANATIONS OF BRITAIN'S ECONOMIC PROBLEMS

Some explanations are not really concerned with providing detailed solutions to specific economic problems because they suggest that the issues are misperceived a problems. A lack of manufacturing growth, for instance,

37

can be replaced by service activities (cf. Gershuny and Miles, 1983). Alternatively, some would suggest that too much overall growth is a bad thing, either because of the environmental costs or because of the impact on the nature and traditions of British society. However, these environmental claims, even if their underlying beliefs are accepted, confuse acceptance of the *status quo* with criticisms of the methods through which resources are allocated and the implicit priorities made within them. A more environmentally sensitive economy, for instance, does not necessitate the large waste of resources associated with the mass unemployment of today.

Other approaches accept the need for, or at least the inevitability of, growth and home in on why it has taken such a sluggish form in Britain. Many economists would argue that the problem lies in an inability of agents to respond quickly enough to the signals of the market economy. When there is a shock to the economic system, such as the oil-price rises of the 1970s, the high value of sterling in the late 1970s/early 1980s, or changes in the relative importance of particular world markets, elements in the British economy block the adjustment of prices and the concomitant transfer of resources necessary to restore the economy to a full-employment, non-accelerating-inflation equilibrium.

The causes of market rigidity are said to be many but emphasis is placed on the role of government and the trade unions. Governments create many problems. They distort adjustments by trying to stave off temporary recessions through expansionary fiscal and monetary policy; through becoming involved in activities undertaken more efficiently by the private sector; through welfare benefits which stop unemployed workers accepting jobs at lower rates of pay; and through a vast array of regulatory controls and legally condoned restrictive practices. Trade unions are said to discourage workers from accepting realistic rates of pay and inhibit the introduction of new working practices. Together governments and

38

trade unions hinder the dissemination of market signals, limit the role of incentives in encouraging investment and effort, and block the need for individuals to make realistic assessments of the state of the economy and their place within it. Such a view of the economy is associated with the *New Classical Economics* (Minford and Matthews, 1987) and with the publications issued by such organisations as the Institute of Economic Affairs. It is also the nearest thing to an intellectual justification for the economic policies of the Thatcher governments of the 1980s.

In this diagnosis the institutional and incentive structures of concern are those associated with the state and other agencies said to limit the effectiveness of the market. Getting rid of claimed rigidities in those spheres is the essence of what has come to be called 'supply-side' economics. No consideration is given to the industrial structure of Britain; nor to most of the institutions through which economic activity is in practice regulated; nor to the class structure of British society; nor even to the actual types of economic activity undertaken. The decline of manufacturing is not a particular problem, for example, as long as it is not caused by market rigidities. A decline in manufacturing in this scenario simply indicates that the economy is adjusting to new forms of activity in which Britain has a contemporary comparative advantage.

Other economists are less sanguine about the speed with which markets adjust, or even doubt whether they can get back to equilibrium without some form of state intervention. They point to the persistent high level of unemployment as an indicator of the limited pace of market adjustment and suggest packages aimed at stimulating demand to speed the process up. These economists might also find unacceptable the distributional implications of unconstrained market processes which throw a large part of the burden of adjustment on limited sectors of society, most notably the unemployed. They possibly might also find unacceptable the distribution of income associated with the final unconstrained market outcome. Governments have a role, therefore, in stimulating the economy to move more quickly towards full employment; in cushioning the poverty associated with low incomes and unemployment; and in regulating the distribution of income amongst wage-earners and profit-receivers through taxation policy and, if necessary, an incomes policy (cf. Bean, Layard and Nickell, 1987). Broadly such an approach can be classified as *Keynesian-style Interventionism*, and is, perhaps, the view most widely held by UK economists.

The overall efficiency of markets is still accepted within this Keynesian perspective. The role of government is to improve the workings of the market by responding to the few situations where they fail to work effectively or fairly. Given the similarity of beliefs about the role of the market between this and the previous school of economists, it is not surprising that their approach to the dilemmas of the British economy have many points in common. As many spheres of economic activity as possible should be made to operate according to free-market principles. Both schools criticize trade unions and state economic activities that do not correspond to market principles. Wages pressure is often blamed for deindustrialisation and high unemployment (cf. Dornbusch and Layard, 1987). This Keynesian school, however, puts less emphasis on ownership. It is acceptable for the state to run major industries or services of the economy as long as their performance does not go against market efficiency criteria. The results of privatisation are consequently viewed with circumspection, because the policy seems more concerned with ownership than with efficiency (Kay and Thompson, 1986). Markets may also be argued to fail in key aspects of social life, such as health, housing and education, which might be provided more efficiently and fairly within the auspices of the 'welfare state' (cf. Barr, 1987).

In the two schools of thought elaborated so far, the institutions and class structure of the British economy are given a deliberately biased treatment. The aspects of the economy with which they are concerned are simply those said to be able to stop the market-allocation process from working – with emphasis put on the state and the trade unions. Other approaches to the economy have concentrated on broader aspects of British society and highlighted features said to create problems for economic development. Explanations in this vein can be called *Social Institutionalist*. Theoretically, rather than having an ideal like the 'market' of the two previous views, institutionalists take historically given social and organisational structures and then apply an analysis based on discovering rigidities, conflicts and disjunctures within them. The key difficulty of this approach is whether the perceived imperfections actually exist or whether they are as important as they are claimed to be.

For some social institutionalists, long-term imbalances between sectors of the economy lead to 'distorted' patterns of development. A much-cited villain is the City. It is said to be biased against investment in manufacturing industry; to impose a short-term horizon on firms' investment decisions through the pressures of the stock exchange; to have at key times encouraged a flight of capital from Britain; and to have a preponderant influence on government policy to the detriment of industry (cf. Ingham, 1984). Empirically, it has been difficult to quantify the precise impact that the City is supposed to have. One reason for this difficulty could be the initial division of the City and industry. It is hard to believe that there is a unity of interest amongst all of industry, opposed to that of the City, as individual enterprises face such a variety of constraints on their operations. There are also social divisions within industries themselves. Workers might have opposite views from their employers about the way in which their industry should develop – the coal industry being one of the best-known examples.

Specification of major divisions within British society needs to be based on an awareness of how those divisions relate to the dynamic of the economy, but unfortunately this is often missing.

Other commentators concerned with the uniqueness of Britain's social structure have focused on cultural biases. Culture, however, is a difficult concept to pin down, and it can easily end up as the dustbin for non-explanations. Wiener (1981), for instance, has claimed that the aping of aristocratic ideals has led to an endemic anti-enterprise ideology in Britain. Aping the aristocracy was common in other European countries during the periods he discusses. Widely accepted beliefs about specific social actions, furthermore, do not necessarily equate with actual social practice or the reasons for it. Who, for example, would nowadays believe that Europe's nineteenth-century empires were 'the white man's burden' required to spread 'civilisation'. It could as easily be claimed that the hallmark of British Establishment culture is a remarkable flexibility of actions and beliefs in the face of perceived necessity, which is why it has survived.

For others, the institutional structure of British society is so complex that it can only be adequately studied at the level of individual industries. It is claimed that, once formed, institutional structures in Britain are so rigid that industries adapt only poorly to new techniques or to changing patterns of world competition (Elbaum and Lazonick, 1987). In this approach, institutional structures become increasingly irrational, but in Britain they do not break down under the pressure of new economic imperatives. But, again, it has been difficult to prove convincingly such irrationality.

A variant on the detailed institutional structure approach suggests that institutional structures set up internal, rational logics on actors within them. The trajectory of industrial development becomes determined by that logic. As the constraints and structures of industries change over time, a detailed historical investigation of each industry is required in order to elucidate its key problems, from which common characteristics across all industries can be generalised. Dangers arise from staying at the level of detailed industry studies and *ad hoc* identification of general problems. Williams *et al.* (1983), for example, place much emphasis on the peculiar structure of demand facing many British industries. They argue that this has discouraged large-scale investment in standardised production techniques. Once again, it is difficult to know whether such characteristics are a consequence or a cause of a specific pattern of industrial development.

Sectoral divisions in the economy and conflicts between social groups form the central component of another approach to understanding British economic development. The decline of manufacturing is a key problem as it imposes a balance-of-payments constraint on future economic growth (Singh, 1977). One of the major difficulties of British industry has been, it is said, the historical fact of periodic major changes in the composition of trade and its geographic structure (Rowthorn and Wells, 1987). Competition between social groups over the national product compounds the problem created by structural imbalances. Incomes policies are needed to limit the effects of such distributional conflict, while governments should concentrate on policies to improve the competitiveness of British industry. The approach is frequently associated with the home of its main proponents, Cambridge, and can be termed *Keynesian Structuralist*. Structuralists highlight the fact that governments should adopt interventionist strategies aimed at altering the fundamental interrelations between various aspects of the economy, rather than smoothing out the (limited) inefficiencies of the market as postulated by the Keynesian Interventionists.

The concern of both Social Institutionalists and Keynesian Structuralists with the social organisation and sectoral divisions of the economy does not encompass the

43

class structure of British society in any noticeable form. Sectioned groups might compete, and interests, like the City, may exude partisan control over economic policy, but the basis on which those groups are formed and compete only stems from the investigator's own interpretation of British society and its key divisions.

Class is central to the last group, which can broadly be called the *Marxists*. Marxists argue that Britain's social and economic development is influenced by fundamental class antagonisms. The central class antagonism is that between capitalists and workers. Divisions of interpretation exist amongst Marxists. The 'imminent collapse of capitalism' thesis is out of fashion. Some Marxists stress the centrality of the conflict over wages and profits, explaining the weakness of British capital in terms of the militancy of its workers (Kilpatrick and Lawson, 1980; Armstrong *et al.*, 1984). The City and the aristocratic nature of the British Establishment have been added by some (Anderson, 1987). Other Marxists suggest that the peculiar structure of the British economy is encapsulated by four features – the City, the preponderance of multinational corporations, a weak labour movement (contrasting with the previous view) and a state that has failed to implement any effective rationalisations of manufacturing industry (Fine and Harris, 1985).

Another perspective called *Regulation Theory* has grown in popularity amongst Marxist commentators in recent years. It sees the development of capitalism on a world scale in terms of major epochs called 'regimes of accumulation'. The period of mass production and consumption is classified as 'Fordism' after Henry Ford's automobile production lines in early twentieth-century Detroit and Ford's advocacy of high living standards for large sections of the working class so that mass-produced cars could find a mass market. Generalisation is then made from cars, and Henry Ford's claims about them, to classifying virtually all forms of production and consumption as Fordist in advanced capitalist societies in the post-1945 era, in a way that has been subject to extensive criticism. According to Regulation Theorists, Fordism, after a long and faltering gestation period between the wars, rose to predominance during the Second World War in the USA and spread throughout the rest of the capitalist world during the 1950s and 1960s (de Vroey, 1984; Lipietz, 1987). After this golden era, Fordism entered a period of sustained crisis during the 1970s, and is slowly being replaced by neo-Fordism. Here, computerisation enables the productive advantages of mass production to be maintained in highly flexible productive systems which can rapidly adapt to producing a range of, say, car models at varying levels of output. Consumption, at the same time, alters towards service activities and more expensive, individualised goods; a lifestyle encapsulated in that new social grotesque, the Yuppie. Society becomes divided into upwardly mobile high-spenders and a low-income stratum that undertakes the poorly paid, menial tasks necessary to the high-tech service economy. For Regulationists, patterns of production and consumption intermingle, but they need to be sustained. They argue that state institutions evolve to regulate the contemporary regime of accumulation, which is why the approach is called regulation theory. Keynesian-style national and international economic policies set up and policed by the USA after the war, for instance, regulated economic activity during the golden years of Fordism.

In the regulation approach, Britain's economic problems stem from an incapacity to adapt quickly enough to the new dominant regimes of accumulation. Fordist production methods were only half-heartedly adopted during the boom years of the 1950s and 1960s, which, it is claimed, is why Britain's growth lagged behind internationally. The transformations currently going on within the British economy and society are another half-hearted shift towards the neo-Fordist regime. The role of the Thatcher government is to help push a new flexibility amongst the workforce and to inculcate a new social ethic commensurable with new patterns of consumption (Murray, 1988; Jessop *et al.*, 1987). The regulation approach bases its theory and analysis, however, on a few broad generalisations (like the description of 'Fordism' and 'neo-Fordism') which many would regard as inadequate to the tasks assigned to them.

Whatever the merits of any of the Marxist approaches, the actual class structure of Britain is treated in all of the above in a rather cursory fashion. Two grand classes, capitalists and workers, feature at the centre, along with a motley collection of social blocks and institutions, such as the City, the state, trade unions, flexible workers and Yuppies, and multinational corporations. Highlighting particular aspects of Britain's social structure might be a reasonable way of homing in on the key issues. But little justification generally is given for the emphasis chosen.

Although all the theories of the British economy surveyed start from different premises and come to distinct conclusions, it can be seen that each focuses on a specific set of blockages or rigidities to explain the distinctiveness of Britain's economic development. At this stage, it is appropriate to consider the special features of the British economy.

PUTTING IN CONTEXT

Before proceeding any further it is worth noting that the explanatory significance of any special characteristic is likely to vary over time. If it could be demonstrated, for instance, that the City had a privileged influence over the conduct of economic policy, it also has to be possible for the Government to affect the variables of concern. In the 1980s, it could be argued that the Government had far less room for manoeuvre than previously over factors like exchange and interest rates because of the internationalisation of financial markets and their extreme volatility.

Paradoxically, as international financial markets increasingly dissociate themselves from the 'real' worlds of trade and production, any claimed power of the City might be waning.

The other major point to remember is that the world economy itself varies considerably over time, and its vicissitudes have a major impact on an economy as open to international trade as that of Britain. Perhaps the most notable feature of the world economy since 1945 is the shift away from record growth rates and expansion of world trade occurring from the earlier 1950s up to 1973 to a much slower pace, especially from 1980 onwards, as can be seen in Figure 3.1. Some of the recent economic 'success' is simply that Britain's growth rate has declined less than others. This could be interpreted either as implying that other economies are now facing up to

Figure 3.1   The Growth of World Trade, 1860–1985[1]

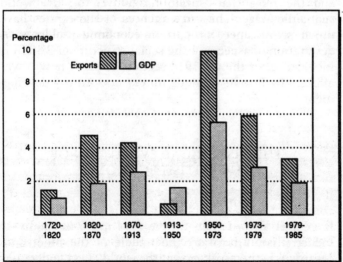

1. Selected major economies.
Source: World Bank (1987).

problems of stagnation that have afflicted Britain for years or that Britain is going through periodic bout of catching up with techniques and practices common elsewhere only later to fall back again. There is no *a priori* reason why the factors necessary to sustain growth in the late 1980s are the same as those which contributed to Britain's slow growth in the 1950s, 1960s and 1970s.

Explanation of the nature of the British economy remains open and highly controversial. All of the approaches outlined above highlighted certain institutional structures of the British economy, which have caused slow growth. Elaboration of some of those special characteristics and their historical origins now follows.

The narrative is divided into three periods that roughly correspond with major shifts in Britain's role in international trade, pre-1914, 1914–51 and 1951 onwards. No great importance should be attached to the specific dates or even to the periodisation. The aim is to reflect how capitalist economies have changed over two centuries and the roles that Britain has played on the world economic stage. The consequences of those roles have much significance for current economic problems. A description of aspects of the social structure of Britain is included, after the pre-1914 section, to show how it was affected by Britain's unique nineteenth-century development.

THE HISTORICAL EVOLUTION OF THE BRITISH ECONOMY

From workshop to world war

It is well known that, as the first major economy to industrialise, Britain by the middle of the nineteenth century was the 'workshop of the world'. Less understood is the effect of industrialisation on Britain's economy and society.

Some points are obvious. Along with industrialisation came large-scale population-growth and a shift of employment from agriculture. City dwelling became the standard way of life, with the urban population concentrated in seven dispersed conurbations, which at their peak in 1931 contained just over 40 per cent of the total population.

The rise of industrial employment was substantial during the nineteenth century but not overwhelmingly so. Already at the end of the eighteenth century, 30 per cent of the working population was employed in industry. In addition, service employment was substantial. A large banking and commercial sector, centred on London, grew up alongside industry, although its direct economic links with industry were limited. Firms generally relied on ploughed-back profits for investment and local county banks for overdrafts and banking facilities. The City was primarily concerned with international trade and finance, including non-British transactions; domestic and international insurance; government borrowing; and the export of capital.

Domestic service was also a major employer, particularly of women. Servants at the end of the nineteenth century constituted a much higher proportion of the population (3.8 per cent) than in other industrialising countries at similar times in their development (cf. USA 2.0 per cent, France 2.4 per cent and Germany 2.7 per cent [McBride, 1976]). This activity declined only in the first decades of the twentieth century with rises in real wages, the advent of domestic appliances, the growing specialisation of women in the domestic labour of the family, and the expansion of other waged employment opportunities for women (see Table 3.1).

Industrialisation up to the last quarter of the nineteenth century in Britain took the form of major improvements in productivity in quite a limited number of sectors – especially in textiles, coal, iron products, metalworking and mechanical engineering. Other sectors

TABLE 3.1 *Employment Patterns in Britain, 1801–1987 (percentage of total working population)*

	Agriculture	Industry[1]	Commerce[2]	Domestic service[3]	Armed forces	Public and other services[4]
1801	35.9	29.7	11.2	9.0	4.8	9.4
1851	21.7	42.9	15.8	10.1	1.4	8.1
1901	8.7	46.3	21.4	9.5	1.1	13.0
1951	5.1	47.6	22.0	2.3	2.5	20.5
1981	2.3	37.5	25.4	0.4	1.0	33.4
1987	1.4	30.6	35.5	n.a.	n.a.	32.5

1. Industry = mining, manufacturing, construction, gas, electricity and water.
2. Commerce = transport, distribution and finance.
3. Domestic service refers to wage labour only, and are excluded from the 1987 data along with the armed forces.
4. 'Public and other services' is a residual category of total employment minus the other categories; at the later dates it primarily consists of public administration, health and educational services.

Sources: 1801–1981, Rowthorn and Wells (1987); 1987, *Department of Employment Gazette.*

expanded considerably but experienced slower technical change, as in construction, the clothing industries and the processing of foodstuffs. The economy was dependent on the dynamism of a few sectors and on their success in world markets. International trade was paramount. Britain in 1899 had a third share of all the world's manufacturing exports and about 60 per cent of the world's merchant fleet. But exports were specialised: 40 per cent of manufacturing exports were textiles (25 per cent cotton alone), 15 per cent were iron and steel products, 10 per cent coal and 7 per cent machinery (Harley and McCloskey, 1981). So this small range of industries provided most exports (72 per cent), and most of those industries in turn were highly dependent on export markets. About 80 per cent of cotton textiles,

50 per cent of iron and steel, and 33 per cent of coal were exported. Each industry was also highly regionally concentrated.

The industrial revolution in Britain was primarily dependent on muscle power combined with the skill of craft workers and their employers in developing new products and ways of working. Standardisation was limited, and the application of science and formal education scanty. The workforce was divided by skill, gender, trade and locality. Much labour was underutilised or out of work. Workers were often low-paid, casually employed and easily dismissed. Employers took advantage of such labour flexibility and adopted labour-intensive, low-fixed-capital processes. Recessions were overwhelmingly borne by the workforce, while firms' low overheads tended to shield them from the worst effects of slumps.

In the last quarter of the nineteenth century, productivity improvements slowed down, and other countries began to catch up on Britain's earlier industrial lead. In some UK industries there were even falls in productivity, most notably in coal, the key provider of energy. British firms were slow to switch away from steam power, so the rising cost of coal hurt them and export markets also.

A second wave of innovations and industrial transformations occurred from 1870 to 1913. The period saw the advent of steel, electricity, refrigeration, organic chemicals, the internal combustion engine, the international telegraph and later telephone. In the inter-war years another range of products was developed including the modern media of cinema, radio and, later, television. New management techniques arose and marketing grew in importance. Standardisation, extensive research and development, 'scientific' management and mass production were at the centre of these industries, and the new techniques were also increasingly being applied to the older industries. Most of the modernisation occurred elsewhere. Manufacturing output in both the USA and Germany overtook Britain's in the decades prior to 1914.

The adverse effects of international competition were felt for the first time. The growth of other economies would obviously lower the share of international trade held by Britain. This was not necessarily a bad thing for British firms; in absolute terms they could have gained substantially from growing markets, by adopting new innovations from abroad and through an improved international division of labour. The problem was that few benefits of other countries' growth reflected back on to Britain's manufacturing base; instead the prime result was extra competition in export markets, and British firms were slowly squeezed out of the markets of the industrialising nations of Europe and North America. In the last quarter of the nineteenth century, Britain's exports of manufactures to Europe and the USA fell by over a third, while manufacturing imports, generally of the most advanced products, from these sources more than doubled. As one commentator has noted, 'instead of looking for new products for her old markets, she (Britain) had sought new markets for her old products' (Hardach, 1987, p. 288).

Associated with the industrialisation of the British economy during the nineteenth century was the expansion of empire. It is remarkable how little attention is given to the Empire in many explanations of the economic and social history of Britain. By the late 1890s, Britain's colonial population was 325 million; in comparison the next two largest imperialist powers (France and the Netherlands) had only around 35 million apiece and the rest below 10 million. (The comparison excludes the contiguous expansion through conquest of both the USA and Russia during the nineteenth century.)

Britain's empire was important for a number of reasons. As world competition in manufactures grew, British producers increasingly relied on Empire markets. Second, and as a consequence of the imperial trading patterns, Britain ran substantial surpluses on its trade with a number of colonies (especially India) to finance its

52

purchases of food and raw materials and advanced manufactures from other countries. Third, and perhaps of particular importance for the history of Britain, was the effect on Britain's social structure. A large empire required a significant number of Britons to be engaged in policing and administration, both domestically and in the colonies. Other aspects of society, as well as political life, took on an imperial gloss. Education at school and university directed the children of the middle class into occupations associated with the Empire, rather than towards industry. Social problems at home, as they became increasingly politically pressing from the late nineteenth century through to the 1950s, were confronted in ways reminiscent of British administrators' reactions to colonial native populations; namely, that social problems are isolated disorders that will succumb to the appropriate administrative measures and exhortations. Finally, Britain's imperial strategy was to help engulf it in two world wars, which considerably weakened its economic position and left a legacy of high military expenditure and research and development through to today.

British nationals in the second half of the century also built up extensive holdings of foreign assets. In the sixty years prior to 1914, an average of 5 per cent of national income was invested overseas. As a result the net stock of overseas holdings rose from 40 per cent of GDP in 1856 to 180 per cent in 1913. By the mid-1870s, property income from abroad was greater than net foreign investments. Receipts reached a peak of 8.5 per cent of national income just prior to the First World War (Matthews *et al.*, 1982). Investment was concentrated on funding the infrastructure and urbanisation of the main centres of European migration in North and South America, Southern Africa and Australia, and was not tied to the Empire. Income from abroad, combined with overseas receipts from financial services and shipping, plus the growth of coal exports in the last quarter of the nineteenth century

– whose effect was somewhat equivalent to North Sea oil in the 1980s – meant that Britain could cope with a significant deterioration in its balance of trade.

These positive financial flows slowly disappeared after the First World War and its financial aftermath. Net overseas assets halved as a proportion of British GDP by 1937, and the Second World War saw the liquidation of the rest. The cushion of net overseas income was thereby lost. There were some variations in the trend. With strong government support, capital exports resumed in the 1920s. Such outflows were one of the Treasury's aims in returning to the Gold Standard. In the changed circumstances capital export put pressure on the balance of payments and contributed to a government policy of high domestic interest rates. Capital exports then declined in the early 1930s, helping the balance of payments and the adoption of the policy of cheap money. In the inter-war years, shipping receipts also plummeted, and the City lost many of its roles as an international financial centre, particularly after 1931 when many of its activities were reduced to dealing with the Sterling Area only.

The social and economic structure of early twentieth-century Britain

British society in the Edwardian era was not only highly stratified but also very fragmented. Class differences were important, but unity within classes was frequently minimal because of regional, industry, job and income differences. Conflicts and social divisions existed even amongst the working class, despite much current romanticism about its erstwhile solidarity. The narrow specialisation of Britain's manufacturing base and export markets highlighted weaknesses of which contemporary observers were not entirely ignorant, but political unity beyond recourse to the Empire was impossible to achieve.

Governments increasingly intervened into people's daily lives with the growth of the welfare state, urban planning and infrastructure provision. Local government was frequently the chosen vehicle, so its role in the economy grew rapidly from the 1890s. But each social problem was treated in isolation, rather than regarded as implying the need for substantial change to contemporary British society. The partial solutions adopted, moreover, were usually grudgingly seen by governments as imposing economic costs rather than conferring long-term benefits as necessary components of a successful modern industrial society. Despite a variety of political programmes from both the Left and the Right, strategies to transform the social and economic structure of Britain to meet the needs of the newly emerging productive forms never featured at the centre of the political agenda. Even the rise of labour was primarily an attempt to give it a rightful voice in the political hierarchy rather than a sustained attempt at social transformation. The formation of the Labour Party itself was encouraged by the dominant trade unions of the day because of the drubbing taken by them from the courts and government in disputes.

A general impression of the economic dimensions of the divisions in Edwardian society can be seen by looking at the share of national income generated by each sector and the share going to each category of income (Tables 3.2 and 3.3). Despite the impression of Britain being one of the world's manufacturing powerhouses during this period, only 27 per cent of GDP was generated by manufacturing in 1913. In 1856, it was only 22 per cent, so the 'workshop of the world' earned less of its total income from manufacturing than does present-day deindustrialised Britain (see Table 3.2). The other main sectors in 1913 were transport, commerce and the public sector, which together contributed almost half of GDP. A greater percentage of the total employment was in industry than its share of GDP, indicating that even in

TABLE 3.2 *National Income by Industry, United Kingdom, 1856–1986 (percentages)*[1]

	1856[2]	*1913*[2]	*1937*	*1951*	*1964*	*1973*	*1980*	*1986*
Agriculture	18	6	4	6	3	3	2	2
Mining, quarrying	5	6	4	4	3	2	2	1
Petroleum and natural gas	–	–	–	–	–	–	4	3
Manufacturing	22	27	30	36	34	30	23	24
Construction	3	3	5	5	7	8	6	6
Gas, electricity and water	–	2	3	2	3	3	3	3
Transport and communications	7	11	10	9	8	9	8	7
Commerce[3]	24	27	30	24	26	27	27	30
Public and professional services	9	10	14	15	16	18	19	16
Ownership of dwellings	13	8	6	3	4	6	6	6

1. Percentages contain rounding errors.
2. 1856 and 1913 at constant 1907 prices, other years at current prices.
3. Commerce includes distributive trades, insurance, banking, finance and business services and miscellaneous services.

Sources: 1856–1973, Matthews, Feinstein and Odling-Smee (1982); 1980, NIESR (1982); 1986, *United Kingdom National Accounts*, HMSO.

the Edwardian era some of the higher-value-added activities were in commerce. Commercial work would have had a high white-collar, if not necessarily well-paid, bias.

Turning to categories of income (Table 3.3), labour's share was much lower in 1913 than today at only 56 per cent of national income compared with around 70 per

TABLE 3.3 *Income Shares, 1856–1973 (percentage of GDP)*

	1856	1913	1937	1951	1973
Wages	44	37	39	42	34
Salaries	7	12	18	20	27
Employers' contributions, etc.	–	1	3	4	7
Self-employed labour income	7	7	6	5	5
Total labour income	58	56	65	71	73
Income from abroad	2	9	4	3	2
Rent	5	6	6	3	7
Farm property income	10	2	1	2	1
Profits	25	27	23	21	17
Total property income	42	44	35	29	27

Source: Matthews *et al.* (1982).

cent in the mid-1980s. By 1913, already a quarter of labour's share was paid in salaries. Labour's share increased in two significant leaps during both world wars, otherwise it has been fairly constant. Wage workers' share continued to fall and the salaried to rise until the present day, reflecting the changing composition of the workforce. Income from property was 44 per cent of national income in 1913. Its share fell most sharply (by 10 per cent) during and immediately after the First World War, reflecting the loss of overseas investment income and a decline in the domestic profit rate. In 1913, only half of property income (i.e. 22 per cent of GNP) was derived from non-farm profits. The euthanasia of the rentier had yet to be achieved, and Keynes's prediction has still not come true today.

Regional data prior to the First World War are rather hazy, but again do not indicate that the greatest amount of 'muck' produced the most 'brass'. The first half of the nineteenth century did see a noticeable convergence of per-capita regional incomes, but they diverged again so that, by 1911/12, average incomes in the South East were over twice as high as in the next region, the agrarian South West. The high average incomes of the South East to a great extent reflected the very unequal distribution of income, the propensity of the rich to live in the London region, and the concentration of middle-class jobs in the metropolis. This gave the London economy a distinctive character. For manual workers, non-factory forms of employment were the norm. Artisanal work was at a premium, pandering especially to the tastes of the rich, and unskilled work was casual and poorly paid. Although the northern regions were the prime source of the enormous wealth realised through industrial production, there was no positive correlation between the more industrialised regions and higher income per head. Some of the regional concentrations of employment were incredible. In 1841, 42 per cent of jobs in Lancashire and 35 per cent in the West Riding were in textiles and clothing alone. Although these concentrations were reduced in the second half of the century, 82 per cent of new textile jobs between 1841 and 1911 were still created in those two regions. The South East also did well in employment growth, capturing 32 per cent of new employment between those census years, two-thirds of it in service industries (Lee, 1986).

In summary, even a brief overview of the economic categories presented in this section show that the economic interests of large sections of the British population in the Edwardian era were not very closely tied to manufacturing industry. Within manufacturing there were also substantial differences of interest, depending on the industry in question, its social composition and regional distribution. Even in the classic heyday of British capitalism, it seems unwise to divide the nation's social structure into the aristocracy and its hangers-on, the City and rentiers, captains of industry and the horny-handed working class, as some commentators have tried to do (cf. Anderson, 1987). Despite, or perhaps because of, losing most of its agrarian population decades before other nations, Britain's social structure was as complex as it is today.

The transformation of the British economy, 1914–51

The industrialising of other nations and the whittling away of Britain's economic lead in the years prior to the First World War created both new forms of production and a new international division of labour. The major world markets were not surprisingly in the countries which became dominated by industrial capitalism. Their firms were the ones demanding the investment and intermediate manufactured goods, and their consumers had the greatest purchasing power. Europe and North America were now major centres of world demand, and a new international division of labour was created with manufacturing countries and primary producers specialising, though of course not mutually exclusively, in particular types of export goods. Economically, therefore, the rise of new industries, products and methods of production and their uneven distribution between the major industrial states was forcing a greater economic integration between countries – particularly in politically fragmented Europe.

Politically, however, forces were pulling countries apart. Imperial designs, geopolitical manoeuvrings and jingoism created intense rivalry between the main industrial powers. The situation was not fundamentally resolved within the non-socialist world until after the Second World War, when the overwhelming economic and military supremacy of the United States enabled its governments to impose their designs on the post-1945 world. Justification for the earlier political rivalry was often couched in economic terms, even if the arguments were frequently spurious or short-sighted. Tariff barriers were erected, particularly against British imports, in many countries after the 1870s, and the race for Empire was sometimes justified in terms of markets and monopolisable sources of key raw materials. As the overwhelming dominant imperial and sea power, Britain could either try to outbid its rivals or push for a new post-imperial economic order. Such choices, with hindsight, may seem clear, but given the social hierarchy of contemporary British society the direction taken was virtually inevitable.

At one level, successive British governments were remarkably successful in their global political strategies. The Empire was considerably expanded between 1870 and 1918, and then defended until post-1945. But the cost to the peoples of the world, to the domestic economy and to future British economic prospects was catastrophic. When Britain was finally forced to accept a new world economic and political order in the 1950s and 1960s, it was from a position of economic weakness rather than of strength.

The First World War saw major losses of world markets for British goods and services. The staple export industries entered severe crisis, but failed to restructure adequately until the 1960s and 1970s, by which time the changing international division of labour has passed them by, as new countries gradually replaced West European ascendancy in textiles, shipbuilding, iron and steel and coal. Services, too, were badly hit as shipping revenues declined, and New York replaced London as the financial capital of the world. Trade rivalry was increased by payments problems created by the collapse of the multilateral world economic system in 1914, and Europe's post-war burdens of debt.

The 1930s slump forced British industry even further back on to domestic and imperial markets. New industries did grow up – chemicals, artificial fibres, and consumer goods, for instance – but they never seemed to be at the forefront of contemporary industrial practice. Technical leads, such as Courtauld's in rayon, were under-exploited, so that initial advantages when they arose were gradually whittled away. Firms merged or grew internally, so that Britain's unique small-enterprise Edwardian industrial structure began to disappear. But mergers were usually defensive – involving financial reconstructions and frequently undertaken to reduce capacity and protect markets – rather than undertaken to achieve radical restructuring and economies of scale. Even in the new industries, products were often technically simple and produced in the old ways rather than by utilising the benefits of mass production.

The inter-war car industry is a prime example. Producers had the advantages of the availability of cheap funds for investment and a highly protected and rapidly expanding home market. Yet cars were produced by a casualised, semi-skilled workforce with only half-hearted application of US-style production and marketing techniques. 'In 1939 the six leading British producers, making roughly 350,000 private cars, turned out more than forty different engine types and an even greater number of chassis and body models, which was considerably more than the number offered by the three leading producers in the United States making perhaps 3,500,000 cars' (Kahn, 1946, quoted in Alford, 1981). Barnett (1987) makes even more far-reaching criticism of aircraft and valve production during the 1940s, amongst a wide range of cited industrial failures.

The Second World War brought state economic intervention on a scale never seen before. During the war years, military needs took precedence in industry. An embryo of post-war society emerged, however, in which the state was to continue playing a major economic role, both in providing basic welfare services and in Keynesian-style economic regulation. A widespread consensus on social and economic priorities was achieved, and many politicians hoped that the state could succeed with minimum interference to property rights and the market mechanism. Keynesian theory, as it was then interpreted, principally meant management of aggregate demand in face of perceived constraints, such as maintaining a stable exchange rate, full employment and balanced trade. The welfare state meant providing minimum standards of consumption goods – like Beveridge's national insurance, council housing, the National Health Service and state education. Beyond the national minima, people could choose to opt out into the private market. Both approaches can be classified as *Liberal Interventionist*. Thatcherism has not so much gone against this perspective; rather, it has reduced the state-provided minima, making market options seem far more attractive.

Post-war nationalisation brought large parts of industry and transportation into the state fold. Telephones, the postal service, airports, the two major airlines, much of the production and distribution of electricity, gas and water were already public industries. Coal, the railways and briefly road freight and steel were nationalised. Later, in the 1960s and 1970s, steel was to be renationalised, as were ports, aerospace and shipbuilding. Government by the end of the 1970s also had substantial stakes in oil production and distribution, and a motley selection of bankrupt or high-tech firms ranging from British Leyland and Rolls-Royce to Amersham International and Inmos. State intervention through ownership itself took specific forms. It relied on profit-centred management constrained by ministerial directive. Workers' control was firmly ruled out, and nationalised industries were progressively used as test beds for new industrial relations strategies – a device which Conservative governments in the 1980s used to great effect. Greatest political consensus was achieved for the acquisition of lame-duck industries or those on which other sectors were heavily reliant.

Britain's economy in the early 1950s reached its maximum reliance on manufacturing industry: 36 per cent of national income originated there, and 48 per cent of all employers worked in an industry of some sort. The emphasis on industry was partly due to the collapse of parts of the service economy and their sources of demand in the pre-war and war years and the exigencies of the war economy. All industries were booming, the old as well as the new – more ships were built in Britain in the early 1950s than ever before, for example. Rapidly escalating raw-material and foodstuff prices made the balance of payments a source of great governmental concern. The 1945 Labour government could encourage a manufactured goods export drive effectively through the use of the detailed physical controls made possible by rationing. In 1951, for example, 78 per cent of UK car output was exported, principally to the Sterling Area rather than to Western Europe. Car exports did not fall below 50 per cent of output until 1955. Serving buoyant overseas demand was encouraged by a swinging 67 per cent purchase tax on home demand, and by controls on the allocation of steel for car bodies. Western European competitors were in ruins, so British industry had enormous advantages. However, a seller's market meant that investment – though it rose above pre-war levels – could be relatively neglected, with the continuation of low-productivity employment practices of many pre-war industries. Cairncross (1985), for instance, argues that the growth of British exports was principally the product of an exogenous rise in world demand for manufactures, rather than of any improvement in British competitiveness. It is not clear, in other words, how much of the diversion of resources into manufacturing in this period was sustainable in the longer term, nor how much the diversion put off the evil day when competition would reappear. After the lifting of controls in the early 1950s,

British industry reverted to its pre-war practices, and continued to rely on Imperial/Commonwealth markets. The proportion of UK exports bound for the colonies (or recently independent ones) in fact reached its peak during these years.

The internationalisation of the world economy

The decade after 1945 was exceptional. The division of the world into trading blocks effectively continued because of chronic shortages of dollars and the continued reliance of Britain on Empire and Commonwealth trade. The USA was both politically and economically over-whelming – at the end of the 1940s its industrial production was as large as the rest of the world's. It helped to sustain demand in the industrial countries by funding much of the investment occurring in Europe and Asia, and helped to head off any balance-of-payments problems countries might face. US action was not altruistic in that its governments demanded conformity to US foreign-policy interests, plus constraints on 'social-ism' and trade unions, while extra demand bolstered US exports and diminished fears of renewed depression. Once reconstruction in war-torn Europe and Asia was near completion, the long post-war boom was well under way.

One consequence of the peculiar situation in the years after 1945 was that countries' economies came as close as they ever would to the Keynesian ideal model of fully employed, domestically centred systems. Production was nationally based. The contemporary international divi-sion of labour consisted of countries' specialising in specific types of commodity and fairly limited trade between nations, while financial systems were nationally orientated.

Once there was a general dismantling of the barriers to international economic relations, erected during the Imperialist era and reinforced by Fascism, the 1930s slump and the needs of war, the domestication of national economies inevitably went into reverse. The organisation of production associated with modern mass-production techniques with their ability to separate out specific functions – including purchases of many subcomponents and services – does not require all respects of production to take place on one site. In fact it is generally more profitable for production to be spread through a variety of locations, and they need not all be within one country. Where the markets served are international, final assembly itself can be spread across various countries to reduce transport costs, to take advantage of wage differentials or to circumvent trade barriers. Technical developments in production techniques, stock control, and management hierarchies, all aided by the use of computers, have continued the trend into the 1980s. Rising wage costs in the most advanced nations, improvements in transportation and the increasing drawing together of world money markets have all aided a reintegration of the world economy and an internationalisation of production.

During the long post-war boom, world trade was a prime stimulus to expansion. International trade, on average, grew one and a half times as fast as world output. Rather than exporting completed commodities, capital was increasingly exported to create new overseas productive facilities. Firms, particularly US ones, set up foreign plants leading to the growth of the multinational company. The process was not new. Production of primary commodities prior to 1939 had often been controlled by foreign capital, while the US Singer sewing machine company set up a production plant in Britain in the late nineteenth century, to be followed by other corporations in electrical engineering and vehicles. Nevertheless, in the post-1945 years, multinationals grew dramatically so that today the value of the foreign output of the multinationals exceeds the value of the manufacturing trade of many countries. At the same time, much international trade now consists of the affiliates of one parent company shipping components or completed goods between each other. In the early 1980s, such shipments counted for over a quarter of total British trade, while foreign and domestic multinationals accounted for over 80 per cent of all exports.

The new international division of labour that grew up from the late 1950s led all nations' economies to become more open to international trade – a process that is continuing. There are obviously considerable differences in the openness of specific economies, depending on resource endowments, the competitive strength of firms producing there, and the response of governments to

TABLE 3.4 *The Opening Up of the World's Economies, 1960–83*

| | Imports of goods and services as % of domestic demand | | | | Imports of manufactures as % of domestic demand for manufactures[1] | | |
	1960	1970	1980	1983	1970	1980	1983[2]
Canada	18	21	28	23	27	31	34
USA	4	6	11	9	6	9	10
Japan	10	10	15	12	5	6	6
France	13	16	24	24	16	23	24
W. Germany	17	20	28	29	19	31	36
Italy	14	17	27	26	16	32	33
Netherlands	47	46	53	57	52	62	68
UK	22	23	26	26	16	28	31
EC (external imports only)	–	10	14	13	nk	nk	nk

1. Most manufactures are internationally traded, whereas many services are not.
2. 1983 estimated.
3. 1982 data.
Source: *HM Treasury Economic Progress Report*, 178, June 1985.

import growth. The USA and Japan are much less open to imports than are the countries of Western Europe, but once intra-EC trade is excluded the magnitudes for the three 'blocks' are not dissimilar (see Table 3.4). US imports have grown rapidly since 1970, and although Japan is still highly resistant to imports it is firmly integrated into the world economic system through its prodigious exports. It should be noted that despite years of deindustrialisation and import penetration Britain's imports as a proportion of domestic demand are on a scale similar to those of France, Italy and West Germany.

The years of crisis

The ending of the post-war boom in the early 1970s exposed the weakness of the British economy. Profit rates had been declining since the mid-1950s. Unemployment started to climb from the mid-1960s as manufacturing firms shed labour in response to their loss of markets and a major bout of corporate restructuring – induced in the second half of the 1960s by government and a merger boom. Inflation also began to creep up. The subsequent turndown in the world economy coincided with the first oil-price rise of 1973. Record balance-of-payments deficits persisted from 1973 until 1976, as the value of imports rose following a 1972–3 government-induced consumer boom (the Barber Boom, as it came to be known), and an oil-price jump; all paid for in rapidly depreciating sterling (the effective exchange rate declined 22 per cent between December 1971 and January 1975). Against this background, Britain in 1973 finally joined the Common Market, Western Europe's main trading block, and by 1978 all trading barriers between Britain and the rest of the EEC were finally removed.

Balance-of-payments problems, a sterling crisis and the

67

intervention of the International Monetary Fund were used as justification by the Labour government in 1976 to abandon the full-employment objective of post-war governments and to espouse a policy of deflation which came to be known as monetarism. Ostensibly a simple policy of controlling the supply of money, monetarism became an excuse for a complex set of deflationary measures. The scale of public expenditure became a government and media obsession. Public-expenditure cuts were aimed at reducing the public-sector borrowing requirements (PSBR) – although there is no theoretical reason why growth in the money supply should be affected by the size of the PSBR, and the empirical correlation between PSBR and the money supply, however defined, is scant. Interest rates rose – although, given the scale of inflation, in real terms they were negative for most of the rest of the 1970s. The Labour government and the later Thatcher administrations added explicit or implicit incomes policies to the deflation armoury, and frequently these were directed at the public sector only.

The 1970s were a period of considerable strike activity – an upward shift experienced in many other countries as well. The three-day week in 1974 and the winter of discontent in 1979 are perhaps the most memorable.

The Thatcher government of 1979 had a clear view of the nation's ills – too much government and too much union power. It introduced a strongly deflationary policy at a time when the value of sterling was rising rapidly and the world economy was on the brink of the greatest depression since the 1930s. The result was a major collapse of employment and output, particularly in manufacturing where employment fell by 21 per cent between December 1979 and December 1982, a loss of a million and a half jobs. Since then sectors of the economy have recovered, along with a recovery in the world economy as a whole, but not to the growth rates experienced in the 1950s and the 1960s.

BRITAIN: A HISTORY OF MAJOR
ECONOMIC CHANGE

This chapter has briefly considered views on Britain's relative economic backwardness, and then examined some central aspects of the country's economic development. What is apparent from that historical survey is the uniqueness of its pattern of development and of its economic institutions and wider social structure.

It is important, however, that Britain's ills should not be put down to a notion of a moribund economy stricken by a malaise that never allowed it to change. Because of its early start in industrialisation and because of its imperialist past, Britain has had to alter its economic structure more than any other advanced capitalist economy. It is the extent of change that is noticeable. Nineteenth-century staples gave way to 'second industrial revolution' consumer and capital goods industries that in their turn went into a crisis from the mid-1960s onwards from which some industries have never recovered. Strong specialisation in manufacturing in the years after 1945 was superseded by the growth of services.

Patterns of overseas trade have reflected and to an extent caused these major shifts. Rowthorn and Wells (1987) classify Britain as one of the few countries that radically shifted its trade specialisation in the post-war years, while most other economies have been able to remain within a similar broad range of specialisation. Changes, however, did not occur through a cataclysmic obliteration of all that existed before. The 'revolution' of the 1980s must be seen with this in mind.

FURTHER READING

The current state of macroeconomic theory can be reviewed in one of the large numbers of macroeconomic texts. Begg, Dornbusch and Fischer (1987) is a clearly written introductory starting point. It is more difficult to find reasonable general accounts of different views on the economy. Most textbooks take the 'there is only one true economic science' line and so tend to play down or ignore approaches that differ from their own. Some books deliberately deal with controversies and try to give an overview of some of them, such as Vane and Caslin (1987). Journals such as *Capital and Class*, from the Conference of Socialist Economists, and the *Cambridge Journal of Economics* are useful reference sources for alternative viewpoints.

The references cited in the text are the best introduction to the opinions of the different schools of economics. For an introduction to Marxist economic thought, see Fine (1988). Coates and Hillard (1987) present papers from a wide variety of perspectives highlighting the 'economic decline' of Britain and reasons for it.

The history of the British economy is covered by a large number of texts. Crouzet (1982) provides a survey of the Victorian economy and debates around it. Hobsbawm (1969) remains a classic overview from the industrial revolution to the mid-1960s, although now it is somewhat dated. Floud and McCloskey (1981) provides useful survey articles for the period 1860–1970; while Lee (1986) is a good overview from the eighteenth century to the 1980s. The international scene is surveyed in Foreman-Peck (1983). Fieldhouse (1973) is a readable introduction to the causes of the imperialist era.

There are many books on the post-1945 period. Some were cited in the text, others are suggested in the appropriate chapters later in the book. Dornbusch and Layard (1987) is a good overview of the position of mainstream economists on the 1980s economy.

4

Trade and Industry
Michael Ball

Two areas in which the British economy has been exposed to major difficulties during most of the post-war era are the trade balance and international competition in world markets.

Periods of economic growth have been brought to a halt by deteriorations in the trade balance. In the 1960s, this characteristic of post-war Britain was dubbed 'stop-go'. Balance-of-payments problems receded with the production of North Sea oil in the late 1970s. But, after a decade of improvement and substantial current-account surpluses recorded from 1980 to 1985, trade deficits resurfaced as a major constraint on growth in 1987–8 with manufactured imports being sucked in by an economic upturn. The Government was forced to switch from an expansionary policy to attempts to restrict demand. Although reminiscent of the early era of 'stop-go', the Chancellor hoped to use high interest rates only, rather than a full Keynesian-style array of fiscal and monetary measures; many were sceptical of the Chancellor's optimism.

Underlying changes in the overall balance of trade since 1945 have been major shifts in the composition of trade. Britain's trade has altered both in the types of goods that are exported and imported and in the countries which are its major trading partners. The prime moving force in recent decades has been the integration of the UK economy with that of the rest of Western Europe. Along with that integration, there has been a long-term decline in the manufactured-goods trade balance.

Deindustrialisation, a move away from manufacturing industry towards service activities, has been associated with Britain's changing trade patterns. Deindustrialisation has been argued to be a beneficial sign of the advanced nature of the British economy and, conversely, the result of a gradual weakening of the manufacturing base which will be the cause of major economic crises in the future.

This chapter examines in detail the changing patterns of trade and the causes of them. The deindustrialisation debate is then considered in depth and the links between it and worries over the balance of trade are drawn out.

TRADE AND THE BALANCE OF PAYMENTS

To understand the problems arising over the balance of payments, we must look at both the current and capital accounts. Overall, the balance of payments must balance, by definition. If the current account is in deficit, a net inflow must exist on the capital account. The positive financial flows may arise from, say, foreigners' funds invested on the money and capital markets; overseas borrowing (from the IMF in the last resort as Britain did in 1976) and asset sales; or through a rundown of the country's exchange reserves.

Adjustments in the balance of payments are directly influenced by the effective exchange rate, as it alters the relative price of imports and exports. How far exports and imports are responsive to price changes, however, is a matter of controversy. Some would argue that the price effects are relatively small, as demand for advanced manufactures is strongly influenced by the nature of the products (such as their quality and their specific attributes) rather than by their price (cf. Thirwall, 1982a). The level of domestic interest rates will also have an important short-run effect on the balance of payments as their relative real levels (i.e. taking account of differences in domestic and foreign inflation rates) will affect the flow of capital into the country and the demand for imports. The exchange rate and interest rates can be influenced by governments through their economic policies.

The changing composition of trade

Britain's balance-of-payments problems can best be understood by concentrating first on the structure of the current account – that is, the goods (visibles) and services (invisibles) imported and exported. During the past century and a half, the product and geographic shifts of trade have been substantial, and the speed of change accelerated considerably after 1970.

Successive generations became accustomed to being told by politicians and media commentators that Britain must export manufactures in order to pay for imports of raw materials and food. Such a pattern of trade was broadly true from the last quarter of the nineteenth century until the 1960s. Even during this period, quite a number of manufactures were imported, but they generally accounted for less than a quarter of imports. The vast bulk of imports was raw materials, to be processed by industry, and foodstuffs. A regime of exporting manufactures to pay for basic commodity imports can be seen clearly in Table 4.1 for the inter-war years and also for the late 1950s. This pattern of trade began to change in the 1960s. Manufactures gradually formed a greater proportion of imports and a smaller proportion of exports. By the early 1970s, over half the goods imported were manufactures; a figure which dramatically increased to almost three-quarters by the mid-1980s.

There are several reasons for the change in the composition of imports. First, incomes have risen substantially since the war. Progressively less of extra income is

TABLE 4.1 *The Changing Composition of Imported Goods, 1935–86 (percentages)*

	1935–8	1956–63	1972–6	1977–80	1986
Food, beverages and tobacco	47	37	18	15	12
Basic materials	26	23	11	9	6
Fuel	5	12	17	13	7
Manufactures	21	28	53	61	73

Sources: 1935–80, NIESR (1982); 1986, *National Institute Economic Review*, November 1987.

spent on food, while more is spent on manufactured goods, so the growing share of manufactures partly reflects shifts in the pattern of consumption associated with greater national prosperity. Another factor has been the large fall in the real price of non-oil primary commodities on world markets. In 1986, real commodity prices were on average less than half of their peak levels in the early and mid-1970s (World Bank, 1987). This has yielded considerable benefits to the trade balance and the UK economy since the value of a given volume of primary commodity imports is much less than a decade earlier, although the existence of the European Community's Common Agricultural Policy has limited the beneficial effects for UK consumers.

The second reason for the shift in import shares is that firms now use raw materials more efficiently because of improved methods of production, and have greater recourse to domestically produced materials such as plastics (now derived from UK oil). So, the raw-material component of most goods today is far less than thirty years ago, and the import content even lower. Increasingly, too, manufacturers work on materials or components that have already gone through at least one manufacturing process – classified as semi-manufactures. Given the new international division of labour, many of these are imported. In 1986, for example, only 64 per cent of Britain's manufactures imports were actually finished goods.

Food imports have declined absolutely as well as proportionately because of the substantial increase in domestic food production arising from the use of intensive farming methods. Increased agricultural productivity has been encouraged by state subsidy and intervention and, more recently, by the Common Agricultural Policy. Food exports were about half the size of imports in 1986, leaving a deficit equivalent to slightly over 1 per cent of GDP, compared to over 7 per cent in the early 1950s. With regard to fuel, imports rose in the 1950s and 1960s because of greater car ownership and oil-fired electricity generation. The oil-price rise of 1973 caused a further hike, but the appearance of North Sea oil led to a sharp fall in imports and major exports of the fuel. The trade benefits of those exports, however, were reduced considerably by the collapse of oil prices in 1985.

Fuel imports are also likely to change in the future given the Government's declared aim of increasing substantially the proportion of electricity generated from nuclear power stations. Whatever the overall merits of such a strategy, one result should be that fuel imports will fall in the long term but in the medium term the balance of trade could be adversely affected by the need to import a considerable part of the generating equipment. British coal has also lost its protected market for power-station coal in the late 1980s, following government policies on encouraging alternative sources and the electricity privatisation programme. The consequence will be a rise in coal imports, although by an unknown volume.

Changes in the composition of imports consequently arose because of sharp declines in the import requirements of non-manufactured commodities; although some

TABLE 4.2 *The Changing Composition of UK Exports, 1975–86 (percentages)*

	1975	1980	1986
Food, drink, tobacco and basic materials	9	10	10
Fuels	6	14	19
Manufactures and miscellaneous	85	76	71

Source: *Bank of England Quarterly Bulletin*, August 1987.

of the falls in raw-material imports have been caused by reduced manufacturing activity in the 1980s.

Looking at exports, the arrival of North Sea oil changed the composition of exports away from manufactures (Table 4.2). Oil, in 1986, constituted almost 20 per cent of commodity exports. Even so, most exports were still manufactures (71 per cent in 1986, down from 85 per cent in 1975).

The changing pattern of trade

Western Europe is now Britain's main trading area. Its rise can be seen in the changing sources of visible imports. By 1986, 65 per cent of Britain's imports came from Western Europe – 52 per cent from the EEC alone. The losers were the non-OPEC Third World, which in 1951 provided almost a third of Britain's imports but only a tenth in 1986. Japan, contrary to widespread opinion, was the source of a mere 6 per cent of imported goods in 1986 (*Annual Abstract of Statistics*, 1988).

During the course of this century, Britain's export markets have also changed considerably. On the eve of the First World War, export markets were broadly spread – albeit with an Imperial bias (Table 4.3a). The inter-war years saw a retreat from markets in Western Europe and much of the rest of the world outside of the Empire. Peak

TABLE 4.3A *Exports by Location, 1913–80 (percentage shares)*

	1913	1937	1955	1956–63	1964–71	1972–6	1977–80
Western Europe	31	26	27	31	44	49	56
Sterling area[1]	33	43	49	39	24	18	17
North America	10	12	11	15	16	14	11
Rest of world	26	19	13	15	16	18	16

1. Countries outside of Europe previously in the sterling block – principally the Empire/Commonwealth.
Source: NIESR (1982).

TABLE 4.3B *Exports by Location, 1980–8 (percentage shares)*

	1980	1984	1988
European Community	43	45	50
Rest of Western Europe	14	12	10
North America	11	16	16
Other developed countries	6	5	5
Oil exporting countries	10	8	7
Other developing countries	12	8	11
Centrally planned economies	3	2	2

Source: *Annual Abstract of Statistics.*

reliance on Empire/Commonwealth markets occurred in the mid-1950s, when they took almost half of all visible exports. In the post-Imperial world, Western Europe has taken a growing export share at the expense of the Commonwealth. Over half of exports now go to Western Europe, while in the mid-1980s almost a fifth went to North America and the booming US market.

The changing structure of the balance of payments

Services, fuel exports and property income from abroad sustained a large visible trade deficit at the turn of the century. Manufacturing exports had to fill the gap left by them in the decades after 1913 and even more so after 1945. Nowadays, the balance of payments again relies heavily on services, fuel exports and property income from abroad. But strong changes are still occurring which could create serious trade problems in the years to come.

The visible trade balance for the decade 1976–86 is shown graphically in Figures 4.1 and 4.2. The rise of oil surpluses after 1979 is clear, although the surplus can be seen to decline following the oil-price fall of 1985 and it will drop even further as oil production has now passed its peak. Quite when the oil account will again be in deficit is a topic of much dispute because depletion rates,

Figure 4.1   The Balance of Payments, 1976–86

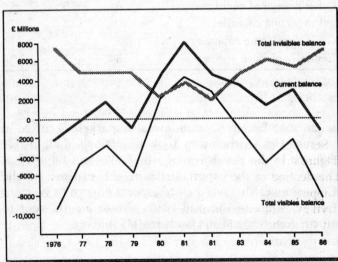

Figure 4.2   Sectoral Trade Balances, 1976–86

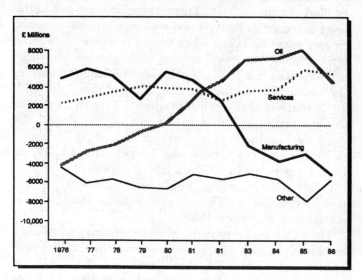

new discoveries and the future price of oil are unpredictable.

Major changes have occurred in the manufacturing balance. There was a dramatic reversal from healthy surpluses in the second half of the 1970s to an increasing deficit from 1983 onwards. In fact, the manufacturing balance has been on a declining trend since the days of record export shares in the early 1950s (Rowthorn and Wells, 1987).

Services overall show a large and increasing surplus (Figure 4.1). But the picture on the service side is mixed. The decline of the merchant fleet has led to traditional shipping surpluses being replaced by substantial deficits. Civil aviation earned substantial surplus up to the 1980s, but since then has been slowly sliding into deficit. Travel and tourism, after major surpluses in the 1970s, are again in deficit. Altogether these three categories were almost

£2000 million in deficit in 1986, compared with a £1000 million surplus in 1976. Travel is highly sensitive to the level of economic activity and exchange-rate movements, so care must be taken when trying to extrapolate long-term trends, but even so the trade picture for these services does not look rosy. It was only the increase in the financial and other services account since the mid-1970s that has kept services in surplus. Even that increase as a proportion of GDP is, in fact, not so great, despite the Big Bang, Euromarkets, and all that. In 1986, the financial and other services surplus was 2.6 per cent of GDP, up from 1.7 per cent in 1976 – a rate of growth far less than the slide in the manufacturing balance from +3.6 per cent to −2.6 per cent of GDP between the same years (*Annual Abstract of Statistics*, 1988).

The other major positive item on the current balance in the mid-1980s has been the net inflow of interest, profits and dividends, which rose over 2.5 times on average between the late 1970s and mid-1980s. As Table 4.4 shows, these items are a consequence of greater flows of capital both into and out of the country. They have led to a rapid increase in payments to foreigners as well as leading to greater receipts from abroad. The payments outflows arise from UK residents and the government borrowing abroad and from investment by foreigners in Britain. To a great extent, the extra flows are associated with the increasing international nature of financial activity. The opening-up of the world's financial markets has led to both greater borrowings from abroad and increased foreign ownership of UK stocks and shares. Inward portfolio investment (i.e. investment in the stock, bond and money markets) was by 1986 40 per cent higher than inward direct investment, whereas previously it had been much lower (Table 4.4).

The take-off of UK investment overseas has been much greater than inward investment, particularly after the abolition of exchange controls in 1979. Many commentators have regarded it as a wholesale flight of capital from

TABLE 4.4 *Cross-Country Transfers and Investment and the British Economy, 1976–86*
(£ million at current prices)

	1976	1978	1980	1982	1984	1986
Interest, profits and dividends balance	1550	821	–219	1078	4216	4686
Transfers balance	–786	–1791	–1995	–1809	–1839	–2193
Overseas investment						
direct	2419	3520	4886	4090	6086	11386
portfolio	–95	1073	3230	6710	9550	22870
Foreign investment in UK						
direct	1653	1962	4355	3027	–181	5420
portfolio	1032	–139	1499	225	1419	8202
Gross domestic fixed capital formation[1]	20114	24851	32277	32807	40202	46104

1. Excludes personal-sector investment which is primarily for new housing.
Source: *Annual Abstract of Statistics*, 1988.

Britain. Between 1978 and 1986, overseas investment rose sevenfold (Table 4.4), although a subsequent appreciation of the pound (especially against the dollar) and the aftermath of the crash in world stock markets produced a large fall in the value of overseas assets during 1987. Throughout the 1980s, none the less, British firms bought up foreign companies and invested in plant and equipment. But the greatest increase (prior to late 1987) was in portfolio investment by financial institutions and the personal sector. In 1986, portfolio investment was twice as high as direct overseas investment, and together they were equivalent to three-quarters of total gross domestic fixed-capital formation (excluding the personal sector).

Exports of capital on such a scale have not been seen in Britain since before 1914, although the return as a proportion of GDP is still quite low – net investment income from abroad was still only 1.6 per cent of GDP in 1986. It would take many years of capital exports on the scale of the mid-1980s to amass a stock of overseas assets of the relative size of Britain's eighty years earlier. Even if on a long-term historical perspective Britain's current overseas assets do not match those of the Edwardian era, they still indicate the longevity of unique patterns in the country's international economic relations. The two countries with the largest international trade surpluses during the 1980s were Japan and West Germany. Yet, in the late 1980s, their net holdings of overseas assets as a proportion of GDP were nowhere near Britain's. Japan's net overseas assets in 1987 were 8 per cent of GDP, West Germany's 12 per cent, and Britain's a much larger 20 per cent; the USA at the same time was in debt to the rest of the world (*Bank of England Quarterly Bulletin*, November 1988). Britain's world role, even if minor in many respects, is still distinct. The legacy of the past remains a fundamental determinant of economic relations today.

The geography of the trade balance

Table 4.5 shows the changing geographic pattern of the balance of trade. It is necessary to bear in mind the state of the overall balance when looking at specific trends; the sharp improvement in the early 1980s, for example, was created by a recession-induced fall in imports. It can be seen that the pattern of payments changed considerably over the decade 1976–86. Deficits in North America and OPEC countries have been transformed into large surpluses. But large deficits exist within Western Europe and other developed countries (which include Japan), while Britain's traditional surplus with the Third World has

82

TABLE 4.5 *The Geography of the Trade Balance, 1976–86*

	1976	1981	1986
EEC			
Balance (£m)	−2403	−599	−9502
Exports as % of imports	−20.9	−2.8	−21.3
Rest of W. Europe			
Balance (£m)	−572	−1458	−4902
Exports as % of imports	−13.2	−18.7	−41.3
North America			
Balance (£m)	−1171	−457	+2074
Exports as % of imports	−27.4	−6.0	+20.6
Other developed countries			
Balance (£m)	−305	−739	−3274
Exports as % of imports	−13.5	−20.1	−47.3
OPEC countries			
Balance (£m)	−1048	+2265	+3319
Exports as % of imports	−24.9	+62.0	+292.8
Other developing countries			
Balance (£m)	−140	+680	−993
Exports as % of imports	−4.0	+12.1	−11.5
Centrally planned economies			
Balance (£m)	−194	+115	−135
Exports as % of imports	−21.0	+11.3	−7.3
World total			
Balance (£m)	−5807	−171	−13058
Exports as % of imports	−18.7	−0.3	−15.2

Source: *Annual Abstract of Statistics*, 1988.

been eroded through the rise of the newly industrialising countries (NICs).

Future trade adjustments will probably be unfavourable. The large surplus with North America will be eroded if the US tackles its huge trade deficit. The surplus with OPEC will disappear as North Sea oil runs out; OPEC's declining oil income has already hit British exports in the 1980s. The trade data in Table 4.5 include North Sea oil exports: without them the picture of trade with Western Europe would have looked far bleaker (although Ekofisk oil boosted the deficit with the non-EC countries of Western Europe).

Countries with which Britain has the worst trade deficits all have advanced manufacturing sectors, especially West Germany and Japan. Imports from both countries rose over fivefold between 1976 and 1986. Of the two, West Germany is by far the more important trading partner, with total trade worth four times as much as with Japan. The deficit with West Germany was also bigger in 1986 (£5600 million compared to Japan's £4100 million). But Japan took only a small amount of British exports in comparison to its exports to Britain, and British exports to Japan even fell by a quarter between 1981 and 1986.

Does the manufacturing deficit matter?

For some, like the House of Lords Committee (1984), the deficit on manufacturing trade spells disaster and shows the weakness and neglect of Britain's manufacturing base. The Treasury holds the opposite view: there is nothing to worry about. This section will consider who is right.

There is no inherent reason why any country should have a deficit or surplus on its trade balance or any constituent part of it, and overall the balance of payments will balance. Unless a surplus on the current account is balanced by an outflow on the capital account, the exchange rate will rise, depressing exports and increasing imports – leading to deflation of the domestic economy. A trade deficit without a compensating capital inflow results in a fall in the exchange rate – exports will be cheaper, but imports more expensive, causing domestic price inflation and a shift of resources from consumption to exporting. But the processes of adjustment are slow, so governments attempt to improve a trade deficit more rapidly, generally by reducing the demand for imports through deflation.

A surplus in the 1980s on the manufacturing balance, given the oil and other surpluses, would have meant an enormous overall surplus – with its consequential depression-of-demand effects in the domestic and international economy. So the idea of the need for a large manufacturing surplus is a historical relic. More exports of whatever category, however, allow greater imports and a payments balance at a higher national income.

The need for more exports is exacerbated in modern Britain by declining export revenues from oil. If oil exports do finally cease, the mix of trade will again change. It is unlikely that extra service exports can fill the gap. Most services are not traded internationally, whereas most manufactures are. International trade is primarily in goods. They were 82 per cent of world trade in 1983 according to the IMF; while half of all trade was in manufactures, only 18 per cent was in services, much of that in travel and transport. Britain already does comparatively well in some international service activities, because of its historical evolution and its current low-wage regime. Yet, in the future, some service sectors' trade balances will worsen as (or if) UK incomes continue to rise. It would cost more, for instance, to visit Britain with higher wages, while the demand for overseas travel would have grown. The fortunes of the financial services sector conversely are intimately tied up with the expansion of the world's capital and money markets. The effects of deregulation and internationalisation in the 1970s and 1980s gave once-and-for-all lifts to international activity. Now it will have to expand more through internal growth, and after the crash of 1987 prospects do not look so good. Other large service earners such as construction are also highly volatile international businesses.

Manufacturing exports look set to remain a central part of Britain's trade in the foreseeable future. The demise of North Sea oil exports will almost certainly require an increase in the export of manufactures if the prospect is to be avoided of successive payment crises 'resolved' by depressing the demand for imports through deflation. But the export picture looks unfavourable given the weakness of manufacturing industry. A major concern is the inability of British manufacturers to expand their penetration of foreign markets to offset the loss of home markets arising from the greater internationalisation of contemporary production. This can be seen from export and import ratios. There have been large increases in both exports as a proportion of UK manufacturers' sales and imports as a proportion of home demand. From 1976 to 1981, the two ratios increased in tandem. Since then the imports share has risen much faster. Has recession and deindustrialisation weakened rather than strengthened British industry?

DEINDUSTRIALISATION

Over the past thirty years manufacturing industry has declined significantly in terms of both its contribution to national income – down from a peak of 36 per cent of GDP in 1951 to 24 per cent in 1986 – and as a source of employment – falling from a peak of 8.5 million workers in 1966 to 5.1 million in 1986. The different timing of the output and employment peaks reflects the pattern of growth in the non-manufacturing economy; most notably, the years since the 1950s have seen the growth of services. Employment in service industries was 14.2 million in 1986, over two-thirds of all jobs. Does this shift in the pattern of economic activity matter? Answers to this question fundamentally depend on arguments about the determinants of economic performance.

Deindustrialisation can be defined in a number of ways.

It could refer to the share of either manufacturing output or employment in the respective totals for the economy as a whole. It could alternatively point to the absolute decline in jobs and/or to a collapse in manufacturing output as well. Finally, manufacturing could be ascribed some privileged economic status, so that deindustrialisation is a shorthand phrase for a general economic weakness transmitted to the economy as a whole through the weak performance of its manufacturing sector. Each conceptualisation has been used in the literature, and the differences can lead to confused interpretations. The definition of the sectors of concern may also create problems. Sometimes the focus is simply the industrial sectors classified in the official statistics as manufacturing; other officially defined production industries, such as gas, electricity and water, may be included; or the net drawn even wider. Misleading implications of classificatory systems may also occur. An example is when there are shifts in the pattern through which specific manufacturing-related functions are undertaken, as with a change from in-house activity in a manufacturing enterprise to hiring specialists belonging to the service sector. Accountancy, marketing, business consultancy and other financial services have all tended to be contracted out more over the years, leading to a shift of employment between the manufacturing and service sectors. Little functional change results, and insofar as the shift has occurred because it is a more efficient way to perform these tasks it would indicate a strengthening rather than a weakening of manufacturing industry.

Generally, deindustrialisation is treated as a relational concept – the share of total economic activity or employment in manufacturing. In this respect all advanced countries have experienced deindustrialisation over the past twenty years. The detailed pattern is complex, varying from country to country and proceeding at a varying pace over time. Britain has fared amongst the worst in its experience of deindustrialisation, experiencing a greater fall in the relative importance of its manufacturing sectors than most other advanced countries. It also started to be subject to deindustrialisation in this sense earlier than elsewhere (Rowthorn and Wells, 1987; Williams *et al.*, 1983).

Shares of employment and output in manufacturing are subject to demand and supply influences which, many people argue, vary systematically over time. Mature economies experience deindustrialisation precisely because they are at an advanced stage of development. This type of argument was initially advanced in the 1950s, and has received a resurgence of support in the late 1980s (cf. World Bank, 1987; Rowthorn and Wells, 1987). The maturity thesis has an intuitive appeal. At early stages of economic development when economic activity is concentrated in low-productivity agriculture, industrial activity is low and backward, and there is a substantial service sector associated with government, servants and commercial activities. During the initial stages of development, all sectors experience a rise in productivity. An agriculture surplus is needed to feed a growing urban proletariat, and labour must be freed by rising productivity in non-manufacturing sectors so that it can work in industry. Manufacturing productivity growth 'takes off', subsequently becoming the prime source of growth, and draws in progressively more workers as output rises even faster than productivity. Competition for labour diffuses rising incomes throughout the growing non-traditional sectors, forcing up costs and prices in sectors where productivity growth is relatively slow. Over time, given its faster productivity growth and the diffusion of rising labour costs, the price of manufactures will fall relative to other sectors, especially services. The demand for services rises, however, with growing incomes, some would say at a faster rate than the demand for manufactures. There comes a time in the growth process where because of the relative price and demand effects, manufacturing's share of national output falls, and labour will be transferred out of it to meet the growing demand for lower productivity services – at this time the economy reaches maturity.

The maturity thesis has great appeal in explaining the worldwide shifts in economic activity that are currently occurring. For it, deindustrialisation is not a curse but a blessing of high GDP per head. Its simplicity and generality, however, raise some doubts as to its universal validity.

One major problem is the implicit assumption of full-employment within the model. If there is widespread unemployment, labour transfers need not take place between economically active sectors, but from the unem-ployed or unwaged. Much of the growth of service employment in Britain in the post-war years, for instance, has drawn women into the labour force, frequently on a part-time basis – a group that previously had very low participation in waged work (see Chapter 6). Britain, in addition, since the mid-1970s has not had full employ-ment, and many of the workers thrown out of work have joined the dole queues rather than move to another sector. Such factors raise questions about processes of adjustment, which the maturity thesis ignores. Adjust-ment, moreover, is not simply to a new fixed equilibrium point but may alter the growth trajectory itself.

Another difficulty is that the model generalises from a closed economy to the very open ones of the contempor-ary capitalist world. World trade in manufactures has been one the major engines of economic growth since the nineteenth century, and is likely to continue to be one. Countries' exports of manufactures and their importance in national income vary considerably in both the First and the Third Worlds. Japan and West Germany and the NICs, for example, have all been highly successful in export markets, whereas other countries have not – trends which are reflected in contemporary patterns of indust-rialisation and deindustrialisation. One of Britain's recur-rent post-war economic weaknesses has been in the manufactured-exports sphere – it is unlikely, therefore, that deindustrialisation in Britain can simply be put down to 'maturity'.

Care must also be taken in assigning to manufacturing industry the greatest productivity per worker. Intuitively, manufacturing processes seem to offer the greatest scope for productivity improvements, but some services still generate much higher value added per person. A difficulty also arises over the basis on which to compare productivity across sectors. Many services are not traded: for example, state education. For such activities, national income accounts simply calculate their economic contribution as being the equivalent of the wages, materials and equipment used up in a given time period. Such services as a result suffer from a negative relative price effect, because with rising incomes it looks as though they necessarily get more expensive over time as input costs rise while output remains the same fixed proportion of input (by statistical definition rather than by what actually occurs in practice). Productivity, in other words, is assumed to be constant over time. Given the size of the public sector in most countries over the past thirty years, a considerable downward statistical bias may in this way have been introduced into overall service productivity and its rate of change. Comparisons are also complicated by the prices at which to compare different sectors. Falling relative prices for manufactures lower the contribution a given output of them makes to national income – so should comparison be made using constant or current prices? No unequivocal answer can be given. Presumptions about productivity change between sectors consequently are difficult to evaluate empirically, yet they are at the core of the maturity thesis.

In the context of Britain in the 1980s, some interesting points about the relative productivity of different sectors can be made, even given the statistical difficulties mentioned above. Manufacturing features higher in employment than in its contribution to GDP, indicating that it is not the highest productivity sector. So the shift in activity away from manufacturing consequently has raised general productivity as represented by GDP per head! (Savage and Biswas, 1986.) Nor has the demand for manufactures declined at the same time as British manufacturing industry, if at all, as can be seen from the high income elasticity of demand for manufactured imports and the concomitant decline in the manufacturing trade balance. The weakness of British manufacturing industry is why it has lost so many domestic markets and failed to expand overseas in compensation. If manufacturing industry had been more successful in home and export markets, its output would have been higher, and so would national income. But greater success would also have raised labour productivity, so it is not clear if manufacturing employment would have been larger; it may have been less (and so corresponded nearer to the maturity thesis).

There are alternative arguments about deindustrialisation. One refers to the pattern of trade specialisation. The specialisation thesis argues that Britain's need to export manufactures in the late 1940s and 1950s forced the country to specialise in manufactures. As the patterns of non-manufacturers' trade had improved in Britain's favour the emphasis on manufacturing was no longer required, so it declined as a proportion of total economic activity (Rowthorn and Wells, 1987). It could be concluded that the British economy has readjusted to a more typical sectoral pattern. The years of high emphasis on manufacturing were the exception – so deindustrialisation is not a problem. Table 3.2 shows the contribution of different sectors to national income at selected years from the nineteenth century to the present day. The 1986 distribution of national income looks very different from 1951 but not so different from 1937. Both commerce and public services show remarkably similar percentage shares in the later 1930s and mid-1980s, and although manufacturing is six points lower in the mid-1980s much of that decline could be said to be due to the negative consequences on manufacturing activity of North Sea oil. The distribution of economic activity in 1986 even does not look that dissimilar from the early years of the twentieth century. Comparing 1913 and 1986, the data show only relatively small shifts away from agriculture, mining, transport and manufacture towards commerce and the public sector. Employment patterns would indicate a much greater change because of differential rates of productivity growth and the ways in which they are calculated. But, in terms of contributions to national income, the shares give credibility to the specialisation thesis.

The content of activity in each of the broad sectors listed in Table 3.2 has altered considerably between 1913 and 1986, so the similarity may be superficial. Whilst it may be true that the proportion of economic activity in manufacturing in the early 1950s was unlikely to be sustained, what limits the usefulness of the specialisation thesis is the subsequent pattern of economic development. If Britain for particular reasons of economic planning, or because of its profitability, did put an extraordinary amount of resources into manufacturing after 1945, it is highly likely that many of the transferred resources were of lower productivity. Britain's already labour-intensive manufacturing processes would have been swollen by an influx of labour, equipment and materials, whose marginal productivity could easily have been lower than the already comparatively poor industrial average; resources that could perhaps have provided better returns if utilised elsewhere in an overstretched economy. Directing resources towards an export drive, in other words, is not the same as improving the long-run competitive position of exporting industries. Without a concomitant strategy of industrial regeneration – absent in post-war Britain – redirection could easily lower long-run competitiveness by removing the coercive effects of competition in input as well as output markets. British producers faced little competition from war-torn Europe and Asia during the export-drive years, which helps to account for the success in terms of the volume of exports of the strategy. If large volumes of low-productivity resources were utilised to achieve the increase in exports in the late 1940s and early 1950s, when they were subsequently withdrawn during the late 1950s and 1960s, a substantial boost to manufacturing productivity should have occurred. It did not happen. The collapse in manufacturing jobs, moreover, has not been a steady one, commensurate with Britain's changing structure of trade. Instead, there have been abrupt downward shifts associated with economic crises in the late 1960s, the mid-1970s and the early 1980s.

Low productivity and an inability to compete in world markets have characterised manufacturing post-1945, so that a significant contribution to deindustrialisation has been the weakness of Britain's manufacturing base. The weakness was exacerbated in the late 1970s by the coming of North Sea oil and restrictive government policies which forced up the value of sterling. The macroeconomic impact of North Sea oil is difficult to assess accurately, and a range of opinion about its effects has emerged (see Bean, 1987; Rowthorn and Wells, 1987). There is general agreement, however, that the decline of manufacturing activity accelerated with the arrival of oil. But there is no consensus on whether the effect was limited to the early 1980s or led to permanent losses.

The consequences of deindustrialisation can be seen in Table 5.1. Unlike in other countries, manufacturing output has never surpassed the peak level achieved in 1973. Employment has slumped and output has remained sluggish. One apparently bright spot is the rapid rise in productivity after the doldrums of the 1970s.

Does deindustrialisation matter? In one clear respect the answer must be no. Manufacturing jobs are often less congenial than others, and the activities and wealth created outside of manufacturing are just as valid and useful as those generated within it. Commentators often argue that manufacturing is vital because it is the source of economic growth, enabling increasing returns in a way not possible in other sectors (e.g. Thirwell, 1982b). But the experience of the UK and in other countries since 1973 shows that other sectors can be far more dynamic than manufacturing. Where manufacturing has a clear privileged position is in export-led growth (as much international trade is in manufactures) or as a means of resolving a balance-of-payments constraint. Deindustrialisation, in fact, has been classified by at least one commentator (Singh, 1977) as the progressive failure of manufacturing exports to pay for the full-employment level of imports. However, even here, other trade options are possible – such as import-substituting activities and expanded trade in non-manufacturing exports – and have occurred in post-war Britain. Non-manufacturing exports and import substitution have limits, though, so manufacturing remains central to trade.

Another way in which manufacturing is endowed with economic superiority is through treating of some forms of economic activity as harmful to future growth. In the mid-1970s there was much emphasis on the growth of the public sector, which was said to 'crowd out' private-sector activity including industry. One well-known variation of the argument (from a non-monetarist perspective) was that of Bacon and Eltis (1976), who claimed that the growth of the public sector drew resources out of industry and resulted in too few producers having to support 'unproductive' public services. Subsequent mass unemployment with a relatively unchanged public sector (privatised industries were part of Bacon and Eltis's 'marketable goods' industrial sector even when they were publicly owned) discredited the claim. Marxists distinguish between productive and unproductive but for different reasons. Any worker who produces surplus value for a capitalist is a productive worker – a category that includes much private- and some public-sector services as well as manufacturing.

What can be concluded about deindustrialisation is that it is important if it indicates that a major sector of the economy is weak, especially one subject to overseas competition. That weakness implies that incomes are lower than they would otherwise have been, either through the loss of internal dynamic effects or through trade constraints. Manufacturing may not be the fountain of all wealth, but it is still an important source.

FURTHER READING

Thirwall (1982a) is a good introduction to mainstream theories on the balance of payments and a history of the post-war era from a policy perspective. Rowthorn and Wells (1987) provide an exhaustive analysis of Britain's changing trade patterns and the balance of payments, linking them to the debate over deindustrialisation.

The references in the text highlight most of the different opinions on deindustrialisation. OECD (1988), chapter 4, provides a statistical overview and an analysis of structural change and economic performance in contemporary Britain.

5

Some Key Economic Issues for the 1990s
Michael Ball

The topics covered in this chapter are grouped under four headings. The first section looks at Britain's major firms and considers the effects of their strong international orientation. The second section examines the role of the City in funding British industry, and considers whether companies operating in Britain face particular handicaps because of the unique operation and economic importance of the City. The focus switches in the third section to the labour market and asks whether there is a relationship between the level of unemployment and the rate of inflation. The final section examines the reasons for the substantial improvement in productivity in British industry during the 1980s.

BIG BUSINESS AND THE MULTINATIONALS

One characteristic of the British economy, noted in Chapter 2, is the scale of its major enterprises and their international orientation. British companies are second only to US firms in the size of their overseas investments, while Britain is a favourite place for multinationals to locate plants. Large firms, multinational corporations and direct overseas investment are interrelated issues, especially given the international orientation of major British companies. What is the effect of them on the UK economy?

Before proceeding further some terminology has to be made clear. 'Multinational corporation' is the term being used here as it is the most common description of firms with multi-country production facilities. But in reality such firms are not really multinational as usually they originate from one country and still have their headquarters there. A few companies have joint international ownership and spread headquarters functions, but they are rare. Two of the most famous examples are Royal Dutch Shell and Unilever, although even with these two companies overall control is tipped in favour of one or other of the international partners. Multinationals in practice are major firms who have spread their activities way beyond their initial country of operation. US firms up to the 1950s and 1960s were by far the most important. But the relative decline of US economic power has been associated with the growth first of European, then of Far Eastern companies.

Some commentators prefer to use the more accurate word 'transnational'; this is the term used by the United Nations, which produces much information on the world activities of such enterprises.

The role of large firms in the British economy

Large firms, most of which are multinationals with overseas activities, are not spread evenly across the economy. Many are in manufacturing. The top 100 private firms produced 37 per cent of net manufacturing output in 1985, a figure slightly down on the 40 per cent of most of the 1970s (*Census of Production, Summary Tables*). Their role in exports is even greater. Seven companies alone produced 20 per cent of manufacturing exports in 1984 (Pratten, 1986); while over 80 per cent of exports originated from multinationals or from their subsidiaries. In employment terms, multinationals also play an important role. In 1981, foreign-owned multi-nationals employed 1 million UK workers, with UK-owned ones employing another 3.5 million at home and 1.4 million workers overseas – at a time when total UK manufacturing employment was 6.2 million (Dunning, 1985).

Large firms exist in areas where there are clear advantages of size. Some will be in industries whose products are traded internationally only to a limited extent – like the public utilities and in retail distribution. But most are active in products where international trade is substantial. Many operate in a narrow range of industries, particularly oil, electrical engineering, electronics, chemicals, vehicles and food.

Britain's large firms are not particularly big by international standards. American companies tend to be much larger – the hundredth-largest US company in the mid-1980s had a turnover ten times the size of the hundredth UK firm. West German firms are also bigger – GEC, the electrical giant, is only half the size of Siemens, its West German equivalent. Only ICI matches the scale of the biggest German firms, yet there are three German chemical companies the size of ICI (Pratten, 1986).

The advantages of size are considerable. Production costs can be reduced through the mass production of a standardised range of products. Scale economies can also be achieved in marketing and sales and in research and development. There are also economies of scope, where benefits are derived from operating in a variety of different product markets. One advantage is that risks can be spread, as for instance with the unknowns associated with the development of a new product. High development and marketing costs may make introduction of a new product too risky for a smaller company to undertake. (Think of what would have happened to the Rover Group if the Metro had completely failed to attract consumers.) The biggest disadvantage of size for a firm's customers, of course, is the threat of monopoly abuse.

The advantages of multinational production, though obviously based on a firm of already considerable size, are said to encompass a wider range of issues. Multinationals are claimed to be some of the most dynamic, technically advanced producers, so investment by them may lead to better than average production facilities and jobs. The inward receipt of investment therefore may lead to a technology transfer, to high-value-added production and the introduction of 'best practice' manufacturing systems. New management and organisational procedures may also be introduced into the host country. Such technological and organisational advances might subsequently be disseminated to indigenous firms, thereby benefiting the economy as a whole. Domestic production by a foreign company may also be import-substituting, benefiting the balance of payments. Conversely, given the international orientation of multinationals, location of a major production facility in a country helps to draw that country into the evolving international division of labour and the benefits such trade brings. Stopford and Turner (1985) argue that the firms investing overseas are the most internationally orientated, and so even outward investment benefits a country as the subsequent boost to trade will tend to be greater than the initial negative impact of the capital transfer.

The disadvantages of multinationals to an extent mirror the benefits in that the role in the international division of labour assigned to a specific country by a multinational may create secondary problems or be of limited direct economic value. A major fear is the control over domestic economic activity given to foreign capital, as well as the abuse of monopoly power. Such fears frequently have general nationalistic undertones, but resorting to nationalism is likely to be of greater benefit to domestic producers frightened of competition than to other strata of society.

Theoretical discussion of multinationals falls into two broad camps. One is based on presumptions about the operation of markets and whether multinationals' actions in them produce socially beneficial or damaging outcomes. The other takes a stance broader than markets focusing on the dynamics of capitalist societies. In theories which concentrate on markets, some suggest that multinationals improve economic efficiency, whilst others are critical of the abuse of monopoly power.

Many of the suggested benefits of multinationals described above can be encompassed within a theory associated with neoclassical economics which suggest that the size, scope and organisational structure of firms is influenced by difficulties associated with market transactions. Real world markets are imperfect. If firms internalise some of the processes most subject to those imperfections, they can increase their profits and improve overall economic efficiency. Internalising those processes increases the size of firms and frequently gives them an international scope, hence the existence of multi-nationals.

Central to the overcoming-of-market-imperfections argument is a belief that firms have little influence on their environment or the markets in which they operate. The credibility of such a view seems weak given the contemporary importance of the multinationals in the economies of specific countries and even at the world scale. The UN estimated, for instance, that a mere 350 multinationals accounted for 28 per cent of the total gross domestic product of the entire capitalist world in 1980 (UNCTC, 1983). The internalisation approach also faces difficulties in justifying the theory as leading to worthwhile empirical statements. Given the complexity of the real world and a lack of data with which to compare internal firm and market processes, resort is often made to evolutionary-style reasoning for justification. 'What exists must be the most efficient otherwise it would not have survived against competing forms of economic organisation' is a common theme in the new industrial economics from which internalisation theory stems.

100

Apart from the poor use of the theory of evolution implied in such statements, they also fall foul of the ability of human beings and the social institutions they create to influence the world in which they exist.

The disadvantages of multinationals have been expounded into a theoretical framework which Jenkins (1987) classifies as 'global reach'. Multinationals in this framework exist because they can use and do abuse their market power, be it over weaker domestic rivals, government or hapless workers and consumers. In contrast to the previous view, multinationals here create, rather than overcome, market imperfections through their monopoly power. Yet, while it might be difficult to believe that large firms have no scope for influencing the economic and social environments within which they operate, to assert that competition hardly works at all seems equally misplaced. IBM, for instance, might attempt to dominate the computer world, particularly through its ability to impose its machine standards on others, yet it has a hard time doing so and has not wholly succeeded. In the real world, competition and monopoly power are not polar opposites.

Marxist views vary. Two replicate in slightly different language the two previous theories. The classic Marxist position, as expounded by Lenin and Bukharin though not by Marx, is similar to the global-reach view. Large firms are international monopolies, used as agents by core capitalism to carve up the rest of the world into a series of competing imperialist blocks, draining economic surplus from the Third World to the advanced capitalist economies. This view again suffers from the exaggerated role given to monopoly power and to the drainage of surplus from the Third World via commodity exchange; while its views on imperialist blocks to an extent match the geopolitics of the first half of the twentieth century, they have far less credibility today. Other Marxists have argued a progressive role for multinationals, similar in its conclusions to internalisation theory. As one of the most organisationally and technically advanced forms of capitalist enterprise, multinationals directly and through their competitive effect improve the level of economic efficiency of the economies in which they operate including those in the Third World (cf. Warren, 1980). Neither of these two Marxists theories takes into account the complex and varied social structures of the countries in which multinationals operate, nor overall development tendencies within global capitalism itself. Such absences have led a number of contemporary Marxists to emphasise in their analysis of multinationals specific characteristics of particular types of society within the context of a trend for capitalism to become more international in its location of production.

Arguments about the increasingly global nature of capitalist production are often used to criticise the possibility of national economic strategies. The internationalisation of production means that domestic economic policy is doomed by its national confines to be unable to affect the activities of the most important producers. Such a position is controversial, however. The level of internationalisation it presupposes has been argued to be exaggerated. There has not been a major change in the locus of production to warrant the claim of a qualitative shift to a new level of internationalisation of production (Gordon, 1988). There have been notable alterations in the output shares of particular nations, such as the rise of Japan and adjustments amongst the European nations, particularly since the forming of the Common Market. But it is questionable whether such movements are any different from those which took place in the nineteenth and early twentieth centuries or whether they imply a significant transformation to international rather than one-country-based production, except in certain cases such as cars. In addition, the new limits to domestic economic policy are also exaggerated by the implication that, prior to the new internationalisation, individual economies were closed to outside influence and subject to control by governments with all-powerful instruments. In the advanced capitalist world neither has ever been the case outside of economics textbooks.

Multinationals and their workforces

There is no evidence that multinationals are systematically worse employers than domestic firms operating in similar conditions, although some, like IBM, are anti-union. For workers, therefore, it makes little difference whether foreign capital owns the enterprise or not – in this sense the old adage about the only thing worse than being exploited by a multinational is not being exploited by one seems to hold. It could be argued, however, that multinationals have less incentive to stay in a country that is not their domestic base. In this way, wages and conditions could be forced down through the threat of withdrawal to a country with a more amenable workforce. Trade unions have felt the need in a number of industries to set up cross-national combines as a way of combating such perceived threats, although the strength of such combines seems limited in practice. Dunning (1985) argues that the limited expansion of multinational activity in Britain in recent years reflects a switch of emphasis to elsewhere in Western Europe, especially of labour-intensive sectors, because of labour troubles, although he offers no concrete evidence. A converse view would argue that the UK is an attractive place for multinationals to locate assembly operations because of low wages and the existence of large (often protected) European Community markets. Such assembly plants take a long time to build up – as was the case with Nissan in the North East – so short-term variations in wages and industrial unrest are unlikely to affect multinationals' plans once formulated.

Investment by multinationals in assembly plants for only a limited set of processes, often for one product alone, sets up fears of the 'branch-plant' syndrome. This fear has a number of aspects. It may be felt that the multinational is interested only in forcing competing governments to offer generous grants, especially for factories in their economically depressed regions. The plant might also only last as long as the life of the product family, retooling for new ones being done elsewhere in the latest favoured location. Branch plants, in addition, may only be a cosmetic device to get round import constraints – a complaint frequently voiced of Japanese assembly operations in Western Europe.

Branch planting can wreak havoc with union strategies towards multinationals. Multinationals may make the siting of a specific plant conditional on agreeing exceptional terms with the unions, which are then used to threaten the whole of the unions' negotiation strategy with the company at other plants. This was the essence of the dispute about the location of a new Ford plant in Dundee in 1988. Ford said it would build the plant only if it could negotiate a single-union agreement outside of the usual bargaining framework for Ford plants in the UK. Some of the major unions objected on the basis that, once national agreements were breached in principle for one new and possibly temporary branch plant, the whole of the national negotiating apparatus would be threatened. In other words, Dundee was seen by these unions as a Trojan Horse which if accepted would quickly lead to much weaker unions in all of Ford's UK plants. There was some comment at the time of the Dundee case that Ford was using the promise of a plant as a means of publicly discrediting the trade unions shortly after they had won a major victory over the company on national pay levels and working conditions. If that was the company's aim, it certainly succeeded in influencing public opinion against the unions. Later in 1988 Ford announced the construction of a new engine plant in South Wales, the largest-ever investment by an overseas multinational in Britain.

Multinationals and the domestic economy

A further series of issues concern the impact of multi-nationals on domestic economic performance. One worry about multinational-owned plants is the degree to which they are integrated into the rest of the economy. Head-quarters might lay down detailed programmes for each affiliate and utilise transfer price arrangements between affiliates whereby the value-added produced in a particu-lar country is not reflected in the prices charged between parts of a multinational's operations spread across diffe-rent countries. Such strategies tend to exclude domestic components suppliers and reduce tax burdens, so that the spin-offs are far more limited than would be the case for an indigenous firm. Much strategic management and research and development may also be undertaken over-seas, limiting the wider gains for economic development.

The macroeconomic effects of multinationals are another source of concern. Their capital flows and sourcing policies may create balance-of-payments prob-lems. If their investment horizons and product develop-ment strategies really are long-term, such firms may be relatively insensitive to the macroeconomic fine-tuning and relative price signals hoped for by policy-makers. The enormous day-to-day flows of money from multi-nationals into and out of specific economies may also be destabilising for exchange rates, as manipulation of foreign payments dates can provide multinationals with handsome profits.

Evidence on the actual performance of multinationals in Britain is mixed, and dogged by the unavailability of data – anecdotes with various degrees of sophistication make up a large proportion of the information used in the voluminous literature on multinationals. The available data tend to back up the idea that multinationals coming to Britain invest in the more dynamic sectors of the economy, and have higher productivity in any sector than indigenous firms (Dunning, 1985). The same is true of UK multinationals investing abroad. Such evidence, however, might simply indicate that more recent investment is of higher productivity than the industry average – which is what growth is all about. Tradewise, overseas direct investment is associated with higher exports rather than less, and foreign-owned multinationals in Britain themselves have a good export record; seventeen of Britain's top fifty exporters are foreign-owned. The trade figures indicate the significance of multinationals in structuring Britain's role in the new international division of labour.

Multinationals owned by British capital exhibit the typically negative characteristic of being concentrated in low-technology industries such as tobacco, building materials, paper, textiles, alcohol and hotels. They are also instrumental in the deindustrialisation process. Stopford and Turner (1985) report the results of a survey of fifty-eight British multinationals' employment patterns from 1973 to 1985. Between them, they shed 600,000 jobs in Britain – nearly a third of all manufacturing jobs lost – while increasing their overseas employment by 200,000. No other country's multinationals were said to have reduced employment in the parent company, while increasing it overseas through that period. Managers of multinationals have defended their actions by saying that they are reducing their exposure to the problems afflicting industry in Britain. But during the same years foreign-owned multinationals increased their UK jobs by 80,000.

Associated with the position of multinationals is the role of large plants; not all large plants are run by multinationals but many are. A number of studies have identified problems in the operation of large plants in Britain (Pratten, 1976; Prais, 1981; Davies and Caves, 1987). Davies and Caves (1987) compares productivity in

US and UK plants in the late 1960s and 1970s. They found that both small and large plants in the UK fared equally badly in comparison to those in the USA, but that the underperformance was greatest for large plants which in Britain failed to achieve the economies of scale gained in the US. The shortfall is particularly significant because large plants on average have much higher productivity levels than smaller ones. By the early 1970s a large number of manufacturing employees worked in them. According to Oulton's (1987) estimates, 42 per cent of manufacturing workers were employed in plants with over 1000 workers in 1973.

Whatever the cause of the poor performance of large UK plants, closures and rundowns hit them disproportionately after 1973, particularly in the early 1980s slump. The number of large plants fell by over 30 per cent between 1979 and 1982. Some of the decrease was caused by higher productivity, but Oulton (1987) has estimated that most arose from total or partial closure. Partial closure could to an extent result from a greater use of subcontracting as has occurred in many industries, but much of it has been a withdrawal from markets — deindustrialisation in the 'failure' sense described above.

Surviving large plants have seen the greatest productivity increases of all manufacturing plants since 1982. But, for two reasons, that does not necessarily mean that all the closed plants were hopeless dead wood. First, the productivity of large plants is so much greater than that in smaller ones that the loss of even the most inefficient large plants could still have led to an overall manufacturing productivity fall. Second, there is no evidence that the plants that have closed were the least efficient. Firms may have closed them because they were unprofitable, but for other reasons than productive inefficiency. Failures in the market-place through poor pricing strategies, product design or quality are other potential explanations. The weakness of the overall group is another. Relative wage levels or capital costs could also have contributed to plant closures and rundowns. A long-term multinational strategy of international restructuring of Western European or even global production facilities away from low-productivity Britain would also have helped the decline. (Remember the outward flight of UK-owned multinationals' capital and employment during this period.) There is no accurate way of knowing what the real causes are.

One final aspect of multinationals' activities links the issues of multinational sourcing and European trade. A large part of Britain's huge manufacturing deficit with other EEC countries arises from the motor industry. The deficit increased substantially after accession as West Europe-bound exports of cars and components stagnated and imports rose dramatically (Dearden, 1986). Ford and General Motors significantly increased their sourcing of UK sales and component requirements from West European plants. Whole imported cars alone for these two companies rose from 1 per cent to 22 per cent of their total UK sales between 1974 and 1984. Taking component imports as well, Jones (1985) claimed that barely a third of General Motors's British sales was value-added in Britain. In 1988, Ford said only about half of its domestic sales were UK-sourced. It should also be remembered that Peugeot, Citroën and Fiat, like British Leyland, were all in severe financial difficulty during the early 1980s slump. British Leyland was pared down, renamed twice, and in 1988 finally sold off as the Rover Group to British Aerospace at a knockdown price. It now sells a small range of cars at low volumes primarily in Britain and cannot independently produce a new model or update any of the key components such as engines and gearboxes (Williams *et al.*, 1987). After restructuring, including the takeover of Citroën by Peugeot, the other West European companies have gone from strength to strength. Changes in the international division of labour, it would seem, have hit the domestic British economy particularly badly.

THE OWNERSHIP AND FINANCING OF INDUSTRY

Anxiety about the ways in which British industry is financed is often couched in terms of a City versus Industry polarisation, in which, it is claimed, the conflict is greatest over the long-term investment needs of manufacturing industry. In the brief discussion of the topic in Chapter 2, it was argued that the existence of such a polarisation cannot be demonstrated empirically and is theoretically suspect. It is worth exploring the reasons for this conclusion in greater depth.

If the City is said to deny industry funds, it has to be proved that there is a special prejudice against industry, so that firms either have to pay a higher than average rate of interest or are severely rationed in the funds they can get despite being prepared to pay the going rate for them. Both these positions seem untenable, have never been demonstrated generally to exist, and imply massive inefficiencies in the financial-services sector arising from a lack of competition – which seems unlikely. Financiers will and do fund any investor who can demonstrate an assured ability to repay the loan at the prevailing rate of interest – industry included. Only when there is a perceived greater than average risk is it likely that funding will be withheld or extra interest charged as a risk premium. Perceptions may contain prejudiced views of the creditworthiness of borrowers, and it has been said that small firms experience some difficulties as do certain types of household in consumer credit (Wilson Committee, 1980). But the overall impact of such prejudices on industry is small.

Another claim is that the City has unreasonable control over government policy against the interests of industry, say, through demanding a high value of sterling, free trade, deflation, and a variety of other anti-industry measures (cf. Ingham, 1984). A number of steps are required to substantiate the claim. In the first place, it has to be demonstrated that the measures perceived to be required by the City are necessarily against the interests of industry. Yet industry itself is unlikely in many cases to have a unified economic interest, particularly if all non-financial sectors are classified as industry. Some manufacturers, for instance, threatened by imports may want trade controls; whereas firms with a wide variety of export markets and international production facilities would be horrified by the threat of a trade war if such controls were introduced. Within companies, divisions of interest can also be substantial. Managers of domestic plants and their workers presumably felt differently from senior management about the rapid rundown in the 1970s of the domestic manufacturing base of UK multi-nationals. Unity, in other words, is as difficult to achieve for firms as it is for trade unions, while 'industry' as a political force is as much of a chimera as the 'Nation'. It is invoked to reinforce someone's political argument rather than constituting a clear entity in itself.

Second, apart from the problems over specifying interests, difficulties for the City-versus-Industry thesis arise over the role of governments. Great faith has to be put in the ability of governments to devise detailed macroeconomic policies to reflect specific interests against others. In some cases, they may be clear as with particular incomes policies or with specific taxation measures – but the effect of an exchange rate or deflationary strategy on particular types of enterprise is not so easy to envisage. Even if these difficulties are assumed away, it still has to be claimed that government policies actually work in the way they are supposed to. Yet controlling the economy is not so easy. Consequently the belief that economic policy strongly benefits the City alone is hard to accept.

The major problem with City-versus-Industry perspectives is the simple dichotomy of interests they imply. In its radical form, the polarisation often involves the conjuring up of something called 'finance capital' whose dimensions are unclear but whose influence is pernicious and all-pervasive. For all believers in the division, any aspect of company financing said to be unbeneficial can be blamed on the City. Having found the scapegoat, however, solutions to the perceived problems must be vague as the processes of capital formation, its funding and the conditions under which capital is used or withdrawn from production are poorly specified. For many anti-City advocates the prime solution to under-investment in British industry is simply to change the ownership of City institutions (e.g. nationalisation) or to force new forms of investment criteria on them. Both policies in themselves, however, may turn out to change very little – as happened with the nationalisation of the banks in France in the early 1980s – or are short-lived because they contain unsustainable contradictory criteria – as occurred with the GLC's Greater London Enterprise Board in the mid-1980s.

Financial influences on firms

Once the crude City-versus-Industry dichotomy is aban-doned, it is possible to consider aspects of company finance and ownership which may adversely affect firms' behaviour. Such features should not be regarded as having been forced on a reluctant industrial capital by financiers but as having emerged through the mutual development of Britain's financial and industrial sectors. In essence, much of the financial sector and industry have grown independently of each other, although growth in both has obviously had common elements. Britain's financial sector, for instance, could not have been dominant in the world in the nineteenth century without the strength of the export trades. But the interdependence has become much weaker now with the internationalisation of finan-cial markets. Different parts of the financial system also have distinct connections with the rest of the economy. While the clearing banks play an important role in domestic payments and credit systems, for example, the City as a whole has been orientated more towards funding governments and international activities.

What has been the actual use of financial services by industrial firms? British industry historically has relied on the banking system only to provide short-term funds to finance stockholdings and trade credit rather than to fund long-term investment in plant and machinery. So overdraft facilities (and some longer-term loans from banks) have been the main direct links between industry and the banking sector (Cotterell, 1983; Harris and Coakley, 1984). Most physical investment is funded through retained profits, with bank credit limited to smoothing out the downturns in retentions caused by short-run profits cycles. Mayer (1987) calculates that retentions financed 91 per cent of physical investment over the period 1949–77, and that there was no discernible shift from this trend in the 1980s.

The use of another part of the financial sector, the Stock Exchange, to fund physical investment has also been very limited. There has even been a decline in corporate bond and equity funding since the early 1950s, so that by the 1980s in aggregate net terms it was non-existent. The fast-growing sectors of industry, in particular, seem to rely on internal funding (Mayer, 1987).

There is no adequate explanation for the overwhelming use of internal funds which is different from the practice in many other countries, but it would seem to arise from a preference of company managers rather than a necessity forced upon them. One advantage to managers of not using extensive bank credit is that they retain greater control – bankers do not have to be persuaded of company plans or given seats on the board, as is often necessary in a country like West Germany where the major banks have close links with industrial companies, including extensive directorships.

A reluctance to use the Stock Exchange for investment funds has to be explained in different terms. One

plausible reason stems from the pattern of share ownership in Britain, and the significance of the secondhand
market in shares. Issuing equities dilutes the ownership
represented by previous shares, and possibly also their
earnings potential. The consequences of dilution may
account for firms' reluctance to issue new shares to fund
investment. For family firms, issuing equities may result
in a loss of control. With larger companies, major
shareholders may not like dilution, as it will lower
earnings per share until the investment starts to bring in
sufficient extra profit, and hence depress the share's price
as well. There are cases, however, when issuing shares is
still attractive. One of the most notable is for takeovers,
where the asset value and earnings potential of the
expanded firm may allay fears of the negative consequences of dilution, while issuing shares is an easy way
of funding the acquisition.

The limited use of long-term debt by British companies
means that there is not a close, stable relationship of
firms to financial institutions lending such funds. Shareholders instead have greater control over the future of a
firm through their ability to sell their shares to a predator.
Such a capital-ownership structure affects the performance criteria adopted by managers. The stock market may
have little influence on the sources of capital for new
investment but it does have an enormous impact on the
ownership and restructuring of British industry. Its
significance is compounded by the ownership structure of
UK equities. In the post-war years, financial institutions,
especially pension funds and insurance companies, have
grown to become the largest owners of company shares.
Their attitude to their shareholdings is particularly
significant for the future of individual companies. They
will be interested long-term dividend incomes, the overall value of their share assets, and the short-term profits
to be made on share purchases and sales. The large
institutions have become important sellers of shares
during takeover battles – they are the recipients of pre-

emptive offers in 'dawn raids' and are wooed by both parties in takeover struggles.

Takeovers now play the dominant role in the restructuring of ownership of British firms – although the practice is relatively recent, becoming general only in the 1960s. Only the USA of the other major developed nations has an equivalent share-ownership market enabling such practices. In countries like West Germany, France and Japan, the ownership and control of companies makes contested takeovers difficult or impossible. The threat of takeover is said to make British firms highly sensitive to the price of their shares. Dividends and investment policies are affected accordingly in order to avoid a temporary drop in share price which may enable a predator to acquire the company cheaply. Firms may cut back investment in order to be able to pay sufficient dividends to stop a fall in share prices. A long-term view of company investment and market strategies may be militated against. UK firms may be victims, therefore, of what is inelegantly called 'short-termism' at a time when imperatives of international production and competition require longer-term strategies, particularly as they are practised by many other countries' multinational corporations. The problem of short-termism, if it is in fact one, has only been of relevance over the past thirty years, although given the increased propensity for takeover and the growth of specialisation takeover consultants its effect may have grown considerably since the 1970s.

A number of commentators have raised the issue of the short-term bias caused by the need to maintain share prices (cf. Williams *et al.*, 1983). It is probable, however, that the bias may also arise within firms as well, given management reward criteria. In a number of countries, managers expect to remain with one company for most of their working lives – Japan being an extreme example. In Britain, partially as a result of the propensity for takeovers, managements are judged on immediate profits records. Managerial prestige, promotion prospects, pay and job security are closely geared to current profits performance. Managers as a result have a strong incentive to take a short-term view of company profitability; if the long-term consequences are disastrous, they are unlikely to be there to face them.

What is the effect of takeovers as the prime means of company restructuring in Britain? It is argued by some that takeovers are a good thing as weaker managements are replaced by stronger, more efficient ones. Counter-claims are made about the short-termism described above, about the threat of removal of successful operations overseas, and about 'asset-stripping' – where companies are acquired for some attractive assets they hold, which are subsequently sold, rather than because the new management can get more out of the business as a going concern. The evidence on takeovers is unclear, but does not augur well, as there is little indication that merged firms have performed any better than the previously independent companies. Conclusive evidence, however, is hard to come by as industrial structures, competitive pressures and the overall state of the economy change over time making it impossible to compare like with like in the pre- and post-merger states.

For much of the 1980s there was a merger boom in Britain in which many firms were acquired to create larger enterprises. Much activity was directed overseas, especially in the USA. On associations, elements of the acquired firms were subsequently sold off, often to fund part of the purchase price, or to bolster corporate profits, or because, in the well-worn and vacuous cliché, the activities were not 'core' parts of the business. An interesting shift in acceptable ideologies is apparent in such practices. In the late 1980s, they are regarded by many as sensible post-takeover strategies; whereas in the late 1960s and 1970s such practices were almost universally castigated as 'asset-stripping' and condemned by people from many walks of life.

Aided by City financial institutions, new phenomena

were also apparent in the takeover world. 'Demerger', for example, entered the English vocabulary. Here companies are purchased in order to break them up into constituent parts to be sold off at a substantial profit. Another semantic innovation of the 1980s was the 'management buyout' in which managers of subsidiaries persuade the parent company and some City institutions to let them take over the subsidiary as a new independent entity. Frequently, the new firms incurred considerable debt to fund the purchase, which encouraged them to sell off all or part of the acquired assets. In a buoyant stock market, takeovers are particularly easy to achieve as shareholders feel reasonably sure that the acquiring firm's shares will continue to increase in value. The 1987 stock market crash temporarily dampened the level of domestic takeovers and made some firms vulnerable to foreign acquisition.

Takeover activity in the 1980s gave the City a poor image with a series of scandals over insider-trading in which employees of the financial institutions use their knowledge of confidential information to purchase shares before their prices rise. (Prior knowledge of information that is likely to lead to falls in a company's share price can also be profitable.) Other scandals involved the deliberate manipulation of the share prices of companies in a takeover battle, the most famous of which was associated with the fiercely contested takeover of Distillers by Guinness, and the subsequent dismissal and trial of the latter's chairman and his associates; a trial that had still not come to court at the time of writing two years after the scandal broke. Whatever the final outcome of the Guinness case, it is generally recognised that the complexity of financial manipulation makes any malpractice lengthy and difficult to prove. This has resulted in calls to reverse the process of deregulation in the City.

One final interesting outcome may have resulted from the restructuring of British industry in the late 1970s and the 1980s. The closure of many large plants, and the large number of takeovers and mergers, together may have altered the composition of British management. Retirements and promotions in the normal course of time change the management personnel of British industry. Yet there was an often-voiced view up to the 1980s that British senior management was drawn from a common stratum, predominantly public-school-educated and Establishment-orientated (see the discussion of the 'business class' in Chapter 13). The social composition and outlook of British management was contrasted with the origins and outlook of managers in countries like the USA. Little analysis has been done of the current social composition of British management or of its training and outlook. Yet it seems probable that a significant transformation of management personnel has occurred. This might account for some of the increase in productivity discussed in the final section.

INFLATION, LABOUR MARKETS AND UNEMPLOYMENT

High rates of inflation in the 1970s finally subsided by the middle of the 1980s. At the same time, unemployment reached unprecedented post-war levels. Many people have come to associate the fall in inflation with the rise in unemployment. High unemployment in this scenario squeezed inflation out of the economic system, although quite how the squeezing was done is a matter of dispute. One of the most famous explanations is the Phillips curve, first mooted in the late 1950s, which suggests that there is a direct inverse relationship between the level of unemployment and the rate of inflation.

There are theoretical and empirical problems with the simple level-of-unemployment/rate-of-inflation parable. The empirical difficulties are associated with two key deviations from the predicted relationship of unemployment and inflation that occurred in the 1980s. Although inflation declined during the 1980s, prices did not continuously fall despite record levels of unemployment. Instead inflation steadied in the second half of the 1980s, creeping up again in 1988. If the onset of mass unemployment is supposed to moderate wage claims, enabling inflation to fall, why did it stop having that effect? Worse still for the excess-labour-supply explanation of the rate of inflation, real wages actually rose much faster in the 1980s than they did in the 1970s despite continued high unemployment.

It would seem that changes in real wages in Britain are not very responsive to the level of unemployment (cf. the estimates in Carruth and Oswald, 1987). Workers, of course, cannot bargain over the level of real wages, which are affected by the rate of inflation as well as the level of money wages. When they or their union representatives make wage demands, they have to anticipate future rates of inflation. It could be that the two periods when real wages did fall, 1975–7 and 1980–1, occurred because wage bargainers did not anticipate inflation correctly or in the first period were unable to transmit those expectations into wage demands because of incomes policies. If those explanations are correct, the empirical relationship between aggregate changes in real wages and the rate of unemployment would be virtually nonexistent.

Neglect of expectations in wage-setting behaviour discredited the simple Phillips relation in the mid-1970s, and led to its replacement by the theory of the *natural rate of unemployment*. It is not the level of unemployment but its relation to the equilibrium or 'natural rate' of unemployment that is important with regard to inflation. First formulated by Milton Friedman as part of his attack on Keynesian demand-management policies, the natural-rate explanation has been accepted by many mainstream economists – at least in its slightly more sophisticated variant called NAIRU, the non-accelerating inflation rate of unemployment. The argument is that, if unemployment is below the natural rate, inflation rises, as excess demand for labour pushes up real wages, and workers quickly adjust their nominal bids to take account of expected inflation. If unemployment is above the natural rate, the excess supply of workers causes wages and hence inflation to fall.

The speed of the process by which workers are supposed to adjust their expectations to the new market situation is one of the disagreements between monetarists, like Milton Friedman, and New Classical economists. Friedman argued that workers would take time to adjust their expectations of inflation to its changing rate, so there would be a short-run Phillips Curve. New Classical economics, with its rational-expectations theory and instantaneous adjustments, has banished even that possibility.

The natural-rate hypothesis has very important implications for government policy because it suggests that at any one point in time there is a fixed-equilibrium level of activity in the economy. If the Government tries to alter that level, say, by reflating to reduce unemployment, all it will succeed in doing is increasing inflation with no effect on unemployment. The theory, therefore, is highly attractive to governments such as those of Callaghan and Thatcher which want to abandon full employment as a policy target.

The natural rate itself is determined by the slopes of the demand for and supply of labour schedules, which it is said are influenced by how willing firms are to invest and by how prepared workers are to work for particular wage levels. Workers' responses to particular wage offers are affected by personal taxation, the costs of not working as determined by the dole and other state benefit levels, and the information they have about job opportunities – which may in the circumstances be unrealistic. Trade unions are said to keep real wages above the market clearing rate creating unemployment.

Although governments cannot shift unemployment below the natural rate through reflation they can try to alter the natural rate itself. 'Supply-side' policies are government measures designed to shift the parameters of labour demand and supply schedules, encouraging growth and lowering the natural rate. Taxation reductions are said to persuade investors to invest more and workers to work harder (although there is precious little empirical evidence to back up the belief); benefits can be reduced and restructured to make not-working a more painful experience; and trade union power can be weakened so that real wages fall to market clearing levels.

Structural economic change as experienced by Britain with deindustrialisation is said to raise the natural rate of unemployment. Workers are thrown out of the declining industries and become 'voluntarily' unemployed while they look for other jobs. During the search process, they have to adjust their expectations of the type of work they can now do and the level of earnings they can now get.

Existence of a natural rate of unemployment might explain the decline in inflation in the early 1980s. It could be argued that the recession in the UK pushed unemployment above its natural rate, forcing a rapid downward revision of wage demands and expectations about inflation. Unfortunately for the natural-rate thesis, unemployment has remained high while inflation has fallen. This combination can only be explained by claiming that the natural rate itself has risen, but that severely weakens the theory's credibility as the idea of a fixed employment equilibrium becomes increasingly difficult to sustain. Furthermore, such a supposed increase in the natural rate took place after the Thatcher government had introduced a number of supply-side policies that should have reduced the natural rate.

Others have argued that unemployment only has a short-run wage-moderating effect. Workers then get used to the fact that it's not their job that is likely to go and stop moderating wage demands (Layard and Nickell, 1987). NAIRU thus becomes a relative concept depending on the rate of change of unemployment rather than on some absolute unemployment level. But, if it is such a relative concept, how can there be something called *the* natural rate of unemployment (Solow, 1987a; Jenkinson, 1987)?

The idea of 'hysteresis' has been used to explain why the natural rate increases. Hysteresis, a term borrowed from physics, is a delay between an event and the effect produced by it. Workers may lose their skills, or capacity may be irrevocably shut during a slump, for instance, permanently lowering the productive capacity of an economy. Hysteresis, however, does not overcome the difficulties facing the idea of a natural rate of activity for an economy. In fact it suggests there are many possible equilibrium points depending on the precise path of adjustment, and possibly no equilibrium point at all. An implication of the hysteresis argument is that government economic policy may be feasible and effective, as governments can intervene to affect the paths of adjustment and consequently their final outcome. This conclusion undermines the whole point of the natural-rate hypothesis which is to deny that government macroeconomic intervention can have any long-run effect, and so the concept loses its didactic force.

Layard and Nickell (1987) argue that the NAIRU has risen in line with unemployment because of the characteristics of the unemployed. Many are long-term unemployed with over twelve months without a job, are often unskilled with low educational attainment, and are at the relative extremes of the employment life-cycle, under twenty-five or over forty-five. These characteristics make them unattractive to employers and possibly 'work-shy'. Whether or not they are actually less employable is an empirical question whose validity has not been settled. But treating the unemployed as having special characteristics does not really rescue the natural-rate thesis. It is

121

a partial segmentation of the labour force on the basis of people's real or supposed characteristics, whereas the natural rate is based on a simple general equilibrium in the labour market. Once labour markets are regarded as segmented, a singular labour market and a general natural rate are by implication replaced by a whole series or potential labour submarkets with their own specific employment/unemployment features. If there are differential effects in separate labour markets, it is possible to have policies towards some of them without having much effect on demand and supply in others, so the door to specific reflationary strategies is opened again.

The argument so far has been based on the idea that the nature of supply of and demand for labour is like that for any other good. As its price is lowered, demand increases and supply falls (in this case, 'price' is the real wage rate). What happens if demand and supply are not so price-responsive? Of particular concern here is the demand for labour. Some economists argue that the demand for labour is not very price responsive, instead labour demand depends on the level of the aggregate demand for the goods they produce which in turn is affected by the general level of incomes. Cutting wages, therefore, rather than pricing people into jobs actually reduces aggregate demand further, creating even more unemployment. This was one of the basic conclusions of Keynes's *General Theory* (Keynes, 1936), which monetarists and New Classical economists in succession have tried to discredit.

Some Keynesians, all Marxists and some other economists argue that there is no continuous downward-sloping labour schedule, nor a natural 'equilibrium' rate of unemployment. Employment is determined instead by the physical capacity of the economy – which is continuously but unevenly changing over time and across sectors; the level and composition of demand; and the ways in which firms are modernising their techniques of production.

Who is right in the explanation of the relationships between wages and employment, and prices and output? It would seem a simple empirical matter to resolve. Most empirical studies indicate that neither firms' investment and cost functions nor their pricing strategies conform to the extreme price sensitivity required in standard neo-classical theory which forms the bedrock of the labour-market analysis underlying the natural-rate hypothesis (cf. Johnson, 1971). The discussion of the long-term strategies of multinationals suggested that their global strategies, while sensitive to longer-run variations in labour costs, were not particularly responsive to short-run wage variations. In the Third World, for example, multinationals often do not seem to adjust their tech-nologies to the lower level of wages prevalent, but continue to use the capital-intensive techniques they apply in advanced capitalist countries; although often the technology is of an older vintage (Jenkins, 1987). Some types of firm or sectors of the economy might be more price sensitive but there is not much information to go on. Yet, despite virtually no supporting evidence on the determination of firms' prices and input demands, neo-classical theory still holds the field in the matter – which perhaps is more a comment on the state of economic theory than a prognosis about the actual workings of the economy.

Other explanations for the rise and fall of inflation have been mooted. One approach is to argue that inflation arises because there is severe conflict between particular social groups over the distribution of the social product. Rowthorn (1980) suggested such a mechanism. Capital-ists and workers fight over the share of national income going as profits and wages. When their demands are greater than the available cake, an inflationary spiral can emerge as capitalists try to sustain their profits by raising prices and passing on higher wage claims in higher prices as well. Workers then respond to the higher prices with higher wage demands. The spiral is broken only when one party has to withdraw from the conflict, and accepts a lower share of national income.

In this conflict approach, the years around the First and Second World Wars could be regarded as a partial defeat for capitalists, as on each occasion the share of wages and salaries in national income rose by almost 10 per cent. The 1950s and 1960s also saw real wages rise continuously and substantially, but improving productivity kept labour's share of national income relatively constant. By the early 1970s, firms' profits were at an all-time low and national income as a whole was cut by the rises in oil prices. The 1970s saw a series of set-piece battles and incomes policies, but essentially an inflationary stalemate as profits failed to revive, while real wages fluctuated around a stagnant level. The early 1980s recession and Thatcherism finally forced workers to discontinue the fight. So the 1980s within this scenario were a defeat for labour after a decade of fierce conflict.

A problem with this conflict explanation is the resilience of real wages in the 1980s, which grew at rates not seen since the 1960s. The conflict approach can be rescued, however, by suggesting that the real losers were the growing tide of unemployed, whose massive cuts in living standards freed enough national income to meet the demands of capitalists and those workers still in employment.

Conflict of itself does not actually say very much, beyond that groups in society have different interests. It only develops causal significance once it is applied with a theory of how the economy operates. The conflict story just narrated took an implicit radical Keynesian view. In it the monetary sector adjusts to suit the requirements of the real economy. It is also perfectly possible to transpose the arguments of natural-rate theorists into a conflict framework. Layard and Nickell's (1987) NAIRU model, for instance, has a strong conflictual ring to it, with unions' target real wages above what is 'feasible' when unemployment is below NAIRU.

124

Some economists have come out strongly with the view that unemployment had nothing at all to do with the fall in inflation. Beckerman (1985) and Beckerman and Jenkinson (1986) argue that the real villain of inflation was the price of primary commodities imported into the industrialised world. They point out that inflation in the 1970s was a phenomenon affecting all the OECD nations, although there were variations around the average rate. During the 1970s, primary commodity prices rose rapidly – not only oil but also foodstuffs and many other raw materials. The high prices encouraged overinvestment in the production of many primary commodities, while recession in the advanced world dampened demand, with the consequence that commodity prices fell substantially. The scale of the rise and fall in commodity prices they calculate matches almost perfectly the rise and fall in the aggregate OECD inflation rates once a lag is introduced and account is taken of the proportion of non-OECD primary commodity imports in an average OECD country's imports. The rise and fall of inflation in this explanation had little to do with the actions of anyone in Britain. The cost of checking inflation was borne by the unemployed. But a far greater burden was imposed on those in primary producer countries, especially in the Third World, where economies were saddled with enormous debt burdens as well, arising from loans incurred partially as a result of the investment in primary commodity production. That investment then intensified the fall in primary commodity prices. It is interesting to note that this is one of the few explanations of inflation that actually recognises that it was a worldwide phenomenon, and not simply specific to Britain.

The final explanation of inflation is the monetarist one. To a great extent it has already been considered since a natural rate of unemployment is central to it. Monetarists believe there is a clear and simple relation between increases in the supply of money and inflation. Given the existence of a natural rate of unemployment, accelerating inflation can only exist if governments supply the money to fund inflationary excess demand in the economy. Firms and workers gradually adjust their inflationary expectations so that real economic activity stays around the natural level whilst prices take off. Inflation can be lowered only by cutting down the growth of the money supply. This leads to a temporary recession but as expectations, prices and wages adjust it disappears.

The Thatcher governments' economic policies are frequently classified as monetarist, but strictly they have not been. The prime reason is the abject failure to control the money supply which consistently and massively overran its targets throughout the decade (Dow, 1987). Failure to control the money supply also led to disenchantment with monetarist theory. According to monetarist predictions Britain should have had rampant inflation throughout the 1980s! Criticism of an inability to define money, let alone control its supply, have been voiced (cf. Kaldor, 1982). Monetarism has also suffered from the problems with the natural-rate-of-unemployment concept raised earlier.

HAS THERE BEEN A PRODUCTIVITY REVOLUTION?

During the 1980s productivity in manufacturing industry rose substantially. As Table 5.1 shows, between 1981 and 1986 labour productivity in manufacturing rose by 30 per cent; whereas between 1973 and 1979 it rose by a mere 4 per cent. Can such a dramatic improvement be seen as the harbinger of a revival of British industry?

A number of explanations of the productivity improvement have been suggested. The first notes that care must be taken when comparing economic data over time because of the importance of *cyclical effects*. Labour productivity tends to be higher in upturns than in

TABLE 5.1 *Indices of UK Manufacturing Activity, 1973–86[1]*

	1973	1975	1979	1981	1986
Manufacturing output (1980=100)	114.2	105.0	109.5	94.0	104.5
Gross fixed investment in manufacturing (£ million at 1980 prices)	6786	6778	7496	4865	6329
Manufacturing employment (1980=100)	114.1	109.2	105.4	90.4	79.2
Output per person employed (1980=100)	100.0	95.9	104.0	103.5	134.3

1. The years chosen represent peaks and troughs in economic activity plus data for the latest available year.

Source: *Economic Trends*

downturns in economy activity for a number of reasons. When the economy is in an upswing production processes are more likely to be utilised at their optimum levels than during a downswing. If employers think a recession is going to be short-lived, they might also hoard labour. Even if they do not, the sharp change in production plans brought on by a severe slump is likely to disrupt production, worsening productivity. Both 1973 and 1979 were cyclical peak years; whereas 1981 was at the bottom of a recession. Some of the productivity growth from 1981 to 1986, therefore, can be attributed to the existence of the mid-1980s economic upturn itself; although at best this can only be part of the explanation.

Another explanation is the impact on productivity of *plant closures*. The recession of the early 1980s led to the full or partial closure of many factories and the scrapping of much plant and equipment. If the lost capacity was the least efficient, the average productivity of what remained would increase simply as an arithmetical consequence rather than because of changes in manufacturing processes themselves. Such a claim has considerable intuitive appeal, and it could easily explain some of the 1980s productivity improvement, but the argument does have limitations. In the first place, the productivity shift would be once-and-for-all and so it cannot explain a continuous rise in productivity. It could be argued that scrapping is continuous, reflecting the gradual process of deindustrialisation in which the early 1980s slump was only an extreme. But that line of reasoning then raises the question of why the productivity-improving effects of plant-scrapping were not seen earlier: for example, in the mid-1970s when manufacturing unemployment rose rapidly. Another difficulty is the presumption that the least productively efficient parts of manufacturing industry are scrapped during economic crisis. Yet plants are owned by firms whose concern is with the overall profitability of their operations – on which productivity will be only one influence. The firm might have had substantial borrowings – for example, have been producing antiquated, unsaleable products – faced a sudden increase in competition or wished to relocated its production facilities overseas. Plants may as a result close for these and other reasons rather than because of their relative inefficiency. In this context, it is worth remembering the earlier discussion of large-plant closures. Large plants are more productive on average than smaller ones, yet they disproportionately closed during the early 1980s recession. The only study of the reasons for their closure was sceptical of them being the most inefficient of the large plants (Oulton, 1987).

Another line of reasoning argues that there has been a major transformation of the content of production as a result of recession and continuing Thatcherism. The loss of productive capacity in this explanation is an unfortunate side-effect of the transformation induced in *industrial attitudes*.

One variant stresses the potential ability of trade unions and workers to hold back the introduction of new technology, to hamper its successful introduction and to work at a slow pace. In clichéd terms, managers are said to have won back the right to manage. Although difficult to quantify, such an overwhelmingly negative view of trade unions and workers on changes in productivity is misplaced. But, in a more limited sense, it could still be said that a workforce's ability to resist managerial changes was weaker than it had been prior to the 1980s recession.

Another attitudinal variant lays emphasis on managerial capacities. British management historically has been unable to organise production effectively, because of either its general low level of training or its attitudes – preferring the quiet life to innovation and confrontation (Nichols, 1986). The 1980s changed all that for managers as the ever present threat of plant and firm closure or the fear of takeover jeopardised their jobs as well as those of the workers they employed.

Attitudes and their impact are exceedingly difficult to quantify – in the field of industrial relations in particular, 'attitudes' can be as much a justification for a course of action as a cause of it. Moreover, even if the changed industrial-relations climate does exist, no statement can be made about the direction of change that arises – that will depend on investment strategies adopted by management. And, once again, even if this type of explanation is correct it cannot explain a continual growth in productivity. Held-up techniques may be introduced or work effort improved only once, although the effects are likely to appear in the aggregate statistics as an improvement in productivity over a number of years, given the likely variability in their impact in individual plants.

Another line of reasoning points to the fact that

comparison of the 1980s with the years from 1973 to 1979 is unfair. The 1970s were the years of crisis rather than the 1980s, and the economy has returned to a period of normalcy at a rate of growth similar to (or slightly less than) that experienced in the 1960s. In the 1970s, profit rates were exceptionally low, oil and commodity prices rocketed and there was intense industrial conflict over inflation's uneven and unforeseen impact. One result was low productivity growth.

Some economists have suggested that the fourfold *rise in the real price of oil* during the 1970s alone could have created the productivity problems. Firms would have been encouraged to economise on oil, scrapping some equipment and utilising possibly less labour-efficient processes, which would show up as a sharp slowdown in productivity. With lagged adjustment, the effect of the oil-price rises would have spread through productivity data into the early 1980s (Posner and Sargent, 1987). If this were true, Britain in the late 1980s would be enjoying the productivity benefits of a reversal of the process, as oil prices fell to the early 1970s level again. Conversely, it could be claimed that the oil-price rises forced firms to innovate, raising rather than lowering productivity, as undoubtedly occurred in energy-intensive but monopolistic industries like bricks and cement.

When considering changes in productivity in Britain it is important to remember the country's low average level of productivity compared to other industrialised countries – a gap that increased for at least thirty years from 1950 to 1980 rather than diminished. Britain's ability to achieve productivity increases by adopting techniques and equipment used elsewhere consequently has grown over the post-war years, so that it should progressively become easier to apply at least a limited number of innovations if someone wished to introduce them, particularly after the hiatus of the 1970s. Productivity rises in the 1980s might be indicating that British firms on average are now introducing some of those 'catch-up' *innovations.* But, even if this is the case, the comparative data in Chapter 3 showed there is still a long way to go.

Catch-up as a cause of productivity increases can be an explanation assigning little or no credit for the improvement to government policy. Rather than being a basis on which firms have been able to introduce innovations, government policy could just as easily have been a constraint on introducing more. Constraints could have occurred for a number of reasons: through the nature of the 'hands-off' industrial policy; through the restriction of aggregate demand for many years, while firms went bankrupt and/or lost markets to overseas competitors; the impact of monopolies policy and the encouragement of takeovers may also have reinforced short-termism; the privatisation programmes could have put strains on key erstwhile nationalised industries and unnecessarily diverted management time and their objectives; the lack of investment in infrastructure could have helped to created congestion and bottlenecks reducing overall potential capacity; an absence of regional policies and measures aimed at house prices could have reinforced costs imposed by the concentration of economic growth in the South East; or, finally, productivity growth may be held back by the failure to introduce sufficiently widespread programmes to upgrade the educational and skills qualifications of the British labour force. On the catch-up scenario, the second two Thatcher administrations may simply have had the good fortune to be in power at a time when British industry was enjoying a spurt of productivity upgrading. Whether it actually created attractive conditions for productivity improvement is another matter.

A more pessimistic scenario on productivity would suggest that British management is simply carrying on with the productivity strategies it knows best and has always used. Production in Britain is labour-intensive and traditional-skills-demanding. Little additional investment occurred for much of the 1980s, as the data on manufacturing investment in Table 5.1 show. Given the weakened ability of workers to resist, however, firms have intensified the speed at which they require them to work and increased the range of tasks they expect any individual operative to undertake. Such a strategy leads to spectacular short-term productivity gains but they inevitably peter out as intensification mounts, and possibly are reversed once labour markets tighten again. Increased industrial unrest in the late 1980s in this scenario is taken as an indicator of growing worker resistance. Labour markets are tightening and the process of intensification is reaching its limits.

Unfortunately, it is very difficult to discriminate between many of the hypotheses about the 1980s 'productivity miracle' outlined above. Insufficient data are available. Hindsight might help, but controversies over the British economic 'slowdown' in the last quarter of the nineteenth century suggest not. One thing to note, however, is that whatever has happened to productivity British firms have withdrawn from many markets and replaced them with few new ones – leading us back into the deindustrialisation debate.

FURTHER READING

An excellent survey of the debates over multinationals is Jenkins (1987). Even though it concentrates on the Third World, the theory chapters and much of the rest are highly relevant to the UK situation. Murray (1981) and Stopford and Turner (1985) are also useful starting-points.

Mayer (1987) attempts to unravel the complexities of whether the City holds back industry. Harris *et al.* (1988) also provides a wide range of statistical material and articles. Ingham (1984) is one of the City's most trenchant critics.

With regard to an introduction to the theory of the

natural rate of unemployment, the Phillips Curve and inflation theory see Begg, Dornbusch and Fischer (1987). Layard and Nickel (1987) is an example of contemporary modified use of the theory, while Jenkinson (1987) introduces some scepticism. Conflict theories of inflation are considered in Rowthorn (1980). Beckerman (1985) stresses the role of commodity prices.

Arguments made about the transformation of the British economy as a product of Thatcherism are dealt with in Chapter 12 below. MacInnes (1987) argues there has been little change. Buiter and Miller (1983) discuss the economic consequences of the early 1980s recession. Oulton (1987) is sceptical about the closure of the words explanation of productivity improvements. Muellbauer (1986) outlines competing hypotheses on productivity change and starts an initial statistical investigation of them. Posner and Sargent (1987) is also a clear exposition of the issues.

PART 2

Labour and Life

6

In Work

Linda McDowell

Waged labour for most people is the prime source of income and it gives purpose and structure to their existence. Jobs determine class locations and influence social attitudes. Many forms of employment give, in addition, access to job-specific goods and services, such as pension rights, insurance schemes and cars. Even for those outside the labour market, by virtue of their age, by choice or excluded by unemployment, the cash nexus and the structure of the working day are a powerful link to the employed population. Many of these 'non-workers' are also, of course, directly or indirectly dependent on wage-earners. Although the types of job available and their characteristics have continually evolved since the industrial revolution, it is argued that more recently the labour market has undergone radical transformation, particularly in the last decade. The origins of recent changes, however, have been discernible throughout the whole post-war period.

Since the mid-1950s, employment, predominantly for men, in the coal industry, shipbuilding, iron and steel, chemicals and engineering has been lost, whereas services have expanded, in both the public and private sectors. The public sector includes employment in central and local government and in the health service; private-sector services include employment in industries as varied as banking and insurance, retailing, hotels and catering and transport and distribution. Expansion of services has been accompanied by a growth in the number of women in waged employment. Indeed, many service-sector jobs are regarded as 'jobs for women'. Related to rises in women's labour-market participation has been a substantial expansion in part-time employment.

Many of the declining, male-employing manufacturing and extractive industries are located in the North East and the North West of England, in Wales and Scotland. There has also been a collapse of manufacturing employment in the large towns, especially in Greater London. New jobs tend to be located elsewhere, so the spatial distribution of jobs has changed and will continue to do so. The purpose of this chapter is to examine the extent and consequences of recent changes in the economy for the structure of the labour force and for individuals' living standards. It has been argued that work has been 'restructured' or 'deskilled' and that new forms of 'flexible specialisation' are apparent. The meaning and extent of these changes will be examined. The chapter will also look at recent arguments about the future of work. The main focus is on waged work, although the nature of domestic labour and the extent of various forms of 'outwork' will be addressed.

DIVISIONS OF LABOUR

In different societies and at different times, the social organisation of work varies. In a peasant society, for example, households provide many of the goods and services which they need themselves. The family is also the most common labour unit within which tasks are shared and assigned, and where the spatial distinction between the home and the workplace is blurred or non-existent. In a contemporary capitalist society like Britain, work is organised differently. A specialised division of labour exists in which goods are made by distinct producers operating at different locations. Although there is a 'public' sector of varying size, most goods and services are produced for market exchange and the basic organising principle of the economy is the search for profit. Workers' incomes enable them to buy most of their daily needs rather than having to make goods and provide services at home for their own individual consumption. This form of organisation of society enables vast increases in productivity compared with more traditional ones, accounting for much of the increase in wealth and rising living standards since the late eighteenth century. Production units are generally privately owned. Their owners usually employ managers to run them. Within firms command-hierarchies exist, with layers of management, specialised personnel and workers. Conflicts may arise at all points in the hierarchy, but particularly between the interests of workers as a whole, or specific groups of them, and the wishes of management.

Waged work is not the only form of 'work' – unpaid domestic work is the most obvious example of other types of work. As with waged labour, a social division of labour is associated with unpaid tasks. In a typical nuclear family in advanced industrial economies, the 'housewife', in particular, bears the brunt of most unpaid work, ensuring that individual members remain fit and healthy, and are able to go out to work or to school every day. Other forms of unpaid work include voluntary work in the community, mutual reciprocation of tasks and other 'informal' means of exchange.

The social organisation of work is subject to change and renegotiation over time: a process that is often the focus of conflict and dispute. Workers may be anxious about their status, job security and rewards. The introduction of new machinery in the early nineteenth century, for example, was met with organised opposition by the Luddites. In more recent decades there has been concern over the impact of new technology on the content of certain jobs, its health implications and the consequence for the economic structure of society. The introduction of different forms of computer-based technology, for instance, has been a significant part of the shift towards a service-based economy in Britain in the 1980s.

WHAT HAS HAPPENED TO JOBS IN BRITAIN?

The structure of employment in post-war Britain has undergone considerable change. Manufacturing employment reached its peak in 1966. Since then there has been a decline from 8.7 million to 5 million workers in manufacturing in 1988. Almost half the fall has occurred since 1979. However, there has been a great expansion in jobs in services. By the mid-1980s over 14 million people worked in service occupations, by far the largest section of the total labour force of 21.4 million employees in Great Britain in 1988.

The distinction between manufacturing and services is not self-evident nor is it watertight. It is based on the differentiation of the production of physical and tangible products – goods or objects – from the production of an intangible service, such as a concert, a hair-cut or a financial transaction in the service sector. It is sometimes assumed that the service sector is 'unproductive' and that only manufacturing produces value: an assumption that is reflected in political debates deploring the loss of 'Britain's industrial base' or warning against 'consuming more than we produce'.

The distinction between manufacturing and services is also reflected in the way in which labour statistics are collected. Figures are available on two bases: an industrial classification and an occupational classification. When the former is used all the workers within a particular industry are classified as part of it. Thus a typist working in the car industry would be included in manufacturing, whereas a typist in the Civil Service is a service employee. Conversely, on the occupational basis, all

typists irrespective of their industrial location are classified as service workers. Whichever classification is used
for comparison, service employment has expanded in
recent decades.

The growth of the service sector

At the end of the 1980s, services employed 14.7 million
workers, over 60 per cent of all non-agricultural workers.
Although growth has been continuous over the post-war
period, it has been made up of differential expansion and
decline in particular activities. There has been an absolute employment decline in transport and communications since the mid-1960s. At the other extreme, insurance, banking and finance, professional and scientific
services experienced the most rapid growth during the
1970s and 1980s. Employment in banking and finance, for
example, expanded by 34 per cent between 1976 and
1986. There has also been growth in some parts of the
public sector like education and medical services. They
increased their employment rapidly during the 1970s but,
as with other types of public-sector service work, have
since experienced a slower rate of growth and even a
decline in some areas, as a consequence of the decisions
by the successive Conservative administrations since
1979 to restrict public spending (see Chapter 12). Privatisation of services such as cleaning, catering and laundry
in the health service provide a good example of the
statistical difficulties in interpreting employment
change. If a laundry service is privatised and taken over
by a large conglomerate, then the workers may be
reclassified to manufacturing despite performing the
same service in the same place, albeit for a different
employer.

Service industries which sell their product to producers
as inputs to further stages of production rather than
directly to consumers are designated producer or intermediate services. It is often difficult to assign service

TABLE 6.1 *The Division of Service Employment between Producer and Consumer Services, Great Britain, 1988*

Type of employment	Number of employees (000s)	producer/ consumer division (%)	
Wholesale distribution	931	100	*
Retail distribution	2085	*	100
Hotels and catering	1144	25	75
Repairs	256	25	75
Transport and distribution	1343	60	40
Banking, finance, insurance, business services, leasing	2406	83	17
Public administration	1599	50	50
Sanitary services	410	10	90
Education	1696	10	90
Research and development	105	100	*
Medical services	1274	*	100
Other services	5820	19	81
Recreation and other cultural services	526	20	80
Personal services	192	*	100
ALL SERVICES	14,706	35	65
ALL INDUSTRIES AND SERVICES	21,464	22	78

Source: *Employment Gazette*, October 1988. The producer/consumer division is based on work by Daniels in Martin and Rowthorn (1986).

activities uniquely to either production or immediate consumption, so a third mixed category is frequently used by analysts of economic change. The producer/consumer division is illustrated in Table 6.1. This division is particularly useful when examining the spatial implications of service-sector growth, a topic considered in a later section. First, alternative explanations for the growth of service-sector employment are examined.

Explanations of service-sector growth

(i) Changes in the technical division of labour: increased horizontal segregation

One explanation of the growth of services is based on analysis of the increasing division of labour. Adherents of the approach argue that much of service-sector growth results from a reclassification of many of the subdivided tasks away from manufacturing to services. By itself, this position implies that in reality there has been little structural change in the British economy. Reclassification, however, is likely to account for only part of employment change.

(ii) The post-industrial thesis

A second, influential explanation of the changing division of labour is based on the work of sociologist Daniel Bell (Bell, 1974). He suggests that advanced industrial societies are moving from an industrial to a post-industrial phase. The views of post-industrial theorists parallel the maturity thesis as a cause of deindustrialisation outlined in the previous chapter. Bell argues that the rise of service-based economies is a consequence of rising real incomes. Demand is stimulated for a whole host of new services, while their provision is facilitated by technological changes that release labour from manufacturing. The socio-economic changes in Britain in the 1950s and 1960s – rising real incomes, the growth of consumption-based spending and the discovery of the teenager as a consumer, at the same time as manufacturing output was rising – seemed to lend support to Bell's thesis. The changes were accompanied by full employment. Stagnation of manufacturing output and rising rates of unemployment in the late 1970s and 1980s conversely have tended to reduce support for Bell's ideas. His optimistic prognosis of continued growth, improved working conditions and greater leisure-time opportunities for all seems unrealistic.

(iii) The self-service economy

One interesting variant of the post-industrial society thesis has been put forward by Gershuny and Miles (1983). They argue that one of the consequences of rising incomes is, in contrast to Bell's ideas, extra demand for consumer goods rather than services in order that households themselves can provide more of their own services. For example, they point to the rising sales of stereo and video recorders as alternatives to buying concert or cinema tickets, to the growth of the do-it-yourself industry, of food processing and freezing in the home as substitutes for purchasing services. The rise in the possession of consumer durables seems to support this argument. Between 1978 and 1986, for example, the ownership of colour televisions almost doubled (to 86 per cent of all households) and spending on TVs and videos over the same period more than doubled in real terms. Almost a third of all households owned a video in 1986. This argument – the growing importance of an economy based on 'self-provisioning' – would seem to imply higher demand for manufactured goods rather than for services and so would appear at first sight to run counter to changes in the structure of employment with growing numbers of service-sector workers. However, relative changes in productivity and the growing penetration of foreign capital in the consumer goods industry in Britain explain why manufacturing employment has not grown at the same rate as demand.

It may also be argued that Gershuny and Miles have constructed a false dichotomy between services and self-provisioning goods. For example, although the ownership of video recorders has doubled in a short period, there has been an associated and remarkable spread of video cassette hire shops – a service-sector activity. There are also important class differentials in the ownership of certain consumer durables and in the patterns of use of services. The people most likely to own a video or a car are also those who most frequently patronise the cinema, theatre or opera or who undertake air travel. Apparently self-provisioning and the purchase of services are not necessarily alternative activities.

It seems clear that none of the alternative arguments provides a complete explanation of the complex set of changes that are taking place in the structure of employment. Labour has been shed from manufacturing, thus a relative increase in service employment is arithmetically inevitable. However, growth in services has been achieved by drawing in new sources of labour rather than by redeploying the workers shed from manufacturing. There has been an absolute, as well as a relative, rise in service employment, partially accounted for by rising incomes within Britain, but also by the pronounced changes in Britain's role in the international division of labour outlined in previous chapters. The rise of the service-based economy has profound consequences for the nature of the labour process, for social divisions in the waged labour force and for the geography of employment opportunities. Each of these factors is now examined in turn.

THE CHANGING NATURE OF
THE LABOUR PROCESS

'The labour process' is a term used to encompass the tasks required to produce a particular good or service. It reflects the nature of particular jobs – their content, the way they are organised, the extent to which workers have autonomy over the execution of the tasks involved, the degree of skill entailed and the relationships implied between workers, supervisors and managers.

In the last few decades there have been enormous changes in the nature of manufacturing and service-sector jobs. Two areas of debate in particular have tried to explain why the changes are taking place. One focuses on losses of skilled work, known clumsily as 'deskilling'. The other is a related debate about the impact of new technology and an associated shift from mass-production assembly-line methods (often known as 'Fordism') to more flexible and specialised forms of industrial organisation.

Deskilling

Modern management's central aim is to gain greater control over what an individual worker does whilst in their employment. Workers are not machines, and can undertake tasks with more or less effort and enthusiasm, and with varying degrees of aptitude and skill. Braverman (1974) claims that the more skilled a job is, the greater control workers have over the way in which their tasks are undertaken. To increase labour productivity, therefore, managers have strong incentive to erode the power conferred on workers by their specialised skills. To achieve greater control, management breaks up the labour process into an increasingly large number of separate tasks, each requiring a minimum level of skill – hence the term 'deskilling' to describe the consequences of job fragmentation. In the deskilling process, Braverman moralistically claims that work is 'degraded'.

Such forms of deskilling were advocated by F. W. Taylor at the end of the nineteenth century. Known as the founder of 'Scientific Management' (see Rose, 1988), Taylor argued that each task should be broken down into its constituent parts, that workers should be allocated to perform a single repetitive routine and that the control and timing of work should be carefully monitored leaving little room for manoeuvre or initiative on the part of the worker. Applications of 'Taylorism', Braverman argues, have not been restricted to manufacturing but have also taken place in the service sector. In office work an often-cited example is where the introduction of word processors 'deskills' secretarial labour.

Braverman's analysis of the degradation of the labour process has, however, been criticised on a number of grounds (see Wood, 1982). First, it is not clear how widely Taylorist principles in their extreme as outlined by Braverman have ever been applied, either within the USA, his case study, or in other advanced industrial economies. Modern management methods encompass far more features than simply a detailed breaking-down of work tasks. Fragmentation of the labour process and mass-production methods anyway were introduced later into Britain than in the USA and have never been widespread throughout all industrial sectors. Secondly, there has been a debate about the degree to which the new computer-assisted technology introduced since the 1960s has reduced or increased the autonomy of individual workers. (The impact of new technology is discussed further in the next section.) Thirdly, Braverman overstated the role of management, both in its adherence to Taylorist principles and in the strength of its new control over the workforce.

Strategies of worker control, other than fragmentation of the labour process, are open to management, including the introduction of wage differentials. Japanese-style quality circles, where each worker undertakes a variety of tasks and is deliberately given a degree of responsibility over their execution, run counter to the fundamentals of Taylorism. The strength of worker organisation and the effectiveness of trade unions influence the ability of management to restructure the labour process. The nature of the market for particular products also affects the degree to which the labour process can be changed. Management is also not concerned solely or centrally with production. Marketing, financial manipulations, takeovers, geographical spreads, product ranges and design are all features of a firm's operations and crucially affect profitability. Management strategies may relegate workforce control to a relatively insignificant place, except in certain set-piece confrontations, designed to reduce union power.

Finally, it has been argued by feminist critics that Braverman's concepts of 'skill' and 'deskilling' are inadequate. Critics point to a coincidence of skill designation and gender of workers. Many of the jobs classified as unskilled are carried out by women. Fiddly assembly jobs in the car components and electronics industries, for example, require a considerable degree of manual dexterity or 'skill', are typically undertaken by women, and often classified as unskilled. When considering deskilling, account must therefore be taken of the social construction of what is appropriate 'women's work', its link to skill levels and the role of male-dominated trade unions in securing the more 'highly skilled' and correspondingly better-paid jobs for men.

A shift from Fordism to post-Fordism

Some commentators argue that we are currently witnessing a shift in advanced industrial societies from Fordist production techniques to new, more flexible forms of organisation of production, sometimes known as post-Fordism. The changes are being stimulated partly by the introduction of new technologies and also by competition from newly industrialising countries in the Far East and Latin America.

Two main schools of thought have developed to explain the shift from Fordism to post-Fordist methods of industrial organisation. One is known as the regulation school based on the work of Aglietta (1979); the other might be termed the institutionalist school and is best-typified by the work of Piore and Sabel (1984) on flexible specialisation. The institutional school was originally developed to counter the emphasis of neoclassical economists on rational decision-making and perfect competition in the market. The new school incorporated into their explanatory framework the impact of sociocultural institutional forms that affect the way markets operate – the role of trade union organisation, for example. The main features of regulationist theory and the general approach of the institutionalists were outlined in Chapter 3. Here the focus is on a specific comparison between the two schools' reasons for believing that there have been significant changes in methods of production.

Both sets of theorists argue that there has been a shift away from the mass-production, mass-market methods of industrial organisation that are labelled Fordism to a new regime of production that is typified by flexibility, small runs and meeting specialised demands. This shift, which, it is argued, is currently occurring in the USA, Japan, Britain and other Western European countries, has been variously called 'the crisis of mass production', from Fordism to neo-Fordism or post-Fordism, or the shift to flexible specialisation.

Although both schools develop a similar description of the changes, their explanatory frameworks are different. The regulationist approach is a variant of Marxist theory that conceptualises capitalist economies as evolving through a series of qualitatively different stages of development, or regimes of accumulation. Their approach involves the search for general laws that are socially determinate. Each regime of accumulation is related to a particular mode of social regulation – so, for example, the Fordist era of mass production was accompanied by the Keynesian welfare state which bolstered industrial wages by 'social wages', through the provision of various types of collective goods and services, such as health, social housing and social security systems. Piore and Sabel, on the other hand, do not see progression between different stages as inevitable but as contingent upon the particular set of circumstances in a country and in the world at the time in question. They envisage change as being a series of breaking-points or divides at which positive choices may be made: hence the title of their book *The Second Industrial Divide: Possibilities for Prosperity*. The first industrial divide occurred when craft-based industrial production was replaced with Fordism. We are now at the second divide, created by the crisis of mass production and the dramatic decline of manufacturing employment in the industrialised West. Piore and Sabel draw on writers who argue that there is no inevitable link between the logic of capitalist accumulation and the nature of the labour process. For example, they cite some of the criticisms of Braverman outlined in the preceding section. It has been suggested, however, that Piore and Sabel themselves are too indeterminate in their view of industrial change. It is highly unlikely that craft methods of production could ever have offered a viable and profitable alternative to the introduction of Fordist methods of mass production of consumer durables in the twentieth-century USA and, to a lesser extent, in Britain. Equally their belief that craft production, although earlier rejected, may form the basis for manufacturing revival, prosperity and greater worker control over the labour process relies on an overromanticised reading of the past.

Both regulationists and institutionalists tend to base their general models of industrial change on what is happening in the consumer goods manufacturing sector rather than on production as a whole. In many countries, small-scale non-assembly-line production remains important. However, it is argued that this form of production tends to typify the capital goods sector that produces the machinery and equipment needed to manufacture consumer goods. Both sets of theorists agree that the production of consumer goods takes a leading role in manufacturing growth. The actual variety and complexity of different forms of industrial organisation in particular capitalist countries is rather cavalierly treated.

Neo-Fordism and flexible specialisation

The solution to the 'crisis of mass production' lies in changes in the organisation of production. Piore and Sabel offer two alternatives. The first is what they call 'multi-national Keynesianism' in which the existing system or regime is propped up by policies to raise purchasing power and so demand for industrial products in the countries of the Third World. The other alternative, which Piore and Sabel favour, is the reorganisation of industrial production based on what they call 'flexible specialisation'. Their analysis is clearly prescriptive, although not seen as a necessary tendency of capitalist development. The regulationists, on the other hand, believe that 'Capitalism can escape from its contemporary organic crisis only by generating a new cohesion, a neo-Fordism' (Aglietta, 1979).

The basic features of flexible specialisation and neo-Fordism, however, are similar, centred around the utilisation of new production technology. New forms of small-scale, small-batch and craft-based production are made possible through the use of electronic information systems and computer inventory ordering. The production of new, customised goods to meet specialised tastes rather than large-scale standardised production for mass markets becomes profitable. A proliferation of small companies compete in 'niche' markets, often offering reskilling or enskilling opportunities to the workers as former craft skills are reintroduced and re-evaluated. Labour, too, is used more flexibly. Firms may seek to achieve 'numerical flexibility' by using temporary workers to meet peaks and troughs of demand. The eventual result may be the creation of a 'core' of skilled, permanently employed workers and a 'periphery' of temporary and casual employers. This aspect of flexibility is taken up again in the next section, in the specific context of Britain.

The move to flexible specialisation or neo-Fordism will

151

be associated with a new managerial style; larger firms may be broken into smaller units, and the introduction of 'just-in-time' inventories enables the production process to be reorganised. The argument is based on generalising certain developments in key industries, like motors, to the economy as a whole. In manufacturing there is a movement towards computer-integrated manufacturing, whereby an entire production system is controlled as a whole from the initial design stages, through the purchase of components, the production process itself, the ancillary office functions to final product delivery.

Some implications of computer-controlled manufacturing can be seen in their introduction to a new Nissan plant in Sunderland in County Durham. The new capital-intensive plant is expected to reduce significantly average production costs per car in Britain and to be a model for future plants. The plant differs from previous car plants in Britain in several ways: first, in its small-town location; second, in the capital intensity of the production processes; and, third, in its labour relations. According to Nissan: 'Labour–management relations will be a cooperative "Japanese-style" arrangement with flexible work rules, a salaried workforce with employment guarantees, and with extensive decision-sharing within work groups.' A single-union deal was signed with the AEU, the engineers' union, but the main negotiating rights remain vested in the company council. Shopfloor discipline is strictly enforced, and the workforce has to work extremely fast. At the core of the Nissan system of production is the 'just-in-time' method. Rather than maintaining a large stock of components, Nissan holds on its own premises just enough parts for seven hours' production. This saves capital and warehouse space. Components are purchased from a single supplier who is tied to Nissan by a part-merger agreement. Components have to be available within two hours and so tight labour discipline also becomes crucial for the suppliers. This system is quite different from 'Fordist' methods of the organisation of mass production which still predominate in the car industry in Britain. Car manufacturers other than Nissan in Britain frequently buy components from several sources, hold stock on the premises and produce vehicles on an assembly-line system with an extreme division of labour. A classic study of the monotony involved in working on the line in a 'Fordist' car assembly plant is Beynon's (1973) study of Ford's Halewood plant in Liverpool, in which the noise and tedium of the day-to-day working routine of male car workers is vividly described. Beynon visited Halewood as an observer. Ten years later, another sociologist, Ruth Cavendish (1982), actually worked for a year on a car-components line doing 'women's work' – fiddly, monotonous assembly tasks- and her book, too, describes in detail the numbing effect this type of organisation of the labour process has on individual workers. During her first few weeks on the line, Cavendish found that she was completely exhausted. Many other studies have reported similar effects. This partly explains why the initial literature describing the move towards greater flexibility was so enthusiastic about the changes as they were envisaged as improving workers' lives and their control over the labour process.

The empirical evidence of 'flexible specialisation', however, is thin, and the arguments of the neo-Fordists and the flexible-specialisation theorists should be questioned. Computer-integrated manufacturing and new-style working practices are still a long way from being the norm in Britain, and agreements about changes in working practices, such as single-union agreements, are not always easy to achieve. A *Financial Times* survey of manufacturing firms in Britain carried out in 1986 (Leadbeater and Lloyd, 1987) found that 59 per cent of employers planned to introduce microelectronics but only 16 per cent aimed to implement Japanese-style just-in-time inventory systems before the 1990s. Innovations in automation are only slowly being introduced, partly because of the relatively small scale of production in this country. Classic Fordist mass production has never been as widespread in Britain as in the United States. For example, almost 70 per cent of components produced by the engineering industry are made in batches of less than fifty (Leadbeater and Lloyd, 1987). At such output levels, the high investment needed to introduce dedicated automation systems would be uneconomic.

The evidence about the increasing fragmentation of markets is also often exaggerated. Although 'designer' products that are less standardised and more personalised have increased their share of the market, there is still an enormous sales expansion in mass-production goods. Good examples are video-cassette recorders, personal stereos, calculators, cameras and microwave ovens, and the expansion of the Japanese economy is based on the mass production of many of these products.

One of the key questions about the introduction of new technology is the impact it has on the organisation of work. Here the literature is speculative for the very reason that these changes are at an early stage. There is evidence that manufacturing firms of the future may be looking for 'multi-skilled' workers rather than one-function specialists and also that the rigid demarcation between shopfloor workers and management may become more permeable. Flexible manufacturing systems require more skilled planning and integration. Skilled computer personnel are needed to devise and maintain the necessary software packages. For economic viability, robots and other complex machines need to operate at full capacity, queues of components waiting to be processed have to be kept short, and breakdowns repaired quickly. The introduction of these forms of computer-based technology is not proving to be easy. Even in the US and Japanese car industries where some of the changes are furthest advanced there have been significant teething problems that have delayed the hoped-for rate of progress by many months. The impact of new technology on jobs is hard to calculate but it seems clear that less skilled manufacturing jobs are most at risk. A Policy Study Institute survey found that of the 34,000 manufacturing jobs lost between 1981 and 1983 because of the introduction of new technology, over two-thirds were unskilled jobs. New forms of training are urgently needed if British industry is to adapt to the new forms of production.

In the service sector, the impact of new technology has primarily been on routine clerical operations. In banking, for example, since the 1960s high-volume routine tasks such as cheque processing have been automated and new forms of automated customer services introduced. The introduction of credit cards has been one consequence of the new technology. Office functions in all sectors of the economy are being radically affected by the rapid diffusion of desktop computers and word processors. For typists, especially if organised on the basis of a pool, the introduction of word processors seems to have intensified the lack of control they already felt over the nature and pains of their work and to have reduced many of the skills previously required, those involved in layout, for example. For secretarial work in the true sense, where the range of tasks, the degree of responsibility and the social-contact element of the job are more important, the evidence of deskilling is less clear (Webster, 1986). It seems that the ratio of secretaries to managers and professionals is decreasing. One reason is that new technology encourages managers and professionals to do tasks previously handed to secretaries. In certain professions, such as publishing and law, conversely, the introduction of standard programmes to perform routine but previously professional tasks leads to a range of jobs being undertaken by clerical workers rather than by skilled editors or professional lawyers.

In the longer term there is enormous scope for changes in routinised, clerical work, particularly in the ability to achieve wider geographic separation of routine and management functions to take advantage of wage differentials. Off-shores data processing in the Caribbean by US firms, for example, is currently being expanded, facilitated by satellite communications networks. Another change in the spatial location of employment arises from the growing opportunities to work from home. Advances in information technology services for shopping, leisure, travel, the media and medical services may eventually revolutionise the organisation of the service sector as a whole and associated consumption patterns in the next few decades. The infrastructural investment needed to carry through a thorough communications revolution is, however, immense.

THE CHANGING CHARACTERISTICS OF THE LABOUR FORCE

By the late 1980s, there are marked differences in the types of job available and in the characteristics of the people who perform them compared with twenty-five years ago. The most obvious, and regrettable, change has been the rise in the number of people without a job at all; a topic discussed in the next chapter.

A second noticeable shift in the labour force has been in its gender composition. In 1959, the employed workforce consisted of 13.8 million men and 7.2 million women. Two-thirds of all waged workers were men. By 1988, the proportion of women in the labour force had risen to 45 per cent. The actual numbers of employees in that year were 11.6 million men and 9.9 million women. During the post-war period, as Table 6.2 shows, women's participation in waged labour has increased at the same time as men's has declined. The growth increase in women's participation is particularly marked among married women. Less than a quarter of all married women worked for wages in the 1950s compared with over half by the end of the 1980s. Married women are so common

TABLE 6.2 *The Changing Gender Distribution of Employees, Great Britain, 1971–88 (millions)*

	1971	1976	1979	1981	1986	1988
All employees	21.6	22.0	22.6	21.4	21.0	21.5
All male	13.4	13.1	13.2	12.3	11.6	11.6
All female	8.2	9.0	9.5	9.1	9.4	9.9
Full-time female	5.5	5.4	5.6	5.3	5.4	5.5
Part-time female	2.8	3.6	3.9	3.8	4.0	4.4

Source: *Employment Gazette*, various dates.

in the labour market that it seems almost unbelievable that until the end of the 1940s married women were formally banned from certain occupations and professions where they now predominate, as in the Civil Service for example. Some jobs are still formally proscribed for women, like coal mining, or extremely difficult to enter, such as skilled building work.

A range of social and economic factors are important in explaining women's rising participation in waged work. Changes in fertility rates and in birth spacing mean that on average women have fewer children in total and spend less time with very young children in their household. Average life expectancy and women's health have improved, as have women's educational qualifications. Expectations and attitudes of both workers and management have also changed. In addition, rising standards of living, the purchase of consumer durables and the expansion of owner occupation has been partly based on the growth in the number of households with more than one wage-earner. The net result of these changes is that more women are available for waged labour, wanting or needing additional income. At the same time, the demand for female labour has expanded. Interestingly, this expansion has occurred at a steady pace over the post-war period and the growth in the number of women in the labour force appears to be unrelated to economic upturns and downswings. Both in periods of high demand for labour, in the 1950s and 1960s, and during the recession in the late 1970s and early 1980s, the demand for women's labour continued to rise. This characteristic runs counter to several explanations of women's increased participation which argue that women's entry into waged labour is a 'temporary' phenomenon linked to phases of the business cycle.

For most women, their attachment to the labour market takes a different form from that of men. Women's life-time participation in waged labour frequently takes a bimodal pattern. Young women tend initially to work full-time before marriage and childbirth, re-entering later in life, often on a part-time basis. The net result for the overall pattern of women's participation is illustrated in

Figure 6.1 Economic Activity Rates by Sex, Great Britain, 1975 and 1985

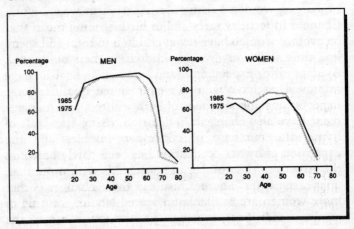

Source: Department of Employment

158

Figure 6.1 where women's activity rates are compared with men's. For all women, however, the number of years spent outside the labour force bearing and raising children has declined significantly in the post-war period. The median time women spend out of waged work after the date of birth of their last child declined from seven and a half years in 1950 to just over three years thirty years later. The age of the youngest child in a family is an important influence on women's labour participation. Less than 30 per cent of women whose youngest child is under school age are employed, rising to over 60 per cent when the youngest is between five and ten and to over 80 per cent when the youngest child reaches school age. So, on average, women spend about two-thirds of their potential working lives in the labour market.

One of the most noticeable features of the current distribution of women and men between occupations is their degree of separation into different subsectors of the economy. In the mid-1980s, half of all employed men work in occupations where the workforce was 90 per cent male and half of all women in occupations was 70 per cent female. Gender segregation is even more marked at the level of the individual firm.

For women working full-time in 1986 about half were in clerical and related jobs, and a further 20 per cent were in professional and related occupations in education, health and welfare. Part-time workers are heavily concentrated in catering, cleaning, hairdressing and other personal service occupations. As well as this segregation of women into particular types of job and industry – known as horizontal segregation – women workers are concentrated in the lower-paid tiers of these jobs. This concentration is known as 'vertical segregation'. These two types of occupational segregation, combined with the high proportion of women who work on a part-time basis (almost half of all women), mean that women's average earnings are well below the average for men. As Figure 6.2 shows, the gross average hourly earnings for women

Figure 6.2 Women's Average Gross Hourly Earnings as a Percentage of Men's, Full-Time Workers, Great Britain, 1970– 86

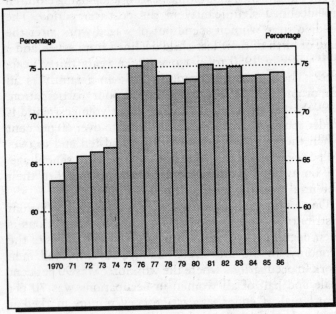

Source: *New Earning Survey*

who are employed full-time have remained about two-thirds of those of men. In 1986, the hourly rates were £3.61 and £4.87 respectively.

The association of women with poorly paid and low-status jobs, and with occupations based on the servicing or caring for clients (like waitresses, receptionists, nurses, secretaries, infant- and junior-school teachers) has led to women as a group being seen as a reserve of cheap labour. This is exacerbated by a widespread assumption that women's jobs are 'secondary' as women work for 'pin money'. Their low cost to employers is enhanced by the fact that part-time workers are ineligible for many of the full-time benefits like sickness pay, holidays, job security and good promotion prospects. As much women's work is low-paid, there is an inducement for employers to construct new jobs as 'women's' jobs, which, in association with the shift to the service economy, helps to explain the marked changes in the gender composition of the labour force.

Other workers also are subject to job segregation and suffer from employment discrimination on the basis of misperceived social characteristics. Members of ethnic minority groups in general tend to be overrepresented in poorly paid occupations. Afro-Caribbean people in particular, both men and women, are more likely to be in manual occupations than the white population: 40 per cent of Afro-Caribbean men and 38 per cent of women were in semi-skilled and unskilled manual jobs in the mid-1980s compared with 28 per cent and 31 per cent of white men and women respectively. When educational attainment is compared, the patterns of discrimination against minority group workers are thrown into sharper profile. Partly because the minority group population is younger, its members are more likely to possess school-leaving certificates than the white population as a whole. The difference is particularly noticeable among women. Older white women lack qualifications on a massive scale. In general, however, the white population is still more likely to possess post-school qualifications than are minority group members. Gender differences in educational attainment are considered in more detail in Chapter 10.

The pattern of life-time attachment to the labour market, often in one industry or occupation, that characterised men's, although not women's, employment histories over most of the post-war period also seems to be breaking down: a theme taken up in the next chapter.

A new geography of employment

The dramatic decline in manufacturing employment since the mid-1960s has taken a spatially uneven form.

Thousands of jobs are lost and gained in all industrial sectors and economic regions every year. It is the net balancing out of these contrasting flows that is of interest here. Stronger regions will either show net job increases or lower declines which improve their position relative to other regions.

In the earliest part of the period – between 1966 and 1971 – loss of manufacturing employment was most marked in Britain's largest cities. Greater London, the West Midlands, Manchester, West Yorkshire and Clydeside together lost net over half a million jobs, almost equivalent to the net decline for the whole country. In contrast non-industrial sub-regions and peripheral areas, such as the Scottish Highlands, Cornwall, East Anglia and rural Northumberland, experienced job increases in manufacturing. This pattern of spatial dispersion was a dramatic reversal of earlier growth trends which were concentrated in the industrial conurbations, although in *absolute terms*, of course, manufacturing employment still largely remained in the biggest cities. But in the early 1970s the pattern of relative peripheral expansion was clear.

Unfortunately, sub-regional data have not been made available since 1977, but regional figures suggest that expansion at the periphery continued throughout the 1970s. The South East and North West's share of manufacturing employment fell rapidly, while the share of the West Midlands – an earlier heartland of manufacturing expansion – remained static until 1975 and then declined; whereas the North, East Anglia, the South West and parts of Wales continued to expand their share relative to the other regions. Even Scotland, Northern Ireland and Yorkshire and Humberside fared better than the South East and North West. Since the end of the 1970s, however, the spatial patterns have changed again and it is now only the southern peripheral regions that are experiencing relative manufacturing growth. The more rural regions in Central Wales, the North and in

Scotland are now losing manufacturing jobs at an accelerating rate, whilst East Anglia in particular continues to improve its relative position. In the most recent past, it appears that growth has strengthened again in the outer South East region.

The changing geographical distribution of manufacturing and spatial variations in the distribution of different types of industrial production may be summarised by the phrase 'the spatial division of labour'. One important element of the Fordism/neo-Fordism debate discussed earlier is the extent to which it is associated with a new spatial division of labour. Writers from both schools in this debate are interested in the geography of employment, at the national and international level. The main argument concerns the extent to which recent changes have led to greater industrial concentration or to patterns of decentralisation. Both schools identify a new international division of labour in which firms in the 'centre' reorganise on Fordist lines but across space: a sort of peripheral Fordism or 'multinational Keynesianism' in Piore and Sabel's terms. Different parts of the labour process are split between countries in the search for low wages in the countries of the Third World. Within Britain, it is argued that a similar division of space has taken place. Routine, low-skill and low-wage processes have been decentralised to the peripheral regions, and specialised research and development (R and D) have been centralised in regions such as the M4 corridor in Berkshire and the Cambridge region (Massey, 1984).

However, within the 'leading edge' sectors characterised by flexible specialisation, spatial reconcentration of all elements of the production process may be taking place. R and D, innovation and the routine labour processes are not easily separated. Scott (1988), writing about the 'new industrial spaces' created by flexible specialisation in areas such as Orange County in the USA and Emilia Romagna in Italy, suggests that spatial links between firms in horizontally and vertically disaggregated production processes are an important part of centralising pressures. Spatially concentrated networks of high-tech firms or of craft-based federated industries arise. Currently, therefore, it seems as if processes of both centralisation and decentralisation may be identified in the spatial restructuring of manufacturing industry.

The service sector is also characterised by countervailing patterns of dispersal and concentration. In overall numbers, the increase in service jobs in the two decades since 1966 has not been sufficient to replace the loss of manufacturing jobs. Hence, there was a net decline across the whole economy of 1,632,000 jobs (excluding self-employment). In addition, many of the new service jobs were part-time and so there has been a significant decline in the total number of hours worked. New service jobs have not been created in the places where manufacturing jobs were lost and so their growth in different areas has been a significant element in restructuring the spatial division of labour in Britain in recent decades. In order to understand the spatial trends in the service sector it is useful to return to the twofold distinction discussed earlier – between consumer and producer services. The former type of service-sector employment by its very definition is responsive to final consumer demand, and its spatial distribution is therefore closely related to the population distribution of the country, although there are varying degrees of under- or over-provision compared with expected levels in particular towns and cities. The location of producer services is related to growth in the industries they serve. Expansion in business services, research and development, finance and banking, advertising and market research is concentrated in the outer South East and East Anglia. It is not surprising that they are also the regions of relative manufacturing growth.

Regional imbalances have long been a feature of the geography of Britain, but their scale since 1979 has led to concern about a growing North–South divide. In early 1987, the Department of Employment published figures of regional job losses and gains. They revealed the extent of job losses in northern parts of the country. Almost 94 per cent of the total jobs lost since 1979 were in Scotland, the North, the Midlands, Wales and Northern Ireland, where 58 per cent of the population live. In the southern part of the country, the South East lost only 1 per cent of its total employment between 1979 and 1986, the South West 2 per cent, while East Anglia actually gained 3 per cent. The absolute losses are illustrated in Figure 6.3. Of the new service-sector jobs created since 1979, two-thirds have been in the South East. There are other measures of the North–South differential. In Table 6.3, differences in the gross domestic product per head in the regions of the UK are shown in the first two columns. The South East stands out well above the national average, and East Anglia is just above. On this measure the South West should be classified with the 'North' rather than with the prosperous 'South' as its GDP per head is almost 20 per cent below that of the South East.

In the other columns of Table 6.3 a further series of indicators of regional inequality are shown. Taken together, the statistics do suggest that there is a North–South divide if the 'South' is defined solely as the South East and East Anglia. This 'South' has the lowest rates of unemployment and the highest GDP and personal income per head. It also seems that East Anglia is closing the gap between itself and the South East. Economists at Lloyds Bank (*Economic Bulletin*, May 1987) have calculated an index of regional variation in personal income to test whether the regional gap is growing over time. This shows that regional disparities have risen in the last ten years, though not by a large amount. Other work suggests that regional variation in wage levels actually declined up to 1980, but increased again since then. Regional unemployment data suggest at first glance an increase in the spread of unemployment rates over time. The difference between the lowest and highest regional unemployment rates in 1975 was 5.1 per cent, whereas by January 1987

Figure 6.3 Regional Employment Changes, 1979–86

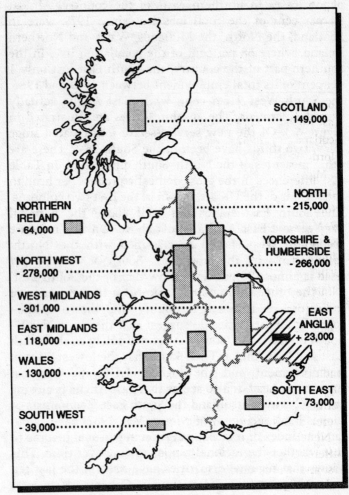

Source: Department of Employment

it had grown to 10.8 per cent. At both dates the South East had the lowest rate, Northern Ireland the highest. However, the gap between the rates when calculated as a proportion of the national average unemployment rate

TABLE 6.3 *Regional Performance Ranked by Various Indicators*

	GDP per head, 1985 £	Personal disposable income per head, 1985 £	Real personal income growth per head, 1975–85	Unemployment as % of working population, Jan. 1987	Long-term unemployment as % of unemployed, Jan. 1987
South East	5831	4725	19.92	8.5	36.2
East Anglia	5118	4244	26.92	9.3	33.5
Scotland	4942	4181	20.86	15.1	39.2
North West	4877	4074	16.95	14.3	44.3
E. Midlands	4861	4066	18.46	11.4	39.2
South West	4763	4152	21.34	10.4	32.7
North	4717	3919	18.24	16.9	44.3
W. Midlands	4690	3997	10.24	13.8	46.3
Yorks. and Humb.	4662	3923	17.70	13.8	42.0
Wales	4509	3778	14.27	14.3	40.6
N. Ireland	3799	3538	18.67	19.3	50.0

National Average 4797
Source: *Economic Trends, Employment Gazette.*

had decreased somewhat. In 1975 the South East rate was 68 per cent of the national average compared with 193 per cent in Northern Ireland. In 1987 the respective rates were 71 and 162 per cent.

Neoclassical economic theory argues that regional differences in income and employment encourage workers and the unemployed to migrate between regions. Indeed, government ministers have suggested it as a partial solution to unemployment in the 'depressed' regions. Norman Tebbit's phrase 'On yer bike' quickly entered the lists of famous quotations but made little sense to unemployed workers with family ties in an area and faced by enormous regional differentials in housing costs. Evidence suggests that net regional migration is very low. Local movements within regions are more common. Indeed, currently there is *out-migration* from the most prosperous region – the South East – into East Anglia and the South West. There are many considerations other than income and wage levels influencing an individual or family's decision to move or not. One significant factor that hinders movement from the less prosperous to the more prosperous regions is the difference in house prices and the availability of rented accommodation. Ties to the local area and to friends and family are also important mobility constraints.

Despite the marked differences, it must not be assumed that the 'South' is uniformly prosperous; nor, indeed, that the 'North' is uniformly depressed. There are significant variations within, as well as between, the regions of the UK and there are also variations within towns and cities. The inner areas of Greater London, for example, have similar problems of run-down industries, urban decay and mass unemployment to those found in parts of the 'North'. Some geographers and sociologists suggest that 'local' differences in the pattern of inequalities are more marked than regional ones and that this is a more appropriate scale for urban and regional analyses.

A core/peripheral labour market?

The combination of social and spatial changes in the structure of labour supply and demand has led certain writers (Atkinson, 1984, 1985; Lash and Urry, 1987; Leadbeater and Lloyd, 1987) to argue that there is now a well-marked distinction between a core of permanently employed, secure and relatively well paid workers and a numerically increasing periphery of workers in temporary, contract and part-time occupations, often poorly paid and with little or no job security. This division is a key element of the flexible firm model alluded to earlier. The core labour force in the manufacturing sector increasingly is multi-skilled and offers 'functional' flexibility, by crossing occupation or task divisions. The periphery provides 'numerical' flexibility through a precarious or insecure labour contract with the firm or by subcontracting. Core workers include the professions, many central and local government officials, and most full-time workers in skilled and unskilled jobs in manufacturing and services. Peripheral workers conversely face uncertain prospects, and short-time or part-time contracts. They include the self-employed and home workers. In Figure 6.4, the relative size of the core and periphery is shown.

Figure 6.4   The Core/Periphery Workforce

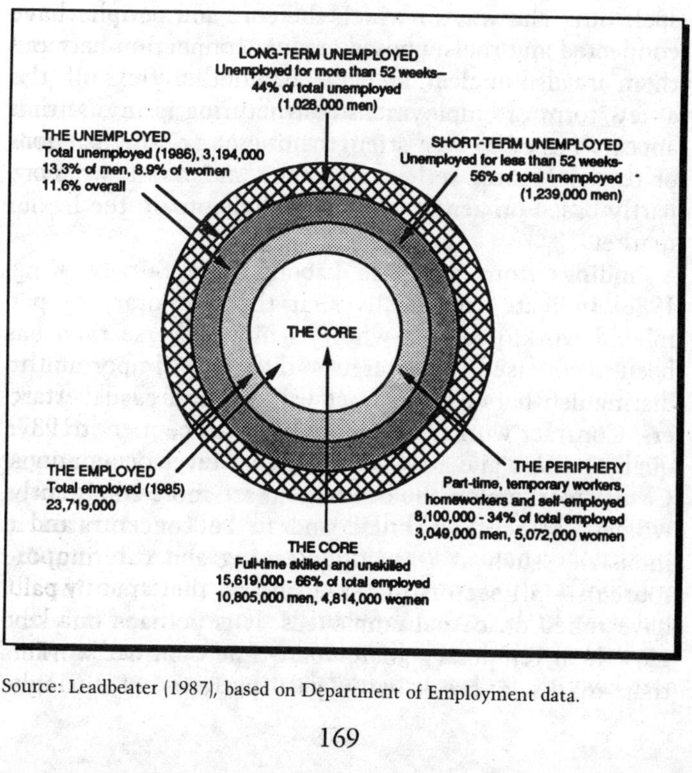

Source: Leadbeater (1987), based on Department of Employment data.

Optimistic commentators regard the division as introducing a much-needed element of flexibility into employment procedures and practices. Less optimistic writers see it as increasing the level of exploitation of the workforce. Many of the unemployed are also on the fringes of the labour market and move in and out of waged work, in much the same way as peripheral workers.

The core/peripheral distinction is primarily a descriptive one, largely dependent on the supposed need for greater flexibility. Most of the literature assumes there is a new trend and proceeds to generalise on this basis. The concept of flexibility is, however, ill-defined. It is used as an all-purpose term, embracing production flexibility, technical flexibility, organisational flexibility, time, wage, financial and marketing flexibility. Although these issues are presumed to be connected, the links are not spelt out. The way in which the core and periphery are connected and the supposed organic connection between them are also unclear. In addition, whether 'flexibility' is a new form of employment restructuring is in doubt. It appears rather to be a strengthening of existing patterns of casual labour, self-employment and home working, partly based on gender and racial divisions in the labour market.

Findings from the 1986 Labour Force Survey (King, 1988) indicate empirically that the temporary or peripheral workforce as a whole is more diverse than has been recognised. King argues that it is important to distinguish between contract workers and casual workers. Contract workers are more likely to be men, to have qualifications and to work in higher-level occupations. Casual workers on the other hand are more likely to be women, black, low-skilled and to be concentrated in industries such as retailing, cleaning and catering and tourism – all sectors of the economy that traditionally have relied on casual employees. It is perhaps only the growth in temporary and/or part-time contract workers that marks a break with past patterns of life-time employment in a single occupation, for men at least. King found the 'contract' pattern most common among young men and she argues 'it would seem that . . . this small group is adapting to changing labour market conditions' although 'they would still prefer the security of permanent employment' (page 247).

Trade unions

Pressures for greater labour flexibility, where they exist, are partly management responses to economic recession, technological change and greater uncertainty. They have led to new working practices and labour–management agreements like single-union and no-strike deals, although their extent is greatly exaggerated in the media. Flexibility evokes a style of management in sympathy with the politics of Thatcherism with its emphasis on competition and insecurity as incentives to greater productivity and individual effort. At the end of 1987 a high-ranking treasury official even shocked the Civil Service unions by proposing new forms of temporary contract for civil servants – previously the apotheosis of the 'core' labour market. The extent to which, however, these changes reflect new forms of employment restructuring is debatable. Sectoral shifts in the economy – particularly towards services that have always relied on this form of labour-market structure – are the major reasons for the changes.

Trade unions have had to respond to labour-market trends, industrial restructuring and high unemployment particularly between 1979 and 1987, in the face of governments determined to reduce their powers. During the 1960s and 1970s there was an expansion of trade-union membership among white-collar workers, especially state employees. Two of the most rapidly growing unions were the National Union of Public Employees (NUPE) which recruits mainly unskilled manual workers

LABOUR AND LIFE

– expanded from 200,000 members in 1960 to 699,000 in 1980 – and the National and Local Government Officers' Association (NALGO) which grew from 274,000 to 782,000 members over the same period by organising amongst white-collar workers. Over the post-war period, union membership among British workers rose steadily until the end of the 1970s when it reached 13,447,000 members, 55 per cent of the working population. Table 6.4a shows the levels of union density since the end of the Second World War. Density measures the number of actual trade union members as a percentage of the total number of potential members. In Table 6.4b the density of membership in different industries is compared. In general, densities are lower in the expanding service-sector industries. The losses of male employment in traditionally highly unionised manufacturing sectors have resulted in a rapid decline of members in certain unions. The Transport and General Workers' Union, for example, lost 800,000 members in less than a decade. Overall union membership fell after 1979 by more than 2 million to just under 11 million members in 1988. The expulsion of the electricians' union (the EEPTU) from the TUC in September 1988 further reduced the number of affiliated union members.

TABLE 6.4A *Trends in Trade Union Membership, United Kingdom, 1949–86*

Year	Number of members (000s)	Density
1949	9318	44.8
1959	9623	44.0
1969	10479	45.3
1979	13447	55.4
1985	11086	39.9
1986	10539	37.0

Source: *Employment Gazette*, various years.

TABLE 6.4B *Union Density by Industrial Sector, United Kingdom, 1984*

	Density
MANUFACTURING INDUSTRIES	
All manufacturing establishments	58
Metals, mineral products	68
Chemicals, manufactured fibres	58
Metal goods, mechanical engineering	55
Electrical and instrument engineering	51
Vehicles and transport equipment	81
Food, drink and tobacco	50
Textiles	53
Leather, footwear and clothing	48
Timber, furniture, paper and printing	59
Rubber, plastics, other manufacturing	40
SERVICE INDUSTRIES	
All service establishments	58
Energy and water	88
Construction	36
Wholesale distribution	32
Retail distribution	34
Hotels, catering, repairs	21
Transport	85
Posts and telecommunications	95
Banking, finance and insurance	43
Business services	21
Public administration	78
Education	69
Medical services	67
Other services	49

Source: Workplace Industrial Relations Survey, 1984; *Employment Gazette*, May 1988.

In an effort to adapt to the changing patterns of employment, union leaders are introducing new initiatives and different structures to retain existing members and to recruit new ones. Several unions are targeting women workers, aware that the interests of men and women are not necessarily identical. Women workers often find it harder to organise. They may be unable to attend meetings because they work part-time and have household and family commitments. Often, too, they feel alienated by the structures of power within trade unions or intimidated by individual male members. These factors are reflected in membership rates. The level of union membership among women workers, particularly those employed on a part-time basis, remains lower than for men. At peak membership levels in 1979, only 41 per cent of women workers were members. The corresponding figure for men was 65 per cent. By 1983 the figures had fallen: membership levels were 57 per cent for men in full-time work, 50 per cent for women in full-time work and 33 per cent for women working part-time.

Trade unions in Britain, in contrast to unions in some West European societies, concentrate predominantly on workplace issues. They are seldom involved in areas such as the provision of housing, although they do campaign around broader social issues such as pensions or women's right to abortion, for example. Their main industrial weapon is withdrawal of labour in industrial disputes. The chief causes of such disputes are questions of pay and redundancy: 59 per cent of days lost in 1986, for example, were over pay issues.

In the decade 1976–85 an annual average of 11.1 million working days were lost through stoppages and strikes. This compares with 1.9 million days in 1986. The annual figures, however, disguise variations in the figures. Large-scale and long-lasting disputes have a significant effect on annual averages but they are not the typical form of stoppage. Over two-thirds of all stoppages in the decade 1976–85 lasted for less than four days. The largest disputes in recent years are as follows:

1979 – the engineering workers' strike
accounted for 54 per cent of all days lost (16m out of 29.5m)

1980 – the national steel strike
accounted for 74 per cent of all days lost (8.8m out of 12.0m)

1984 – the miners' strike
accounted for 83 per cent of all days lost (22.4m out of 27.1m)

1985 – continuation of the miners' strike
accounted for 63 per cent of all days lost (4m out of 6.4m)

1986 – the teachers' strike
accounted for 16 per cent of all days lost (0.31m out of 1.9m)

These figures show how important it is to consider the size of major stoppages in each period when making comparisons between years.

Contrary to the popular belief that strikes are the 'English disease', the number of working days lost in Britain in recent years does not exceed the number lost in many other advanced industrial nations. Amongst the OECD countries, between 1976 and 1985 the highest incidence of working days lost per employee was in Spain and Italy. The lowest was in Japan, and Britain fell in the intermediate group in these years.

In an interesting comparison of OECD countries, Freeman (1988) attempted to assess whether differences between countries in trade union density and other aspects of labour-market institutions affected economic performance. It is often suggested that high unionisation in Britain is one reason for relatively poor industrial performance. Union densities vary markedly between the member countries, ranging from 98 per cent in Denmark and 95 per cent in Sweden in 1984/5, 52 per cent in the UK, 51 per cent in Italy and 45 per cent in West Germany to a low of 18 per cent in the USA, well below the second-lowest country, France, with only 28 per cent of workers unionised. Freeman found that over time there had been a tendency towards a polarised position with union density rising in already highly unionised countries and falling where workers were weakly organised. Interestingly, it was also the countries at either extreme that had the best levels of economic performance on a range of measures. It is difficult, therefore, to conclude that unionisation *per se* has an adverse effect on economic performance.

THE FUTURE OF WORK?

It seems clear that the expectation of full-time continuous employment in the same occupation over a lifetime is an unrealistic one for a growing number of men, as it always has been for the majority of women. This leads to a question of what the future pattern of work is going to be in Britain. It has been argued (Pahl, 1984) that full-time waged labour for a large proportion of the population of 'working age' is a historically and culturally specific phenomenon, restricted to advanced capitalist economies in the post-war decades. This period is apparently over on Great Britain, although the structure of the labour market in Japan throws doubts on the generality of the timing. What is more interesting about Pahl's argument is the recognition that, as feminist scholars have consistently argued for a decade or more, work consists of more than just waged labour. As the feminist slogan so nicely puts it 'capitalism needs domestic labour, too'. Work may be undertaken in different ways, in different spheres, and may or may not be financially rewarded. As was argued at the beginning of this chapter, the overall amount of work undertaken in an economy is divided between domestic labour, formal waged labour and a casual or informal sector where labour may be exchanged for goods and services in kind as well as for money paid on an irregular basis. This division between the three spheres varies over time and between places. It is also associated with a gender division of labour. On the whole, domestic labour is undertaken by women, although in many economies the rigid division between men and women, and between waged and unwaged labour is not so well defined as it was in the immediate post-war decades in Britain.

The boundaries are now more fluid in Britain, too. New forms of work, its location and methods of organisation are challenging current conceptions about waged work. The recent growth in home-working is a clear instance of the shifting boundaries (Allen and Walkowitz, 1987). Despite the widespread belief that 'outwork' disappeared with industrialisation in Britain, it is estimated that there are more than a million home-workers in the country at the end of the 1980s, many of whom are paid below legal rates and are unregistered.

It may be the time to ask a series of new questions about the division of work between different sections of the labour force or over workers' life-times. Unfortunately it is probable that present trends will lead only to new areas of poorly paid and insecure work and the increased significance of racial and gender divisions in the labour force and society at large. However, changes in the structure of the population, in particular the declining numbers of young people who will be entering the labour market over the next decade, may provide a counterweight to the growth of insecure and exploited forms of waged work. At the end of the 1980s, as unemployment began to fall and the demand for labour grew, the possibility of labour shortages emerged. Increased competition for highly skilled, well-educated workers may force employers to reconsider their strategies. The Confederation of British Industry argued that increased investment in education and training is urgently needed to enable the current labour force to adapt to future changes. Whatever the relative changes in skilled and unskilled employment in different sectors of the economy, it seems clear that the pattern of a job for life in a single industry or occupation is now a phenomenon of the past for the majority of British workers.

FURTHER READING

Braverman (1974) has been one of the most influential authors of the numerous books that have been published over the last twenty years about the changing nature of waged work. Braverman's thesis that work is being degraded and deskilled has stimulated a large number of studies to test his ideas. One of the best ways to gain a notion of the dimensions of these debates is to read some of the chapters in one or both of the following two collections of case studies, undertaken in the main by sociologists.

Wood (1982) and Purcell *et al.* (1986) contain collections of detailed, mainly empirically based papers examining dimensions of the changing labour process.

An important aspect of the restructuring of waged work in recent decades has been the growing participation of women. There are now several good books on women's employment at both a general theoretical and a statistical level, and several fascinating and detailed case studies of the particular types of work that women do in different sectors of the economy and in different industries. An excellent summary of the different theories that are used to explain women's labour-force participation is the book by Dex (1985).

A collection edited by *Feminist Review, Waged Work: A Reader* (1986), is a useful introduction to a range of contemporary debates — about the links between sex and skill designations, the use of male power at work, the impact of equal opportunities legislation and several other issues.

Rubery (1988) is a cross-national study of the impact of economic restructuring on women's work in Britain, the USA, France and Italy. Westwood (1984) is an excellent example of the growing number of participant observation studies undertaken by feminists in a range of different work situations. It is a lively and readable account of the lives of women working on a hosiery factory floor in the early 1980s in the East Midlands.

Contemporary scholars disagree about the extent to which the future of waged work will diverge from past patterns. Arguments rage about the definition and extent of flexibility, restructuring and casualisation, and whether or not these processes are leading to new forms of work that are more or less oppressive than old forms. A central text in these debates, which takes the view that the current changes will improve the lot of many workers, is a US study by Piore and Sabel (1984). The debate about flexibility is summarised and well critiqued in two papers by Anna Pollert (1988a and b). Both articles include an excellent bibliography of books and articles about the changing nature of work.

In Britain, two books by R. E. Pahl assessing the changing structure of work have recently appeared. The first (Pahl, 1984) is in two parts. The first part is a historical survey of the structure and distribution of waged work since industrialisation, demonstrating the specificity of the contemporary view that the most usual, and important, form of work is full-time employment in the formal economy. The second half of the book is a case study of the impact of changing work patterns on individual households in a small area of South-East England. Pahl's second book (1988) is an edited collection of papers that explores historical changes in work processes in a comparative perspective and surveys the key theoretical debates.

An accessible book about the changing geographical division of work in contemporary Britain is Massey (1984). Two other books about the changing geography of work, although based primarily on US examples, are worth looking at. They are Scott and Storper (1986) and Wolch and Dear (1988). An edited collection of readings about British economic change is Martin and Rowthorn (1986).

Finally, one way to help keep up to date with the latest official employment figures and debates about changes in waged work is to read the *Employment Gazette*, a monthly publication from the Department of Employment.

7

Out of Work
Linda McDowell

In the previous chapter the changing characteristics of the
people and of the activities that constitute 'work' or,
more accurately, waged labour in Britain today were
examined. In this chapter the focus is on the reverse side
of the coin – on the people and activities that constitute
the rest of everyday life. For, in Britain today, a growing
proportion of the population is not directly involved in
waged labour, although because of patterns of household
dependence many of these people are enmeshed in wage
relations. Part of the expanding group of the non-waged
is made up of elderly people whose direct income
contribution to society has already been made. Average
life expectancy in 1987 was seventy-seven years for
women and seventy-one for men. Increased life expectancy in recent years has meant that the proportion of
people over sixty in the population is growing. Another
major group exists at the opposite end of the age spectrum
– children and young people who have not yet entered the
labour market. The official school-leaving age was raised
to sixteen in 1972. The proportion of sixteen-year-olds
who remain at school or enter some form of further
education or training continued to rise after 1972.

In 1986, 45 per cent of sixteen-year-olds were in full-
time education compared with 40 per cent a decade
earlier. The number in employment, on the other hand,
fell from 53 per cent to 15 per cent over the same ten-
year period. In 1986, 27 per cent of sixteen-year-olds were

on the Youth Training Scheme and 12 per cent of all sixteen-year-olds were unemployed. Unemployment rates among school leavers, but particularly among young blacks, rose throughout the early and mid-1980s to a peak in 1986, when 136,600 school leavers in Great Britain were unemployed. Youth employment began to decline from that date, partly as a consequence of growing demand for young workers, but also because of a decline in the total number of school leavers. Unemployment has also affected increasing numbers of adult workers from the early 1980s. The number of both short-term and long-term unemployed adults rose by the mid-1980s to exceptionally high levels (3.06 million), so millions have involuntarily joined the unwaged during the 1980s.

One purpose of this chapter is to look at the social characteristics of the non-waged population and to consider the effects of not having a wage on standards of living in different parts of the country. A critical evaluation will also be made of the concept of unemployment itself. Having done this, the focus turns to the impact of economic change, sketched out in previous chapters, on life outside the world of business and industry. Rising participation by women in the labour market, mass unemployment and the problem of never experiencing work have fundamentally affected the daily lives of many families and individuals. On a wider scale the shifting interface between waged employment and the rest of society has an impact on the nature of communities and their political and social organisation.

THE 'DEPENDENT' POPULATION

Dependency has a clear meaning in demographic analysis. The 'dependent' population consists of children under school-leaving age, women aged sixty and over and men aged sixty-five and over, that is, the proportion of the population below the official school-leaving age and above the official retirement age. Its size is usually expressed in relation to the population of working age. In 1986 there were just over sixty-three dependants for every hundred people of working age. Table 7.1 shows the composition of the dependent population and how it has changed over time. The number of children has declined considerably since 1971, the post-retirement group slightly, whereas the number of the very old (seventy-five and over) has increased. Life expectancy should continue to rise while fertility rates will rise very little. So, although the overall population projected for 2025 is expected to be not much higher than it was in 1971 or in 1986, the proportion of the elderly will be larger.

TABLE 7.1 *Dependent Population per 100 Population of Working Age, United Kingdom, 1971–86*

| | | Dependants aged | | | |
	0–15	60/65–74[1]	75–84	85+	All ages
1971	43.8	19.9	6.6	1.5	71.8
1981	37.1	20.0	7.9	1.8	66.8
1986	33.5	19.0	8.5	2.0	63.1
PROJECTION					
2025	34.1	23.3	11.3	3.9	72.6

1. 60–74 for women, 65–74 for men
Source: *Social Trends* 18 (1988).

The size and composition of the population have an important impact on the demand for social services, welfare benefits and payments and the overall level of public expenditure. For example, the decline in the number of children aged five to fifteen affects the provision of schools and the number of teachers required, whereas the rising number of the elderly affects the

TABLE 7.2 *Selected Social and Economic Needs of Population Groups: by Age, United Kingdom, 1971–2025*

	Population index (1986 = 100)				Needs of different age groups
	1971	1981	1986	2025	
People aged					
Under 1	120	97	100	101	Maternity services, health visiting, preventative medicine.
1–4	127	94	100	105	Day care, nursery education.
5–15	121	113	100	101	Compulsory education.
16–19	85	105	100	78	Further and higher education, training, employment.
15–44 (women)	86	95	100	89	Maternity services.
20–49	90	94	100	94	Employment, housing, transport.
50–59/64	109	104	100	130	Pre-retirement training, early retirement.
60/65–74	98	102	100	122	Retirement pensions.
75–84	73	90	100	132	Pensions, health care, home helps, sheltered housing, retirement homes.
85 or over	68	84	100	191	

Source: *Social Trends* 18 (1988)

demand for health services, the need for sheltered housing and the resources allocated to pensions. Table 7.2 shows how different services are required at particular stages in the life cycle and also the projected size of the specific groups needing different services. In Figure 7.1 the division of the population into age groups is shown in the form of a population pyramid. The pyramid shows how past differences in birth rates determine current and

Figure 7.1   Population by Sex and Age, 1988 and 2025

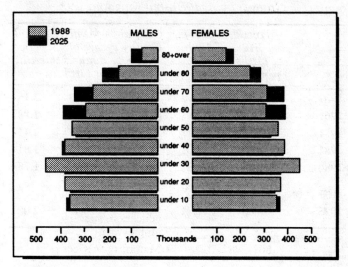

Source: *Social Trends* 18 (1988)

future age structures. By 2025, the peak in births in 1964 will give rise to a peak of sixty-year-olds reaching retirement age and increasingly dependent on pensions. In the mid-1980s this group was in its early twenties and part of the working-age population. It can also be seen from the pyramid that women are more likely than men to survive into very old age.

THE YOUNG

Throughout the post-war period the birth rate has varied considerably. The total number of live births in 1986 (755,000) was close to that in 1951 (797,000) but in the two and a half decades in between the birth rate rose and fell again (Table 7.3). Despite the numerical similarities, both the crude birth rate and the fertility rate were lower

TABLE 7.3 *Live Births: Totals and Rates, United Kingdom, 1951–86*

	Total live births (000s)	Crude birth rate	General fertility rate	Mean age of mothers at birth	Total period fertility rate
1951	797	15.9	73.0	28.4	2.15
1961	944	17.9	90.6	27.6	2.78
1971	902	16.1	84.3	26.4	2.41
1981	731	13.0	62.1	27.2	1.81
1986	755	13.3	61.1	27.7	1.78
PROJECTION					
2025	760	12.7	67.4	28.1	2.00

Source: *Social Trends*, 18 (1988).

in 1986 compared with the early 1950s; while the average number of children each woman would expect to bear fell to below two in 1986. The birth rate is projected to climb slightly to reach two again by 2025 – at which level the total population is just replacing itself. Since the 1950s many women have delayed starting their families, especially women in higher income groups. Consequently the number of children borne by women in their mid- to late thirties rose throughout the post-war period, particularly during the 1970s. Concomitantly, the number of births to younger women fell. For example, for women aged twenty to twenty-four the number of births per thousand fell by over 39 per cent between 1971 and 1986.

Birth rates vary between different social groups in the United Kingdom. Before the Second World War, there were marked occupational and social-class differentials in birth rates but these have since narrowed. Ethnic differences remain. Black women have slightly higher birth rates, and so there is a larger dependent population among

TABLE 7.4 *Fertility Rates, Parity and Illegitimacy: by Country of Birth of Mother, England and Wales, 1971–86*

MOTHER'S PLACE OF BIRTH	Total period fertility rates			Percentage of all births Legitimate and to women with 3 or more previous live-born children			Illegitimate		
	1971	1981	1986	1971	1981	1986	1971	1981	1986
United Kingdom	2.3	1.7	1.7	9.2	5.3	5.1	8.1	13.4	22.9
India	4.1	3.1	2.9	25.6	14.3	13.3	1.7	1.2	1.7
Pakistan and Bangladesh	8.8	6.5	5.6	43.0	36.4	42.1	0.8	0.5	0.6
Caribbean	3.3	2.0	1.8	25.8	9.3	7.9	36.3	50.0	48.3
East Africa	2.4	2.1	2.0	8.2	6.1	5.9	3.7	2.4	3.4
Rest of Africa	3.8	3.4	2.8	24.1	14.6	11.3	4.6	13.0	22.1
Other New Commonwealth	2.6	2.0	2.0	12.2	4.5	5.4	5.2	6.3	9.9
Rest of the World	2.7	2.0	1.9	12.6	8.4	8.3	8.9	9.4	13.7
ALL COUNTRIES	2.4	1.8	1.8	10.4	6.5	6.5	8.4	12.8	21.4

Source: Office of Population Censuses and Surveys.

ethnic minority groups. Table 7.4 shows the differences in live births to women of different origins. Fertility rates nevertheless have declined for all categories of women. The fertility rate for women born in the Caribbean, for example, fell by almost half between 1971 and 1986, to a level that is hardly above that for UK-born women.

Data for women born outside the UK obviously do not represent the whole picture for ethnic minority groups as they exclude information for second-generation families and beyond. The size and composition of their dependent population, therefore, is related to the time of peak immigration for the group in question. The peak period of in-migration to Britain from the Caribbean was during the 1950s and 1960s, while for people born in Bangladesh and Pakistan it was during the 1960s and early 1970s. As the initial immigrant population ages, an increasingly large proportion of each group will have been born in the United Kingdom. By 1986, 43 per cent of members of all ethnic minority groups in Great Britain had been born

TABLE 7.5 *Children and Older People by Ethnic Group, United Kingdom, 1984–6 (percentages)*

Ethnic group	Children 0–15	Older people 60 and over	Dependent population[1]	Total population (000s)
White	20	21	41	51,107
All white minorities	34	4	38	2,432
West Indian or Guyanese	26	6	32	534
Indian	32	5	37	760
Pakistani	44	2	46	397
Bangladeshi	50	1	51	103
Chinese	28	5	33	115
African	26	4	30	103
Arab	17	5	22	66
Mixed	53	3	56	235
Other	28	4	32	119
Not stated	29	17	46	691
TOTAL POPULATION	21	20	41	54,230

1. This figure is an approximation to the 'dependent' population as defined earlier in this chapter as it includes men aged between 60 and 64 who are part of the 'working' population.
Source: *Social Trends*, 18 (1988).

here. Most of them are British and so indistinguishable from white British women in official statistics.

The Afro-Caribbean and Asian populations in Britain, however, still have different age structures from that of the white population. In 1986, for example, 21 per cent of the white population was aged sixty and over, compared with 6 per cent of people with West Indian and Guyanese backgrounds, the first of the different groups of black migrants to Britain in the post-war period. In Table 7.5 the proportion of children and older people among ethnic minority groups is compared with the same proportions among the white population. It can be seen that the composition of the dependent group is noticeably different for specific ethnic minority populations. Whereas the white population is an ageing one, other groups have a much higher proportion of children among their dependants. The differences obviously affect relative needs for particular social services. Proportionately the ethnic minority population will continue to be heavier users of the education service for several years to come. The white population are correspondingly greater users of the National Health Service. It is also important to take into account the absolute size of the different groups. In total, the 'black' population (as defined on the basis of skin colour rather than on place of birth) accounts for only 4.8 per cent of the total population of Great Britain.

THE ELDERLY

In the population as a whole the elderly have become a larger proportion throughout this century. Their numbers have also increased in real terms. This is a consequence of greater life expectancy, particularly among women, and the falling birth rate. The gender differential in life expectancy is reflected in household structures among the elderly population. Whereas most elderly men live

TABLE 7.6 *Elderly People and Household Type, England and Wales, 1986 (percentages)*[1]

Age	Living with spouse		Living alone		Living with others	
	Men	Women	Men	Women	Men	Women
65–69	80	57	13	33	7	10
70–74	75	44	21	44	5	11
75–80	70	30	21	55	9	15
80+	52	12	35	61	13	27
All elderly	73	38	20	47	7	15

1. Sample size 1,504.
Source: General Household Survey, 1986. Table adapted from EOC (1987) *Men and Women in Britain: A Statistical Profile*, HMSO.

with their wives, the majority of elderly women live alone (Table 7.6). The growing number of older people in the population shows itself in rising public expenditure on contributory and non-contributory benefits (for further information, see Chapter 11). The value, and hence the cost to the government, of state pensions was cut in 1979 when the earnings-related formula for annual updating was abandoned. The value of the basic state pension has fallen, partly as a consequence of the Government's emphasis on private-sector schemes. In 1988, the idea that the basic state pension might become a selective rather than universal benefit was floated. Despite denials from the Treasury that this was planned, it is clear that the cost of supporting the rising number of old people will remain an important political issue into the next century.

For old people themselves, the level of state and private support after retirement from waged work is a crucial element in their standard of living. Research by Seebohm Rowntree in York at the beginning of the twentieth century demonstrated how economic well-being fluctuates for most people over their life cycle. This pattern is still apparent towards the end of the century. A typical family has a well-marked life-cycle pattern of peaks and troughs in its prosperity. Despite the introduction of state pensions and other forms of financial support during this century, many elderly people have found that old age is a period of relative or absolute poverty. At the present time reliance on state pensions compared with earnings significantly reduces the income levels of pensioner households. In 1987, taking the average household income as 1.00, the disposable income of families headed by a sixty-five-to-seventy-four-year-old was 0.55, compared with 1.3 for families with a head aged forty-five to fifty-four, the most prosperous age group. For the very old, seventy-five plus, the figure drops to 0.44.

In old age, however, as at other stages in the life cycle, there are marked class differentials in income levels among the elderly. Men, in particular, who were previously in well-paid jobs and who contributed to earnings-related occupational pension schemes throughout their working lives, are better off than those solely reliant on state pensions. Alterations to the State Earnings Related Pension introduced in the Social Security Act 1986 will increase the differential over time. There are also marked differences in the possession of wealth by elderly people, partially a reflection of their previous housing careers. Owner-occupiers, especially in the South East of the country, have a potentially disposable asset often worth a great deal.

The elderly in Britain, as a group, however, are significantly poorer than their compatriots in other advanced industrial nations. Hedstrom and Ringen (1987) have calculated the disposable income for different age groups (adjusted for family size) in relation to the national mean in seven countries. Table 7.7 shows their results. The relative adjusted income of the 65–74 age group in Britain is only 76 per cent of the population average and in the 75+ group it fell to 67 per cent. As Hedstrom and Ringen point out, 'These figures should be compared to

TABLE 7.7 *Adjusted Disposable Income[1] of Different Age Groups in Relation to the National Mean, 1980*

Age	−24	25–34	35–44	45–54	55–64	65–74	75+	Total	SD
Canada	0.87	0.96	0.96	1.11	1.15	0.94	0.81	1.00	0.11
Germany	0.86	0.88	0.95	1.30	1.07	0.84	0.77	1.00	0.17
Israel	1.02	1.03	0.91	1.00	1.23	0.92	0.96	1.00	0.10
Norway	0.81	0.96	0.99	1.04	1.18	1.01	0.79	1.00	0.12
Sweden	0.86	1.00	0.98	1.12	1.17	0.96	0.78	1.00	0.13
UK	0.99	0.97	0.97	1.20	1.17	0.76	0.67	1.00	0.18
USA	0.77	0.93	0.95	1.13	1.21	0.99	0.84	1.00	0.14
Mean	0.88	0.96	0.96	1.13	1.17	0.92	0.80	—	—

1. The adjustment of disposable income for family size is done with the use of the following equivalence scale:

Number of family members:	1	2	3	4	10+
Equivalences factor:	0.50	0.75	1.00	1.25	3.00

Source: Hedstrom and Ringen (1987), based on data from the Luxembourg Income Study.

94 per cent and 82 per cent which are the averages of the relative incomes of the elderly in the other six nations'.

CHANGES IN FAMILY STRUCTURE

There have been changes in family and household structures paralleling the changes in birth rates, the timing of childbearing and the rising number of the elderly. The media present contradictory images of contemporary trends. On the one hand, there is a constant barrage of advertisements based on the 'ideal' nuclear family, consisting of Mum at home examining the washing or the kitchen floor, Dad at the office or some unspecified place where he earns the family wage, and two wholesome children interested mainly in break-fast cereals. The press, on the other hand, is full of stories about delinquency, marriage breakdown, rising illegitimacy rates and child abuse. Governmental pronouncements on social problems and social policies are based on a series of propositions about the need to strengthen 'the family' with an implicit assumption of its constitution.

Information is available to examine the nature of family structures and to consider whether the family is

Figure 7.2   Household and People by Type of Household, Great Britain, 1985

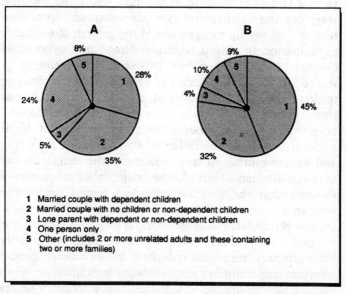

Source: *General Household Survey*, 1985

breaking down. Figure 7.2 shows (*a*) the distribution of individuals between particular household forms; and (*b*) the proportion of the total that each of these household types makes up. Taken together, the two charts reveal that the number of people who lived alone in the mid-1980s was almost as great as the people living in

193

'families'. At that date, nearly a quarter of all households were one-person households compared with only one-tenth in 1951. Most single people living alone are elderly. Only 3 per cent of young men and women (aged between sixteen and twenty-four), for example, lived alone in 1985. Many of the younger ones, of course, still lived with their parents.

Despite the growth of the one-person household, most people in Britain still live in traditional nuclear families. But the advertisers' 'two kids' ideal is a minority form: in the mid-1980s, in fact, only 8 per cent of households were a family consisting of an employed father, a non-wage-earning mother and two dependent children. One reason why the figure is so low is the growth of women's participation in waged labour, outlined in the previous chapter. Despite women's extensive involvement in waged labour, a major survey of social attitudes in Britain, undertaken in 1986 (Jowell *et al.*, 1987), reported that three-quarters of all adults interviewed thought that the best working arrangements for a couple with children under five were for the father to work full-time for wages and for the mother to stay at home. If the children were between five and sixteen, the majority of respondents thought that the ideal arrangement would be for the woman to enter the labour market on a part-time basis. So several decades of wage-earning mothers, and of the women's movement, seem to have made remarkably little impact on most people's views about gender relations and women's responsibility for childcare. Even the majority of women who themselves worked for wages agreed with the statement that women with children should either stay at home or work for wages on only a part-time basis.

Most British children continue to live with one or more sibling and their married parents, that is, in a traditional 'nuclear' family. However, there have been changes in the last few years. The proportion of children living with a single parent, for example, rose from 8 per cent in 1972 to 13 per cent in 1985. Most of these children live with their mother.

WOMEN, CHILDREN AND MARRIAGE

The majority of women living in Britain today have or will have children. It is estimated that the proportion of women born in 1950 who will never have children is only 14 per cent. This compares with 20 per cent of those born in 1920 and 10 per cent of those born in 1945 – the cohort least likely to remain childless. Most women also continue to bear children within marriage. Only 22 per cent of women aged sixteen and over in Britain today are unmarried. However in recent decades, while marriage remains popular, the divorce rate has risen, but so too have remarriages. In 1986 over a third of all marriages were remarriages compared with less than half this figure twenty-five years earlier. The proportion of couples who cohabit has also increased, particularly in the last decade. Between 1979 and 1985, the number of women aged between eighteen and forty-nine cohabiting with a man doubled (from 2.7 to 5.0 per cent of the age group). This change is reflected in 'illegitimacy' rates, which appear to have risen sharply in recent years – from 61,000 to 158,000 in the ten years from 1976, or one in five of all live births in 1986. This rise seems to give support to arguments about the 'moral decline' of Britain. Two-thirds of all these births, however, were registered by both parents in 1986, compared with only half in 1976, suggesting that cohabitation is the predominant family form, little different from the conventional nuclear family, apart from its legal status.

FAMILY STRUCTURE AND PROSPERITY

Children born into households consisting of two adults appear to have the greatest prospect of relative material security. Different family types have been affected by the scourge of unemployment to different degrees. In 1986, 86 per cent of married men with children were employed, compared with 57 per cent of lone fathers and only 37 per cent of lone mothers. Over half of employed single mothers worked part-time only. This reflects women's continuing responsibility for childcare and the limited provision of inexpensive full-time alternatives. The differential in average total family income between single parents and married couples is marked. The gap is enhanced by the tendency in many dual-headed families for the woman partner also to work for wages. Between 1973 and 1979, the proportion of married couples of working age where both were in employment rose from 52 to 57 per cent. It actually declined slightly after that date, mainly because of the rise in male unemployment.

UNEMPLOYMENT

Rising unemployment during the first seven years of the 1980s was the main cause of the increases in the non-dependent, unwaged population during the decade. Before looking at the effects of unemployment, it is necessary first to look at how unemployment is defined and, second, at how unemployment has differentially affected sections of the population.

Defining unemployment

Official statistics on unemployment serve a variety of purposes. Finding out how many people are unemployed is only one of them, and over the past decade it would seem to be the least important.

The prime reason why the Government collects unemployment statistics is administrative. The number of people registered as unemployed and the duration of time on the register are necessary for the payment of benefit and determining the types of benefit for which the claimant is eligible. The link of unemployment data to the state social security system excludes certain groups from the unemployment totals and includes others who might be claiming whilst working in the informal economy. The latter by definition are difficult to identify but could easily be numerically overwhelmed by those looking for types of waged work that make them ineligible for benefit.

To be registered as unemployed and so to be counted among the official statistics is dependent on exclusion from only certain types of waged work. Women, who have been doing casual work, housework, or seasonal work, for example, never appear at all in official statistics, whether of the employed or of the unemployed. Similarly, young people in casual or marginalised employment are often excluded, usually because they fail to register to claim benefits.

Official unemployment data are the only consistent and continuous means of asking wider questions about the scale of unemployment. Administrative changes, however, affect who is drawn within the data net. And, as unemployment is such a contentious political issue, governments have strong incentives to reclassify groups so that they are not included within the officially unemployed. Before October 1982, for instance, people who registered as being available for work, even if ineligible for benefits, were counted in the unemployment totals. After that date, only people claiming benefits were counted. Approximately half of the people excluded by that reclassification were married women.

During the 1980s further changes have reduced the groups eligible to register as unemployed. School leavers and men over sixty were taken out of the official statistics in 1983. The change removed 162,000 from the total. Work-experience schemes such as the Youth Training

Scheme introduced in the same year, and various Manpower Services Commission projects that basically topped up benefits for participants, also resulted in people being withdrawn from the registers. In 1986, a set of increasingly stringent requirements defining 'availability' for work was introduced. Claimants may be refused benefit on the grounds of placing 'unreasonable restrictions' on their availability, such as specifying employment within a particular area, failure to demonstrate pre-existing childcare arrangements, or asking for part-time employment. The net result has been to reduce the official numbers of the unemployed compared with the number of people out of work and actively seeking employment. The 1986 changes, for example, reduced the total count by 50,000.

A fundamental problem with the unemployment data is ambiguity in the meanings of 'employment' and 'work' discussed in the previous chapter. Is, for instance, a work-experience scheme equivalent to a permanent job, or is domestic, informal and part-time work any less valid than full-time waged work? No unequivocal answer can be given as the nature of work depends on the questions asked about the tasks people undertake in their lives, on the social role represented by those tasks and on the inquirer's and societal attitudes to specific types of work. If there are ambiguities over the meaning of 'work', its opposite, 'out-of-work', faces similar problems.

One striking definition of unemployment is that of neoclassical economists who believe in the 'natural rate of unemployment', considered in Chapter 4. They argue that a person is only involuntarily unemployed if they cannot get work of any sort at the prevailing rate for the job. They claim that many people who say they are available for work may not in fact be so, as they are only prepared to work at rates higher than those available at market equilibrium. Alternatively, workers may be holding out for jobs in declining industries, occupations or particular localities, rather than taking jobs elsewhere.

For them, consequently, most unemployment is voluntary. The strident popularisation of such definitions is reflected in sections of the press and in their apparent impact on recent official redefinitions of unemployment. Whilst there may be some truth in the fact that some people may only be looking for impossible jobs or unrealistically high wages, such a broad definition of voluntary unemployment seems an unrealistic assessment of people's opportunity to find work. The definition depends on assumptions about labour-market homogeneity and price flexibility that were questioned earlier when considering the natural-rate thesis in Chapter 5. More adequate definitions of unemployment must recognize the reality of people's lives and the set of social roles and obligations they fulfil, as well as regional differences in the availability and types of waged work.

A proportion of claimants drawing benefit do so illegally while they are working in paid employment, perhaps in the informal sector. The totals obviously are hard to estimate. However, investigations during 1988 amongst certain groups of workers, including London taxi drivers and East Coast fishermen, resulted in approximately 55,000 people withdrawing their claims for unemployment benefit. DHSS officials believed that this number was only a small proportion of those working in the 'black economy'. Ironically, then, the state benefit system may help to prop up low-paid private-sector employment. The more general issue is whether unemployment and social security benefits are too high (encouraging people not to work) or too low (at or below a minimum subsistence level, forcing people to work at the same time as drawing benefit). The relationship of benefit levels to wage rates and their effect on labour-force participation is not clear. Nor is there any general social agreement about what is an adequate minimum income for individuals and households at the current time.

Because under- and over-estimates of unemployment

are impossible to assess with any accuracy, the following discussion is, of necessity, based on official unemployment totals.

The extent and impact of unemployment

For most of the post-war period, the total number of officially defined unemployed people was less than half a million and the long-term unemployed (defined as people without paid employment for a year or more) were a small proportion of this number – usually under 50,000. From the late 1970s, the extent of unemployment increased significantly (Figure 7.3), reaching a peak in 1986. The

Figure 7.3   Workforce and Workforce in Employment, Great Britain, 1976–88

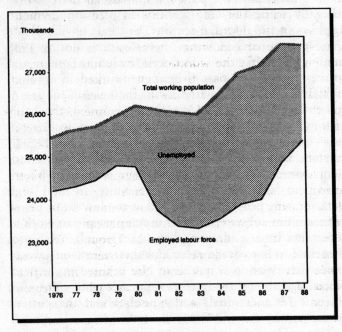

Source: Department of Employment

200

rate of increase was most marked in the depressed years at the turn of the decade. In 1981, for example, there were twice as many unemployed claimants as in 1979. Unemployment rates peaked in 1986, when over 3 million people were officially registered as unemployed. Despite a further change in the method of compiling statistics introduced in February of that year to reduce the 'over-recording' of claimants, 11.9 per cent of the insured workforce were officially unemployed in 1986. The number of long-term unemployed reached a total of 1.4 million, two out of every five unemployed people. Since 1986, unemployment totals have begun to fall (at the time of writing at the end of 1988 registered unemployment was 2.29 million, 8.1 per cent of the workforce [including the self-employed]). During the 1930s a similar number of workers were unemployed, nearly 3 million at the peak level, although the proportion – 22 per cent of the insured workforce – was much higher as the total workforce was smaller.

The chance of becoming unemployed is not spread evenly throughout the workforce. Those most likely to be unemployed are younger or older workers, although younger workers on average are unemployed for shorter periods. Table 7.8 shows age-specific unemployment rates by duration. Members of ethnic minority groups, people in manual employment, particularly unskilled manual employment, and workers in certain parts of the country are more likely to become unemployed. A survey carried out by the Policy Studies Institute in the early 1980s (Brown, 1983) found unemployment rates of 13 per cent for whites, 25 per cent for Afro-Caribbean people and 20 per cent among those of Asian background. The rate of increase in registered unemployment over the previous decade has been 515 per cent for ethnic minorities compared with 309 per cent increase as a whole. Figures 7.4 and 7.5 compare the position of black and white men and women in the mid-1980s. By 1988 when unemployment started to decline, the differentials for black and

TABLE 7.8 *Unemployed Claimants: by Sex, Age and Duration, United Kingdom, July 1987*

| | Duration of unemployment (weeks) | | | | | | |
	Up to 2	2–8	9–26	27–52	53–104	Over 104	Total
MALES							
16–19	9.5	17.6	28.4	24.3	15.3	4.9	212.5
20–24	11.0	14.3	21.9	18.2	15.7	18.8	390.8
25–34	5.2	9.8	18.8	16.8	17.0	32.4	491.2
35–49	4.0	7.8	16.3	14.4	15.7	41.7	479.1
50–59	2.8	5.3	14.0	14.3	17.4	46.2	369.2
60 or over	5.6	10.2	26.3	32.2	13.6	12.2	65.8
All men	6.1	10.2	19.2	17.4	16.2	30.9	2,008.5
FEMALES							
16–19	10.6	17.2	26.5	25.3	15.3	4.9	151.4
20–24	14.7	16.1	23.5	20.0	11.7	14.0	220.7
25–34	7.4	13.6	28.3	26.6	12.3	11.7	220.6
35–49	7.0	11.3	22.8	19.8	16.9	22.2	172.0
50 or over	3.1	5.6	13.3	15.2	17.4	45.5	133.2
All women	9.0	13.2	23.6	21.8	14.3	18.1	898.0

Source: Department of Employment.

white workers remained marked and had even increased for certain groups. For all ethnic minorities the rate of unemployment was exactly twice that for white workers – 20 per cent compared with 10 per cent. The hardest-hit were those of Pakistani and Bangladeshi origin, with a 31 per cent unemployment rate against 22 per cent for Afro-Caribbean people and 16 per cent for those of Indian origin (Figures 7.4 and 7.5).

Regional differences in unemployment rates are also considerable, in large part because of geographical differences in the economic structure. Between 1984 and 1987

Figure 7.4   Male Unemployment Rates by Ethnic Origin and Age, Great Britain, Spring 1984, 1985 and 1986

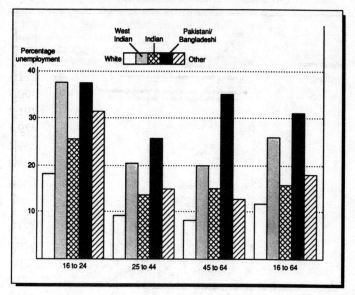

Source: Department of Employment.

the likelihood of becoming unemployed was highest in Scotland and the North and lowest in the South East, while the likelihood of ceasing to be unemployed was highest in East Anglia and the South West and, more unexpectedly, by the end of the period in the North West. Differential rates of increase also occurred between workers in different types of employment. For example, in 1983 as many as one-third of all men in semi-skilled jobs had spent time unemployed in the previous twelve months. This figure was four times as great as for men in non-manual work, compared with a threefold difference in 1977.

A number of employment and training measures have been developed in response to high unemployment in the

Figure 7.5   Female Unemployment Rates by Ethnic Origin and Age, Great Britain, Spring 1984, 1985 and 1986

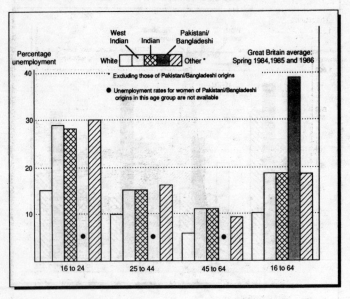

Source: Department of Employment.

1970s and 1980s (see Figure 7.6). The total number of people participating in the schemes peaked at 1.1 million in 1981, mainly because there were 875,000 individuals supported by the Temporary Short-Time Working Compensation Scheme which ended in 1984. The Youth Training Scheme (YTS) was introduced in 1983 providing training and work experience for sixteen- and seventeen-year-olds. Almost 1.2 million young people joined the scheme between April 1983 and March 1986. During that time, the number who were in a job three months after leaving the scheme rose from over a half to just under three-quarters, many of them in the occupation in which they had received training. In 1986, YTS schemes were extended to two years rather than one. The number of

Figure 7.6 *Unemployment and Training Measures, 1976–86*

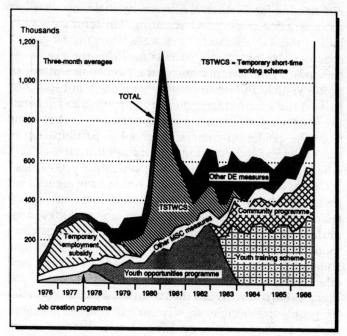

Source: *Social Trends*, 18 (1988).

trainees increased by over 75,000 between December 1986 and December 1987. However, only 28,000 of the increased number were girls. The inadequacy of technical and vocational training for girls has long been a feature of the schemes. In recognition of this criticism, the Manpower Services Commission, then running the YTS schemes, published an Equal Opportunities Code in November 1987 for participating organisations. One way of promoting greater equality was the introduction of reserved places and single-sex schemes in non-traditional areas of work in which women are underrepresented. At the end of 1987, sixty-one reserved-place training schemes covered building trades, various aspects of engineering and other traditionally male occupations such as gamekeeping and seafaring. Unfortunately only half of the 357 reserved places were taken up. Single-sex schemes also had mixed success in filling the places. At the end of 1987, twenty-one of the twenty-five places in motor vehicle and repair courses were taken but less than half on the schemes for joinery and painting and decorating. Part of the difficulty in filling these places may come from the gender differences at school in participation in the Technical and Vocational Education Initiative (TVEI), where girls tend to opt for typing and home economics.

Critics of the YTS scheme as a whole have argued that many of the young people received little on-the-job training and were exploited as cheap labour. Assessment of the content of vocational training schemes in different industrial sectors has revealed their inadequacy and shown that in many cases the first year of YTS is not used effectively. Indeed, in a report on retailing (Jarvis and Prais, 1988) it was argued that vocational training policies for people under eighteen were so bad that they were in danger of producing 'a certificated semi-literate underclass' because of their concentration on practical skills assessed in the workplace, as opposed to written and practical tests on more general educational subjects. In comparisons of British and French training for engineering craftsmen and technicians and retail training, the National Institute for Economic and Social Research found far higher standards in France. The number of young people attaining vocational qualifications of a comparable standard was nine times higher in France. Similar criticisms have been levelled at schemes for the adult and long-term unemployed. The Restart Programme aimed at the long-term unemployed was started in 1986 and aimed at boosting the morale and confidence of people who have been out of work for six months or more. Some job training is offered and a Jobstart allowance of £20 a week if a full-time job is taken with a gross weekly wage of under £80. This allowance has been criticised as a subsidy to those employers who pay extremely low wages. In addition, the Restart Programme seems to reduce unemployment totals for another, questionable, reason. In the eighteen months to April 1988, 10 per cent of claimants stopped claiming benefits rather than attend the Restart interviews arranged for them.

By the late 1980s the variety of employment and training schemes was enormous, the product of *ad hoc* initiatives and responses to particular problems. From the end of 1988 it was planned to replace the thirty or so training and employment schemes by one: an adult training programme run by the Training Commission, a new body to replace the Manpower Services Commission. Participants, between the ages of eighteen and fifty and previously unemployed for six months or more, were to be paid £5 to £10 a week more than benefit levels. However, in autumn 1988, at its annual conference, the Trades Union Congress withdrew its support from the scheme and barely two weeks after its initiation Norman Fowler, the minister then responsible, proposed to abolish the Commission. Its functions were to be passed to a new agency within the Department of Employment.

Aggregate statistics cannot reveal the implications of unemployment for the standard of living and access to opportunities of those individuals who become unemployed and their families. A range of psychological and sociological research has shown that unemployment is essentially a negative experience for the 3–4 million people without waged work in the mid- to late 1980s. This is despite the often vigorous and determined responses made by individuals on becoming unemployed and frequently even, for an initial period at least, a feeling of escape from the monotony of the work routine or the drudgery of an unpleasant job. Financial support by the state to the unemployed is not generous. In 1988 a single person was entitled to only £28 a week unemployment pay; a married man to £52.70. Becoming unemployed challenges and undermines many people's self-respect and sense of purpose. The Government is determined to reduce the total number of the unemployed, but in ways which many people think conflict with notions of social justice. Its policies aim at 'pricing workers into a job', restoring 'incentives' and reducing the differential between income support and low wages. In Chapters 9 and 10 the role of the state is considered in further detail.

The majority of those vulnerable to unemployment have few resources with which to protect themselves. The effects of living without waged work in Britain today vary depending on who it is who becomes unemployed. Problems, life-styles and prospects may be very different for women, long-term unemployed men, school leavers and the elderly. Class differences may also be important. The consequences for the jobless middle class may differ from those for individuals whose previous experience of waged work was temporary or disrupted. Individual, family and local circumstances may also vary. The impact of becoming unemployed in Sunderland, say, may be quite different from being unemployed in Slough.

Most unemployment research that has dealt with some of these issues has focused on men, and mainly on working-class men, in part because this was the group most affected by unemployment until recent years but also because of the perceived centrality of waged work in men's lives. The preceding chapter discussed the ways in which assumptions about women's roles affect the structure of the labour market. The same assumptions mean that unemployment is not seen as such a crisis for women. Women's unemployment is less 'visible' as, after all, it is argued, they frequently have their family role to fall back on.

Unemployment can have disastrous personal consequences. Psychologists assessing the impact of long-term unemployment on men (Fryer and Warr, 1984) found that the unemployed suffered progressive loss of their mental agility, comprehension, memory and general alertness.

Middle-aged men were affected more seriously than teenagers and men nearing retirement age. These men, in particular, expected to be at the height of their careers and suffered great loss of self-esteem. Physical health, as well as mental abilities, was affected. Most of the sample reported a deterioration in their well-being, including worsening angina, headaches, high blood pressure and ulcers. The unemployed men interviewed in this and in other studies also reported that they felt failures, as if other people despised and blamed them, and this caused problems of severe depression, loss of identity and increased tension within their households. Income losses are substantial. Among the middle-aged working-class men in the sample (954 men in all) on average total household income was about half the level of the man's previously earned income.

Unemployment alters family circumstances and the strategies adopted to deal with the changes. One of the impacts, which initially may seem contradictory, is that the wives of unemployed men may leave the paid workforce. Warr and Jackson (1984) found that it was noticeable that a far lower proportion of the wives of long-term unemployed men were themselves in waged work than amongst those wives of men who were out of work for only short periods. This is partly a consequence of how the benefit system works but also because of particular strategies adopted by women to assist their menfolk who were physically ill or depressed and to bolster their image of their 'worth' and 'masculinity' (Cooke, 1987).

The ideal that the male partner in a family should be the breadwinner is strongly engrained in the fabric of British society. Men's economic dependency presents a challenge to conventional gender divisions, but studies of the family relations of men made redundant – steel workers in South Wales, for example (Harris, C. C. *et al.*, 1987), and steel and shipyard workers in the North East (Morris, 1987) – have revealed little evidence of change in the conventional distribution of domestic tasks in the home. Women continue to carry out the vast majority of jobs in the home despite men spending much more time there. Campbell (1984) has summed up this contradiction as follows: 'They [women] need the men to change, and yet feel the need to protect men in crisis' (p. 61). Studies among younger women, in particular Beurat and Makings's (1987) study of 'courting' couples, where the women were in waged labour and their male partners were unemployed, have found evidence of changing attitudes and practices. None of the women in Beurat and Makings's sample (which was only small – twenty-five couples in total – so the results have to be treated with caution) was prepared to marry and shoulder the economic burden of being the breadwinner. However, these women did provide for their boyfriends on dates and on holiday in ways which, through various subterfuges, managed to retain intact male pride and some semblance that these men were providing for their girlfriends rather than vice versa.

Other studies of young people, particularly those still living with their parents, make much more pessimistic reading. There was an enormous increase in the extent of youth unemployment from the early 1980s and many young people leaving school faced the prospect of several years on the dole or in temporary training and work-experience schemes. The lack of opportunities for young black people is particularly severe. According to official figures published by the Department of Employment in 1988, an average of 32 per cent of sixteen- to twenty-four-year-old men from the ethnic minority groups were out of work at any one time in the period between 1984 and 1986. This compared with 18 per cent of young white men in the same age group. Among young men of West Indian and Pakistani origin, the rate was 37 per cent, even assuming all these young men were officially registered as unemployed. The position for young women was almost as bad. Some 31 per cent of ethnic minority women were unemployed compared with 15 per cent of white women aged sixteen to twenty-four.

Young people, like older workers, have been affected by the structural economic shifts, recession, deskilling and the occupational composition of the economy outlined earlier. But youth unemployment has risen faster than the levels for older workers. This feature is usual in periods of recession. Young people, especially school leavers, are particularly affected when firms stop recruiting. In addition their relative lack of skills and inexperience, at a time of labour surplus, may make them a less attractive proposition than other workers, although of course they are cheap labour. The reduction by employers in training and apprentice schemes that lead into secure employment has mainly hit the young, although there are now a number of government-sponsored schemes available. Young people are also proportionately affected by last-in-first-out lay-off policies. However, unemployment among young workers began to fall rapidly in the second half of the 1980s. By mid-1988, the number of school leavers among the unemployed was 34,000 compared with 136,600 at its peak in September 1986. The numbers of fifteen-to-nineteen-year-olds in the population as a whole fell during the 1980s, and a decline will be a feature of the population structure for several decades. A fall of 22 per cent in this age group is projected between 1985 and 2025, with a growing shortage of young workers predicted. Many firms are now looking for other categories of worker to recruit and train. As married women returning to work are one of the favourite targets, the gender composition of the labour market seems set to continue to change in women's favour.

For the young unemployed themselves, levels of income support are extremely low, and benefit changes introduced between 1986 and 1988 are based on an assumption of growing parental responsibility, despite the fact that eighteen-year-olds legally are adults. Consequently the benefit system enforces patterns of dependency between parents and children in the same way as it does between men and women. Brah (1986), in a study of unemployed Asian young people, has found evidence that this dependence leads to boredom, depression, anxiety and anger as well as to severe financial difficulties. Brah argued that the male-breadwinner ideology, which is extremely significant among Asian families, was a central element in many of the social and psychological pressures which the unemployed male respondents described as affecting them. In an earlier study of young white men out of work, Willis (1984) considered that these problems amounted to a 'male gender crisis'. Young Asian women without waged labour found their overall independence severely restricted. Studies of both Asian and Afro-Caribbean young people found evidence that the social and economic pressures of unemployment were increased by the racist nature of British society. Racial attacks, harassment, discrimination and changes in immigration and nationality laws have become a more marked feature of British life during the 1980s. Unemployment heightened these young people's sense of themselves as blacks and, indeed, social contacts between black and white young people seem to be severely reduced once they leave school.

Young people, both black and white, are not merely passive victims of the processes of social and economic change but also attempt to resist, challenge and change the structures that have produced their current poverty and dissatisfaction. Aggregate figures show that, as youth unemployment has risen and the likelihood of gaining full-time employment at sixteen has fallen, the number of young people undertaking some form of education beyond the official school-leaving age has increased. For the majority of respondents to surveys, however, being unemployed is an alienating and negative experience. Belief by young people in ideas such as justice and fairness (Allatt and Yeandle, 1986) results in anger and apathy but above all a sense of moral outrage at all the waste of talent represented by the aggregate totals.

Unemployment, despite releasing individuals from the routines of waged work and so 'freeing' time, evidently does not mean that the unemployed are able to engage in various forms of unpaid work or the mutual exchanges of goods and services with others in the same situation. Indeed, the sociologist Pahl (1984), who initially believed that what he called self-provisioning and mutual exchange among the unemployed was widespread, found, in a study of the changing division of labour and the impact of unemployment in the Isle of Sheppey (part of Kent), that quite the opposite was the case. Contrary to his own initial hypothesis, it was the very households where the majority of members were in waged work who were most active in the informal exchange of goods and services within the local economy and in self-provisioning. This latter entails buying tools and equipment to provide services previously purchased in the market such as entertainment or home improvements. The low household incomes of the families hit by unemployment were not sufficient to enable them to buy or maintain the necessary equipment. Pahl believes that his findings also provide a counterargument to those who suggest there is a growing 'black' or informal economy in Britain.

The geographical impact of unemployment

Unemployment, as well as disrupting family relationships, affects wider social and political relations in different parts of the country. Social and cultural divisions in local areas are reshaped by economic change and unemployment. Most studies of the geographically uneven impact rely on regional-level analysis as there are few explicitly comparative studies on a more local scale. Official statistics of regional variations reveal an apparent deepening of the North–South divide. In 1987, for example, registered unemployment in the Northern region was almost double the South East rate – 14.2 per cent of the workforce compared with 7.3 per cent. But there were also marked variations within regions. Parts of the prosperous South-East region, like the Thanet area of Kent, for example, had unemployment rates well above the national average.

Evidence on the North–South divide and social and cultural variations within Britain has led to opposing conclusions on whether Britain is becoming an increasingly homogeneous or heterogeneous country. Adherents of the growing-regional-diversity thesis point to the significant variations in such factors as voting patterns, where the Labour vote is solidly concentrated in the North of the country. In the 1987 general election, Labour won all but 10 seats in Scotland and 96 out of 153 in the North (the North West, Northern and Yorkshire/Humberside regions) but only 26 out of 260 seats in the South (the South East, East Anglia and the South West). Regional house-price differentials between these areas also widened during the 1980s, to such an extent that, at the end of 1987, a prospective house purchaser in Mansfield or Doncaster could buy five semi-detached houses for the price of one in London.

Two sets of counterarguments are made in relation to the idea of a growing North–South polarisation in Britain. One line points to the enormous variations that exist within regions and suggests that a North–South dichotomy is too simple. On many of the indicators the clearest divide is between Greater London and elsewhere. House prices, average incomes, and the proportion of the population with a degree, to take three indicators, are significantly higher here than elsewhere. But some of the poorest individuals and households also live in London, and boroughs such as Tower Hamlets and Hackney rank consistently at or near the top of national indicators of social and economic deprivation. Other critiques of the North–South divide point to a decline in local variations. Some of their arguments are based on the penetration of an increasingly national culture throughout Britain, through the national media, for example, and growing central control over local government. There is also less diversity in the structure of regional economies as the service sector has expanded and increasing numbers of women have entered the labour market (Walby, 1986; Warde, 1985).

It is clear that Britain is a society in which there are deeply contested views of 'national' culture and that these partially map on to regional differences. Wright (1987), Hewison (1987) and others claim that sets of supposedly national values – images of the countryside, and a particular view of the past – are actually based on the class-specific attitudes of the rich and powerful. These are then packaged and sold through the 'heritage industry'. One effect has been to sanitize and iron out regional differences – even trips around abandoned coal mines have become part of the heritage industry in the same way as trips around 'Shakespeare country'. But this set of essentially rural-based and middle-class values summed up in Ian Nairn's phrase 'deep England' is contested in a number of ways, by young people (youth culture) and particularly through the self-conscious rejection of 'British' values by many of the black population. Gilroy's book *There Ain't No Black in the Union Jack* (1987) is a vivid demonstration of the oppositional culture of parts of the Afro-British community.

Exclusion of large numbers of unemployed workers and their families, sometimes called the underclass, from the benefits enjoyed by the majority of the population leads to persistent class and regional differences. The enormous rise in unemployment during the early 1980s reinforced existing inequalities. The theme of class and inequality is taken up in the final section of this book.

FURTHER READING

Allen *et al.* (1986) is a collection of twelve papers dealing with different aspects of unemployment: how to interpret the figures, the impact on different types of workers and some policy implications. The bibliography contains numerous references to other useful sources for those wishing to read further.

For those interested in the impact of unemployment on workers who are made redundant, Angela Coyle's (1984) book is an interesting corrective to the predominant emphasis in the literature on men's experiences.

Two useful books looking at general change, rather than at unemployment in particular, over the life cycle are Bryman *et al.* (1987) which deals with theoretical approaches to lifetime change, popular ideas about life-cycle stages including babyhood and old age, and resources and transfers over time; and Allatt *et al.* (1987) which looks specifically at the changes that take place during women's lives.

Abercrombie and Warde (1988) is an introductory book that deals with many of the issues raised in this chapter and elsewhere in this book. Its primarily sociological emphasis makes it a useful complement to our approach.

Finally, *Social Trends*, published annually by the Central Statistical Office, HMSO, London, is the best source of information on many areas of everyday life. Annual statistics from government departments of official bodies are collated in a single volume and enable the picture of social change to be continually updated. Each annual volume also includes an essay on an aspect of contemporary social change.

PART 3

Housing, Health and Education

8

Housing: The State and the Market
Michael Ball

Tenure, following usual practice, is used in this chapter as the prime means of structuring the discussion. Private renting, council housing, housing associations and owner-occupation are examined in turn. 'Tenure' describes the form of ownership of a dwelling and the rights of possession conferred on the people living in it. Many of the arguments about housing in Britain revolve around the advantages and disadvantages of specific tenures, and what the policy of the state should be towards them. However, the supposedly private tenures are to a considerable degree regulated by the state. Similarly, public housing has never totally broken with pressures of the market and the private agencies that operate there. There is also more to housing provision than an array of potential tenures.

In this century housing tenure in Britain has changed dramatically. The legal, economic, social and ideological meanings of specific tenures have altered – some of these transformations are elaborated below. The most obvious change has been in the proportion of households living in specific tenures (Table 8.1). Private housing has remained the dominant tenure form throughout the period. Renting from a private landlord has constantly declined, while owner-occupation has increased to take its place. Public housing expanded substantially from 1920 to 1980, but since then it has decreased in significance.

TABLE 8.1 *Housing Stock and Tenure, 1914–86*

| | Per cent of total stock in Britain | | | | | |
	1914	1938	1960	1971	1979	1986
Privately rented[1]	90	58	32	19	13	10
Local authority	negligible	10	25	29	32	27
Owner-occupied	10	32	44	53	55	63
Out of a total stock of million:	7.9	11.4	14.6	17.1	20.8	22.1

1. Private rental includes other minor tenures as well, the most important of which are Housing Associations, which had 2.5 per cent of the stock in 1986.
Sources: HPR (1977), *Annual Abstract of Statistics*.

Whatever the tenure, housing is a highly socialised consumption good. It necessitates systems of property and possession, so that other people can be excluded from the space one household designates as home. Houses exist in proximity to each other, and their characteristics depend on the wider physical and social environment in which they are built. Their usefulness is affected by such features as their design, quality of construction and the characteristics of the neighbourhood and local environment. Each dwelling has, in addition, to be plugged into the physical infrastructure of a built environment – roads and other transportation systems, water and sewerage networks, gas and electricity provision and telecommunications facilities. The housing net, however, is usually drawn tightly around the issue of tenure. The broader physical context of housing provision is usually shunted off into the framework of land-use planning.

PRIVATE RENTAL HOUSING

Up to 1920 almost everybody lived in a home rented from a private landlord. New building for rent virtually ceased after that date. A large stock of rental dwellings existed by then, but the net stock has since slowly declined. As recently as 1960, almost a third of the stock was still privately rented (Table 8.1). Over the years, however, many landlords found it more profitable to sell to owner-occupiers; while millions of the worst rental dwellings were demolished in slum clearance programmes. By 1986, under 8 per cent of the population rented privately.

The tenure contains some of the worst housing conditions – 36 per cent of furnished tenancies lacked a fixed bath or shower in 1985, while 31 per cent had no inside WC. Some expensive, high-quality rental accommodation exists, but it is predominantly the tenure of the elderly who have lived in their dwelling for years and the tenure of last resort for those who cannot get accommodation elsewhere, because of either youth or poverty or failure to satisfy the criteria for entry into council or housing association property. For the elderly stuck in poor accommodation no alternative future is in prospect. For younger households, however, living in the tenure might only be transitional before moving on to home ownership or (less likely) public housing. A survey in 1985, for example, found that a third of all households with a head under twenty-five years old rented privately (*Social Trends*, 1988).

Why has the tenure been so reduced? Some, including the present government, put the blame squarely on rent controls. First introduced in 1915, a variety of measures since then have effectively restricted rents and given tenants legal security of tenure. An inability to charge market rents or offer the accommodation to other prospective tenants who are prepared to pay more has made privately rented housing hopelessly uneconomic, the critics of control claim (Minford *et al.*, 1987; Black and Stafford, 1988). The Conservatives' 1988 Housing Act aims to rid the tenure of most of these controls (for details, see Chapter 12).

The correlation between the decline of the private rental stock and the years of rent control is one of the empirical cornerstones of the anti-rent-control argument. Obviously, if rents are restricted, the sector as a whole becomes less profitable. But when looking at the case against rent controls many other factors have to be considered. In particular, it is unclear in practice that higher rents would induce much extra supply. The decline of the rental sector instead is in part a product of conscious political factors, like the decisions to embark upon major slum-clearance programmes, to build mass public housing and to subsidise heavily the growth of owner-occupation. But there were also reasons inherent in the nature of rental housing provision in Britain that contributed substantially to the tenure's decline. As it is widely believed that the tenure would have survived at a major level but for political interference with the attractiveness of specific tenures, emphasis in the following analysis will be placed on the inherent economic problems of the structure of private rental housing provision.

The empirical evidence of the continual existence of strong rent control since 1915 itself is open to doubt. While some form of rent control has existed almost continuously since then, the extent of the controls and the security-of-tenure provisions have varied considerably. Uncontrolled sectors (such as furnished accommodation for many years) or previous relaxations of controls have not stemmed the tenure's decline. In the inter-war years, for instance, new rental housing was for the most part uncontrolled. Yet despite chronic housing shortages little new rental housing was built, except in the last few years of the 1930s when the demand for owner-occupied housing began to tail off. Decontrol of a significant part of the rental stock for a few years after 1957 had a similar desultory effect, even leading to a fall in the supply of

rental accommodation as decontrol enabled landlords to
sell out to owner-occupiers.

Many people argue that the real reason for the decline
of rental housing is that other tenures are heavily
subsidised whereas it is not. Owner-occupiers get tax
reliefs, while councils and housing associations receive
direct state subsidies. Only once the tax/subsidy arrangements are neutral between tenures would most households contemplate renting and investors be interested in
letting housing. The argument has merits. The subsidies
to housing are huge and now overwhelmingly go to
owner-occupation. But this was not always the case. In
the inter-war years, home ownership expanded rapidly
yet the subsidies to owner-occupation were generally
small (see the discussion of owner-occupation below).
The mortgage interest rate was for many years also much
higher than the general cost of capital. The financing of
owner-occupation, therefore, was frequently more expensive than the interest costs faced by a company embark-
ing on house rental. Few people wanted to be tenants or
landlords. Present-day rental housing is also subsidised,
although not by as much as owner-occupation. Low-
income households can claim housing benefit to offset
their rents. Such subsidies, not surprisingly, encourage
landlords to raise their rents, so some of the benefit is
appropriated by landlords rather than accruing solely to
tenants. When rents rise, as they are likely to do after the
1988 Housing Act, the subsidy rises commensurately – a
feature which the Government has implicitly recognised
by introducing maximum limits on the scale of housing
benefits. In addition, since 1988, small-scale landlords
can receive generous subsidies under the business expansion scheme; a subsidy which building societies are also
taking advantage of.

Housing landlords have never been popular. Most
people object to paying rent directly to another individual
or a private company for accommodation, and invariably
suspect unreasonable profiteering. Conflicts between

landlords and tenants are well documented from the nineteenth century onwards. The animosity felt by tenants has a basis in the economics of private landlordism, as will be explained below. Rent controls and unequal subsidies have probably only speeded up the decline of the tenure, the cause of which lies in fundamental weaknesses in the traditional British rental system.

One feature of the structure of private rental provision is the social composition of landlords. Most landlords are, and always have been, small-scale, owning a few houses at most. Such enterprises are generally chronically undercapitalised, and often can barely maintain their properties. In the nineteenth century, many middle-class people are said to have invested in rental accommodation for lack of any other alternative. When other savings media became available in the early years of this century, these potential types of landlord deserted housing in droves.

Small-scale private landlordism is highly inefficient. Few landlords have efficient management skills or care about acquiring them – any conflict between landlord and tenant is exacerbated by such inefficiency. There are, furthermore, considerable scale economies in managing rental property, which private landlordism has never managed to achieve. The incentive to maintain property beyond fairly minimal standards is also generally weak (except in the luxury sector, where some major companies did invest particularly in the inter-war years).

Private landlordism creates problems for the construction industry as well. Its demand for new housing is highly unpredictable and lumpy (the nineteenth-century housebuilding industry was the most backward part of the construction industry for this reason). But perhaps what makes private landlordism so unsustainable is the intense distributional conflict it engenders. With increasing prosperity, the cost of housing rises as more people want to use the scarce space in the crowded and closely spread cities of a country like Britain. In a market rental system, rising rents distribute some of the benefits of increasing prosperity away from tenants to landlords. The rent increases are soon capitalised into the purchase price of rental dwellings. In order to increase the supply of rental accommodation, therefore, individual landlords have to pay the going price for dwellings, which keeps the profitability of doing so close to the general competitive rate. Higher rents do not tend to induce much extra supply, but get dissipated in rising property values and land prices. The distributional arbitrariness and unfairness of the economic benefits of private landlordism make landlords a weak political group. Individual tenant–landlord problems, of which there are many, get drawn into a wider debate over the beneficiaries of economic growth. Landlords are an easy target as they can be attacked without threatening the concept of private property.

In summary, the history of rental housing in Britain suggests that a revival of private rental housing is likely to be a highly inefficient means of housing provision, and would reintroduce a major source of social conflict.

COUNCIL HOUSING

At its peak in the late 1970s the council sector housed about 32 per cent of all households in Britain. One of the major planks of Conservative housing policies in the 1980s has been to dismantle the tenure. Initially this was done through selling council houses, and then in the late 1980s through proposals for the transfer of whole estates to private landlords and housing associations. In 1987, however, there were still almost 6 million council dwellings. Council housebuilding for many years was closely associated with slum-clearance programmes. From 1961 to 1970 each year on average 65,000 slums were cleared and 166,000 council dwellings built. In 1986, only 10,000 slums were demolished and a mere 24,000 council dwellings constructed.

The history of council housing is long and varied. Some local authorities built dwellings from about the middle of the nineteenth century, and interest greatly increased after local government reform in the 1890s. But it was not until after the introduction of central government subsidies in 1919 that a major expansion occurred. The Coalition Government's decision to subsidise council housing can be seen as the logical outcome of a process or growing recognition amongst opinion-formers of the inadequacies of private rental housing and the need to subsidise working-class housing. Alternatively, it can be seen as the outcome of intense agitation by working-class organisations and communities against appalling housing conditions. Another suggestion is that subsidised council housing was an ideological device aimed at keeping the 'Bolsheviks at bay'; an argument backed up by noting that the subsidies offered were savagely cut within two years of being introduced. It is, however, unlikely that the growth of council housing can be attributed to any simple, singular cause.

Since its inception after the First World War, the scale and form of subsidy have varied; sometimes influenced by political differences and by a propensity to see public housebuilding as a soft option for the expenditure axe. Labour up until the 1980s was seen as the party favourable to the tenure, although Conservative governments up to Mrs Thatcher helped fund the building of millions of council homes.

Council housing has fulfilled a number of roles. Either general-needs provision or slum clearance has provided the impetus, but never the sole reason, for the tenure's expansion at different periods. In the early years, much was built for the general needs of the better-off working class and lower middle class; poorer households could not afford the rents. This role, particularly in suburban estates and new and expanded towns, continued up to the

1980s. In the 1930s, slum clearance was a major aim. There was some decanting of population to the suburbs, but high-density flatted accommodation was built in the inner cities – some of it the worst housing in Britain today. Later slum-clearance drives gave council housing a similar role. In the later 1950s high-rise and deck-access systems began to make their appearance, often built from proprietary 'industrialised' systems. The inner areas of many of Britain's cities were transformed by the clearances and rebuilding, and in some cities, especially in Scotland, some high-rise suburbs emerged as well. Slum clearance and provision for general needs have meant that for most of its existence council housing has accommodated a broad range of the population, and has had a social mix similar to that of owner-occupation apart from the extremes of wealth and poverty.

The industrialised building experiment of the 1950s and 1960s was a disaster, generally producing expensive, poorly built flats in drab soulless environments. Within a few years, many of the buildings were found to have chronic design faults. Expensive heating systems and water condensation and penetration are the worst problems faced by tenants living in them. Demolition and costly remedial works have been necessary and far more needs to be done as the remaining structures age. The Modern Movement and British architects are usually blamed for the industrialised-system disaster, but often they were not responsible. Most systems were foreign, needing little architectural input, and they were erected by building companies which often cut corners, perhaps by using lower quality than specified materials or poorly trained, undersupervised labour. Councils were encouraged to use the systems by central government which was keen on achieving productivity breakthroughs in housebuilding. Cases where architects were in control, however, neither looked nor fared any better. By the mid-1970s, many design lessons had been learnt; in many cases too late as public-expenditure cutbacks lowered standards and the rate of new building slowed dramatically.

For many, inner-city slum-clearance flats and their problems epitomise council housing. The reality, however, is far different from this imagery. In the mid-1980s, almost two-thirds of council dwellings were houses, around a quarter low-rise flats and a mere 6 per cent high-rise flats. The houses, moreover, are generally in suburban estates; many of them designed on garden-suburb lines at much lower densities than modern private estates. It has, in fact, been this type of council property that has been most popular in the 1980s 'Right-to-Buy' programme.

Turning to rents, policies here have changed over time with shifts in the general financing of council housing and contemporary government attitudes towards tenants. Since the mid-1930s, local authorities have been able to pool the costs and revenues attributable to their housing stocks. Encouraged by central government, the practice became general in the 1950s. One result is that the rents charged for specific dwellings bear little relation to the cost of providing and maintaining them. For tenants living in older properties, rents are considerably higher than the historic costs of the accommodation, whereas on newer and refurbished dwellings they tend to be lower. The result has, in effect, been that many council tenants have never received any subsidy but instead have cross-subsidised other households in the tenure. Some neo-classical economists, however, still argue that they are subsidised as they have not generally paid the full 'market' rent. The accounting principles of council housing similarly lead to wide differences in rent levels between local authorities. Rents are to a great extent determined by the historical accident of when the stock was built, rather than by the political complexion of local government. Rents in London have always generally been much higher than elsewhere because of high building and land costs.

Up to the late 1960s, much central-government subsidy directly offset the cost of new construction. This encouraged councils to build more houses and to conform to central-government housing directives, while it helped ameloriate the tenant cross-subsidy effect. Financial reforms have meant that since then subsidies have not been related specifically to new building but are used instead to make up deficits in councils' Housing Revenue Accounts. The policy shift was justified in terms of subsidising people not bricks and mortar, but gave central government much greater control over council housing finance and rent setting. At the same time, individual rent rebates were introduced and later retermed 'housing benefit'. Means testing, in other words, came late to council housing.

For most of the 1950s and 1960s rents rose faster than inflation. But in the inflationary years of the 1970s they trailed way behind, partly through central government directives aimed at controlling inflation and partly because of the failure of a policy of fair rents, aimed at bringing market principles into council rent determination. From contributing around 75 per cent of council housing income throughout the 1960s, rebated rents contributed less than a third by 1984. Inflation had wreaked havoc with local authority housing finance. Another cause of the declining rental contribution has been the increasing concentration of lower income households in the tenure. One consistent policy of the Thatcher administration has been to force up the level of rents, which since 1979 have actually risen faster than the rate of house-price inflation. Between 1979 and 1986, for example, council rents rose by an average of 265 per cent and house prices by 175 per cent. Many councils now make substantial accounting profits from housing rental and subsidise their rate accounts with them. Given that housing benefit has risen as a result of the increased rents, the paradox has arisen for some local authorities of central government implicitly subsidising their rate accounts through the backdoor of their Housing Revenue Accounts. Conservative councils have been the prime gainers from the effect.

Council housing is firmly enmeshed within the private sector. Councils in effect took over the role of the private landlord. Local authority building departments have done most repair and maintenance, but the vast majority of the new building has been undertaken by private building contractors on tendering procedures that often have made local authorities a 'soft option'. A particularly inefficient system of building management was foisted on the tenure, in which managerial responsibility is confusingly shared by an architect and a building firm. Conformity to central government regulations and directives is necessary. Sometimes the sector is used as a place for experiments in building techniques as with concrete and timber-frame industrialised systems: in all, a recipe for high-cost, low-quality building, none of which is inherent to public housing as such.

Apart from a brief post-war period, land has had to be acquired at market prices. This further inflated housing costs and led to some set-piece battles over where the next suburban council estate was going to be. Constraints on suburban sites encouraged high-density inner-city building. If finance is included as well, it can be seen that many aspects of 'public' housing in Britain have involved private agencies. A true public housing service has never existed in Britain.

The case for public housing rests on a number of factors. The fundamental claim is that council housing is provided on the basis of need rather than on the ability-to-pay criteria of the private market. Whatever its problems, council housing has provided millions of low-income households with good-quality, low-cost housing. Assessing and defining needs is a difficult task, involving value judgements as well as quantitative measures. Local authorities' housing allocation decisions have been criticised for being inequitable or missing out some of those most in need. But the criticism itself recognises and supports the fundamental importance of the criteria of allocation based on need. Criticisms of the homogeneity that council housing may bring to certain localities, the ghettoisation of the poor or the lack of social mix are also criticisms of specific allocation policies rather than rejection of non-market principles of allocation.

Associated with the argument about need is the ability of public-sector housing to target subsidies directly to housebuilding or specific households, instead of seeing much of the subsidy leak into rising rents or house prices as occurs in private markets – a process which imposes additional costs on other households living in those tenures. Another economic advantage suggested is cheaper management costs derived from the economies of scale associated with large housing stocks. Some commentators have claimed the largest authorities have reached a scale where diseconomies are reached, but there is little empirical evidence to go on. Transactions costs are also far less in comparison to the private sector, especially owner-occupation with its myriad of exchange professionals and the lack of knowledge on the part of house-purchasers and -sellers.

One complaint against local authority housing is the insensitivity of housing management. Racial prejudice has been found in some allocation procedures. Tenants may be treated as the 'undeserving poor'. Repairs or requests for transfer may be ignored or responded to only slowly. It is difficult to quantify such factors and so know how prevalent they are. Surveys show that most tenants prefer having the local authority to another landlord but are to varying degrees dissatisfied with the service they get. Local authorities have sometimes responded by decentralising housing management and repair services to neighbourhood units and by increasing the training given to staff. The experiments have had mixed success.

How far public-expenditure cutbacks or bureaucratic inefficiency are to blame for particular tenant problems is virtually impossible to discover.

By the late 1980s, council housing faced severe problems. The sale of over a million dwellings in the 1980s and the virtual halt on new building at a time of acute housing crisis for low-income households are altering the social composition of council tenants. Increasingly commentators are suggesting that the tenure is becoming a ghetto for the dispossessed and the poor (Forrest and Murie, 1988). A vast backlog of repairs is required, £19 billion according to a government survey in 1985 (DOE, 1985). But with the Government keen on bringing back the private landlord little chance of improvement seems in prospect at least for a few years.

OTHER SOCIAL HOUSING

Council housing, following practice in other European countries, is increasingly regarded as part of 'social housing'. 'Social housing' is a very loose term. There are two overlapping definitions, which create considerable terminology confusion. One classifies social housing as being the provision of housing on a low- or non-profit basis. The other specifically earmarks the provision of accommodation for low-income households by agencies that are regulated and subsidised by the state (but they can still be profit-maximising). The two definitions reflect distinct attitudes to housing. The former is based on a critique of capitalist forms of housing provision; the latter is based on an ideology of the welfare 'safety net' and the acceptable means of providing it to targeted groups. Neither definition specifies the tenures concerned, and in Europe there have been a large number of owner-occupied social housing projects. In Britain, only housing for rent is usually discussed. Council housing has overwhelmingly dominated the sector, but the switch to the term 'social housing' in recent years has been an ideological device to show the existence of other forms. The 1980s Conservative governments, not surprisingly, championed the safety-net definition of social housing, being keen to show that there are alternatives to council housing.

Renting from a housing association is the most common social housing alternative, although it is a much smaller sector than council housing: in 1986, only 2.5 per cent of households rented from a housing association compared to 26.7 per cent from a local authority. Housing associations have a long history stretching back to the nineteenth century. Although with varied aims, they generally accommodate people with special needs or with problems poorly catered for in other tenures. The homeless, single parents, battered wives, the very poor, the elderly and the handicapped are typical examples. As such, housing associations are very much part of the voluntary social services sector, set up by concerned groups or individuals to help their fellow-citizens in need. The tenure houses some of the lowest income, most disadvantaged people in the country. Some unscrupulous operators have taken advantage of the benefits derived from forming a housing association, while some of the bigger ones have lost their philanthropic roots and have become little different from other private-sector landlords. In the main, however, the sector has performed a valuable and unique social role.

The current form of housing association emerged from a series of reforms in the 1960s and 1970s. Most are registered and overseen by the Housing Corporation. Central government grants throughout the 1970s and 1980s covered most construction costs, so the sector is the most highly subsidised per unit of all. New building expanded rapidly from the late 1960s but has rarely reached 20,000 dwellings a year. Like council housing, housing associations have suffered from public expenditure cuts in the 1980s. Cutbacks in the formulas determining government funding in 1987 and 1988 threaten further expansion of the tenure's role, particularly in meeting social needs in high-cost areas like London.

There is periodic debate over whether housing associations constitute a better alternative to council housing. In 1988, government ministers thought so and wanted housing associations to take over council estates; though many in the movement were keener to maintain their specialist role. For those who do not like state involvement, housing associations seem like a good alternative, but they tend to forget how heavily state-subsidised the sector is. Housing associations are accountable only to their governing bodies, which are neither democratically appointed nor controlled by tenants. The lack of accountability for many is an argument that the sector should not become a major force in rental provision. For all their faults, local authority tenants at least can campaign against and vote out unresponsive councils.

OWNER-OCCUPATION

Owner-occupation is the tenure in which the majority of British households live. By 1988, 66 per cent of dwellings in Britain were owner-occupied, but there are marked regional differences in the amount of home-ownership. In Scotland only 43 per cent of dwellings were owner-occupied in 1987 because of a traditional policy of extensive council housebuilding. The percentage is lower still in parts of Britain's major cities and much higher in rural districts and most medium-sized towns. Overall, owner-occupation is greatest in southern Britain.

Prior to the First World War less than 10 per cent of households owned the dwelling in which they lived. The mutual origins of the building societies and the ownership structures of some of the new industrial towns built in the late nineteenth century (such as some new mining communities) meant that even in the nineteenth century some skilled working-class households were home-owners. So the tenure has never been the preserve of the rich. Traditional rural societies also tend to have high home-ownership rates, even if most of the houses are rudimentary structures.

Owner-occupation became a mass tenure at the same time as council housing, and its initial growth in the 1920s was aided by substantial government housebuilding subsidies. In the 1930s there was a large owner-occupied housebuilding boom, which helped to drag the British economy out of the depths of depression. Between 1927 and 1936, the price of new houses fell by almost a fifth, bringing them within the reach of the upper echelons of the working class (Bowley, 1945). A building boom was triggered off on a scale never seen before or since. At its peak in 1934, 292,000 houses were built for owner-occupation, many of them in southern England. Concern at the loss of agricultural land, suburban sprawl and transport inefficiencies led to the development of green belts around most major cities, and was a major reason for the introduction of state land-use planning controls in the 1947 Town and Country Planning Act. The parallels with current debates about housing development in southern England are obvious, particularly as the 1980s witnessed a major reduction in the powers and role of public land-use planning. Most of the inter-war boom was unsubsidised as many new home-owners paid little or no income tax and so did not benefit from mortgage tax relief, while if they were income-tax payers they also had to pay schedule A tax on the imputed annual rental value of their home.

Home-ownership grew again from the mid-1950s onwards. Private-sector housebuilding peaked in the mid-1960s at about 220,000; by 1981 it had dropped to 120,000; but in the later 1980s boom output recovered to around 175,000 a year. The considerable rise in real incomes since 1945 and the growing burden of direct taxation meant that mortgage tax relief was a significant factor during this second phase of expansion. In 1963, schedule A taxation was abolished; many economists would like to see it reintroduced to lower tax incentives given to owner-occupiers (King and Atkinson, 1980). Abolition of rates based on property values and their replacement with the community charge, which is a tax on individuals, will remove the final major tax on owner-occupied housing. One consequence will be upward pressure on house prices of around 5 per cent according to Treasury estimates and up to 20 per cent according to independent estimates. The only special tax remaining on home-ownership is stamp duty imposed at the time of purchase. Although VAT has to be paid on some items, like transactions costs and home improvements, new housebuilding is exempt from VAT unlike most other consumer durables.

From the 1920s onwards an increasing number of private rental properties were sold to owner-occupiers. Up to the 1970s, much of the conversion consisted of removing multi-occupants and selling to a single household. This process helped contribute to the large fall in urban populations. The rising cost of home-ownership since then, however, has led to the conversion of many single family houses back into owner-occupied flats (albeit of a generally higher standard), contributing again to the growth of inner-city populations, particularly in the case of London.

Since the 1950s the falls in house prices of the inter-war years have never been repeated. It was also common for the purchase price of rental housing to fall during depressions prior to 1914. Over the past thirty years, rising house prices have become a new, and seemingly permanent, feature of owner-occupation. If house prices are looked at in real terms the picture is different. Since the early 1970s the housing market has been subject to periodic booms and slumps. They roughly correspond to the general level of economic activity. Prices rise when disposable incomes are rising and credit is easily available, and stagnate when the rate of increase in incomes tails off. The most rapid boom was in 1972–3, when real house prices rose by 25 per cent a year. The subsequent slump conversely meant that real house prices by 1977 were over 33 per cent less than their 1973 peak. Another boom occurred at the end of the 1970s, followed by a slump during the early 1980s recession. The most recent boom from the mid-1980s onwards has been the longest and, unlike previous ones, for much of the time was concentrated in the South East. In late 1988, this boom began to peter out, with falls in house prices reported in some of the districts of the South East that had earlier experienced the greatest price-rises. More generally, the market is likely to readjust in ways similar to the end of the previous booms. Yet, given the scale of house-price rises in the South East, often very high mortgage-to-income ratios, high real interest rates and a comparatively low rate of inflation, a long period of house-price stagnation or fall cannot be ruled out for the early 1990s.

Rising house prices are said to be one of the major economic benefits of owner-occupation as they confer increasing wealth on home-owners. They have certainly led to major shifts in the official estimates of wealth. In 1986, owner-occupied houses (net of mortgage debt) constituted 32 per cent of all personal-sector net wealth, up from 22 per cent in 1972 (Social Trends, 1988). As home-ownership is widespread, this has contributed to a shift in the distribution of wealth away from the richest households (a point considered further in Chapter 13). For individual households, however, house-price rises are a mixed blessing.

Over the longer term, house prices have risen faster than the rate of inflation. But, as they vary considerably in the short run, the time of purchase significantly influences the real increases in wealth received by home-owners. Owner-occupiers who purchased a dwelling in 1973, for example, on average did not see the real value of their house return to its 1973 level again until 1987, because of the steep fall in real house prices during the mid-1970s. Added to this temporal effect is the considerable variation in the rate of change of house prices between regions and even quite small local areas in the same city. Some areas, because of a mixture of high local employment and an inability of low-income home-owners to maintain their dwellings, have actually seen significant real price falls in the 1980s. Variations in price-changes affect all areas of the market, but given the significance on prices of high local unemployment and the regionally unbalanced nature of growth in the 1980s the prime beneficiaries of price rises have tended to be higher-income groups living in southern England. It could be said that the wealth gains from home-ownership are allocated on the principles of a lottery, but one in which the odds are strongly stacked towards those living in the South and those on higher incomes.

Owner-occupied dwellings are classified as marketable wealth, as home-owners in principle can sell at any time and realise that wealth. But the reality of home-ownership is more complicated as for most people there is no housing alternative to purchase. Unless a household buys a cheaper dwelling or dissolves through death or breakup, housing wealth cannot be realised. It still has some immediate benefit, however, because it can be used as collateral for borrowing. This is particularly advantageous if the borrowing involves a mortgage, which carries significantly lower rates of interest than other types of personal borrowing especially when subject to interest tax relief. In addition, housing wealth gets home-owners on to the 'housing ladder' because when buying similar-priced houses they are sheltered from the additional purchase costs imposed on new entrants with rising prices. Despite enjoying such benefits, some home-owners still bear some of the burden of house-price rises as the absolute cost of trading-up increases, especially when prices rise at different relative rates. The last effect has been brought into stark relief in the 1980s with the increasing divergence of prices in southern England above those elsewhere. By the end of 1987, average house prices in London (the most expensive region) were almost two and half times those in the northern region (the cheapest). The owner-occupied housing market had become a major barrier to employment mobility, making it almost impossible for many home-owners from the North to move to London or anywhere in the South.

Most people who trade down and can actually realise some of their housing wealth are the elderly. It could easily be argued, given the scale of housing costs for first-time buyers, that younger home-owners through house purchase are being induced into forced savings, the proceeds of which they can only realise much later in their lives if ever. One characterisation of this process would suggest that home-owners in effect are in a bizarre pension scheme, the costs of which are borne by younger ones and the benefits enjoyed by the elderly (or their usually middle-aged legatees) who happened to buy houses that considerably appreciated in value. The redistribution is from the young to the old, but it tends to benefit only the better-off elderly, increasing income disparities amongst the old. These processes can have major social implications. Couples, for instance, may put off having children until they are firmly established in the owner-occupied market. Once children arrive, both parents may continue to work because of high mortgage payments, whereas one or other would prefer to devote more time to childcare.

The effect of forced saving in the process of house purchase is greatly enhanced by the traditional form of mortgage repayment and general price inflation. Repayments are based on the prevailing interest rate and mortgage advanced. Inflation raises nominal interest rates and erodes the real value of outstanding debt. The real pattern of costs consequently is loaded towards the early years of a mortgage (a process called 'front-loading'); the greater the rate of inflation, the more is the loading of the real costs of repayment on to the early years.

Home-owners with mortgages derive one considerable state subsidy – mortgage interest tax relief. Of course, the 38 per cent of home-owners who own their dwelling outright do not directly enjoy this subsidy, so its benefits are unevenly spread amongst home-owners. Even so, the cost of mortgage tax relief has risen substantially over the past decade with increases in home-ownership and house prices. In 1985/6, it stood at around £5000 million. In that year, three-quarters of the relief went to home-owners on above-average incomes, and its incidence would have overwhelmingly been concentrated in the high-price regions of southern England; so it is a subsidy that is both highly regressive and encourages regional imbalances. Overall, owner-occupation is subsidised far more than council housing, even if rent rebates are included in the comparison and excluded are tax breaks to building societies, housebuilders and landowners plus the public infrastructural costs associated with owner-occupation.

Estimates of the distributional effect of mortgage tax interest relief are further complicated by the second-round effects the subsidy may have. As the tax relief is only given on mortgages for house purchase, the finance of house purchase is biased towards mortgage borrowing. One effect of the subsidy therefore is to encourage more households to take out mortgages and to take out larger ones than they might have otherwise envisaged. The institutions lending mortgages (such as building societies) gain from this stimulus to the demand for their products. In addition, the subsidy has the effect of reducing mortgagees' interest costs by their marginal tax rates, reducing their sensitivity to changes in mortgage interest rates. Lenders can take advantage of the greater interest rate insensitivity and charge higher interest rates. Some of the effect of mortgage interest tax relief consequently leaks through to mortgage finance institutions. Other leakages exists as well. Mortgage interest tax relief induces a greater demand for owner-occupation, and pushes up the overall price of houses. This benefits those who already own a dwelling, estate agents and others operating in the housing market, housebuilders and landowners. Precise calculation of these leakage effects, however, is impossible, as they crucially depend on the price responsiveness of the supply of mortgage credit, housebuilding and residential land; although they are likely to be large.

Discussion of the distributional incidence of mortgage interest tax relief requires consideration of the agencies involved in providing owner-occupied housing. In combination they help to determine the cost of new dwellings, the price of existing dwellings, maintenance and renovation expenses, and other costs associated with finance and purchase. The way in which owner-occupation operates in Britain is distinct from other countries to varying degrees because of unique characteristics of the institutions involved. No other country, for instance, has speculative builders on the relative scale and importance of the major housebuilders in Britain. The British housebuilding industry itself is less efficient than its counterparts in many other major industrialised countries. The type of mortgage instrument issued in Britain and the building society movement itself have few counterparts elsewhere. Given the distinct institutional structure of owner-occupied housing provision, it is not surprising that the experience of home-ownership has been different elsewhere – in terms of its scale, the existence of housing alternatives, the financial benefits to individual households and the overall taxation and distributional outcomes. Much of what is supposed to be immutable about home-ownership when viewed from the British experience does not look so permanent when a broader international perspective is considered, including the inevitability of house-price rises.

241

Many issues have been left untouched in this chapter. One concerns debates over the political perceptions induced in voters living in the different tenures (see Chapter 14). A number of general points, however, can be drawn out.

First, housing conditions in Britain have improved substantially in the post-war years. On all traditional public health criteria, the British are much better housed in the late 1980s than forty years before. Overcrowding, slumdom and a lack of basic amenities are now a fact of history for the vast majority of the population; although poor-quality housing, shared and limited living space, and desolate physical environments still have to be endured by millions of people. State subsidies have played a key role in that transformation, particularly through slum clearance and the provision of council housing, but also through the subsidies to owner-occupation. There is considerable evidence, however, that the improvement ground to a halt and maybe was even reversed during the 1980s (Malpass, 1986). Much of the cause was the rundown of council housing and the inability of the private sector to provide an alternative for many of those for whom public housing caters.

Second, despite a major owner-occupied housebuilding boom in the late 1980s new output was still way below the level needed to meet reasoned estimates of need (throughout the 1980s the government has refused to estimate the shortfall). New housing was also over-whelmingly being provided for middle-to-high-income households in owner-occupation, rather than for those in greatest need. The old housing vacated by those moving into newly built homes does not trickle down the housing ladder; this intuitive New Right theory has been discredited by every empirical investigation made of its supposed effect. Furthermore, the cost of housing rose substantially throughout the 1980s, partially because of rent increases and partially because of rising house prices and real interest rates. Again the greatest increase in costs was borne by some of the least advantaged, although with considerable interpersonal and regional variation. Council tenants saw their rents rise and housing benefit for many cut. Private tenants will after the 1988 Act experience a similar effect, as all rental tenures are subject to increases towards 'market level' rents. Amongst home-owners, while rising interest rates affected all borrowers, price rises and 'front-loading' meant that the greatest losers were first-time buyers, those trying to move to a more expensive region and those who suddenly experienced a large drop in their income, such as the unemployed.

Some of the consequences of a growing housing malaise can be seen from some general statistics. Homelessness became a major social problem in Britain in a way it had not been for a generation. During 1986, almost a quarter of a million households began the lengthy, distressing and frequently unsuccessful process of being officially designated as homeless. In the same year, 22,000 households were living in temporary accommodation. Over £45 million was spent on accommodating the homeless in that financial year. London has a particularly acute housing shortage; and there over £16 million was spent on bed-and-breakfast accommodation alone (*Social Trends*, 1988). Mortgage problems also grew dramatically in the 1980s. In June 1987, 64,000 mortgages with building societies were six months or more in arrears (up sixfold since 1979); while 23,000 houses were taken into possession by the societies (up ninefold since 1979) (*BSA Bulletin* 54). Other evidence of housing distress can be seen in the state of the housing stock with an estimated £19 million or more required to bring the public stock into good repair in the mid-1980s and £27.5 million on improving and repairing private-sector substandard housing (ALA, 1988).

Disparities in housing worsened considerably during

the 1980s, be it in terms of wealth realised, Exchequer subsidy, housing costs in relation to disposable income, the quality of housing enjoyed or the ability to exercise choice through moving to a new location. It is difficult to see how better housing for the rich can in any sense benefit the poor, rather than deny them even more resources necessary to improve their situation. As has been shown above, the distributional impact of the current forms of provision are very diverse, yet clearly regressive on average. No contemporary system of provision is particularly efficient, especially in terms of construction and maintenance costs and the effects on labour-market mobility. Government policies in the 1980s, outlined in Chapter 10, exacerbated inequalities in housing.

FURTHER READING

There are many introductory housing books. Most concentrate on a history of policy and tend to be weak on housing finance. Murie and Malpass (1987) is a good one, though. Black and Stafford (1988) pushes the neo-liberal line on regulating housing via the market. Arguments about the need to look at the agents involved in housing provision are made in Ball (1986); see also Ball (1983 and 1988) for investigations on specific aspects of British housing provision and the role of the construction industry. Le Grand (1982) considers the distributional implications of contemporary forms of housing provision, as well as other aspects of the welfare state, and finds them regressive. Hindess (1987) suggests conversely that Le Grand overemphasises egalitarian intent in the design of the social service provision. An international comparison of the changing nature of housing provision is given in Ball, Harlow and Martens (1988).

Shelter's journal *Roof* is a good place to keep up with

housing debates. *Housing Studies* specialises in more in-depth articles.

9

The Provision of Health Care
Linda McDowell

Compared with housing, the role of the state in the provision of health services and education appears more central. Despite the existence of a small private sector in both areas, the vast majority of the British population is dependent upon state-provided health care and attends state-funded or state-maintained schools and institutions of further and higher education.

The ways in which health care and education are financed and provided in Britain were at the forefront of political debates in the late 1980s. The particular set of proposals at issue – based on personal and private finance and forms of private organisation and management as alternatives or additions to the public sector – are the focus of Chapter 12. The division of responsibilities between the public and private sectors, however, has been a constant theme in the debate about the welfare state since its inception and in the decades before 1944. As the preceding discussion of the finance and provision of housing has demonstrated, the division is often more complex than it is perceived to be. Yet simple dichotomies that disguise the reality of different forms of subsidy arrangements tend to polarise both public opinion and policy options into adherents and opponents of state provision. The arguments about the nature of provision and access to publicly and privately provided health care and education are the focus of this and the succeeding chapter.

THE HISTORY OF
THE NATIONAL HEALTH SERVICE

Most people in Britain today depend on the state-provided National Health Service (NHS) for their health care. The origins of the NHS lie in two major pieces of legislation that were introduced thirty-five years apart. In 1911, the National Health Insurance Act initiated an insurance-based system that at its widest extent covered somewhat less than half the British population. The limitations of an insurance-based system – where care was related to income through ability to take out cover – became obvious in the three decades between its inception and the introduction of a free universal system in 1948. The working class in general, but working-class women in particular, were excluded from health care in the early part of the twentieth century. In 1939, a damning indictment of the consequences for maternal and child health was published as a result of an inquiry into the health of working-class wives (Spring Rice, 1939).

By the end of the Second World War, there was popular and political support for a comprehensive and free health service. Health care was to be provided by the state as a form of welfare and as a public utility. Throughout the previous century numerous interventions in the general area of public health, from measures to control contagious diseases to public sanitation and bye-law provisions to improve housing standards, were based on the recognition that health is a public good. This recognition was reinforced by awareness of the poor general health of working-class conscripts in the two world wars. The good health of the majority benefits society as a whole, while the converse also holds true. The 'choice' of one person to remain ill may affect the health of others. This is most obvious in the case of infectious diseases.

The avowed objectives of the proposed state-provided, universal service was to ensure equity in the availability and distribution of goods and to ration services and resources according to clinical need. Decisions about the allocation of resources were to be made by the state, which would be the main employer of doctors and other professionals who provide and run the medical service. This model of health care has become known as 'paternalistic rationality' (Calnan, 1988). It may be contrasted with a second model in which health care is a private good rather than a public utility, provided and allocated on the basis of market forces. Here the emphasis is on consumer sovereignty and individual choice. Care is financed primarily by fees for the service and paid for privately or through insurance-based schemes. Professionals tend to be self-employed individuals or small groups of entrepreneurs competing with each other. Although the health care systems of few countries in the world conform to either of these ideal types, the National Health Service as originally envisaged is a prime example of the first model and that of the United States of America typifies the second. In Britain at the present time the new emphasis on consumer choice in health care provision and a search for alternative sources of funding are pushing the near-state monopoly towards a mixed economy model. However, this shift is a recent development and it is important first to understand the history of provision in post-war Britain.

In the first post-war Labour government, Aneurin Bevan was appointed Minister of Health. His immediate task was to attempt to reorganise the piecemeal system of medical provision and health care that was then in existence to meet the requirements of an equitable, universal service. Throughout the nineteenth century and the first half of the twentieth, a geographically uneven system of locally administered services had developed. The continuation of local authority control was strongly resisted by the medical profession, partly because of the status implications. The pre-war distinction between public and private hospitals was based on a considerable disparity of prestige and facilities. But the possibility of local authority control was also rejected for financial reasons. The enormous cost of universal provision would have required a massive subvention of central government funds to local authorities.

The National Health Service Act passed in 1946 established a centrally controlled system with a tripartite structure of administration. Twenty regional hospital boards administered both local authority and voluntary hospitals that were nationalised; executive councils organised the dental, ophthalmic, pharmaceutical and general practitioner services, and at the lowest tier, local authority welfare services included vaccination and immunisation services, maternity and childcare, domestic help, health visiting, home nursing and ambulances. An adverse feature of the division of responsibility was the fracturing of a patient's relationship with channels of treatment. In essence, despite reorganisation of the tiers of administration and variations in their geographical coverage at various dates in the intervening decades, this division of care has remained a feature of the system to date.

The mood of doctors after the war was out of step with public support for the new plans for health. From the publication of the White Paper *A National Health Service* in 1944 until the inception of the service in 1948, the doctors' professional body, the British Medical Association, campaigned against a national, state-run service. General practitioners, in particular, remained adamant in their opposition to becoming state employees. Bevan negotiated a compromise by buying off the opposition of the elite of the profession – hospital consultants. As he freely admitted, he 'stuffed their mouths with gold' to achieve this end. Consultants were to be allowed to work part-time in hospitals for high salaries while continuing private practice and using pay beds in public hospitals for their own fee-paying private patients. General practitioners were paid on a capitation basis and did not become state-salaried employees. Both elements of this system remain in place today.

The new national health system was financed primarily by the state through general taxation. An element of national health insurance was preserved with part of the national insurance contribution of employers and employees funding a proportion of the cost of the health service. This led to the common and continuing myth that the NHS is paid for out of insurance contributions. The overall share of national insurance contributions has never exceeded 20 per cent of the total cost of the NHS. The dual source of funding, and the pros and cons of insurance-based *vis-à-vis* state-financed health care remain central features of contemporary debates about alternative funds for the NHS.

Resources, access and demands

A key issue of the new service that has continued to exercise health service planning to the present time was how to extend the coverage of care so that it became universal. In 1946 there were marked class and geographical inequalities in access to health care. A second major issue was financing. Initial estimates of the costs of the service proved to be totally inadequate. Demand for medicines, for dental services, and for spectacles exceeded projections severalfold. The 1944 estimate for ophthalmic services, for example, was £1 million a year; actual expenditure in the first year of operation was £22 million. The question of charging for services became a central part of the political agenda, and some element of charging was felt to be inevitable. The incoming Conservative administration in 1951, in fact, introduced prescription charges but did not dismantle the basic structure and principle of access to free care that lay behind the establishment of the NHS.

The question of *demand* for a free good, such as health care originally was, or for a good that is not priced in the market, is one that has become a central part of welfare economics, and a hot political issue. Critics of free universal provision argue that the demand for health care is effectively limitless. Even Bevan, the architect of free universal provision who resigned over the introduction of prescription charges, remarked in the late 1940s, 'I shudder to think of the ceaseless cascade of medicine which is pouring down British throats at the present time.' The definition and measurement of demand for health care are problematic, partly as there is no agreement about how to define good health but also because continued technological advances make new forms of treatment possible and so alter the definition of what is possible. However, it is clear that there are flaws in assuming that the theoretical concept of infinite demand is applicable in reality. In the real world, the idea that there could be infinite funding for the health service is patently a nonsense. The level of expenditure on different services is a political decision made by ministers and their advisers. The level of NHS funding reflects the priorities of the time. Currently, defence spending takes as much of the national budget as the health service (for more details about government spending, see Chapter 12). But also demand for health is not inflated infinitely by the fact that it is free at the point of demand. Most people do not choose to be ill nor do they try to use services just because they are available. They are not admitted to hospital because they choose to be, but after clinical diagnosis and, often, waiting in a queue.

However, difficult questions of how to allocate and distribute scarce resources in a cash-limited service and how to order priorities for each form of care and provision still have to be answered. It is hard to explain why certain types of treatment such as acupuncture, homeopathy or most psychoanalysis are provided outside the publicly financed sector, although powerful professional interests are part of the answer. In addition, there are also pressures from private firms with interests in health, such as the drug companies, to increase spending on particular forms of intervention. Certain 'high-tech' areas of the profession have gained in status at the expense of what have become known as the 'Cinderella' services of geriatric medicine and mental health care. A corollary of the emphasis on particular types of medicine has been an increasing geographical concentration in the provision of health care, particularly in the hospital service. Capital-intensive specialities demand high investment and, in a cash-limited service, it is uneconomic to provide facilities, for cardiac care, for example, at every local hospital. In the last decade there has been a move to close small cottage hospitals and to concentrate provision in large District General Hospitals in Britain's major towns and cities. For patients, who generally have to arrange their own travel to hospital, except in an emergency, the greater availability of particular types of care is offset by increased access costs.

Opponents of public provision of health care, as well as worrying about limitless demand, argue that the introduction of market mechanisms would lead to a more efficient allocation of resources between services. Through the market, individuals would be able to signal their preferences. As well as supposedly leading to greater efficiency and economy, a moral belief in the superiority of 'choice' and consumer sovereignty lies behind these arguments. Opponents counter that liberty and freedom to choose suitable health care is an illusion. Fundamental inequalities in the distribution of income structure lead to unequal access to health care. Further, it is argued that patients cannot possibly acquire sufficient knowledge either of symptoms or of the available treatments to be able to make an informed choice of what is appropriate to their needs. In calculating the economic advantages of a market-based model, the enormous administrative burden involved in itemising, costing and billing each element involved in a course of treatment is often forgotten.

The polarisation of the debate between state or public provision and market or private provision, however, disguises one of the key issues facing the National Health Service in the late 1980s. Whatever the structure of provision, in a cost-limited, mixed-economy health service it is clear that the allocation of care between different categories of patient must be effected by some mechanism or other. The current rationing system is based on queues for care within each regional health authority. The length of the queue for particular operations varies both within and between areas depending on the availability of resources and specialists. Within the North West Thames Regional Health Authority, for example, in the early 1980s the waiting time for a hip replacement operation varied from a few days in the London Borough of Hammersmith in the south of the region to well over a year in Bedford in the north of the region. This variation is not uncommon. A proposal for a voucher system to facilitate cross-regional flows of patients has been proposed as part of the review of the NHS established in 1988. Currently, a modified version of this system exists whereby general practitioners may refer their patients to a consultant in another health authority if they have the available information about differential waiting-lists. However, this is a matter of informal networks rather than a structured system of cross-regional flows. Questions of accessibility for the patient, and patients' relatives, will become important if greater mobility across the boundaries of regional health authorities is encouraged.

The current system of rationing and allocation of alternative forms of provision – that paternalistic rationality referred to earlier – relies largely on the professional judgement of doctors and health service administrators. Decisions are primarily based on a trade-off between clinical effectiveness and economic

253

efficiency. An attempt to quantify the basis of these decisions and to add into the cost–benefit equation an estimate of the additional length and quality of life of the recipient of care has been made by health economists working at the University of York (Williams, 1987). A quantifiable indicator (a QUALI) has been developed in an attempt to provide a basis for a more equitable comparison between different forms of treatment, a recognition of the risks involved and the potential enhancement of length and quality of life that would ensue. However, attributing quantifiable values to such concepts as the 'quality of life', before and after medical treatment, is a notoriously difficult area. The opinions of doctors, administrators and patients about the value and effectiveness of particular types of medicine often differ markedly.

One of the criticisms of the current provision of health care in Britain is that it is insufficiently responsive to the needs and wishes of the lay population – the consumer of health care. Arguments about the need to take into account the perspective of patients tend to be tied to political beliefs. There are those who argue that the health service should be a more democratic and accountable service. Greater consultation and patient participation would counteract the powerful interests of the profession and the state. Alternatively, from a different political perspective, the emphasis is placed on consumer sovereignty and the need for provision to respond more directly to patients' preferences and expressed demands. In the last ten years the principle that the state should provide a free-at-the-point-of-access universal health service has been challenged, as part of the campaign to alter the nature and role of the welfare state as a whole in contemporary Britain. A political emphasis on the moral superiority of self-reliance and individual responsibility has encouraged the growth of private health insurance, alternative forms of funding and new methods of provision. Medical care is seen as a product just like any other marketable good rather than as an inalienable right to good health. The views of the medical profession, however, have been somewhat at odds with this political sea-change.

The third argument for the shift to greater lay involvement stems from changes within the medical profession, particularly among general practitioners. A British Medical Association-sponsored committee (General Medical Services Committee, 1979) reaffirmed at the end of the 1970s a humanitarian view of medical practice that places the needs and wishes of the patient at the centre of health care. Although surveys of the general public and of patients show generally high levels of satisfaction with the NHS, respondents to questionnaire surveys often express dissatisfaction with 'scientific' medicine. In a study in the mid-1980s (Halpern, 1985), it was found that over a quarter of the sample used one or more forms of 'alternative' medicine such as an osteopath, herbalist or acupuncturist. In addition, patients often resent the incompleteness of the information which they are given and find doctors authoritarian and arrogant (Calnan, 1987). In a consumer comparison of public and private health care, Taylor-Gooby (1986) found that many of his sample were dissatisfied with the waiting-lists and staffing levels in the NHS. However, the majority of respondents felt that the provision of publicly and privately financed care is not incompatible and favoured the provision of both forms. The expansion of private provision in recent years is discussed at the end of the chapter. Before that, however, the origins and persistence of geographical and social inequalities in health care are examined.

Geographical inequalities

When the NHS was set up in 1948 there were marked geographical inequalities in the distribution of medical services. Certain areas of the country had far more hospital beds and general practitioners per head than others. In general the more affluent areas of the South East were much better off than the rest of the country. This pattern persisted throughout the 1950s and 1960s, despite attempts to reduce the differentials. From the inception of the service, for example, there were restrictions on the establishment of new general practices in 'overdoctored' areas. There were also regional variations in health spending, partly in an attempt to reduce differentials but mainly, in the first decade of the operation of the NHS, as a reflection of existing regional inequalities in provision.

Until the mid-1960s the structure and the levels of provision by the NHS established in the late 1940s remained in place with little major change. Indeed, during the first half of the 1950s health spending as a proportion of GNP at current prices actually fell – from 4.1 to 3.4 per cent. From then on it rose slowly until a capital spending programme was initiated in the mid-1960s. But in 1964 health spending – at 3.9 per cent – was still below the share in 1950. From that date spending rose as a major hospital building programme, initiated by the Conservatives, was carried out under the Labour Government. Capital spending on hospitals, and also on the introduction of health centres to reduce the number of general practitioners working alone, rose throughout the 1960s but current spending in real terms hardly increased at all. Throughout this decade, despite the building programme, regional inequalities remained. Indeed, about 40 per cent of the large schemes that were in progress at the end of the decade were in the London region. In current spending there was some attempt to redress regional imbalances, and here three of the four poorest Hospital Boards improved their position. Continued redress of financial inequalities, and questions about strengthening the democratic decision-making within the Boards, later to become Regional Health Authorities, became the issues of the 1970s.

A working party within the Department of Health and Social Security was set up to investigate the extent of inequalities in provision. The role of the Resource Allocation Working Party (or RAWP, as it became known) was 'to ensure, through resource allocation, that there would eventually be equal opportunity of access to health care for people at equal risk' (DHSS, 1976). But the concepts of need, access and equality are difficult to define. In their report, published in 1976, the working party proposed a statistical formula as a method of distributing total financial resources between the regions. The formula was based on the total population of a region, weighted by standardised mortality ratios and the propensity of different groups (defined by age and gender) to use health services. Usage was a surrogate measure of need, for, as the working party pointed out, the actual, and uneven, provision of services influences demand, that is, the number of cases that are actually treated. On the basis of the formula (which also took into account flows across regional boundaries, the extra costs of care in the London region and the extra costs of teaching hospitals) a target allocation was compared with the actual allocation to a region and plans drawn up for some measure of regional equalisation.

A limited measure of regional redistribution of resources has been achieved since the publication of the report, particularly away from the four Thames regions. However, in mid-1988, as a part of a general review of the NHS, the RAWP formula was reassessed. In particular, a new indicator of social deprivation and a measure of local morbidity, or sickness, were proposed. The addition of these two measures would have the effect of re-emphasising needs of the London area and of taking cash away from some of the northern regions that had gained under the old formula. It is clear that measuring the need for health services and allocating limited resources can never be an objective statistical exercise but will always raise sensitive political issues.

Equality in health

The RAWP report was an important step in attempting to deal with equality of provision. It tried to define equality and to measure need. However, equality of opportunity for access to health care is not the only measure of equality. Equality may mean equal access to available care but it might also mean equal treatment for equal cases, equal quality of care or equal access to the service for equal needs. This latter definition may mean that there needs to be different types of service in different areas to respond to geographical differences in patterns of health. There perhaps also should be positive discrimination in services in favour of those in greatest need to achieve a greater measure of equality between individuals.

In 1977 the Secretary of State for Social Services appointed a Research Working Group to assess the evidence about inequalities in health and to draw out the policy implications. The group was chaired by Sir Douglas Black, President of the Royal College of Physicians. Its report, which was completed in 1980 but not published until two years later (Townsend and Davidson, 1982), has become known as *The Black Report*. Together with *The Health Divide* (Whitehead, 1988), the final report of the Health Council before it was abolished in 1987, this report provided evidence not only of the persistence of regional or geographical variations in disease and mortality rates in the 1970s and 1980s but also of marked social inequalities between individuals in the same region. The publication of both reports was unwelcome to the Conservative governments of the time and they were given a frosty reception. The Black Report was in fact initially suppressed. The findings of these reports clearly were embarrassing to an administration that was attempting to restructure health services provision along more 'competitive' lines.

TABLE 9.1 *Standardised Mortality Rates¹ by Region and Occupational Class, Great Britain, 1979–80 plus 1982–3*

Region/country	Men aged 20–64		Women aged 20–59	
	I and II	IV and V	I and II	IV and V
North	81	152	80	136
Wales	79	144	79	125
Scotland	87	157	91	141
North West	83	146	86	135
Yorks. and Humb.	79	134	78	120
West Midlands	74	122	73	110
South East	67	112	71	100
East Midlands	74	122	73	110
South West	69	108	70	96
East Anglia	65	93	69	81
GREAT BRITAIN	74	129	76	116

1. SMR for all men and women in Great Britain for 1979–80 plus 1982–3 is 100.
Source: Townsend and Davidson (1982).

The Black Report found regional differences in mortality, with rates increasing from the South and South East to the North and North West. The Health Council report found that these persisted into the 1980s (Table 9.1). The rates are partially a reflection of the social-class composition of the regions. The regions with the highest death rates had more working-class residents but also exhibited the widest gap in death rates between the Registrar-General's occupational classes I and II (professional and managerial groups) and IV and V (semi-skilled and unskilled workers). Greater poverty, poorer housing conditions, diet and a greater likelihood of people living in the North to smoke are all contributory factors in the North–South divide in health. Heart disease, a major cause of death for men, is more prevalent in northern regions. For women, regional differences are less marked, in part because the occupations of women show less regional variation. The major causes of death for women – breast and lung cancer – are, in fact, more common in the south of the country. An urban–rural differentiation, however, is also important, with higher death rates among women living in towns and cities.

Differentials in health and health care: class, race and gender

The organisation of provision and geographical variations in patterns of disease and mortality are not the sole explanations for inequalities in health and health care. Social inequalities in health remain significant in Britain at the end of the 1980s. Indeed, it appears that class-based differentials, between men at least, have been widening throughout the post-war period (Table 9.2). The experience of individuals in social class V relative to other men appears to have worsened between the 1930s and the

TABLE 9.2 *Standardised Mortality Rates of Men by Occupational Class, Great Britain, 1930s–1970s*

| | Men aged 15–64 | | | | |
	1930–2	1949–53	1959–63	1970–2	1979–83
Professional (I)	90	86	76	77	66
Managerial (II)	94	92	81	81	74
Skilled manual and non-manual (III)	97	101	100	104	98
Partly skilled (IV)	102	104	103	114	114
Unskilled (V)	111	118	143	137	159

Source: Townsend and Davidson (1982).

1970s, despite the introduction of the NHS. However, there are inequalities between and within the social classes, ethnic groups, rural and urban populations, and between men and women, different age groups and people of different ages. As analysts seldom look at all these factors in combination, it is difficult to judge what lies behind the demonstration of a simple occupational class-based difference in Table 9.2.

The Black Report looked at four different types of explanation for inequalities in health: artefact explanations; theories of natural or social selection; materialist or structuralist explanations; and cultural/behavioural explanations. The artefact explanation suggests that the statistical associations between health and social class as measured by the Registrar-General's classification of occupations are a statistical artefact. The measure of social class used artificially inflates the size and importance of health differences. It is argued that the apparent failure of health inequalities between the classes to diminish in the post-war period can be explained by the changing distribution of the population between the class groups and because the nature of the occupations open to the labour force have changed so markedly, comparisons with earlier decades become meaningless.

In natural or social selection explanations, health is seen as the causal variable and occupational class the dependent one. It is argued that an individual's class position is a consequence of his health, robustness or vigour. The materialist and structuralist explanations reverse the relationship and emphasise the role of economic and associated sociostructural factors in the distribution of health and well-being. Deeply embedded structures of inequality in the distribution of income and material rewards influence not only health and access to health care but, as seen later in this chapter, also the distribution of education success. Table 9.3 indicates an interrelationship between these variables. Housing tenure, educational achievement and access to cars are all

TABLE 9.3 *Standardised Mortality Rates of Men and Women by Housing Tenure, Education and Access to Cars, England and Wales, 1971–81*

Socio-economic indicator	Men aged 15–64 at death	Women aged 15–59 at death
HOUSING TENURE[1]		
Owner-occupied	84	83
Privately rented	109	106
Local authority	115	117
EDUCATION[2]		
Degree	59	66
Non-degree higher qualification	80	78
A levels only	91	80
None or not stated	103	102
ACCESS TO CARS		
One or more cars	85	83
No access to a car	121	135

1. Aged 15 and over in 1971.
2. Aged 18 to 70 in 1971.
Source: Based on unpublished work by P. O. Goldblatt reported in Whitehead (1988). Crown copyright reserved.

related to mortality ratios. Good health or, rather, a long life is clearly linked to general living standards. As Chapter 7 showed, the proportion of the population with relatively low incomes and dependent on state benefits has grown in recent decades and unemployment may have a deleterious effect on the health of the unemployed and on their families.

Health and well-being over the life cycle

Inequalities in health start at an early age. Despite a marked overall decline, class differentials in infant mortality have not significantly narrowed in the post-war

TABLE 9.4 *Trends in Infant Mortality by Occupational Class, England and Wales, 1930–84*

	Infant deaths per 1000 legitimate live births				
Social class	1930–2	1948–53	1970–2	1978–9	1984
I	32	19	12	10	6.5
V	80	42	31	18	13

Source: Townsend and Davidson (1982).

period. Table 9.4 shows infant mortality rates over time for classes I and V. It indicates how important in reducing infant deaths were the introduction of the NHS in 1948 and the extension of maternal and child health care in succeeding decades. Class inequalities in rates of death at birth and in the first year of life are paralleled in the incidence of low birth-weight.

Throughout childhood, the most frequent cause of death is from accidents and their rate also differs between classes. The Black Report points to the material circumstances that make working-class children more prone to accidents. They include less adequate housing and a greater likelihood of living in a polluted environment, as well as lower levels of car-ownership and telephones – both resources that make communication in emergencies easier. In addition, middle-class parents tend to have greater knowledge, skills and verbal resources that ensure that they and their children get a greater share of the available resources. Finally, there is evidence that material deprivation affects the physical development of children and that ill health in childhood may persist throughout adult life.

During working life, health differences between people are strongly related to their occupation. One of the clearest divides is between men in manual and non-manual occupations. Men undertaking manual work are subject to greater risks of accident in their everyday life. They are also more likely to smoke. Countering these

263

class differences is the greater incidence of stress-related diseases among men in sedentary and management-related occupations.

In old age, inequalities in earlier years are reflected in differential mortality rates. As the Black Report succinctly noted, 'the bodies of men seem to exhibit the effects of wear and tear sooner than those of women and those of manual workers sooner than those of non-manual, and the manifestations of degeneration in disease become more frequent. . . . In the collective effort of social production, some workers' bodies wear out first.' Poverty and health among pensioners is closely related; those with good occupational pensions and secure housing conditions are better able to look after themselves in retirement. Thus inequalities in health are perpetuated from cradle to grave.

Ethnic origin and health

Health differentials also exist between the black and white populations and between different ethnic minority groups. They partly reflect differences in the overall class position of the minority population as a whole but also result from specific health issues facing minority groups. Investigation of the health of ethnic minorities in Britain, however, is hampered by the way in which the data are collected, because most statistics are collected on the basis of country of birth and so do not differentiate the British-born children of ethnic minority groups.

The Health Divide pointed to evidence about the greater incidence of certain diseases and health-related problems among particular minority groups (Table 9.5). The Immigrant Mortality Study (Marmot *et al.*, 1984) on which this table is based included individuals over twenty years of age who had been born outside England and Wales. Some of the findings are difficult to interpret. The high incidence of heart disease among men from the

TABLE 9.5 *Summary of Main Findings of the Immigrant Mortality Study, England and Wales, 1970–8*

Mortality by cause	Comparison with death rates for England and Wales
Tuberculosis	*High* in immigrants from the Indian subcontinent, Ireland, the Caribbean, Africa and Scotland
Liver cancer	*High* in immigrants from the Indian subcontinent, the Caribbean and Africa
Cancer of the stomach, large intestine and breast	*Low* among Indians
Ischaemic heart disease	*High* in immigrants from the Indian subcontinent
Hypertension and stroke	*Strikingly high* among immigrants from the Caribbean and Africa
Diabetes	*High* among immigrants born in the Caribbean and the Indian subcontinent
Obstructive lung disease	*Low* in all immigrants
Maternal mortality	*High* in immigrants from Africa, the Caribbean and to a lesser extent the Indian subcontinent
Violence and accidents	*High* in all immigrant groups

Source: adapted from Marmot *et al.* (1984).

Indian subcontinent, for example, is not related to drinking and smoking as it is amongst British-born men.

Analyses of information about the health of babies born to women in different ethnic groups reveal significant variations. Figure 9.1 shows stillbirth, perinatal, neonatal and post-neonatal mortality by country of birth of the mother. For all of them, mortality rates are higher for babies born to mothers from Pakistan and Bangladesh

Figure 9.1   Outcome of Pregnancy by Mother's Country of Birth

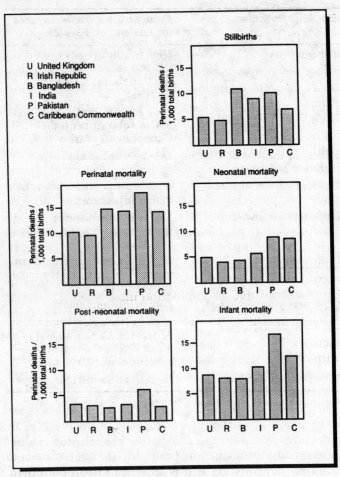

Source: OPCS (1986).

(OPCS, 1986). Investigations of the reasons for the higher rates suggest that risk factors for Asian women include low maternal weight, anaemia, the greater likelihood of late births, large numbers of children and infrequent ante-natal attendance (Gillies *et al.*, 1984).

The health balance sheet

While there is no doubt that the health of the population as a whole has improved since the 1940s, marked differences between social groups related to their material circumstances remain evident in Britain today. Targets for health for all by the year 2000 have been set by the World Health Organisation. The European targets were endorsed by member countries in 1984. Among them was an expressed desire to reduce social inequalities in health. One of the major issues facing Britain, and other advanced industrial nations, is the rising cost of supporting the growing elderly population. If the British government is seriously committed to reducing differentials in health and in access to health care, the extent of the inequalities suggests that resources have to be increased and redistri-buted and positive discrimination introduced. The NHS, at the end of the 1980s, faced a major crisis – cuts in services, financial shortfalls, the enforced privatisation of ancillary services (catering, cleaning and laundry). The British Medical Association was forced to announce that it could not guarantee adequate care in hospitals badly affected by cuts.

In 1988 a House of Commons select committee was set up to review the structure and funding of the NHS. In an early interim report, the committee commented favour-ably on the efficiency of the British health service compared with its US and West European counterparts, despite underfunding of the NHS throughout the 1980s. However, it seems clear that the current Conservative administration, with its emphasis on individual responsi-bility and its commitment to market provision, will continue to encourage moves towards insurance-based private provision of health care.

THE PRIVATE MARKET IN HEALTH CARE

During the 1980s there was a significant expansion of private health care in two main areas: the private hospital sector for acute care and private residential nursing homes for the elderly. The geographical distribution of the expansion has been uneven. Private hospitals are predominantly in the South East of England, largely reflecting the distribution of the affluent population but also related to the location of large teaching hospitals. Nursing homes are concentrated in retirement areas, many of these, too, in the South and South East, particularly on the coast. Many have developed in response to new DHSS benefit regulations whereby a per-capita sum is paid for each resident. In 1988 the weekly benefit was between £180 and £200. Firms in the private sector regard the sum as totally inadequate. The managing director of Nestor-BNA, a rapidly expanding company that runs hospitals and nursing homes for the affluent, contrasted it with the £25,000 a year paid by residents of one of the group's nursing homes in Oxfordshire. DHSS grant-aided private nursing homes often provide poor care and rely on part-time, very low paid workers (Phillips and Vincent, 1986).

Private hospital provision has developed largely in response to the demands from people covered by private health insurance. Since 1979 the number of individuals covered has more than doubled. A particularly important factor in the increase has been employment-related membership of health insurance schemes, with private employers offering insurance in 'employment packages', and some trade unions have negotiated reduced subscriptions for their members. In the 1980s there was a 54 per cent increase in the number of private beds outside the NHS and the number of private hospitals rose by 35 per cent (Higgins, 1988a). The increases, however, have been from a small base. Less than 10 per cent of the population of Britain had private health insurance in 1988, and beds in private hospitals accounted for only 3 per cent of all acute beds. The size of the private health sector is thus comparable with that in education and is far smaller than the private sector of the housing market.

The likelihood of belonging to an insurance scheme and benefiting from private treatment is inversely related to needs. As a group the insured tend to be healthier than average and to require less treatment. This is a reflection partly of their social class but also of the policy of the insurance companies who are concerned to minimise their risks and maximise their profits. The chronically sick are usually unable to obtain cover, and many expensive forms of treatment are not available privately. The greatest beneficiaries of private medicine are middle-aged men from social classes I and II and their dependants. Just over 1 per cent of classes IV and V and 3 per cent of class III have private health insurance compared with almost 25 per cent of social classes I and II.

Changes to the employment contracts of NHS consultants in 1980 encouraged the growth of the private sector. From that date full-time hospital doctors were permitted to undertake private practice. Although few health authorities keep accurate records, it has been estimated that 85 per cent of all hospital consultants in 1988 treated some private patients and that their additional earnings from the private sector averaged £30,000 per annum (Higgins, 1988a). The arrangement imposes large costs on the NHS. Consultants' time is lost and many consultants operate on their private patients in NHS hospitals, where support services are good, and then discharge them for convalescence to the private sector.

The NHS suffers from the loss of a small number of nurses each year to the private sector. But in a general sense, too, the National Health Service suffers from the view that private-sector medicine should be encouraged. The relationship of staff and patients, and co-operation between the different categories of staff, medical and non-medical, are adversely affected by the moves towards private provision. Many ancillary workers, for example, affected by the privatisation of laundry, catering and cleaning, feel that there has been a qualitative change in the nature of their work, as well as changes in wage rates and terms and conditions of service. Rather than being an integral part of a caring system, they now recognise that they are casual workers (Hunt, 1987). The advantages of moving towards private provision are not clear. International comparisons show that the idea that private-sector medicine will benefit the majority of people needing health care is incorrect. Higgins (1988a) has shown that the growth of the private sector alters the balance of control over health provision, shifting power towards insurance companies and employers whose overriding motive is profit. Consequently certain forms of health care are overprovided, whereas others become a scarce commodity. International comparisons show the NHS in a good light. Compared with the United States, for example, the NHS has lower administrative costs, more effective cost-containment, provides better value for money and results in equally favourable, if not better, health outcomes. In the USA, administrative costs alone accounted for over 20 per cent of total spending in 1988, compared with 3.8 per cent for administration in the NHS. However, a number of alternatives to the current method of financing health provision remained under active consideration at the end of the 1980s.

Internal markets

In an internal market, the District Health Authorities within each region would no longer be the providers of health but would become agencies for buying or arranging health care. At the beginning of each year, the authority would be given a cash allocation and would shop around amongst health care providers – both public and private hospitals and clinics – wherever costs were lowest or waiting-lists shortest. Each of the providers would be in competition for patients. Each would be free to set its own charges and determine its own specialities. Despite the purported advantages of the scheme – that competition reduces costs and equalises waiting-lists across the country – the National Association of Health Authorities and the NHS Management Board consider the proposals would lead to greater inefficiency and inequality. There would be an enormously increased administrative burden in recording and billing each item to different health authorities. But, more important, an internal market would return the NHS to a system similar to that before 1948. Richer parts of the country attracted a disproportionate share of resources, GPs and the better-endowed teaching hospitals. It has already been shown that geographic inequalities are a significant element in health differences and that they are hard to eradicate. Even now, there are marked differences in, for example, the age of hospitals in different parts of the country and consequently in their maintenance and running costs. Hence, the level of profits in each district would vary. It is unclear whether profits would be redistributed across the country as a whole or accrue to each individual district or region.

Alternative funding

Various methods of alternative funding have been suggested and several have already been introduced. The proposals are principally of two kinds: either charities or lotteries raising money for the NHS or methods of charging patients and selling services.

Encouragement of charity is an important element in the Conservative government's strategy for the health and social services. On a visit to Great Ormond Street Hospital for Sick Children in London in April 1988, Mrs Thatcher said, 'The voluntary spirit of personal giving is part of the British character. You should never denigrate it. It is one of the things that made Britain the country that it is' (*The Times*, 28 April 1988). The Hospital for Sick Children has launched an enormous and relatively successful appeal for funds, necessitated by underfunding. In 1983 Tadworth Court, an annexe of the hospital, had to be sold to a private charitable trust. This trust refused to recognise the NHS unions and wage structure and said that wage rates would have to depend on the state of their finances.

Charitable appeals, of themselves, are an important opportunity for the public to support particular causes. However, if charities become substitutes for, instead of supplements to, adequate government funding a number of difficult issues are raised. These include whether charitable funds should be used to pay wages and meet the costs of running the basic infrastructure rather than for specific items of equipment or specialised research; how to maintain rational planning and overall provision when certain types of medicine attract charitable support more easily than others; how to maintain an even geographic spread of services (the children's hospital in Manchester was shocked to discover in 1988 that the Great Ormond Street Wishing Well appeal was diverting charitable funds for sick children from their region to London). As well as the danger of diminishing returns if a series of appeals are launched successively or in competition, an increased reliance on charity raises philosophical questions about the rights of citizens to free, universal health care without the indignity of having to depend on the charity of others.

Raising funds by an NHS lottery has also been suggested. MP Simon Burns introduced a Ten Minute Rule bill in 1986 to initiate a national lottery. It was defeated but despite this a scheme was launched in 1988 which the Home Office, at the request of the Gaming Board, were in the process of investigating at the end of that year. Raising funds by lotteries leads to the same questions about distribution as are raised by charitable funds, with the additional question of who profits, and to what extent, from organising the lottery.

Charging for services

A number of methods of increasing the amount that individuals contribute directly to their health care have been suggested. The disadvantages of private medical insurance were outlined in a preceding section. However, the Government plans to increase the proportion of the population currently covered by proposals such as tax concessions and vouchers for health. Both systems will involve the strengthening of a two-tier health system and result in differential access to care based on ability to pay. The schemes also introduce a distinction between public services which individuals may choose to opt out of – similar proposals for the education service will be outlined in the next section – and those which remain universal such as defence.

Additional income-generation schemes are also under consideration. They include the provision for sale of a wide range of services such as hairdressing, banking and meals. Provision of a wider range of services for patients may be beneficial. However, it is important that the basic and free provision of services such as meals is not undermined. It is also proposed that clinical services should be sold. Items not routinely available such as cancer screening may be offered in NHS hospitals to private individuals, from Britain or abroad, or to firms. The only existing large-scale sale of services – pay beds – has not been successful, but even if profits were generated by the sale of other services it is not clear whether individual authorities would retain them as additional income or whether the Treasury would reduce its contribution. In the autumn statement of 1987, for example, the Chancellor calculated an amount health authorities were expected to raise for themselves and deducted this from the Government's contribution. Whatever proposals are introduced, it is clear that the idea of a universal state-funded health service is under attack.

FURTHER READING

The Black Report is probably the most important document that has been published about health since the establishment of the NHS. It is available in paperback, edited by Townsend and Davidson (1982). In 1988 it was reprinted with *The Health Divide* (Whitehead, 1988) as a single volume entitled *Inequalities in Health* (Penguin, London).

An edited collection by Wilkinson (1986) provides further information about class differences in health, and Culyer and Jonsson (1986) is a comparison of alternative forms of provision.

Critical perspectives on the health service and the medical profession are to be found in two books, both published by Pluto Press in 1979 but still relevant today. They are Doyal (1979) and Ehrenreich and English (1979).

The *Lancet*, despite being a 'house' journal, often contains interesting articles on social aspects of medicine and health that are accessible to the layperson.

10

Divisions in Education
Linda McDowell

THE EDUCATION SYSTEM

As with the health service, at the end of the 1980s, questions about universal provision, alternative sources of funding and the opportunity to opt out of state-provided services are under discussion in the education system. In both schools and the higher education system, new forms of provision and funding are proposed. These challenge the assumptions of a school system that, in the main, owes its features to reforms introduced in the immediately post-war period and a higher education system that was expanded in the 1960s.

The history of school provision

Throughout the nineteenth century the state gradually extended its intervention in schooling, originally provided mainly by charitable institutions and the church. The motives for intervention were mixed. Some were moral and political. They included a desire to instil social deference and the 'right' attitudes in the growing working class, the fear of the propaganda of 'agitators' succeeding because of the ignorance of the mass of the population, and a strong impulse to encourage Christian morality with its message of accepting one's lot in this life. Other motives were economic. As the century progressed, for example, there was a growing need for a more highly educated workforce. In 1870 an Education Act was passed establishing in principle the right of every child to some form of schooling. School boards were set up to provided non-denominational elementary schools, financed from local rates and central government grants. Board schools co-existed with voluntary, often church-run, schools which received increased state funding. By 1900, 54 per cent of children were educated in board schools. Initially, children were charged fees for attendance but they were virtually abolished for elementary schooling in 1891.

Secondary education was not introduced for the majority until the twentieth century. Higher schools were established under the 1902 Act and extended in 1916. A report in 1926 firmly established the division at eleven between elementary and secondary education. In the inter-war years, however, education was a minor part of government's intervention in social policy and there were no major Education Acts between 1918 and 1944.

The 1944 Education Act was introduced by R. A. Butler and hence is often known as the Butler Act. When debated in Parliament not a single vote against the proposals was recorded. According to Fraser's (1973) history of this period, the Act represented a 'brave attempt to create some system in English education after decades of more pragmatic evolution'. A Ministry of Education was set up and charged with developing a national education system. The term 'elementary', with its pejorative overtones, was dropped in favour of three stages of educational development: primary, secondary and further. All local education authorities – replacing school boards – were to provide all stages, and fees for state schools were abolished. Education became compulsory and free for all children between the ages of five and fifteen, the school-leaving age in 1945. The Act also included a provision to raise the school-leaving age to sixteen as soon as possible, an action that was in fact delayed until 1972.

The voluntary – or maintained – church sector was brought under stricter control. The Act also made provision for nursery schools and colleges of further education catering for sixteen-to-eighteen-year-olds on a part-time basis. The system of state provision was established alongside the existing private sector – rather misleadingly called 'public schools'. Until the introduction of the comprehensive reorganisation programme from 1965, there was also an intermediate category of direct-grant schools, partly funded by the state but also reliant on private money and fee income.

One of the stated aims of the 1944 Education Act was to reduce the class differentials in access to education. 'Secondary Education for All' became a rallying cry in the Labour Party. As R. H. Tawney persuasively argued in 1931, 'The hereditary curse upon English education is its organisation upon lines of social class' (quoted in Halsey et al., 1980). Post-war education policy was based on an attempt to reduce inequality of opportunity and the associated waste of talents and also to continue to imbue all children with the values of a shared culture. It had one further aim: to make the education system responsive to the needs of the economy. In the event, the goals of social justice and economic efficiency proved hard to reconcile.

Until the advent of comprehensive schools in the 1960s, secondary education was provided in three distinct ways – in grammar, technical and secondary modern schools. This tripartite division, although not laid down in the 1944 Act, had been proposed in earlier reports, particularly the Spens Report 1938, and confirmed by the Norwood Committee in 1943. The three types of school were believed to fit neatly with the aptitudes of different groups of children. They were set up to have 'parity of esteem' and to offer children comparable, if distinct, opportunities. Each type of school was intended to be of equal merit but, in the event, the tripartite division proved to strengthen rather than challenge class differentials in education and in Britain as a whole.

The division was based on meritocratic conceptions of social justice. In post-war Britain, poised for economic expansion and fired by beliefs in scientific rationality, it was argued that ability, which it was assumed could be accurately measured on IQ scales, should be rewarded and encouraged. Children with high IQs, whatever their class background, were to benefit from a grammar-school education and possibly a university education. Those with lesser abilities would be more appropriately educated in technical colleges and secondary modern schools. These educational divisions were believed by policy-makers to be appropriate to the new, more complex, social division of labour that was developing with its growing need for managers and technicians as well as less skilled workers.

Equality of schooling: comprehensive reform

The liberal theory of equality of opportunity that lay behind the 1944 Education Act has been criticised. Its limitations in a fundamentally unequal society have led critics to suggest that 'positive discrimination' is needed to overcome initial differences between children from different backgrounds (Young, 1958; Plowden, 1967). Sociologist Pierre Bourdieu (1974) has been a strong advocate of educational priority programmes. He argues that children enter schools unequally endowed with 'cultural capital' and that schooling then reinforces the initial inequalities. Similar arguments are made about the 'middle-class bias' of the language and curriculum content of conventional education (Bernstein, 1977). Children from working-class backgrounds do not possess the cultural attributes associated with a middle-class family background and so are less likely to achieve educational success. Such critics believe that the aim of education policy should be to achieve educational equality between children from different class backgrounds rather than equality of opportunity.

The debate about the aims of education has taken a particular form in Britain. It has centred on a battle over comprehensive education in which it is assumed that meritocracy and selectivity are bedfellows as are equality and comprehensives, although this is by no means self-evident. In the mid-1960s a programme was initiated to replace the tripartite system of schools with a single local comprehensive school with a wide catchment area. In 1965, 92 per cent of the state secondary school children were in schools organised on tripartite lines. Ten years later, three-quarters were in comprehensive schools. The arguments behind the transition had both educational and social content. The 11-plus examination used to separate children into grammar schools and others had come to be regarded as an inappropriate method of selection as children develop at different rates. A single hurdle, albeit with a second chance at thirteen, meant that it was difficult for the late developer to change streams. On social grounds, comprehensive schools were seen as a way of reducing class and racial divisions in Britain, as children from diverse backgrounds would be educated together. In addition, the tripartite system had not served the economy well and the comprehensive system was seen to be a better way of producing skilled and flexible workers.

The comprehensive programme was introduced at a varying pace by local education authorities – school education remains a local government responsibility, although the 1988 Education Act enables schools to 'opt out' of local control and also increases central government influence through the introduction of a national curriculum. Even now, its success is still difficult to evaluate as in many areas the supporters of grammar schools fought a long rearguard action. Indeed, selective grammar schools still exist in several areas and many comprehensive schools continue to bear the legacy of their previous role as either a grammar or secondary modern school. In addition, there is a significant private sector. Residential segregation, with neighbourhoods occupied by households with common social characteristics, also hinders the achievement of a wide social diversity among the pupils of comprehensive schools. Schools tend to reflect the class composition of their catchment areas.

Opponents of the principle of comprehensive education continue to advocate testing and selectivity. They argue that clever working-class children in deprived areas have little or no opportunity for an academic education and that, in general, equality, as opposed to equality of opportunity, means a levelling-down of achievement. The right-wing Black Papers (not to be confused with the Black Report on health) published in 1975 (Cox and Boyson, 1975) are the best-known example of the attack on comprehensive education. One of the editors, Caroline Cox, has been influential in more recent debates about reintroducing a greater element of selectivity into schools, whereas Boyson was for a time in the 1980s a junior minister at the Department of Education and Science.

Behind the arguments for selectivity is a belief that the abilities and learning potential of different groups in society are psychologically or genetically determined rather than a reflection of cultural factors: opposing views often encapsulated in the terms 'nature v. nurture' or 'hereditary v. environment'. The work of Jensen (1973) and Eysenck (1971) is often cited as evidence that educational ability is genetically determined, although the validity of the latter's research results have been questioned. Counterarguments are found in the work of Douglas (1964 and 1968) and Jencks et al. (1972) highlighting the importance of home background, and Rutter *et al.* (1979) who found significant differences between the achievements of schools within the same authority regardless of the class background of their intake.

Inequality in education

Several studies indicate a marked persistence of interlocking sets of social inequalities in Britain (Brown, 1983; Rutter and Madge, 1976). Social class has continued to be associated with length of education and levels of achievement. The class background of university students, for example, has changed little in the post-war period, although the number of students has increased. A thorough examination of the links between social class and equality of educational opportunity, based on a large data set, was published in 1980 by A. H. Halsey and his colleagues. Their work was based on the personal and educational biographies of 10,000 men living in England and Wales in 1972 which were collected as part of a large-scale survey of social mobility in Britain since the war. Five questions lay behind Halsey's study: What have been the class differences in access to education? How far has the British education system achieved its professed goal of meritocracy? What is the relative importance of different factors such as IQ, social class and cultural capital in attaining educational success? What are the likely consequences of comprehensive reform for achievement of goals such as equality of opportunity and equality of results? Is the structure of the education system important?

Based on comparisons of four cohorts of men born at different dates between 1913 and 1952, the study compared the relationship between social class and educational opportunity over time. The first two groups of men had been to school before 1944, the other two after. Taking into account the overall expansion of places in universities and selective schools since the war, Halsey *et al.* found that the rate of increase of student numbers remained almost constant between classes. The consequence is that class differentials in access to university remained unchanged over the forty-year period. The sons of fathers in social classes I and II held on to their disproportionate share of educational resources.

In an effort to establish the causes of inequality in education, the authors separated material factors, measured by income levels, from cultural background or, in Bourdieu's terms, 'cultural capital'. Cultural factors were measured on the basis of the parents' educational level, on the assumption that children of 'educated' parents would be more predisposed towards educational success as well as being assisted by their parents in coping with the system. Up to the age of eleven, cultural background was found to be the most important factor influencing a boy's progress; after that age, income became important. Working-class parents are less able to bear the cost of keeping their sons in education after the school leaving age.

When evaluating the impact of type of school, Halsey *et al.* found, contrary to US evidence (Jencks *et al.*, 1972), that the type of secondary school attended was important. Boys at secondary modern schools were far more likely to leave school as early as possible than boys from either grammar or public schools; whereas boys at public, direct-grant and grammar schools in descending order were more likely to gain O- and A-level passes or their equivalent. The differences, however, were largely a reflection of the social composition of the entrants. Controlling for social class, an individual at any of the selective schools was equally likely to achieve examination success, but the proportion of boys so doing was higher in public and direct-grant schools than in state-maintained schools because of the class composition of such schools.

The authors concluded their work with a note of cautious optimism despite the fact that the results of their survey confirmed the still-enormous significance of social class and family background for children's educational success. They hoped that the transition from a tripartite system to a comprehensive one would reduce educational inequality, while recognising the continue importance of the private sector. In the words of the authors: 'the private schools . . . exact their uncalculated but enormous toll of reduced political pressure from middle-class parents, of stimulus from expert teachers and response from motivated pupils. The private market starves the comprehensives of the resources they need to attain high standards.' In addition, they recognised that the combination of residential segregation and streaming within individual schools tends to reproduce previous patterns of class-based inequality.

Since Halsey's work, spending on the state education system has not risen as fast as in earlier decades. Government expenditure on education in the United Kingdom as a proportion of GDP fell in the 1980s from 5.5 per cent to 4.8 per cent between 1980–1 and 1985–6. Overall state spending on education has remained almost static in real terms in the decade between 1978 and 1988, rising from £18.4 million at the first date to £19.9 million ten years later, but falling to a low of £15.7 million in the financial year 1982–3. Local authority expenditure accounts for the major part of total education expenditure (£15 million out of a total of £17.5 million in 1985–6). In the country as a whole, the average state expenditure on a primary-school pupil in the school year 1985–6 was £815, on a secondary-school pupil it was £1175, but there are considerable variations around these averages. The prospect of school reorganisation, entailing greater selectivity and the introduction of opportunities for schools to 'opt out' of the local system altogether with central funding will increase the variations between areas.

In Table 10.1 the actual and projected numbers and distribution of school pupils are shown. The number of primary-school children increased slightly in 1986 and is

TABLE 10.1 *Pupils by Type of School, United Kingdom, 1961–91 (thousands)*

	No. at January of each year				Projection
	1961	1971	1981	1986	1991
Public-sector schools					
Nursery schools	31	50	89	96	100
Primary schools	4906	5902	5171	4635	4864
Secondary schools	3165	3555	4606	4080	3473
Assisted and independent schools	680	621	619	607	543
Special schools	77	103	147	128	113

Source: *Social Trends*, 18 (1988).

projected to continue to do so until 1998 whereas numbers in secondary schools fell between 1981 and 1986 and are projected to continue to do so until 1991, when they will begin to rise again. The fall in the numbers of school leavers has led to anxieties in several areas of the economy. An extremely high proportion of the girls leaving school at the end of the 1980s, for example, would have to be recruited into nursing to maintain the required numbers in the profession. In 1988 an advertising campaign to recruit both young men and young women into nursing was launched. In the same year, the Council for British Industry expressed worries about the shortfall in graduate recruits in many areas of the economy at a time when employment opportunities for graduates are increasing. In Table 10.2 the effect of the comprehensive programme is revealed in the changing structure of secondary education. The majority of children by the mid-1980s were educated in comprehensive schools. The non-maintained (that is, public) schools provided places for 6.9 per cent of all pupils – a proportion that had risen from 5.8 per cent in 1976. Class sizes in public schools (Table 10.2) have consistently been smaller than in state

TABLE 10.2 *Pupils in Secondary Education, England and Wales, 1971–86 (percentages and thousands)*

	1971		1981		1986	
Maintained secondary schools	E	W	E	W	E	W
Middle deemed secondary	1.9	0.1	7.0	0.1	6.6	0.1
Modern	38.0	22.3	6.0	1.8	4.2	0.6
Grammar	18.4	15.4	3.4	1.3	3.0	0.5
Technical	1.3	–	0.3	–	0.1	–
Comprehensive	34.4	58.5	82.5	96.6	85.4	98.5
Other	6.0	3.7	0.9	0.3	0.7	0.3
TOTAL PUPILS	2953	191	3840	240	3389	218

Source: *Social Trends*, 18 (1988).

TABLE 10.3 *Pupil–Teacher Ratios, United Kingdom, 1971–86 (numbers)*

	1971	1981	1986
Public-sector schools			
Nursery	26.6	21.5	21.7
Primary	27.1	22.3	22.0
Secondary	17.8	16.4	15.2
All public-sector schools	23.2	19.0	18.5
Non-maintained schools	14.0	13.2	11.6
Special schools	10.5	7.5	6.7
All schools	22.0	18.2	17.4

Source: *Social Trends*, 18 (1988).

schools, although in both sectors the fall in the numbers of secondary-school pupils has been reflected in declining class-sizes since 1971.

As pupils attending the remaining grammar schools and most independent schools are selected on the basis of educational ability (as well as their parents' ability to pay the fees of private-sector schools), their likelihood of leaving school with examination qualifications is greater than for pupils attending comprehensive schools which draw on a wider ability-range. The proportion of all school leavers with at least one GCE O-level pass or equivalent, however, has risen over time. In the decade 1976 to 1986, for example, the proportion of male leavers with this level of achievement rose from 49 per cent to 53 per cent; while among female school leavers it rose from 53 per cent to 59 per cent. In 1988 a new single examination to replace the O-level and CSE system was introduced – the GCSE examination. It is designed to encourage pupils of all abilities to follow suitable courses

TABLE 10.4 *School Leavers: Highest Qualification by Sex, United Kingdom, 1975–76 and 1985–86 (percentages and thousands)*

	Boys		Girls	
	1975/76	1985/86	1975/76	1985/86
Percentage with 2 or more A levels/3 or more H grades	14.3	14.9	12.1	14.2
1 A level/1 or 2 H grades	3.5	3.6	4.0	4.3
5 or more O levels (grades A to C)	7.2	10.0	9.4	11.9
1 to 4 O levels (grades A to C)	23.9	24.4	27.0	28.7
1 or more O levels (grades D or E) or CSE (grades 2 to 5)	29.9	34.0	28.4	30.9
No GCE/SCE or CSE	21.2	13.2	19.1	10.0
TOTAL SCHOOL LEAVERS	423	444	400	427

Source: Department of Education and Science.

and have them recognised with certificates. The GCE system was originally designed for the top 20 per cent of the ability range and CSE for the next 40 per cent. In the academic year 1985–6, however, almost 90 per cent of all school leavers achieved at least one graded result at either GCE or CSE (Table 10.4).

GENDER INEQUALITIES IN SCHOOLING

Halsey's study compared the educational experiences only of boys. In common with most studies of social mobility, it is assumed that the women's different pattern of attachment to the labour force over their life-time raises insoluble problems for analyses of the links between education and class position. There are significant differences between boys' and girls' school lives and their levels of educational achievement, although Table 10.4 shows that the gap between the examination achievement of boys and girls has narrowed over time. The percentage of school leavers with two or more A-level passes indicates the proportion of young people eligible for higher education: almost 15 per cent of the boys and just over 14 per cent of girls. But these aggregate figures conceal important gender differences in subject choice, at both O and A level. At O level girls are more likely than boys to take arts and language options and boys more likely than girls to obtain passes in maths and science, with the exception of biology which, perhaps because of its links with nursing, has long been regarded as an acceptable science option for girls. At A level similar differences are apparent and they are mirrored in the choice of subjects to study at degree level (Table 10.5). Women are proportionately far more concentrated in arts subjects.

Gender differences in access and subject choice reflect both societal attitudes about the appropriate roles for each sex and the nature and content of classroom

TABLE 10.5 *Higher-Education Qualifications: Subject Group, Type of Qualification and Sex, United Kingdom, 1985 (thousands)*

	Arts	Science	Education	Other	Total
Postgraduate					
Males	10	11	5	–	26
Females	6	3	6	–	15
First degree					
Males	36	38	2	4	80
Females	36	14	5	4	60
Below degree level					
Males	22	30	2	–	55
Females	15	7	2	–	25
All					
Males	67	80	9	4	161
Females	57	24	14	4	99

Source: Department of Education and Science.

teaching and the curriculum. Spender and Sarah (1980) and Stanworth (1983) have demonstrated how in mixed schools boys command the lion's share of the teachers' attention and that teachers tend to use materials that more closely relate to and reflect boys' experience. The content of the curriculum often excludes or trivialises women and their concerns. Girls educated in single-sex schools tend to achieve better examination grades and, within mixed schools, it has been shown that their achievements are higher in maths and science subjects when they are taught separately.

Gender inequalities in higher and further education

Despite the small differences in the numbers of boys and girls gaining two or more A levels, significantly more

TABLE 10.6 *Higher Education – Full-Time Students by Origin, Sex and Age, United Kingdom, 1970–85 (thousands)*

	Males			Females		
	1970	1980	1985	1970	1980	1985
UK students						
Universities	152.2	165.8	156.8	65.0	107.5	113.7
Polytechnics	102.0	111.9	143.5	113.1	96.4	132.2
From abroad	20.0	40.7	38.4	4.4	12.6	15.3

Source: Department of Education and Science.

eighteen-year-old boys enter higher-education, although the gender differential has narrowed over time. Women accounted for 41 per cent of all higher education students (full- and part-time) in 1985–6 compared with 33 per cent in 1970–1. Table 10.6 shows the distribution of full-time students between institutions, their origins and their sex. Gender differences are even more marked at the post-graduate than the undergraduate level: 26,000 men were awarded a postgraduate degree in 1985 compared with 15,000 women. At first-degree level, the respective figures were 80,000 and 60,000. On vocational, non-advanced and day-release courses, women are even more in a minority.

THE STRUCTURE OF HIGHER EDUCATION

The higher education system in Britain in the late 1980s more nearly mirrors the tripartite school system of the immediately post-war decades than the current comprehensive system. Higher education for all has never been a rallying cry, and in the mid-1980s only about 10 per cent of all nineteen-to-twenty-four-year-olds were full-time students, 14 per cent of the age group received some form of higher education. As the previous section showed, fewer women than men continue with full-time study after school and the British proportions compare unfavourably with those for other West European countries (Table 10.7).

TABLE 10.7 *Full-Time Students Aged 19 to 24 as Percentages of the Age Cohort, European Comparisons, 1970–86*

	Women				Men			
	1970–1	1975–6	1980–1	1985–6	1970–1	1975–6	1980–1	1985–6
Belgium	11	15	19	25	18	20	23	28
Denmark	16	25	24	26	22	27	24	26
West Germany	10	16	18	21	18	25	24	27
Greece	7	11	12	–	15	18	16	–
Spain	6	12	17	24	17	21	21	24
France	13	18	20	25	17	20	20	24
Ireland	7	8	11	14	13	13	14	16
Italy	11	16	19	19	17	25	24	20
Netherlands	7	11	14	17	18	23	25	24
Portugal	8	9	9	–	9	10	11	–
United Kingdom	7	9	9	9	11	13	12	12

Source: Eurostat.

British students may study at degree level in one of three types of institution – universities, polytechnics and higher education colleges. In addition, further education – that is, non-degree level – is provided at a range of other types of college. Until the mid-1960s, universities catered for the small elite of middle-class children and a tiny number of working-class children of exceptional ability who won scholarships. Until the universal system of maintenance grants introduced early in the 1960s most students were reliant on their parents for financial support. For the less academically able, teacher-training colleges provided non-degree-level higher education, viewed as particularly appropriate for women. Finally, further-education colleges which grew out of the enormous post-war expansion of technical colleges in the 1940s and 1950s not only incorporated training (that is vocationally orientated courses) for workers but also admitted the overflow from universities. Although not offering degrees now, further-education colleges used to do so. In 1956 a White Paper legitimised the expansion of degree-level education outside the universities by initiating the Colleges of Advanced Technology (CATs), later to be incorporated into the university system. An elite of nine CATs, later to become ten with the addition of Brunel in 1962, were established and the remaining technical colleges became 'regional' colleges overseen by the National Council for Technological Awards. These colleges were the forerunners of the present polytechnics.

In 1961 the Robbins Committee was set up in response to the rising demand for higher education. The scale of post-war technological development, particularly in the USA and the USSR, had become apparent to the British government of the time who saw the need to modernise British industry. In addition, increased affluence and the expansion of white-collar employment, the 'embourgeoisement' of the working class, led to increased numbers of people who aspired to higher education for themselves or for their children. The Robbins Report in 1963 recommended the upgrading of the ten CATs to universities to fulfil the first set of demands, and the establishment of several small, new collegiate universities, in the mould of Oxbridge, to meet the latter.

The Robbins Report recommended that the regional technical colleges should be able to provide degrees, not merely diplomas, for all courses, not just technology, by a variety of methods of study, full- and part-time and sandwich courses. The degrees were to be granted by the Council for National Academic Awards (CNAA). Although Robbins intended that some of these colleges were eventually to become universities (he suggested ten by 1980), in the event they became the polytechnics, established under the binary policy for higher education introduced by the Labour government in the 1966 White Paper. Sixty colleges of technology, building, art and commerce were incorporated into thirty new polytechnics. The new institutions were not to emulate the university pattern but to cater for a wide range of student ability and subjects, drawing on a regional catchment area and responding to local industrial needs. One of the criticisms of their development over the following twenty years has been that they have not succeeded in this aim but have concentrated to a large extent on degree-level work.

The university and polytechnic systems have, until 1988, been financed and administered in distinct ways. The polytechnics – often known as the public sector of higher education despite universities also being funded mainly by the state – were administered by local authorities and jointly funded by central and local government. Their degrees are awarded by the CNAA. The universities, or the autonomous sector, with the exception of the Open University, received their funds from the University Grants Committee, a state-funded body mainly composed of representatives from universities. Each university awards its own degrees under royal charter.

Access to university increased from the mid-1960s, although, as already noted, the intake remained predominantly middle-class. The establishment of the new universities was reflected in the rise of the proportion of eighteen-year-olds at university from 4 per cent in 1959 to 7 per cent in 1968. The growth of the polytechnics added to the increase in the numbers studying at degree level. By 1985 there were nearly five times as many full-time students as thirty years earlier (almost 600,000 in total). However, as already indicated in Table 8.11, this number is low compared to other countries of a comparable size, such as France and West Germany. In Britain, the universities, in particular, have maintained a restrictive attitude to the range of subjects permissible. In addition, they have tended to hold on to an exclusive concept of the ideal student and type of study – full-time degree courses for school leavers. Robinson (1968) argued that this restriction is 'part of the characteristic boarding school tradition of British universities which is still very much alive' (p. 47). The establishment of the new universities in the 1960s as campus-based, often collegiate, institutions in small towns such as Colchester, York and Lancaster revealed the ideal model of a university. Nothing could have more clearly suggested the disdain of universities for mass-educational provision in large industrial centres. This – obviously inferior – task was to be left to the polytechnics. One partial response to the needs of other types of student – older, in work, needing credit transfers or vocational updating – was the foundation of the Open University in 1969 (Tunstall, 1974) which complemented the work of Birkbeck College in London, the only university offering part-time and evening study.

The basic features of the binary divide remained intact until the coincidence of a radical right government interested in investigating alternative methods of funding to reduce state expenditure on higher education and a decline in the number of eighteen-year-olds opened up a new discussion about accessibility. In their use of the term, however, the Government and the institutions of higher education had different aims. The former wanted value for money, the latter more students, or at least to maintain their numbers. The period of rapid expansion had long come to an end and the universities and polytechnics were beginning to feel the need to look at different types of student to sustain their demand for more places and funds.

It was from the early 1970s that the change in the climate, from expansion to retraction, may be dated. The key principle of the Robbins Report, that higher education should be open to all those qualified to enter, was augmented by a debate about the links between higher education and the needs of the economy. The Government began to demand economically useful skills and relevant training. Early in the 1970s, a White Paper (DES, 1972) contained the indication that higher education 'should be related more directly to the decisions which will face them [students] in their careers'. By 1985 this hint had hardened to a demand, made by William Waldegrave, then Minister for Higher Education, in a speech at Bristol Polytechnic (May 1985), that 'government, industry and the higher education system *must* [my emphasis] work together to match the output of qualified personnel with industry's needs'.

New forms of financing and control over universities and polytechnics were proposed, some of which were introduced throughout the 1980s. The University Grants Committee began a major restructuring of the universities from 1981. Financial cuts were made and the performance of departments and institutions ranked and monitored. Greater selectivity was the key word and the concentration of high-level teaching and research in a small number of elite institutions was proposed. In the public sector the National Advisory Body for local authority higher education (as it then was) was created in 1982 to allocate students and funds to public-sector colleges and polytechnics. In 1987, these institutions became 'independent' when they were removed from local authority control. At the same time two new funding bodies were created to oversee the universities and polytechnics, each with strong commercial and industrial representation. Funds were to be allocated by contracts rather than by grants. Institutions have to bid for funds which they may lose if they fail to deliver the promised service.

An innovation is the involvement of the Government's training agency (formerly the Manpower Services Commission) in higher education, rather than restricting its attention to training at non-advanced levels. Funds will be available for 'enterprise' at undergraduate level and for courses in new technology and in areas where skills shortages have been identified.

Many of these changes challenge the conventional definition of academic freedom. Institutions are no longer completely free to choose what they teach, success is increasingly measured by economic criteria, and wares have to be marketed to bolster revenue. This increases pressure to concentrate on particular subjects at the expense of 'less relevant' areas. The ability of the Government to persuade the universities and polytechnics to teach what it thinks industry and commerce need is also debatable. It is difficult to predict future industrial needs, as the history of the MSC's different training schemes in the decade and a half of its existence illustrates. TOPs and YOPs have risen and fallen (see Figure 7.6) and there have been many programmes of youth training with different aims, titles and contents. In many cases colleges and local authorities have started courses and recruited staff only to find government funding withdrawn before alternative sources could be identified.

Student loans

Late in 1988, the conclusions of a two-year review of student support were published. The Government proposed to change the system of mandatory maintenance grants on cost grounds. The change was justified by an ideological commitment to greater self-reliance and independence in society generally and a policy of 'targeting' benefits by selective payments to those in greater need rather than by providing universal benefits. The Government justifies the change in terms of expanding higher education. It is argued that neither parents nor the state should be expected to fund any further increase in student numbers. Rather, loans will provide the necessary flexibility to cope with a more diverse range of entrants as the number of school leavers falls.

The White Paper outlining the new system, to be introduced from 1990, ran into considerable opposition. Ranked against the scheme were the university vice-chancellors, the directors of polytechnics, the National Union of Students and the unions representing teaching staff. The Confederation of British Industry expressed scepticism and the banks who were to run the scheme were angry at the lack of consultation with their representatives.

Several arguments against loans may be raised. These include the suggestion that the participation of women, ethnic minorities, mature students and students from disadvantaged backgrounds will be discouraged; that the differential rewards of certain jobs and careers will influence subject choice; that students would have to work part-time as they studied and so their work would suffer; that the costs will be passed on to employers in demands for higher salaries; and that the administration of repayment schemes would be cumbersome and costly. The Government's response to many of these criticisms was an annexe to the White Paper in which it was argued that as repayments were to be linked to earnings students would not be deterred. In particular it was promised that women would not have to repay their loan while out of the labour market raising a family, nor would the loan be means-tested against spouses' incomes. The argument that working-class students would be deterred by loans was dismissed as 'an unproved cultural assumption', while mature students were assumed to have additional resources. The annexe pointed out that all social classes currently are dependent on credit. In other countries where student loans and part-time work while studying are common, drop-out rates are much higher than is currently the case in Britain. This is especially so in the USA, where defaulting on loan repayments is also a problem. However, the Government believes that low drop-out rates in Britain are 'not necessarily a product of the present grant regime'. It is pointed out that, with top-up loans, students would lose more if they failed to complete their studies. Defaulters would be prosecuted, although repayments may be deferred if income falls.

It is thus clear that the White Paper challenges conventional ideas about the nature of higher education. Further radical change is also proposed. One system under discussion is vouchers for education, for schooling and higher education. The proposal is similar to that for vouchers for health.

Voucher schemes

The basic feature of voucher schemes is that each eligible individual would be able to claim a voucher entitling a certain number of years of education (or access to health care). These vouchers are tradable and, in certain variants of the plan, may be topped up through individual contributions or by insurance schemes. The adherents of vouchers believe that they provide a means of responding to demand for particular types of education or course. Popular schools, colleges, polytechnics and universities would be able to expand as students trade their vouchers in for education in these institutions, whereas unpopular places would have to close.

There are arguments for and against the voucher system. In the case of higher education, for example, the Government argues that it will give to universities and polytechnics the greater autonomy which they have long argued for. A corollary may be reduced state funding. The university vice-chancellors and polytechnic directors who believe vouchers will bring greater autonomy, however, may find that this is not the case. From a leaked paper by Robert Jackson, Minister for Higher Education in 1988, it became clear that the Treasury will insist on allocating vouchers according to its estimations of future needs for particular skills. A quota system, for example, for doctors, dentists, scientists and engineers is proposed.

There is nothing inherent in the idea of vouchers *per se* that entails particular consequences. Supporters of vouchers from other political persuasions argue that they may be used selectively to discriminate positively in favour of categories of student who currently are not well represented in higher education. Working-class or black students may be encouraged by offering them 'enhanced' vouchers. The ideological complexion of the Conservative government in power at the end of the 1980s makes it more likely that ability to pay will be the main, if not the sole, criterion of a voucher top-up scheme. An element of admission according to ability to pay already exists as several universities and polytechnics admit overseas students, for whom they charge higher fees, with lower grades than home students.

Schools for the future?

It is not only higher education that is being restructured. At the end of the 1980s the extent and structure of state provision of school education is also being reassessed. Despite the ideological commitment of the Conservative administrations in power since 1979 to market provision and reduce the role of the state, less than 10 per cent of all schoolchildren were educated in the private sector at the end of the 1980s. However, questions about a greater degree of selectivity in state schools, about increasing the involvement of parents as governors, about the introduction and content of a new national curriculum and the freedom of teachers to raise 'controversial' issues such as sexual preferences or nuclear power are being raised.

In the Education Reform Bill introduced during 1987 a clause to allow schools to opt out of local authority control was introduced. It seems clear that central government sees local authorities and teachers as some-how having abused their power and failed to provide an education appropriate for most children in the last decades of the twentieth century. It appears as if the option will raise a difficult dilemma for the Secretary of State for Education. Although only a small number of schools had indicated their intention to opt out at the end of 1988, the majority of them were under threat of closure by the local education authorities because of falling school rolls. Both closure and opt-out plans go to the Secretary of State for decision and the merits of individual cases against plans for total state provision in an area have to be decided.

The shape of the education system, and of the health service, in the 1990s will depend on the extent to which the third term of Conservative government under Margaret Thatcher results in a radical reassessment of the role of the market in the provision of previously collectively provided goods and services. The aims and success of 'Thatcherism' are evaluated in Chapter 13 where it is argued that several of the changes in policy since 1979 have longer antecedents than is commonly recognised. However, in the areas of education and health, there remains a fundamental difference between the Conservative administrations that have been in power since 1979 and the beliefs of the Labour opposition. A commitment to a free and universal health service and education system remains a central plank of the Labour Party's platform. The extent to which these services will be transformed in the 1990s will depend on the balance of political power. It is clear, however, that there remains strong popular support for the current method of provision, particularly in the health service. Despite this, the third Conservative government in the 1980s seems determined to introduce 'market' principles into the allocation and provision of health care, with proposals for cash-limited general practices and self-governing hospitals.

FURTHER READING

Nothing like the Black Report has been published on the education service, although the Plowden Report (1967) is an interesting document, if rather dated now. Burgess (1986) is a useful introduction to the sociology of education. Stanworth (1983) is a good, short introduction to the ways in which teachers treat boys and girls differently and Rutter *et al.* (1979) deals more generally with the impact of schools on their pupils. The study by Halsey *et al.* referred to in the chapter is an interesting study of mobility based on a sample of several thousand men and boys.

Finally the *Journal of Social Policy* published quarterly by the Social Administration Association often contains interesting articles about education and other areas of social policy, including health and housing.

PART 4

Politics and the State

11

Steered by the State?
Fred Gray

The state fulfils a number of basic roles. Of paramount importance is the maintenance and reproduction of society and of the state itself. This includes a number of tasks such as defence of territory, maintaining internal law and order, and regulating social and economic processes and change. This is achieved by the state exercising its power and authority.

States are not necessarily successful in these objectives. At an extreme, some states (such as those of Tsarist Russia, Nazi Germany and Socialist Chile) fail to ensure their own survival and are replaced by radically different systems of political authority. Moving from the level of epic struggle, for all its authority it is clear that state intervention may be ineffectual or unsuccessful. Part of the reason is that the state is not independent of society. As Coates (1984) puts it: 'the modern state faces a highly structured universe, from which it has to recruit its own personnel, from which it takes its own agenda of problems, over which it has to preside, to whose imperatives it is subject, and by which in the end it will be judged'.

Most social and political scientists would accept these characterisations of the state. Here, though, agreement ceases and arguments begin about how best to theorise the state. Writing and talking about the state in general and the British state in particular are bound up with a number of difficulties. An enormous literature exists about the state. Much of it is hard to understand. Part of the problem is that it deals with abstractions from the real world. The debates make use of the same words and terms (including 'the state' itself) but often attach different meanings to them. Alternative theories take a different perspective on the state's role. All political 'isms', from anarchism through conservatism and liberalism to socialism, contain within them one or more theories of the state, different views about what the state can do, its relationship to the private sector and 'civil society', and prescriptions for change.

Theories are abstractions. We should not expect to find a concrete, clearly defined entity called the British state. Theorising about the state, therefore, presents the problem — common in the social sciences — of dealing simultaneously with abstractions and the 'real world'. The void between the two is revealed when theories of the state are matched with what is empirically observable. We cannot even take for granted the real world. There is no easy or correct path to linking theory with 'facts'; rather, facts are 'theory-impregnated'. Just as different political standpoints predispose researchers towards particular theories, so specific theories lead to the selection or privileging of certain kinds of fact.

This book is not the place for a comprehensive review and assessment of state theory. Instead the intention is to explore a number of key issues by focusing in turn on what three of the most important theoretical strands — pluralism, Marxism and the New Right — contribute to an understanding of the state's role in social and economic change.

Several themes run through the chapter. One is a discussion of alternative definitions and views about the state's role in change. The state is a slippery and elusive concept; few definitions are immune from criticism. Equally there is a diversity of approaches to state power, how the state responds to or implements change, and with what consequences. A second theme concerns the most appropriate means of conceptualising political power in Britain. Which groups are able to channel change to their own best interests? A third concern is with the relationship between political and economic power, the state and the market, and public and private sectors.

PLURALISM, DEMOCRACY AND THE POLICY PROCESS

Pluralism rests on the assumption that political power is fragmented and widely dispersed. The political system is seen as an independent sphere isolated from the economic. Pluralist theorists do not always examine the state explicitly. Sometimes the term 'state' is used synonymously with 'government' or 'central government', and taken as the central political power which mirrors, accommodates or referees competing demands. Political actors, their demands and their degree of success are of central concern.

At an extreme, pluralists stress the democratic nature of politics in Britain, and see government as the voice of the people. This position has been widely criticised. At best Britain is a representative democracy in which Parliament, rather than the people, is sovereign. Put another way, democracy could be said to mean little more than the right to put a cross on a ballot paper every few years. But even this portrayal of British democracy is dubious. The electoral system is far from fair. Political parties may take power with the support of less than half the electorate, and many adults are effectively disenfranchised. Equally important, a great deal of political power is not under democratic control.

Democracy has important implications for the shape and power of the state; ultimately governments can be voted out of office. Popular consent has to be won or bought with suitable policies. During the 1970s a number of theorists argued that there was a mounting crisis of the state (Held, 1984b). The crisis centred around the state's inability to deliver the goods necessary to maintain consensus. Pluralists and those on the New Right developed the thesis of the 'overload of government' with too many complex tasks, and Marxists that of 'legitimation crisis', with large sections of society refusing to accept the sanctity of law or the representativeness of government. These notions have been overtaken by events, and replaced by other concerns, particularly issues to do with the limits of state intervention and relationships between economic and political power.

More subtle pluralist analysis eschews the idea that politics in Britain is centred on the election of Members of Parliament by individuals voting in secret ballots. Instead emphasis is on 'pressure groups' or 'interest groups' competing with each other in the democratic process. A detailed focus is placed on specific issues and groups competing over them, with competition examined throughout the policy process. The thrust is on what Jordan and Richardson (1987) call 'negotiative' politics and the 'constraints that bind, hamper and limit any government' in the policy process. Typically constraints are seen in terms of elections and voting; pressure and interest groups; party politics; bureaucratic systems, the civil service and public administration; the role of prime minister and cabinet; and the place of Parliament. Pluralism of this type provides the foundation for most studies of British politics.

Orthodox political scientists cast a wide net. Some authors concentrate on a multitude of different groups voicing a wide range of concerns. Others argue that pressure groups have vastly unequal powers and leverage on government, and that it is more appropriate to highlight key groupings such as trade unions and employers' organisations. The most refined analysis of this type is corporatism, suggesting that politics in advanced societies is increasingly reduced to negotiations

306

between 'corporate' bodies representing the interests of particular sections of society – most notably business interests, organised labour and state bureaucrats (Middlemas, 1979; Thompson, 1984). Consensus bargaining excludes large sections of society and negates the workings of 'representative democracy'. The empirical existence of corporatism has been subject to dispute, but even adherents of the perspective would accept that such 'Tripartitism', if it existed, is now on the wane. For corporatists, political developments from the late 1970s have weakened organised labour, and given capital heightened influence within the state.

Most political analysts accept that Parliament is weak and ineffectual in comparison with the executive and government. Some suggest that 'government' itself should be disaggregated and examined in terms of its internal policy-making process. Conflicts may be highlighted within cabinet and government. During the mid-1980s an example was the battle between traditional interventionist Conservatives and those advocating Liberal New Right policies. Ministries and departments also struggle each year over the extent, and their share, of public expenditure – in what is sometimes called budgetary politics. Here stress is placed on the power of the Treasury (and Bank of England) to thwart the expenditure plans of big-spending departments, while the latter assert the worth and value of their programmes above others – the Home Office, for example, struggling with the Department of Education, and Defence with Environment. An increasing number of studies consider the role of the Civil Service, arguing that it can erect considerable barriers to the formulation of government policy (as claimed by politicians such as Richard Crossman and Tony Benn).

Orthodox political science studies, grounded in empirical detail, highlight many of the complexities, contingencies and constraints in the policy-making process, with valuable insights for an understanding of how government manages social and economic change. Yet there is reason for dissatisfaction. First, there is considerable disagreement as to how power in the policy process is distributed between the various actors, groups and arenas, and how the distribution has changed over time. Second, the approach tends to overlook issues of policy implementation and assessment, what happens once the policies are in place. Third, key questions such as how to theorise political power in Britain, and the relationship between economy and politics, suffer from neglect. Fourth, the state gets left behind – in many cases no value is seen in having an explicit theory of the state.

The disunited state

Criticisms may be made of the pluralist account of political power. Since the industrial revolution the social forces represented in the British state have evolved in a number of ways. Some social entities – the monarchy, church, landowning gentry, private landlords, and certain types of capitalist – have lost part of their direct power within the state. Others – such as banking and commercial capital, organised labour, the middle classes, and professional interest groups – have gained power. State power is a social relationship which changes as the balance of social forces in a society alters (Jessop, 1982). Most non-pluralist commentators agree that political power is polarised and concentrated, although how and where is debated. Those on the New Right stress the power of organised labour and the state bureaucracy. In contrast, many Marxists argue that power remains in the hands of a 'dominant class', to use Miliband's (1982) phrase, serving the interests of a capitalist state and economy.

Another weakness of many pluralist accounts is that the institutional form of the state is taken for granted. A number of authors with alternative theoretical perspectives (such as Miliband, 1969) counter this view, explicitly defining the state as a set of institutions. All the immense political, coercive, legal, administrative and financial powers of central government, it is argued, depend on other state institutions. A central government disillusioned with the pace and nature of change may attempt to reform existing state institutions or introduce new ones. Major watersheds in the shaping and reorganisation of state institutions may be identified. The 'one nation project' after the Second World War involved setting up new state institutions, including the National Health Service, environmental planning bodies, new town development corporations, and the Arts Council; reforming existing institutions, as in education; and abandoning others, including the last institutional vestiges of the Poor Law. The result of institutional restructuring was the Keynesian welfare state. State regulation of the economy was intended to overcome stagnation and balance-of-payments problems, and secure full employment. The state also intervened more deeply into social life, nurturing people from 'the cradle to the grave', and meeting popular aspirations for improved education, housing and social welfare. The 1980s are seen by many as another watershed in the structure of the state.

An institutional approach provides a wider definition of the state than in pluralist accounts. Yet the institutional perspective may also be criticised. Central government is usually still seen to be of paramount importance, as the institutional pivot of the state. Coates (1984), for example, treats the component institutions of the state as a cohesive whole managed and regulated by government, and under its 'formal and actual control'. But which institutions should be included in this definition? Some commentators see the church and the media as parts of the state, while others draw a much tighter boundary. It is impossible to provide a comprehensive and workable empirical definition of state institutions because of the basic problems of attempting to identify and equate an abstraction – the state – with empirical observations. Even real institutions may be hidden from view. One example is those agencies of the 'secret state' (Thompson, 1980) which are often literally beyond the law. Their existence may be officially denied. MI5, MI6 and Special Branch controversially engage in vetting, surveillance and 'security', and attempt to control political dissent and subversion in a wide range of spheres including industrial conflict.

Institutions are in themselves empty and without power. They only take on life through the actions of people, as individuals and members of social groups and classes. Incorporating the notion of social relations into the institutionalist framework provides a powerful tool with which to understand the development of the British state, the constraints on policy and conflicts within the state itself. It suggests that state institutions are locations of political struggles, in which conflicting groups battle for power, attempting to use state institutions to mould change in their interests. Alternative state institutions may be run by distinct social groups, and so reflect conflicting interests. The ethos, aims and personnel of particular institutions may be counter to the direction in which those in other parts of the state apparatus may wish to go, and therefore create barriers to change.

Conflicts within the state are partly geographical. Some state institutions are specifically able to respond to and achieve local diversity. Regional and local government are good examples, sometimes seen as 'local states'. *Local authorities*, as the name implies, retain some independence from central government, and have major roles in providing education, social services, housing, and environmental planning. Local state institutions reflect the interests of politically powerful local groups, so councils may attempt to implement policies counter to the wishes of central government. Indeed, since the mid-1970s there has been conflict between central and local government over rate-capping, council house sales, local expenditure, education and the privatisation of services. The intractable problems of Northern Ireland and places like West Belfast are extreme instances of the weakness of government in specific local contexts. The territorial organisation of the United Kingdom into four separate nations (England, Northern Ireland, Scotland and Wales) has continuing political significance. The power of government centred on London to promote or respond to change is at times tenuous.

The sovereignty and independence of the British state are constrained by the European Community. For instance, agricultural policy in Britain, and especially the crucial issue of farm subsidies, is determined at the European level. With the development of the single European market in 1992, the presumption is that Europe will have much the same economic weight and strengths as Japan and the USA. The consequences of European integration are open to debate – one result might be to consign Britain to the periphery of a West European multinational state.

MARXISM, CLASS AND THE CAPITALIST STATE

Marxist accounts assert that political power and the structure of the state are closely linked to the economic organisation of society, particularly its class structure. Although Marxists disagree about the degree to which the economic determines the political, for them the overriding characteristic of Britain is that it is a capitalist society in which the major antagonism is between capital and labour. Marxist perspectives on class are further discussed in Chapter 14.

Marxists recognise that capitalism has evolved, from the nineteenth-century archetype of many small-scale industrial capitalists to a system in which competition is circumscribed by large firms or coercive financial interests. Commentators have described the modern structure of British society as constituting 'late capitalism', 'advanced capitalism', 'state monopoly capitalism' or 'finance capitalism'. Each description of contemporary capitalism implies a particular view of the state and state activity. The notion of advanced capitalism, for example, highlights the increasingly global character of Western economic processes, high levels of labour productivity, the emergence of giant firms and the growth of sophisticated labour organisations. A global view helps pin-point key problems faced by the British state – those of attempting to grapple with economic change which has fundamental effects on domestic class relations and the global strengths or weaknesses of British capital.

Marxist accounts may be criticised for reducing the state to the economy. Criticisms include economic determinism – the 'reading-off' of the role of the state from the manner in which capitalism develops; and functionalism – seeing the state as an 'instrument' in the hands of a capitalist ruling class. In response to these criticisms, some Marxists highlight the gap between abstract theories and historical and geographical specificities, and suggest that 'the economy cannot predict or determine more precisely than "tendentially" ' (Hall, 1984). Recognition of the influence of the non-economic has led to the idea of the 'relative autonomy' of the state and political sphere from the economy, while other Marxists go further and assert the independence of politics.

There has been considerable debate on the Left about the possibility of fundamental change within the present system of economic relations and political authority in Britain. In one view, Labour may win victories but never threaten capitalism. If a threat arose, the state would use coercive force to ensure its own survival and that of the social system in which it is rooted. Another view on the Left argues that control of government could be a means of achieving radical reform of political and economic relations, and that Parliament can be used as a vehicle for achieving socialism.

A critique of Labourism

Analysis of the politics of the Labour Party by Marxist political theorists has focused on a critique of Labourism. It is argued that there have always been two major and conflicting strands within the Labour Party. One is avowedly socialist, calling for the transformation of society through common ownership of the means of production and democratic planning. Labourism is the other. Whilst paying lip-service to the goals of socialism, it is more interested in improving the condition of the trade-union-organised working class within capitalism.

Labourism's political demand is that the state should introduce policies providing immediate benefits to the organised working class. The legitimate interests of trade unions and their members should be recognised through legislation over trade union rights and negotiation of key economic and social policies. Management of the economy should ensure economic growth and full employment. Nationalisation should be used to improve industrial efficiency, to reduce monopolistic abuse and to facilitate macroeconomic management.

Some concern is given to the redistribution of income, but in general Labourism has shunned major redistributions of wealth and income. Minimum-wage policies, for instance, have received little support, while great emphasis is put on the importance of free collective bargaining. Internationally, Labourism has supported the supremacy of British power. Colonialism was not opposed except when expediency demanded it, as with India in the 1940s. More recently little practical emphasis has been put on transforming the international relations which keep so many people in the Third World poor.

313

The Keynes–Beveridge style of macropolicy within a welfare state framework fits the interests of Labourism. These policies enabled a merging in the Labour Party of the interests of middle-class social reformers, represented by such individuals as Clement Attlee and institutions like the Fabian Society, with the concerns of the majority of trade union leaders. Both Keynes and Beveridge were Liberals. Paradoxically, the trade unions in the first decade of this century set up the precursor of the Labour Party in alliance with groups like Fabians and some small socialist parties because of the difficulty of persuading Liberal governments to overturn anti-trade-union legislation.

Critics of Labourism highlight the ambiguity forced upon the Labour Party. It has to claim both to be a socialist party and the party that can manage British capitalism the most efficiently in the interests of the widest proportion of society. The problem is that the two claims are incompatible, with the added difficulty that capitalism cannot successfully be managed to benefit the groups that Labourists claim to represent. Capitalism cannot be managed because of its inherent unplanned characteristics. Sharp inequality is a feature of its economic forces, and national economic strategies are increasingly circumvented by the global mobility of capital. As Labourism predominates in the Labour Party, the Party is doomed to fail when in power through unrealistic economic policies. Economic crises force Labour governments to attack the economic aspirations of trade unionists and working people as a whole. Socialists in the party are blamed for disunity, when defending those interests or suggesting alternative strategies to combat crisis. On this analysis, the late 1980s 'new realism' of some trade unions and the Labour leadership was a redressing of old Labourist strategies. Added to them was a greater pessimism about what can be achieved in managed capitalism.

In a number of respects there are parallels between Left critiques of Labourism and the New Right critique of the so-called post-war consensus (see below). The 'socialism' which Mrs Thatcher claimed to want to destroy in fact is the Labourist strategy outlined above. In contrast to the New Right, socialists argue that it is the market and capitalist institutions active in it that deny many people's freedoms and self-expression. Low incomes, poverty, sharp inequality, discrimination, mass unemployment, monotonous jobs, limited education and training, poor social services and a scant regard for the environment are all inevitable consequences of relying on the market as the guiding force of society. Some form of state orchestration of the economy is required to overcome the inadequacies of capitalism.

There are differences among socialists over what 'state orchestration' means. For some, particularly Trotskyists, only world revolution and 'workers' power' are the solutions. Struggle guided by the undemocratic executive of a party is the only means of gaining improvement. Given that disagreement over policy or tactics in such a framework leads to immediate expulsion, Trotskyist groupings are forever splitting or entering other political groupings. Most other socialists reject the simplicity of the Trotskyite analysis, and see scope in a society like Britain's for substantial social transformation without the need for violent revolution and militaristic-style discipline.

From the late 1960s onwards there has been a major expansion of 'libertarian' socialism. Libertarians emphasise the importance of personal freedoms and self-fulfilment, concerned to achieve a democratic organisation of society on socialistic lines. They argue for greater democracy in contemporary society, and feel that practical demonstration of the benefits of socialist principles is both feasible and necessary in contemporary Britain. Experimenting with different models of socialist and democratic practice is encouraged. Libertarian socialists have been active within the Labour Party and in campaigns outside of it.

315

Libertarian socialists frequently base their politics on personal experiences in specific social movements where collective but democratic demands have led to significant social change or awakened people's consciousness to the feasibility of change. Such movements encompass complex issues – including feminism, anti-racism, gay and lesbian rights, Third World liberation struggles, community action, world peace and the environment. By no means all members of such groups are socialists; in fact, many are not and would see the practices of traditional socialist groupings as antithetical to their aims. But many, none the less, view as important the linking of class-based issues, associated with the nature of capitalist production, with such campaigns if their aims are to succeed. While denying that all the problems of the world are simply products of capitalism, socialists argue that the nature of personal exploitation and discrimination can only be understood in the context of the economic forces of society.

In the 1980s there was disagreement amongst socialists over the strategies required to bring about political change in Britain. Several objectives were suggested as most important: removing Mrs Thatcher through a centre-left all-party alliance; electing a Labour government; fighting for socialist policies within the Labour Party; ignoring the Labour Party for campaigns or other groupings; or dreaming of the existence of a genuinely socialist party.

Ideology and the state

Many Marxists argue that ideologies play a major part in securing economic and social order and control. The state has a key role in promoting and maintaining them. Ideology is also a difficult concept to define. It is concerned with how people think and what they believe about society and expect from it. Non-Marxist discussions of 'socialisation' and 'legitimation' refer to ideology

316

by another name. Through ideology, categories are defined, sanctioned and enforced by the state. Examples include the definition of public and private issues, what is legitimate and illegitimate behaviour, what constitutes work and not working, what is legal and illegal. Ideologies are successful when such distinctions are generally taken for granted.

The private sector cannot exist without state support. Private property and the rights associated with it are maintained by the state. At the same time, as Held (1984a) argues, private property is depoliticised and treated 'as if it were not a proper subject of politics. The structure of the economy is regarded as non-political, such that the massive division between those that own and control the means of production, and those who must live by wage labour, is regarded as the outcome of free private contracts, not as a matter for the state. But by defending private property in the means of production, the state already has taken a side.'

The state also helps to define the private realm within 'civil society'. This has important implications for how far the state intervenes in, for example, home and family life (McIntosh, 1984). A result is that domestic and sexual violence within the home are usually considered as a private matter between men and women. Definitions of public/private are also crucially important in policies for transport, education, housing and health care. Similarly, the state is the final arbiter of the 'public interest' and what constitutes public order (or disorder).

The state plays a key role in defining the boundaries of socially acceptable behaviour, often backed by the force of law. Getting married is ideologically acceptable, while homosexuality has been unacceptable for most of this century. What is recognised as meaningful and financially rewarding work also depends on the sanction of the state. Unpaid domestic labour in the home, typically carried out by women, remains largely ignored in official employment definitions, statistics and policies, with a major impact on the place of women and men in the home and wider society.

A central issue in the discussion of ideology is how it is formed and transmitted. Many authors argue that the inculcation of ideas and attitudes begins at school (if not before). Pupils are encouraged to accept the restrictions of the education system, the authority of teachers and the value of what is being taught. On leaving school it continues both in work and out of work. Three 'agencies' used to be singled out as the most important transmittors of ideology (or socialisers of individuals and groups): the family, the community and the church. Most commentators accept that they have now been replaced by the media and education system, and a number of other state institutions.

How powerful is ideology? In opposition to the notion of a dominant and hegemonic ideology, some writers (Abercrombie *et al.*, 1980; Held, 1984a) argue that historical evidence shows there is neither a common value system nor a one-dimensional ideology. Rather, any so-called dominant ideology may only be accepted by the middle and upper classes.

Challenges are made to dominant ideological perspectives. In schools truancy, violence, and poor educational attainment, particularly amongst working-class children, show how ineffective the ideological goals of school and education can be. Many black people accept neither the authority of the police nor the neutrality and fairness of the law, protesting that the police and the law are racist. The ideal of citizenship means little to the people who do not vote. At work, people threatened with redundancy may take collective action, ignoring the supposed imperative of their position as individuals selling their labour in the market-place.

Protests by powerless groups can often be ignored by the state, as its control of ideas remains dominant. On occasions, however, the state is forced into a response. Concessions may be made, or sanctions imposed to force

318

people back into line. Ultimately, physical force is used to reimpose the state's domination and political authority.

Ideologies also reflect the power of competing social and economic interests. As the distribution of power changes, so, too, will ideologies. During the 1960s and 1970s the women's movement and the gay movement were partially successful in challenging definitions of acceptable behaviour. During the 1980s, as both groups lost power, there were reversals.

It is doubtful whether the agencies and institutions supposedly transmitting ideology stress the same values and beliefs – the church may emphasise one set of values, the education system another. Ideological distinctions and definitions also alter over time. During the First and Second World Wars, for example, women found that they were suddenly valued by the state as productive workers, encouraged to leave their homes for paid employment. In the Second World War, the state took over some of the family and home-centred responsibilities held by women, providing communal eating-places, child care, and other supposedly domestic facilities. These interventions may change ideological expectations. Many women were reluctant to return home after the wars. The emergence and growth of the welfare state after the Second World War produced a general acceptance that the state should provide health care, education and social security. Since the late 1970s central government has cut parts of this provision, but with limited success because most people retain their welfare state expectations. Radical policy changes are only likely to succeed if there are commensurate changes in ideological beliefs.

THE NEW RIGHT, THE STATE AND THE MARKET

The political theories having greatest impact on Western countries in the last quarter of the twentieth century are those from what has become known as the New Right. In fact New Right ideas are far from new and far from unitary. Their origins can be traced to the eighteenth century and before. New Right ideas contain contradictions and conflicting positions between the two main strands of Liberalism and Conservatism. Liberalism argues for the restoration of the traditional Liberal values of individualism, free market forces and limited government. Conservatism consists of claims about government being used to establish societal order and authority based on social, religious and moral Conservatism (Figure 11.1).

Figure 11.1 Liberalism and Conservatism in the New Right

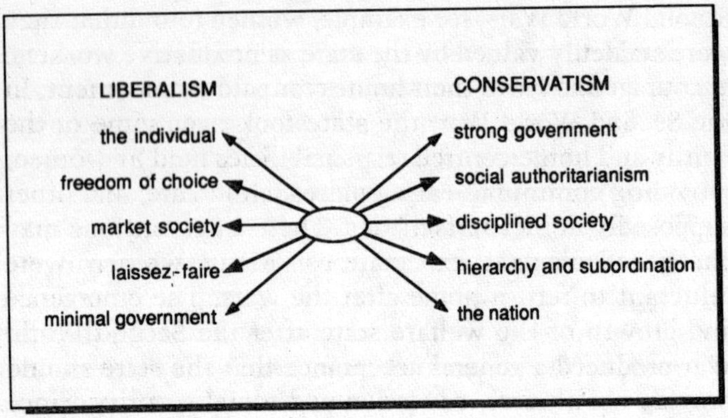

LIBERALISM	CONSERVATISM
the individual	strong government
freedom of choice	social authoritarianism
market society	disciplined society
laissez-faire	hierarchy and subordination
minimal government	the nation

Source: Belsey (1986).

All New Right theorists see individual 'freedom' and market competition as the motors of social and economic progress. On the basis of their views of the efficacy of individual actions in markets, they make clear, although contradictory, prescriptive assertions about the proper role of the state in society. The overriding New Right position is that the relationship between state and economy has moved too far in favour of the state. Political authority distorts the authority of the market.

New Right liberals argue for minimal state intervention and maximum individual and market freedom. Minimal state regulation is required because the economic sphere contains built-in self-governing mechanisms, through market competition. The market provides its own rationale, ultimately working for the greater societal good and guaranteeing individual political freedom. Just how 'minimal' the state should be is contested. At the extreme it is asserted that the state should merely defend national territory, others (monetarists) believe that it should be limited to controlling the money supply, while some libertarians argue the state should protect private property rights but no more. Conservatives on the New Right, in contrast, assert the importance of strong central government, well defined and policed laws and strict social morality to protect the market and individual rights. So, despite a common economic analysis, there is an ambiguity between and within the liberal and conservative wings over the role of the state.

New Right ideas have had a marked impact on British politics. During the 1970s and 1980s British governments introduced New Right policies in attempts to break the established post-war pattern of political relationships. In the mid-1970s, for example, the then Labour government introduced a number of policies, including tight controls on public expenditure, which are nowadays thought of as New Right in character. However, most commentators argue that the rift with the past has been strongest since the election of Mrs Thatcher's first Conservative government in 1979.

New Right explanations are accepted by many in the Conservative Party, and form the basis of recent Conservative governments' political rhetoric. Sir Keith Joseph, an influential Conservative politician in the 1970s and early 1980s, for instance, used New Right ideas in urging the removal of the six 'poisons' of 'excessive government spending, high direct taxation, egalitarianism, excessive nationalisation, a political trade union movement, and an anti-enterprise culture'.

The impact of New Right ideas is partly a consequence of the prominence and influence of New Right intellectuals. Organisations such as the Institute of Economic Affairs (founded as early as 1955), the Centre for Policy Studies and the Adam Smith Institute all disseminate the New Right ideas of authors such as Hayek and Friedman, often translating them into policy proposals aimed at government. In addition, however, it is possible to argue that the conditions were ripe for New Right theories to have an impact: they provided a set of ideas to explain and rationalise changes already at work and being forced on government and state in Britain. The extent to which the three Conservative governments headed by Mrs Thatcher have implemented New Right policies is assessed in the next chapter.

State intervention and the private sector

One element of Liberal New Right analysis, the idea that a complex society such as Britain could reinstate a minimal state, seems particularly impractical. As Held (1984a) points out: 'With the development of capitalism the state entered into the very fabric of the economy by reinforcing and codifying – through legislation, administration and supervision – its structure and practices. It thus constituted and complemented, as it still does, economic relations.' The free market needs the state and vice versa, and in modern societies the two have become inseparable although the precise relationship and balance between them has changed over time.

For much of the nineteenth century the state's main domestic role was to sustain the political and class structure of imperial Britain. Territorial defence and the maintenance of internal law and order were of major importance. Economic intervention was limited, although the state was involved in crucial activities such as regulating weights and measures, providing a monetary system, and protecting private property rights. Nowadays these basic facilitative roles remain, although becoming more complex as the economy has evolved. Without this intervention the British economy would be severely disrupted.

Over time, state intervention in the economy has increased. For much of the post-war period, for example, state activity in Britain was directed toward Keynesian demand management, based on the idea that economic growth could be managed and stabilised by 'fine tuning' the broad economic aggregates, particularly through control and adjustment of government revenues and expenditures (Thompson, 1984). One implication of the Keynesian position is that economic theory, when translated into practice, could be used to maintain full employment. It is possible, however, to turn the proposition on its head and argue that the possibility of maintaining full employment in the overstretched post-war economy led to a commitment to do it.

At times the state intervenes directly in market processes, rather than facilitating or supporting them. Nationalisation of key firms and industries is a prime example, being a central part of state activity for much of the post-war period. In the early post-war years, nationalisation was used as a tool for economic planning, and as a means of attempting to alter the system of economic ownership and economic relationships. Coal was nationalised in 1948, electricity in 1947, gas in 1948, iron and steel in 1949 and transport in 1947. In the 1960s and 1970s nationalisation was used in a different way, to ensure the survival or restructuring of sectors or of companies (such as steel and shipbuilding, Rolls-Royce and British Leyland). As the objectives of nationalisation changed, so did their management. In the 1980s a large number of state-run industries were denationalised, with most of the remaining ones being run on market lines and operating according to the dictates of profit-and-loss balance sheets and accounts. There are exceptions, such as the nuclear power industry, which point to government pragmatism in some circumstances.

Modern states are also involved in ensuring the availability of the elements necessary for production and other forms of economic activity. Most typical is the availability of a suitable workforce, an activity outside the control of individual enterprises. Much state intervention in education, health care and housing facilitates the provision of an adequate labour supply. State activity in this area of 'collective consumption' acts to cut across and amend market provision. The state may also be centrally involved in infrastructure development (including supplying transport, communications and energy), and fields such as law-and-order services including prisons and police forces.

State intervention may favour particular parts of the private sector through a variety of methods including company law; monetary policies; subsidies, credit and grants; defence expenditure; and policies on competition and monopolies. A well-documented example is government spending on defence contracts (Lovering, 1985; Lovering and Boddy, 1988; Simmie and James, 1986). Defence spending has a geographical bias favouring private firms in the south of England, and especially relatively prosperous localities such as the London and Bristol regions. In the Bristol case, for instance, expenditure on defence contracts outweighs government regional assistance going to neighbouring South Wales with its far higher rates of unemployment and factory closure.

The increasing interdependence of the state and the private sector is reflected in the gradual if uneven rise of state expenditure as a proportion of national income over the last century (Figure 11.2). In the late nineteenth century the state took less than 10 per cent of national income through taxation to finance public expenditure. Today the figure is about 40 per cent. Public expenditure

Figure 11.2   State Expenditure as a Percentage of Gross
Domestic Product, 1890–1986

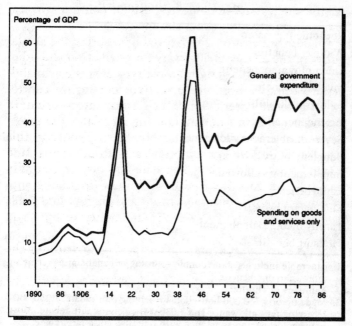

Source: Adapted from Chart 5.6, HMSO (1988b), Volume I.

rose steeply during the First and Second World Wars, and
then failed to return to pre-war levels. The continuation
of greater spending after the 1914–18 war highlights the
emergence of substantial intervention in areas such as
education, housing and the then embryonic social security system. The post-1945 levels were affected by the
development of the welfare state and continued high
defence expenditure. Figure 11.2 also shows the important differences between total state spending and that
proportion actually spent on goods and services. The gap
between the two in large part indicates the significance
of 'transfer' payments, including money spent on pensions and social security.

TABLE 11.1 *Estimated Average Numbers of People Receiving Selected Social Security Benefits at Any One Time, 1987–8 (thousands)[1]*

Retirement pension	9735
Widows' benefits	380
Unemployment benefit	845
Invalidity benefit	935
Industrial disability benefit	200
Attendance allowance	635
Severe disablement allowance	265
Supplementary pension	1875
Supplementary allowance	3285
Child benefit[2]	12090
One-parent benefit	635
Family income supplement	210
Housing benefit[3]	12040

1. The table includes some double counting of beneficiaries receiving more than one benefit.
2. Numbers of children.
3. Made up of 3,760,000 households receiving rent rebate, 1,250,000 receiving rent allowance and 7,030,000 receiving rate rebate. Most households getting assistance with rent also got a rate rebate.
Source: Table 15.6, HMSO (1988a), Volume II.

In distributing transfer payments the state provides much of the incomes of the unemployed, elderly, sick and poor (Table 11.1), amending the income distribution generated in the private sector. Some benefits are universal rather than income-related. Most, however, are 'means-tested' depending on earnings and savings, and are 'targeted' on the poorest sections of the population. The best available estimate of those totally dependent on state benefits is the number of recipients of income support. In 1987–8 the estimated figure was 5.2 million, including 2 million elderly people and 1.9 million unemployed people. On average, 64 per cent of the income of people in the bottom quarter of the income distribution came from state benefits in 1984–5 (HMSO, 1987). Social security is the largest item of government expenditure.

Public-sector employment is another aspect of the state's economic role (Therborn, 1984). In 1986–7 5.5 million people, or about 22 per cent of the population in work, were employed in the public sector. Despite falling by 14 per cent since 1978–9, state employment remains a central feature of the British economy, and the focus of significant conflicts over pay and conditions. These figures relate to a narrow institutional view of the state, and exclude private-sector employment which is either indirectly or directly dependent on the state. Examples range from workers in armaments factories, through those making bandages for hospitals and text-books for schools, to the less obvious cases of shopkeep-ers and taxi-drivers whose businesses are patronised by people with state-funded incomes.

The relationships between the public and private sectors are clearly not immutable. Some Western coun-tries, such as Sweden, have more comprehensive and direct state intervention than Britain; others, like France and the United States, have left more to the private sector. The state has an impact on most dimensions of the economy. But private market processes also make themselves felt in most public goods and services. State education, health care and social services, for example, have significant private rivals. Even the police force in Britain is complemented by a growing private security business. Within the state sector, goods and services are bought from the private market. The NHS, for example, is crucially dependent on private medical suppliers.

The New Right's fears of the state overwhelming the private market seem empirically misplaced. Private com-panies have wide discretion over production decisions – including what to produce, where to locate production, what labour to use, and what technologies to employ. The state may facilitate, induce, support, cajole, join in with, direct, and in some circumstances take over private firms, but not to the extent that private ownership and the market system are fundamentally threatened.

Examination of national economic policies during the post-war period reveals many failed government plans for economic change (Pollard, 1983). The 1945 Labour government was forced to curtail its programme of economic and social reform. In the mid-1960s, another Labour government found its 'National Plan' for the modernisation of British industry defeated. In the early 1970s, changes in economic policy forced on the Conservative government of Edward Heath introduced the phrase 'U-turn' into political discourse.

These examples emphasise one of the major themes of this chapter: the paradox of the state in Britain. On the one hand, the state has immense political, legal, administrative, financial and ideological power and influence which affect most dimensions of society. On the other hand, the state itself reflects British society and is restrained by it. This is seen in how the wider societal content helps determine what the state does and its degree of success, and also the changing make-up of the state, whether measured in terms of institutions or social relationships.

FURTHER READING

For anyone wishing to chart their own path through state theory, a number of guides and syntheses are available, including Dunleavy and O'Leary (1987), Cox, Furlong and Page (1985), McLennan, Held and Hall (1984), Jordan (1985) and Ham and Hill (1984).

Accessible orthodox political science studies of British politics include Kavanagh (1985), Jordan and Richardson (1987), Mackintosh (1982) and Moran (1985).

A useful account of the territorial organisation of the British state is in Dearlove and Saunders (1984).

Miliband's classic book on the state in capitalist societies (1969) and his more recent (1982) study, and Coates's (1984) account of British politics provide stimulating Marxist perspectives to the state in Britain. Not all Marxists would agree with their approaches.

Readable assessments of the New Right are Green's (1987) sympathetic account and King's (1987) and Levitas's (1986) critical studies. Kavanagh (1987) and Levitas (1986) discuss the most important individuals and groups involved in the propagation of New Right ideas.

12

Thatcherism and Change
Fred Gray

'Thatcherism' is often seen as the major motor of change in British society in the 1980s. But it is a term used in contradictory ways.

A popular view is that Mrs Thatcher single-handedly has radically altered Britain. The problem with a 'Mrs Thatcher's Britain' approach is that the complexities of social change are swept away. It ignores the social, economic and political context within which Thatcherism exists. Other advanced capitalist countries have experienced similar changes, and Mrs Thatcher cannot be congratulated or blamed for changes throughout the Western world.

'Mrs Thatcher as a unique political leader' is an alternative definition of Thatcherism. It has been adopted by sycophantic biographers, and Thatcher herself in the use of the royal 'We'. Here Thatcherism is equated with a particular style and content of leadership including stress on her own childhood experience and moral beliefs, conviction politics, the return to Victorian values, an emphasis on the individual, family and private enterprise, the turning away from consensus and antipathy towards some dimensions of the state and bodies such as trade unions. The underlying assumption is that recent British history is a product of a single individual.

In another view Thatcherism is broadened to constitute

government and the state (as in 'the Thatcherite state')
rather than just an individual. When Thatcherism is
equated with the three Conservative administrations led
by Mrs Thatcher, attention is focused on a set of policies
aimed at restructuring the state (weakening in some areas
and strengthening it in others), altering the balance
between the public and private sectors to give greater
weight to the latter, and placing more emphasis on the
individual, family and market mechanisms. One criticism of Thatcherism as a description of government is that
it ignores the fact that the objectives of policies have
changed over time under Mrs Thatcher, sometimes on
the basis of pragmatism and 'political reality'. Another
inadequacy of government and state conceptualisations
of Thatcherism is that, if the arguments made in the
previous chapter about the limited power of politicians
and governments and the complexities of the modern
state are accepted, we should have low expectations of
the power of Thatcherism.

Another approach, taken by some intellectuals on the
left, sees Thatcherism as a temporary and exceptional
'authoritarian-populist' form of the state (Hall, 1979).
Advocates of 'Thatcherism as a state form' argue that
authoritarian populism emerged in response to an acute
economic crisis. At the time a political vacuum existed,
caused by the disintegration of consensus and the decline
of Labourism. Since then the state has become increasingly authoritarian; for example, by strengthening law
and order and increasing central control. Ideologically it
has tried to create popular consent even for measures that
are against the broad interests of the populace. This
attempted ideological hegemony has emphasised 'traditional' values based on personal responsibility, the family
and the nation.

Thatcherism as authoritarian populism has been criticised for assuming 'an ideological homogeneity in the
conception and pursuit of policies which does not exist'
(King, 1987). It also plays down the intrinsically contra-

dictory relationship between the Conservative and Liberal strands of New Right thinking. How Thatcherism has changed over time is ignored: 'The authoritarian populist approach demonstrates how Thatcherism has attempted to establish a chain of equivalences among themes such as monetarism, the strong state, law and order, the family, etc. But it also tends to reify these linkages and to ignore their changing emphasis and contents' (Jessop *et al.*, 1984; see also the reply by Hall, 1985). It is equally difficult to argue that there has been popular consent or acceptance of Thatcherism, or that a new ideological hegemony has been achieved.

Other criticisms stress the limited nature of the concept of authoritarian populism (Atkins, 1986). Authoritarianism and populism are not exceptional state forms, and undue attention is placed on political processes. The theory does not fully explore the restructuring of capital (rather than labour) over the post-war period, not only in Britain and Europe but in the other parts of the world. Despite criticisms, however, the authoritarian-populism definition of Thatcherism is important. It has strongly influenced debates in both the Labour and Communist parties.

There is, then, no definition of Thatcherism which is convincing. But Thatcherism remains a powerful term. For descriptive ease, the Conservative governments and their policies since 1979 will be called Thatcherism. We do not accept the view that Conservative policies would have been much different if there had been another Prime Minister. Nor do we accept that there has been a politically inspired social revolution creating a new relationship between state, society and the individual. Changes are undoubtedly occurring, but to ascribe them solely to government is to fall into an instrumentalist view of the state.

The aim of the rest of this chapter is to provide an assessment of the practical impact of 1980s Tory administrations on British society.

THE BATTLE FOR IDEAS

Most government action in the 1980s has been informed and justified by New Right ideas. These ideas have been translated, albeit in a distorted manner, into a set of policies, and have provided the core set of beliefs used to justify Thatcherism and the changing social and economic landscape of Britain. Their use is clearest in political rhetoric. The welfare state is attacked as a playground for 'scroungers', trade unions are seen as 'the enemy within', radical Labour councils are tagged the 'Loony Left', and demands by the low-paid for higher wages 'price people out of jobs'. In contrast, New Right alternatives are praised with exhortations about the virtues of the market, 'Victorian values', the family, 'getting on your bike', and the importance of higher salaries and lower taxes to encourage 'wealth creators'.

The diversity of New Right thought has not been a problem for Thatcherism. Rather, alternative New Right ideas have been used pragmatically. The Liberal free-market tradition is drawn on in arguing against the welfare state, while the Conservative authoritarian strand is used, for instance, to justify the increased emphasis on law and order.

The ideology of Thatcherism has been endorsed and taken even further by much of the popular press. It has also had an impact on most dimensions of formal politics in Britain. By 1988, for example, sections of the Labour Party including the leadership had accepted that a sea-change in politics had taken place. Specific issues (such as council house sales and trade union reform) and the general role of 'the market' were endorsed in a way that would have been anathema to the Labour Party a decade earlier. What of the wider ideological impact? Has there been a general movement away from belief in the state intervention in social and economic life towards acceptance of a more central role for individualism and the market-place?

333

Assessment of the long-lasting consequences of Thatcherism on people's ideas and beliefs is difficult. Surveys of people's opinions are difficult to interpret. A great deal depends on when polls are taken, and on the context, order and wording of questions. Essentially similar questions may lead to varying responses between surveys. Another problem is discovering causes of change in people's opinions. People's ideas and views may have altered for reasons other than Thatcherism. Opinion polls point to some movement to the right on issues such as nationalisation, trade union reform, and law and order (although the proportion in favour of capital punishment has fallen). Key events during the 1980s also appear to reveal support for Thatcherism. Some polls suggested strong support for the Government during the crucial confrontation with the miners in 1984–5. And nationalist (and pro-government) fervour was high during the Falklands War of 1982.

Miners' strikes and wars with South American republics are relatively infrequent. Other survey evidence from a range of sources suggests that throughout the 1980s an increasing majority of people favoured state provision of and extra spending on health, social services, education and the other mainstream components of the welfare state (Jowell *et al.*, 1987). There was less support for programmes favouring disadvantaged groups such as the unemployed, the homeless and single parents. So opinion-poll and survey evidence indicates that Thatcherism has had a patchy success, and nothing as substantial as the 'populism' assumed by some left-wing commentators.

There is evidence that even the supposedly popular policy successes of Thatcherism have been partial. By the end of 1986 more than 800,000 people had bought their council dwellings under the 1980 'right-to-buy' legislation. However, right-to-buy sales peaked in 1982 and have dwindled since, albeit in an uneven manner. Although the percentage of dwellings in public ownership has fallen from 31.5 in 1979 to 26.1 in 1987, 5.8 million dwellings were still in the public sector in late 1987. Less than one in seven public-sector households have taken the opportunity to buy their homes. In early 1989 there were an estimated 9 million adult shareholders, treble the number in 1979. But 'popular capitalism' measured in this way is still not very popular set against the 78 per cent of adult non-shareholders. Moreover, many successful applicants quickly sold their shares in denationalised industries (the number of British Gas shareholders, for example, falling from 4.4 million in 1986 to 2.7 million in 1989). The stock market crash of late 1987 which coincided with the BP share flotation casts doubt on whether people will readily apply for shares in the future. Over much the same period the number of people covered by private medical insurance rose steeply to 5.2 million. Yet, the fastest rate of growth in private medical insurance occurred in the early 1980s, with most of the 10 per cent of people involved covered by group schemes initiated by employers and trade unions.

Voting behaviour is often seen as the best index of political success. The British electoral process is such that governments receive less than half the vote. But voting figures hardly suggest mass acceptance of Thatcherism. Rather, with a divided opposition, a first-past-the-post electoral system, and a geography of party support and constituency boundaries favouring the Conservative Party, Thatcherism has done enough to achieve the backing of an electorally significant minority. In the 1987 general election, for example, 13.8 million people voted Conservative, 18.7 million voted for other parties and 11 million did not vote. So, on a turnout of 74.5 per cent, 42.3 per cent of those voting did so for the Conservative party, enabling it to win a comfortable majority of 374 out of 650 parliamentary seats. In all three elections won by Mrs Thatcher, the Conservative percentage of the vote has been lower than for any other election in the post-war period.

ECONOMIC POLICY AND THE TRADE UNIONS

Central to the Thatcher governments' economic policies, at least during the first five years, was control of the money supply. Failure to control money supply was said to be the main reason for inflation during the 1970s. The first Thatcher government set annual money-supply targets of 5–9 per cent in 1982–3 and 4–8 per cent in 1983–4. The policy failed. Money supply grew annually by just over 11 per cent in 1982 and 1983. By 1987 the figure had risen to almost 20 per cent. In 1985 the policy of money-supply control as originally envisaged was abandoned. Despite the failure to control money supply, inflation did fall. The implication is that either monetarist theory is faulty and there is no easy relationship between money supply and inflation, or that the translation of the theory into practical policy was inadequate. Chapter 5 reviews alternative explanations of the fall in inflation.

Trade union power has worried many Conservatives for a long time, particularly after the Heath government's unsuccessful confrontation with the National Union of Mineworkers in 1973–4. Ideas, such as those of Hayek (1980), simply strengthened the belief in the need to curtail the unions.

There have been a number of dimensions to attempts to restructure the unions. First, intensive publicity, blaming unions for restrictive practices, unemployment, and excessive wage levels, and urging that unions should be both moderate and non-political. Second, a legislative programme aimed at curtailing union power. The 1980 Employment Act gave non-union members the right to sue both union and employers for damages if excluded by a closed-shop (that is, union members only) agreement. It made future closed shops dependent on the support of 80 per cent of employees, provided finance for postal balloting, and restricted the number and location of pickets in disputes. In the same year, the payment of social security benefits to strikers' families was reduced. A 1982 Act made provision for secret votes for strike action. Unions became liable for damages and faced sequestration of their assets in unlawful strikes. The 1984 Trade Union Act extended the provisions for secret ballots – before industrial action, in leadership elections, and over political funds for campaigning, lobbying and supporting a political party. Further restrictive union legislation progressed through Parliament in 1988.

A third departure has been the decision to dissolve union input into government, informally ('beer and sandwiches at Number Ten') and formally. A fourth dimension of government curtailment of trade unions has been a willingness to confront public-sector unions. The most significant defeat, achieved with backing from the police and the judiciary, was of the NUM during the miners' strike of 1984–5.

A dominant view, on both the Left and the Right, of the impact on unions is that Thatcherism has imposed a new industrial relations framework on what are now weak and disunited unions. Supporters of this position point to a decline of strikes in manufacturing, a rapid fall in union membership, failure of many public-sector strikes, savage changes in certain industries like printing and shipping, and battles between unions over strike-free or single-union agreements with employers. Yet many aspects of Thatcherism's supposedly 'new' industrial relations are old (including decentralised collective bargaining) or far from universal (such as no-strike agreements). While Thatcherism has hit hard at the social justice and welfare role of unions at the national level – for example, over minimum wages, and broader government social and economic policy matters – at the workplace level Thatcherism has often meant 'business as usual' for the unions.

Surveys show that union organisation in workplaces is largely intact, and that unions' collective bargaining power has often not been weakened (MacInnes, 1987).

Tactics may sometimes have changed, but it is debatable whether arguments over 'New Realism' within the union movement are a result of shifts in political balance within specific unions or a product of external forces. One thing is clear. For many workers throughout most of the 1980s real wages rose substantially, which was not true in the 1970s. So the major cause of strikes, demands for pay increases, ameliorated. The political role of unions has changed but not disappeared. For example, most union members voted to maintain their unions' political funds. Most unions still contribute substantially to the Labour Party.

Thatcherism's attempt to change the trade unions has taken place at a time of massive unemployment and industrial restructuring. It is difficult to separate the impact of government policies from other changes affecting unions. Thatcherism has actually pushed some unions into greater confrontation with employers. In 1988, and with unemployment, particularly in southern Britain, on the decrease, industrial strife re-emerged in the car industry. Ford workers, for the first time in more than a decade, struck successfully over wages and working practices. In the same year nurses took unprecedented industrial action, protesting about their own pay and the financial position of the NHS.

PUBLIC EXPENDITURE

Throughout the 1980s Conservative governments proclaimed their wish to reduce public spending. Advocates incorrectly argued that cutting public expenditure would reduce money-supply growth and lower inflation. It was also thought that public spending placed an undue burden on private activity. Taxes should be minimised to encourage entrepreneurial spirit and work incentives.

Conservative strategists highlighted inadequacies in the welfare state, the major item of public expenditure

338

(Atkinson *et al.*, 1987). Welfare spending was assumed to encourage unemployment, as it was argued that benefits were too high relative to wages. Similarly, the welfare state leads to a 'dependency' culture. Benefits in cash and kind (such as free school meals) and the system of council house allocation 'induce' the formation of one-parent families. Elsewhere, 'scroungers' abused the welfare state. An alternative and contradictory argument was that the welfare state (and particularly education and health services) mainly benefited the relatively privileged. There was also criticism of the quality and delivery of many services.

It is useful to distinguish between statements of intent and what has actually occurred. Indeed, although the primary objective of cutting public spending remained throughout the Thatcher years, there has been an important if subtle change of emphasis. Early on the intention was 'to reduce public expenditure progressively in volume terms' (HMSO, 1980), the implication being that, discounting inflation, spending should actually fall. By 1988 the Government's principal expenditure aim was somewhat different, to 'hold its rate of growth below the growth of the economy as a whole and thus reduce public spending as a proportion of national income' (HMSO, 1988a).

To some extent abhorrence of public expenditure had weakened by Mrs Thatcher's third term. Not all state spending was bad, but it did depend on the health of the private sector. The private sector needed to be revitalised, for example, by tax cuts, before the public sector could spend. Interestingly, despite the objective of reducing personal taxation, for most people taxation, direct and indirect, increased under Mrs Thatcher both absolutely and proportionately, at least until 1988. Only the very highest earners now pay far less tax, with the highest income-tax band falling from 83 per cent in 1980 to 40 per cent in 1988. Even the 'tax cutting' 1988 Budget greatly favoured high earners, with the income tax bill for the top 1 per cent of earners being reduced by £1880 million, compared with £1730 million for the bottom 70 per cent.

How successful, then, have Mrs Thatcher's governments been in reducing public expenditure? As a proportion of total national income – defined as gross domestic product (GDP) – public expenditure at first rose from less than 44 per cent in 1978–9 to a plateau of about 46 per cent during the first part of the 1980s. Since 1985–6 the proportion has fallen quite sharply (Figure 12.1). Public expenditure in real terms, however, has continued to rise (Figure 12.2). The best Thatcherism can claim to have achieved in restricting public expenditure in real terms is that its rate of growth has been less steep than in the

Figure 12.1   Public Expenditure as a Percentage of GDP, United Kingdom, 1963–4 to 1990–1

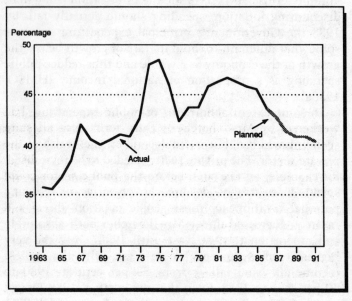

Source: Chart 5.4, HMSO (1988b), Volume I.

Figure 12.2   Public Expenditure in Real Terms, United Kingdom, 1963–4 to 1990–1

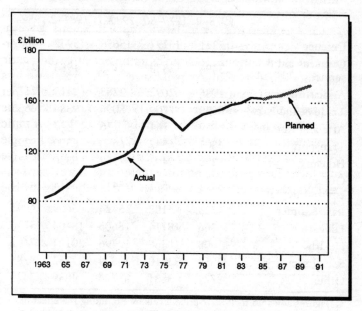

Source: Adapted from Chart 5.3, HMSO (1988b), Volume I.

twelve or so years prior to 1974. Even this achievement, if it is thought to be one, is insubstantial when set against the real reductions experienced during the Labour government of the mid- to late 1970s.

The proportionate fall in expenditure since the mid-1980s is largely a consequence of economic growth which continued into 1989. National income rose more steeply than public expenditure, with public expenditure as a proportion of GDP consequently being forced down. Because proportionate public expenditure is dependent on the vagaries of economic activity and growth rates, it is particularly difficult for governments to control. As in the early 1980s, upward pressure on public expenditure tends

TABLE 12.1 *Public Expenditure by Programme in Real Terms, United Kingdom, 1978–9 to 1987–8[1] (£ millions)*

	1978–9	1979–80	1980–1	1981–2	1982–3
Defence	15221	15297	15655	15942	14509
Overseas aid & services[2]	3496	3370	2108	1983	2107
Agriculture etc.	1985	2092	2283	2113	2173
Trade & industry[3]	8633	7709	8096	9384	6656
Arts and libraries	759	764	776	773	720
Transport	6301	6547	6653	6500	5299
Housing	8722	9402	7952	5330	3838
Other environmental	5461	5571	5412	5014	4503
Law & order	4738	5108	5324	5659	4993
Education	18366	18114	18605	18404	15710
Health	17908	18360	19796	20107	17402
Social security	32854	33210	33824	37382	33785
Other	3777	3831	3774	4059	3425

1. Figures adjusted to 1986–7 price levels by excluding the effect of general inflation.
2. Including contributions to the European Communities of £1.330 million in 1987–8.

to increase during recessions – at just the time when national income is growing slowly if at all. One reason is that recession leads to higher unemployment and increased social security spending. Rapid economic growth also creates uncertainties in planning public expenditure. In March 1988, for example, expenditure for 1987–8 was estimated to be 42.5 per cent of GDP. Because economic growth was greater than expected, the actual figure, announced in November 1988, was a full percentage point less, standing at a twenty-year low of 41.5. What happens to public expenditure in the future will be crucially dependent on national economic performance and changes in the level of national income. Sustained

TABLE 12.1 *continued*

	1983–4	1984–5	1985–6	1986–7	1987–8
Defence	17642	18740	17955	18149	17907
Overseas aid & services[2]	2883	3036	2667	3015	3282
Agriculture	2758	2628	2872	2182	2378
Trade & industry[3]	7706	9667	6961	7177	5952
Arts and libraries	862	888	868	955	980
Transport	6025	6042	5604	5713	5516
Housing	4976	4787	4052	3779	3500
Other environmental	5446	5376	4903	4960	4933
Law & order	6194	6637	6304	6904	7448
Education	18673	18513	17529	19178	19891
Health	20873	21371	20704	22267	23095
Social security	41344	42828	42763	45805	45457
Other	3092	3250	3206	3570	3781

3. Includes energy and employment.
Source: Abstracted from Table 2.12, HMSO (1986), and Table 2.7, HMSO (1988b), Volume I, using cash deflator from Table 5.1, ibid.

economic growth will allow the proportion to decrease. An economic slump will probably quickly reverse the trend.

Amid the overall pattern of public spending there have been some radical shifts between different spending programmes (Table 12.1 and Figure 12.3). The five principal losers have been housing (declining by a massive 59.9 per cent), trade and industry, transport, other environmental, and overseas aid and services. The major gainers have been law and order and social security (growing by 57.1 and 38.4 per cent respectively), followed by arts and libraries, health, agriculture, defence and education.

Figure 12.3   Percentage Changes in Public Expenditure, United Kingdom, 1978–9 to 1987–8[1]

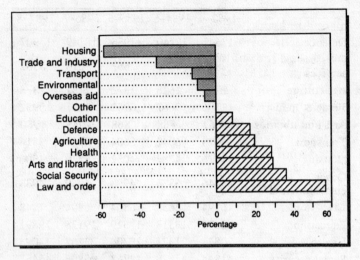

1. Original figures adjusted to 1986–7 price levels by excluding the effect of general inflation
Source: As for Table 12.1.

Some changes perhaps come as no surprise. The increases for defence and law and order reflect the traditional and persistent Conservative stress on these themes given even greater weight with Thatcherism's concern to secure a 'strong state'. Given the Government's rhetoric, a remarkable feature of public expenditure during the 1980s has been the often substantial spending increases on many welfare state programmes (the one obvious exception is housing). This information seems to contradict the view of many commentators that the welfare state is being dissolved or abolished.

Some increases in welfare spending are easy to explain. By far the biggest item is social security. Over the period from 1978–9 to 1987–8, the social security share of total public expenditure increased from 25.6 per cent to 31.5 per cent. In part the change reflects spiralling unemployment during the first half of the 1980s, with much higher total benefit payments to the unemployed. Deflationary policies had the unintended consequence of raising public expenditure. At the same time the numbers of pensioners and other groups such as single-parent families rose steeply, again increasing the social security budget. Such groups also make heavy demands on the health and social services (although costs in the NHS have also risen because of the use of new technologies, treatments and drugs). Rising demands have therefore forced up a number of central elements of welfare spending. Governments have limited the rise by imposing selective cuts. It is consequently possible for the Government to point to overall increases in its welfare state spending, while its critics can highlight the real decline in levels of benefits or the low quality of services in key areas.

With the exception of housing, the programmes bearing the brunt of expenditure cuts have not been major components of the welfare state. Some changes reflect the application of New Right ideas about the state's role in the economy. The fall in trade and industry expenditure, for example, largely results from declines in regional aid and direct support for both publicly and privately owned industries. Yet, contrary to New Right beliefs, trade and industry spent far more on employment and training initiatives, with expenditure rising by 73 per cent between 1978–9 and 1987–8. Overseas aid presents a similarly complicated picture, with traditional aid to developing countries static and low, but Britain's 'contribution' to the European Community (appearing ruefully under the 'overseas aid' heading) increasing from £235 million in 1980–1 to £1330 million in 1987–8.

Even the reduction in housing expenditure, singled out by some commentators as the clearest sign of Thatcherism at work, is not what it seems. Most of the reduction is on local authority housing, but other housing expenditure (not appearing under the 'housing' heading) has soared. Expenditure on 'housing benefit' to help people pay rent and rates grew because of rising council rents combined with increasing eligibility in both public and private rented sectors because of low incomes. Total housing benefit expenditure (hidden under the 'social security' heading) was estimated in 1987–8 to be £3746 million. Also absent is revenue forgone as tax relief on mortgage interest, the major hidden owner-occupation subsidy. Mortage tax relief in 1987–8 was an estimated £4513 million. Most reasoned analysis, from whatever political viewpoint, accepts that the overall result is to raise house prices, making entry into owner-occupation more, not less difficult. Despite the political strength of the owner-occupation lobby both within and outside government, by the late 1980s the implication of this message was accepted to a limited degree by the Government. The £30,000 mortage level on which tax relief was eligible remained unchanged for a number of years. In addition, limited reductions announced in the 1988 budget in the scope of the tax relief were expected to save £200 million a year (although still a figure less than the cuts in housing benefit announced in the same year).

Housing benefits and mortgage tax relief together totalled £8259 million compared to the declared £3500 million 'housing' spending in 1987–8. They are subsidies to the consumption rather than the production of housing. They demonstrate a movement, dating from the late 1960s, toward increased public spending on housing consumption, and also on expenditure in the private sector. In both cases the expenditure is hard to justify on the basis of New Right ideas.

The Thatcher governments' wish to reduce public spending has been overridden by rising demands not only from the elderly, unemployed, sick and poor, but also from politically important groups such as owner-occupiers. Political reality and pragmatism have had far stronger impacts on public expenditure than New Right philosophy and policy proposals. None of this is to suggest that the welfare state has survived unscathed. Moreover, evidence shows that reform of the state has become more radical the longer Thatcher has been in power.

There have been some important shifts between and within major spending programmes during Thatcherism, but nothing akin to the massive changes which took place between the late 1930s and early 1950s (see Figure 11.2). Even when compared to the 1970s, the overall magnitude of the state's financial involvement in society has not changed. Those arguing for a minimal state have been disappointed. There has, nevertheless, been some change in the state's role, particularly as provider of services and owner of major industries.

Public-sector employment partly reflects such changes, falling by 14 per cent between 1978–9 and 1986–7 (Figure 12.4). Even so, 22 per cent of all employees still worked for the state in 1986–7. The largest decrease, of 43 per cent, was in public corporations, reflecting the privatisation of nationalised industries. The number of people working in the Civil Service fell by 19 per cent, largely in Whitehall and offices such as the Department of Health and Social Security. In contrast, the local authority sector, the largest form of public employment, rose marginally. There were increases in employment in both the armed forces and the National Health Service (the latter being the biggest single employer in Europe).

Aggregate employment figures hide the rising demands made on public-sector employees during the 1980s. Many public-sector employees faced increased workloads. The use of state services by members of the public, whether DHSS claimants, social service clients, homeless applicants, hospital patients, or prison inmates, grew over the decade. For staff, the effects of rising demand are often compounded by the requirements of financial stringency and institutional reorganisation. The consequences were

347

Figure 12.4   Public-Sector Employees, 1978–9 to 1986–7

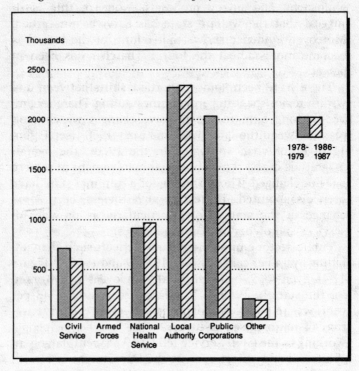

Source: Chart 2.15, HMSO (1988b), Volume I.

reflected in growing discontent amongst teachers; health service staff including porters, nurses, doctors and consultants; DHSS benefit-office workers; and even prison officers.

REFORM OF THE WELFARE STATE

There have been wide-ranging reforms of the welfare state under Mrs Thatcher. Services have been privatised, contracted out, or subject to competitive tendering. Expenditure has been scrutinised for 'value for money'.

Some universal benefits (such as child benefit) and means-tested benefits have not increased in line with inflation. Income-related benefits have been given a greater emphasis. Other benefits have been abolished, including DHSS 'exceptional needs' payments and free school meals. An earlier policy of increasing pensions in line with either inflation or earnings, whichever was higher, was abandoned in favour of raising them in line with inflation alone. As a result, spending on pensions in 1988 was £4 billion less than it would have been. By 1986 the unemployed were receiving £2.8 billion less benefits than they would have been entitled to under the 1979 rules (MacInnes, 1987). Recipients have been more rigorously vetted and controlled. For the unemployed, stricter 'eligibility for work' rules have been introduced and benefits withdrawn when they are not met. In 1988 60,000 young unemployed people who did not take up training places had their benefits withdrawn. Some user charges have risen much faster than the rate of inflation, while new ones have been introduced. Prescription charges increased by over 1000 per cent between 1979 and 1988, and in 1988 means-tested charges were introduced for sight tests and dental checks. Pay in the welfare state has also been tightly controlled.

The biggest spending programme, social security, was substantially restructured in April 1988 when the provisions of the Social Security Act 1986 were introduced. The Government's objectives in carrying out the most far-reaching reforms sicne the war were to direct help towards those thought to be in genuine need, to simplify the range of benefits, and to reduce the social security share of public spending. Reducing social security spending involved either restricting eligibility or cutting payment levels. This led to considerable opposition, including much from within the Conservative Party. The cuts often had a severe impact on individual claimants. The second aim of the 1988 reforms was partially achieved: the benefit system was simplified, although it is still complex. It was less clear that reform succeeded in targeting funds to those most in need. Part of the problem is that defining terms such as 'genuine need' depends on value judgements. In addition, take-up of many means-tested benefits has been poor.

The 1988 reforms had a number of elements. Benefits for state earnings-related pensions were scaled down, and accompanied by measures encouraging people to opt out of the state scheme. Supplementary benefit and pensions were reshaped and renamed 'income support'. Maternity and death grants, previously universal, were made income-related. Family income supplement (FIS) was replaced by a new family credit scheme for low-income working people with children. Family credit was more generous and aimed to reach twice as many families (400,000) as FIS. Yet take-up was low, and 500,000 families' entitlement to free school meals under FIS was abolished. Exceptional-needs payments (for instance, for cookers or blankets) were replaced by a system of discretionary loans and grants from a limited social fund. Radical changes aimed to cut housing benefit by £650 million. One million households stopped receiving it altogether, and 5.7 million lost some of their benefit (following opposition within Parliament this was subsequently reduced to 5.3 million). The reduction was achieved by using stricter income and savings rules: by, for example, reducing housing benefit progressively as personal savings increased above £3000. In the case of rate rebates, a so-called 20 per cent rule abolished the previous 100 per cent rebate for the very poorest. In its place every household had to pay all of its water rate and a minimum 20 per cent of its domestic rate.

The changes generated political opposition. The Government argued that funds would be redirected to the worst off, while opponents pointed to the large number who would suffer benefit-loss. In the case of supplementary benefit (now income support) the Government argued that 46 per cent of claimants would gain and only

35 per cent lose; in contrast the Benefits Research Unit of Nottingham University thought only 17 per cent would gain and 60 per cent would suffer. There was also contradictory evidence about the impact on particular social groups. On the basis of government statements, the 'deserving poor' – families with children, single parents, pensioners, and some groups of people with disabilities – were to be given more help. Younger people, unemployed childless people, and carers looking after the old or disabled were thought to be less deserving and more able to help themselves. While the Government said that it was favouring low-income families with children, the Child Poverty Action Group's own research suggested that this group lost substantially.

The social fund received the most vehement criticism. First, it was argued that the cash-limited total of £203 million in the first year was about £150 million less than the amount spent on single exceptional-needs grants. Second, in distributing the social fund across Britain the North and inner cities lost out to typically Conservative-controlled towns in the south of England. Third, legal right to emergency help from the state was removed – all social fund payments are discretionary and not subject to an independent right of appeal. Fourth, the fund appeared to be designed to complement the work of charities rather than vice versa. Fifth, 70 per cent of social fund payments were recoverable loans, with repayments subsequently being stopped from claimants' benefits. The irony here is that the poorest – by definition those most in need – were least likely to get help because of being excluded by their inability to repay loans.

The longer-term public-expenditure consequences of the 1988 social security reforms are unclear. It is equally difficult to assess whether the complexity of reform adds up to a radically different social security system. Some commentators think that Britain now has a qualitatively different benefit system that is more selective and no longer ensures a minimum universal support for all individuals. However, it is also possible to argue that, although there have been gainers and losers from the 1988 reforms, the basic structure of social security is unchanged as is the state of commitment to it. The poverty safety-net remains, although more people fall through its now wider mesh than did in the past. What is certain is that for an increasing proportion of claimants state benefits will be inadequate for their minimum needs. Responses will be diverse. Some people will be driven to despair: family break-up, domestic violence, divorce and even suicide could result. In other cases people, such as some of the single homeless, will opt out of the state benefit system completely. Others will continue to claim benefit but take on paid employment in the informal economy.

Health, education and housing – other central dimensions of the welfare state – have been subject to considerable political debate and legislative reform under Thatcherism. The state of the National Health Service assumed major political significance in the late 1980s. In the face of intense debate and mounting popular support, in 1987 and 1988 spending was increased significantly (by £2.2 billion a year), the money being used to fund a nurses' pay award and other expenditure. A major government review of the finance and organisation of the health service was announced in 1988. The Government presented the resulting White Paper, *Working for Patients* (HMSO, 1989), as proposals for maintaining a publicly funded service delivering health care on the basis of need rather than of ability to pay, while also improving financial accountability, and shifting power away from political and administrative vested interests and towards individual hospitals, GPs and patients. Some critics argued that the proposed management changes and schemes for internal competition and financial control would increase costs and administrative burdens and harm the delivery of health care. Other critics thought the attempt was being made to introduce radical funding and structural changes which, in turn, would herald the privatisation of the NHS. If implemented, the White Paper proposals will result in the most significant post-war changes to the organisation and delivery of health care in Britain. A publicly funded national health service would remain, however, with the liberal New Right vision of its replacement by a privatised system still far from being realised.

In the same period a wide-ranging Education Reform Act legislated for major educational change in England and Wales (separate although generally similar reforms were proposed for Scotland and Northern Ireland). Within schools the Government imposed a national curriculum with core subjects and provision for compulsory testing of all children. Head teachers and governors were given budgetary control of their schools, at least at the level of determining how a school's income was to be spent between books, teachers and heating. The local authorities' right to determine pupil numbers in individual schools without regard to parental demand was removed. Parents and governors were given the right to 'opt out' of local education authority control and become grant-maintained schools receiving money direct from government, running their own affairs and hiring and firing teachers. The Inner London Education Authority was abolished despite the wish of a majority of London parents for it to continue. The organisation, administration and funding of further and higher educational establishments such as universities and polytechnics was reformed in a number of ways, including the removal of academic tenure, abolition of local-authority control of polytechnics, and the replacement of the University Grants Committee by a new body under stronger central-government control and with private-sector representation.

Education policy contained a diversity of beliefs and objectives. Existing education power-blocs were attacked. Local authority control at all levels of education was eroded. Professional interest groups, such as school and university teachers, found their position weakened. Some other groups were given greater power, particularly parents, governors and representatives of the business community. Some changes sought to bring greater competition and consumer sovereignty into state education. Once again, however, the opportunity to implement more radical New Right ideas (such as the use of a voucher system to increase choice) was not taken up. Underlying many of the reforms was a strong centralising tendency. Central government assumed greater control over the finance and organisation of education, right down to details about what subjects should be taught in schools, for how long and with what result.

The impact of the Conservatives' third-term education reforms is uncertain. It is unknown, for example, how many schools will opt out and the effects of them doing so; whether the application of market processes will have any significant consequences for education in Britain; how the national curriculum and testing will change the educational experience of children; and the extent to which further and higher education will be transformed. Only some years after the legislation can its results be evaluated.

In the case of housing, a 1988 Housing Act and other proposed legislation included reforms directed at further weakening council housing, bolstering the private rented sector, and encouraging alternative social housing in the form of housing associations and co-operatives. Sections of the 1988 Act were designed to lessen security of tenure in the private rented sector, lift rent control, and give tenants greater protection against harassment. Council tenants acquired the right to transfer to other landlords (although many critics of the Act argued tenants would have no real say). New, centrally appointed Housing Action Trusts with wide-ranging powers were set up to take over, improve and perhaps sell off run-down council estates.

Some aspects of the 1988 housing reforms arose from government concern that despite the success of the 1980 'right-to-buy' legislation and other policies a major council sector had survived. Whether the Housing Act enables the Conservative government to replace council housing with other forms of tenure – including a new 'social rented sector' backed by private finance – remains to be seen. It is unlikely that the Act will lead to the reversal of the seventy-year-old decline in the private rented sector (see Chapter 8).

The developments in the late 1980s herald the most significant changes to the welfare state since its inception, but how great the changes will be in practice, and their consequences for public spending are unknown. Some of their objectives are incompatible. In many cases power will move towards either government or private enterprises, with consumers (say, as parents or as tenants) having little real sovereignty. In other situations consumers will be split into distinct groups, some with increased opportunities, others with reduced ones. In the opting-out proposals for schools, for example, it is likely that middle-class or better-off parents will gain. Most reforms have a New Right tint to them, but the best assessment is that the welfare state will be remoulded, in some dimensions radically, but certainly not abandoned.

PRIVATISATION

Privatisation covers a range of policies. Some involve transferring parts of the state to the private sector. Others lower or abolish state controls over the private sector. Yet others aim to bring market criteria into the state.

Denationalisation – moving public enterprises into the private sector – was not an important part of the Conservatives' 1979 election manifesto, only becoming a major policy initiative during Mrs Thatcher's second term. Following the sale of the British Airports Authority

TABLE 12.2 *Denationalisation under the Thatcher Governments*

Year(s)	Company or Concern
1979, 1983, 1987	British Petroleum (oil)
1981, 1985	British Aerospace (aerospace)
1981	British Sugar Corporation (sugar refining)
1982	National Freight Corporation (road haulage)
1981, 1983, 1985	Cable and Wireless (telecommunications)
1982	Amersham International (radio and chemicals)
1982, 1985	Britoil (oil)
1983, 1985	Associated British Seaports (seaports)
1983	International Aeradio (aviation communications)
1983	British Rail Hotels (hotels)
1984	Enterprise Oil (oil)
1984	Jaguar (cars)
1984	Sealink (ferrys and harbour)
1984	British Telecom (telecommunications)
1987	British Airways (airway)
1984, 1986	British Gas (gas and oil)
1986, 1987	Royal Naval Dockyards (dockyards)
1987	British Airports Authority (airports)
1986	National Bus Company (bus services)
1986	Royal Ordnance Factories (arms and munitions)
1987	National Seed Development Organisation and Plant Breeding Institute (agricultural research)
1987	Rolls-Royce (aero-engines)
1988	Rover Group (cars)
1988	British Steel (steel)

Other denationalisations in progress or proposed in early 1989 include:
Girobank (banking), National Engineering Laboratory (engineering research and development), Short Brothers (aviation), Harland & Woolf (shipbuilding), electricity generation and supply industry, British Rail, water supply and distribution industry.

in 1987, more than a third of public-sector industry has been transferred to the private sector (Table 12.2). 650,000 employees were involved, the single most important contribution to the total reduction in state employment over the period.

Largely as a consequence of the denationalisation programme, the number of people owning shares increased from 7 per cent in 1979 to 22 per cent in early 1989. Wider share-ownership is argued by the Government to give people a stake in the system and spread the distribution of wealth in society. In the case of employee share-ownership, other advantages are claimed such as giving workers an incentive to see that the company succeeds, and a belief that industrial unrest is reduced. A number of denationalisations also generated large revenues used to finance public expenditure and tax cuts. Between 1982 and 1987 denationalisation and other privatisation activities yielded £10.8 billion: a further £5 billion being expected by 1991.

Share offers to the public were well publicised, as with the infamous British Gas 'Tell Sid' campaign. Yet many transfers to the private sector relied heavily on institutional investors in Britain and abroad. Institutional investors were left with all but a tiny number of the British Petroleum shares sold in October 1987 at the time of the stock market crash. The sale of British Steel a year later was also aimed at the institutions. In other cases sales were to management consortia (the subsidiaries of the National Bus Company) or private companies (including Sealink, British Rail Hotels, and the National Seed Development Organisation and Plant Breeding Institute). Interestingly, British Aerospace, one of the first denationalised concerns, subsequently bought both the Royal Ordnance factories and the Rover Group.

For the Government, the most financially beneficial and easiest privatisations were of concerns which were both relatively successful in profit-and-loss terms and/or had only recently been nationalised. Some industries nationalised shortly after the Second World War, such as rail, coal, water and electricity, have proved more difficult to transfer to the private sector. Heavily loss-making corporations, like the Rover Group, have only been denationalised after most of their debts have been written off and other financial inducements offered to the purchaser.

When assessing the effect of denationalisation on corporate performance much depends on what criteria are used. Some businesses have yielded increased profits, but often solely because of price increases (British Gas and British Telecom are two examples). For the car-making firm Jaguar – which was profitable anyway, before denationalisation – privatisation coincided with a rising dollar making its cars attractive in the USA, the biggest market. Sometimes denationalisation has been followed by a substantial restructuring of a company. Sealink, for example, closed unprofitable ferry routes. British Aerospace valued a number of the newly acquired Royal Ordnance factories at over £400 million. The valuation at privatisation had been £45 million.

Neither increased profitability nor restructuring is a logical concomitant of moving a business from the public to the private sector. Most nationalised industries are run on similar market principles to private firms. There is no economic reason why industries should be more profitable when transferred from the public to the private sector. In 1988, as a preliminary to the denationalisation of the electricity industry, electricity prices were pushed up far above the rate of inflation to enhance profitability. Restructuring of state-run industries can be as fundamental as anything achieved in the private sector – witness the immense changes in the coal and rail industries during the 1960s and the 1980s.

Another New Right reason for denationalisation is that it provides the opportunity to break up state monopolies and increase competition. Paradoxically, many denationalisations in Britain have simply transferred public-sector monopolies to the private sector. Kay and Thompson (1987) not surprisingly argue that this type of denationalisation is 'unlikely to be very beneficial'. A notable instance of private monopoly was British Airways post-privatisation acquisition of its chief domestic competitor, justified on the grounds of competition in its international markets.

Consumer experience of denationalised companies has often been negative. Apart from price rises, many services have shown little improvement or they have actually worsened (on this count British Telecom received immense criticism for its failure to maintain the public callbox network). Of the millions of new individual shareholders, some sold their shares very quickly and made handsome financial gains. Others benefited from concessions such as discounts on telephone bills. Following the stock market crash of 1987, however, it seems less likely that future denationalisations will attract masses of small individual investors. Unless attractive incentives to buy shares are offered, Sid will probably stay well away. Neither does employee share-ownership necessarily reduce industrial unrest. British Telecom engineers successfully took strike action shortly after privatisation. Similarly, in 1988 industrial unrest loomed on the shopfloor of Jaguar following the company's attempt to respond to falling profits by restructuring working practices.

Denationalisation has fundamentally altered the extent of state activity in Britain. Despite early threats from the Labour Party to renationalise everything, by 1988 many of the most powerful groups within the Labour Party had abandoned nationalisation, at least in its post-war guise, as an appropriate policy tool or political objective. For some, the essential issue is now one of control rather than ownership. Interestingly, the Thatcher governments retained some control over denationalised concerns, often via statutory regulations, competitions policy, or direct or indirect financial support. Some sell-offs were partial

– the Government retained ownership of the land and fixed assets of the Royal Naval Dockyards. Elsewhere 'golden shares' were retained to avoid foreign takeover. In the case of the 1987 BP sale, a foreign government purchasing almost one-quarter of the shares available was subsequently forced to reduce its holding to 10 per cent.

Other privatisation policies have forced state institutions into the *sale of assets*, ranging from the sale of land by the Land Settlement Association, through the sale of plantations by the Forestry Commission, to the sale of land and property by New Town Development Corporations and the Commission for the New Towns. Some sales were preliminary to winding-up – the best instance being the bodies running the English New Towns. In earlier post-war years the New Towns programme was often highlighted by planners and academics as the major environmental planning achievement of the Keynesian welfare state. But the single most politically successful privatisation policy of this type was that compelling local authorities to sell council houses.

For many council tenants buying is attractive. Large discounts are available on the 'market price' of properties. Owner-occupation allows greater control over use and improvements such as the installation of central heating and the colour of the front door. For a small but significant minority, however, home-ownership proved disastrous. Some former tenants, especially those subsequently unemployed, found mortgage repayments and maintenance costs unbearably high. When evicted by the building society or other mortgage lender, they end up back in the local authority sector.

Sales legislation and strict controls on the finance for council house repair and building meant local authorities found it increasingly difficult to maintain an adequate housing service. Typically sales have been of the best-quality housing, often in suburban cottage estates, with most of the purchasers having relatively high incomes. Despite considerable capital receipts from sales, local councils have been unable readily to use them for building or repair because of central government restrictions. Local authorities are being forced into a 'welfare' role, rehousing homeless families (but often few others), with people in the council sector living in often poorly designed and inadequately maintained properties in near-'ghetto' conditions.

Deregulation is a further form of privatisation, involving the removal of statutory restraints, in either the public or private sector, on competition in the supply of goods and services. Deregulation measures were introduced for industries such as telecommunications and electricity and gas supply, and some aspects of the postal services. The deregulation of broadcasting was announced in 1988, although in the same year the Government strengthened other elements of its control over the media, setting up a Broadcasting Standards Council and imposing restrictions on the reporting of Northern Ireland politics.

The consequences of deregulation have been varied. In some cases the original dominant corporations (such as British Telecom) retained their near-monopoly positions. In contrast, deregulation has had a marked impact on long-distance express coaches and bus transport, although the market share of the previously publicly owned companies has changed little. Particularly in some towns and cities, the deregulation of buses following the 1985 Transport Act led to rival companies engaging in unseemly fights for customers, racing each other from one bus-stop to another. After a period of shake-out, the previously dominant company in an area has generally seen off much of the competition, but with socially useful loss-making routes closed (including many in rural areas), higher fares, and smaller workforces on lower pay and in poorer conditions.

Deregulation also involves contracting out and competitive tendering of publicly financed services. Emphasis has been on the health service (including hospital laundry, cleaning and catering services) and local councils (for instance, school dinners and refuse collection). Lower costs have usually resulted, although in some notorious cases only at the expense of a much lower quality of service and/or a cut in the wages of already low-paid workers. This aspect of deregulation (which paradoxically depends on increased central regulation) has so far been implemented on a relatively small scale, and in many cases internal tenders from workers and management rather than from private firms have won contracts.

At its core, privatisation, especially of the welfare state, has to do with substituting a socialised, non-market system of provision for a profit-orientated, market-based one. All critics (and a fair number of advocates) of private provision accept that it leads to greater inequality. Privatisation has had most impact on the easiest targets, that is, those activities carried out by the state most amenable to market processes. Elsewhere within the state, where non-market provision is stronger, privatisation has been less effective. There have been policy proposals aimed at radical change; for example, a voucher system has long been proposed as the best means of privatising state education (Blaug, 1984). Such radical initiatives have been discussed but not as yet implemented by Mrs Thatcher's government. Instead, privatisation within the welfare state has usually been an incremental affair.

CENTRALISATION

Centralisation describes the tendency for central government to draw powers to itself or to its nominated bodies. Most forms of privatisation have involved centralisation.

The most prominent aspect of centralisation during the 1980s was the manner in which local government was increasingly controlled by central government. The attack on local autonomy is noteworthy for its diversity

362

and extent and for its cumulative character. Apart from the centralising measure applying to housing, public transport and education described earlier, greater central control has been exerted elsewhere including land-use planning and civil defence. Most important is the extension of control over all forms of public expenditure and revenue.

With planning, the Secretary of State for the Environment adopted a more interventionist approach to the structure plans drawn up at the county level and designed to provide a medium-term framework for land-use change. Structure plans, especially for areas of growth such as south-east England, have often been overridden and altered by central government. Most of the local authorities involved have been Conservative-controlled. Planning appeals to the Environment Secretary by private developers, who, say, want to build out-of-town supermarkets or housing estates on green-field sites, now have a greater chance of success. Green belts around big cities came under intense central government review in the mid-1980s, although by 1988 (and following protests from pressure groups and local authorities in the affected areas) a climbdown had taken place, with central government declaring its intention to preserve existing green belts. Public inquiries into development proposals were also sometimes curtailed or overridden. A notable example was the decision not to hold a public inquiry into the Channel Tunnel. The overall consequence of the centralisation of planning has been to weaken the control of development by local councils and residents and, in turn, to give developers more power to build as and when they wish. The planning profession itself pragmatically adapted to the new realism and supported many private-sector initiatives.

Central government's most sustained attack on local autonomy has come in the area of local government finance and expenditure. Severe controls have been placed on the ability of councils to raise money or to spend it as they wish. The major source of revenue, government grants, has been restructured and cut back. Rates income has been restricted. The Audit Commission was introduced to police local authority finance and to discipline recalcitrant councils and councillors. A number of local councils, some Conservative-controlled but mostly Labour inner-city authorities, such as Liverpool and some London boroughs, were 'rate-capped' for exceeding centrally determined spending limits. Some local authorities decided to defy the Government and break the law, but all ultimately gave in to central legal and financial pressure. The councillors involved were disqualified from office, surcharged, and their personal assets seized by the courts.

The rates issue has been an important part of the relationship between central and local government during the 1980s. In the 1970s the Conservatives announced their wish to replace rates with another system for raising local revenue. At the end of Mrs Thatcher's second term the decision was taken to replace rates in Scotland by a new form of local taxation, the 'Community Charge' or 'poll tax', a flat-rate charge levied on all adults resident in an area. Both for England and Wales, for which legislation was introduced after the 1987 election, and Scotland, the poll tax policy led to immense opposition, sometimes from Conservative MPs and peers.

A major criticism of the community charge is its inequitable basis. It takes no account of income or ability to pay, a low-income family living in a council house paying more than a single millionaire living in the same locality. Rates are a direct tax on housing, so their abolition will raise private-sector rents and house prices. The flat-rate community charge will also vary between local authorities. There are further implications for civil liberties and electoral registration. In an attempt to gain a high coverage of the tax, numerous ways of tracking down people are to be introduced, including a system of national surveillance on the movement of individuals.

Community Charge Registration Officers can request information from any local authority department, with access denied only to police, social work and medical files. Such measures are expensive, so the tax will not be cheap to collect; much higher, in fact, than rates. Even before the legislation came into force, some people tried to avoid the charge by not registering to vote. Other arguments against the new tax revolve around the impact on local autonomy and the ability of councils to raise revenue and provide services to local people. The charge on individual residents is subject to central capping in the same way as rates. At the same time local authorities lose control of industrial and business rates with the introduction of a new centrally determined and nationally uniform business rate.

Underlying the decision to abolish rates and substitute the community-charge tax is the idea that everyone should pay for the local services they use. Supporters of the new tax believe that once and for all it will demonstrate to local people the folly of 'unnecessary' local authority expenditure, and consequently make them more likely to vote for financially conservative – and hence politically Conservative – councillors.

Central government's attack on local finance and expenditure reveals much of Thatcherism's antipathy towards local government. Antipathy springs partly from belief in the need to minimise public expenditure. Local authorities are central providers of welfare services. Their work is dominated by public, non-market provision so often criticised by Mrs Thatcher's supporters. All local authorities therefore represented an implicit political challenge to Thatcherism.

During the early 1980s, many Labour councils challenged the Government more explicitly in terms of both practical policies and ideology. Their strategies were described as local socialism, city socialism or New Left alternatives. Initiatives over women, race, public transport, local enterprise boards and employment were all directly counter to the programme of central government. In trying to bypass central government financial controls and increase local authority revenues, some councils moved into 'creative accountancy', leasing or selling to private-sector financial institutions property such as council houses, town halls and parking meters.

Central government countered by labelling councils as part of the 'Loony Left', asserting that ratepayers were being ignored, and that council policies helped destroy the local economy. The metropolitan authorities were abolished in 1986, including the Greater London Council. Experiments have also been made with new local administrative forms – Urban Development Corporations (UDCs), Enterprise Zones and Freeports – less restrained by controls over land-use planning and development, rates, and health and safety-at-work legislation.

The centralisation of local government under Mrs Thatcher has decreased local democratic control. Locally elected councils have been curtailed, while powerful but locally unaccountable bodies have been set up. This is apparent with the London Docklands Development Corporation which (despite opposition from local councils and many groups of local residents) has overseen and coordinated the social, economic, and land-use transformation of much of the East End from a dominantly working-class and decayed industrial area into a yuppyfied extension of the City of London.

The London Docklands illustrate one of the contradictions of Thatcherism's reshaping of the state. Reducing the influence of particular state institutions and giving new emphasis to the private market has only been achieved by concentrating power into the hands of central government. It is clearly wrong to argue that the state has been weakened under Mrs Thatcher: some parts have been, but others have been given new strength. The centralisation of power increases the possibility of a future government implementing an alternative programme of change.

Law and order has been at the forefront of political debate
and rhetoric since 1979. It corresponds to the conservative New Right emphasis on 'upholding the rule of law
absolutely' in order to protect individual freedoms and
private property. The rise of law and order can alternatively be interpreted as part of the growth of the
Thatcherite authoritarian-populist state discussed in the
introduction to this chapter. There is evidence, presented
below, that the police and judiciary have become increasingly authoritarian. At the same time the debate on law
and order has been partial and populist. Government and
media focus on street crime, crimes against the person,
inner-city theft and burglary, and social security fraud.
They use strong stereotypes of muggers (often equated
with black people), welfare scroungers, and anti-social
behaviour in the inner city. A range of other crimes are
ignored or downplayed, including white-collar crimes
like company fraud and tax evasion, domestic violence,
and racist crimes against black people. Until 1988 the
populist debate has little to say about the rise of violent
crime committed by young people from affluent suburban
homes. Contrary to popular stereotypes, for example, in
1987 the London Borough of Bexley headed a South East
London 'league table' of crimes against the person which
rose by 60 per cent in the year from 1986. According to a
local police superintendent these crimes were mostly
committed 'by young men in their late teens and early
twenties, who drive cars, have jobs and can afford to get
drunk on a Friday night' (*Policing London*, 1987).

New law and order measures have been considerable.
Public spending on law and order grew in real terms by
57.1 per cent between 1978–9 and 1987–8. Full-time
police officers rose by 10,000, and police pay considerably
improved. The prison population increased from 49,700
in 1979 to 54,200 in 1986. Extra prisons are being built to

accommodate them and to alleviate worsening conditions. New punishment schemes have been implemented, like the 'short, sharp, shock' administered to young people in detention centres. Others are proposed, such as the electronic tagging of offenders. There has been a major programme of legislative reform. The 1982 Criminal Justice Act allowed more extensive and flexible sentencing powers. The 1984 Police and Criminal Evidence Act gave the police much greater powers to stop, search, arrest and detain people. The Public Order Act of 1986 gave police new powers over marches and processions and 'static' assemblies and pickets, as well as making it easier to evict and charge trespassers and an offence to publish, distribute or possess racist material. A wide-ranging Criminal Justice Act in 1988 continued reform, including powers for police to stop and search people suspected of carrying knives and similar objects 'without good reason' and ending the centuries-old right of the defence to peremptorily challenge jurors.

Despite the commitment to law and order, the 1980s have been characterised by growing lawlessness and disorder. For many people this has been the most frightening social change. Serious offences recorded by the police in England and Wales rose by 52 per cent between 1979 and 1986, from 2.5 million to 3.9 million, with particularly steep increases for burglary, robbery, theft and fraud. The annual rate of increase in notifiable offences between 1979 and 1986 was 6.5 per cent, compared with under 5 per cent during the 1970s. Over the same period the 'clear-up' rates for serious offences in England and Wales (although not Scotland) fell from 41 per cent to 32 per cent.

Many Conservative politicians reject the idea that crime is related to unemployment, poverty or government policies. Indeed, to make such an admission would be to engage in self-criticism and to acknowledge that law-and-order failures were at least in part a consequence of other dimensions of government policy. Other explanations for crime are stressed. For example, Norman Tebbit's (1985) much quoted public view is that the 1980s crime wave was 'triggered in the era and attitudes of post-war funk which gave birth to the permissive society which, in turn, generated today's violent society . . . . Thus was sown the wind, and we are now reaping the whirlwind.' There are, of course, close links here with Mrs Thatcher's desire for a return to Victorian values. Taylor (1987) sees such statements as part of 'a new moral and cultural rhetoric on the right . . . [which] attempts to explain present conditions of social disorder almost mystically'.

Against Tebbit's view is the manner in which rising crime figures followed the increase in unemployment during the first half of the 1980s. Moreover, the much lower rate of increase (of 1 per cent) in crime recorded for 1987 might be interpreted as shadowing the reduction in the number of people out of work which began in 1986. But what, if any, is the causal relationship between crime and unemployment? Taylor (1987) highlights 'the general condition of the capitalist economy', while others suggest that both are indices of the spread of poverty, deprivation and inequality. The Bexley example, and rural and 'yuppie' riots in 1987 and 1988, however, show that some crimes cut across social and economic divisions, and are concentrated amongst teenagers and younger adults. Similarly, 'white-collar' crimes have grown as much as many 'working-class' crimes.

Since 1979 there has been a growth of civil disorder on a scale unparalleled in the post-war period. This general heading includes football 'hooliganism', and also major urban riots, in areas such as St Paul's, Bristol (1980 and 1982), Brixton (1981 and 1985), Toxteth (1981 and 1982) and Moss Side (1981), Notting Hill Gate (1982), Handsworth (1985) and Tottenham (1985). Civil disorder may also arise during public demonstrations, mass protests and industrial picketing. Violent confrontations have often occurred between protesters and police, including the 1984–5 miners' strike, the 1986–7 Wapping print dispute, protests by the Greenham Common peace women and other anti-nuclear groups, and the Stonehenge 'hippy convoys'.

New forms of policing and legal tactics have been developed – with police units specially trained in riot and crowd control; the use of riot shields and batons; an increase in the use of firearms; explicitly confrontationary actions; national co-operation and co-ordination between police forces; considerable use of new technology to record, monitor and control people; roadblocks at which people are turned back or arrested; and the use of bail conditions preventing free movement and some types of political activity.

Police and legal systems increasingly have overt political roles. Political dissent by 'extremists', 'agitators' and 'the enemy within' has become an important aspect of policing. Targets include trade unionists, the anti-nuclear movement, immigrants, and threats to 'national security' and official secrets. Other legislative reforms, such as the community charge, the outlawing of the 'promotion' of homosexual material by local authorities (in Clause 28 of the 1988 Local Government Act) and the move to means-tested social security benefit, are also bound up with extra central assessment, monitoring, surveillance, control and coercion. Changes in the legal and judicial system have reduced the rights of defendants. Most notably, in late 1988 the Government proposed to end the right of defendants to remain silent while being questioned and not to have their silence taken into account at trial. For many commentators the cumulative result is a rapid erosion of civil liberties in contemporary Britain.

When first announced, the end of the Right of Silence was presented as a response to the ability of Northern Ireland terrorists to frustrate the due process of law. It was argued that terrorists were trained to remain silent under questioning and to present new evidence once in court. The Public Order Act was a response to the growing public disorder of the 1980s. Mass picketing and riots have induced new types of policing. Such illustrations suggest that the machinery of the law and order system simply keeps pace with the changing nature of lawlessness and disorder. Other examples suggest this is not an adequate explanation, and that law and order problems are heightened by the new forms of policing, sentencing and legislation. Although a response to the situation in Northern Ireland, the proposal to end the Right of Silence also covered the remainder of the United Kingdom. Similarly, policing during the 1980s generally appeared to become more repressive. An immediate cause of some riots was racist and confrontationary street policing, and crowd control by the police has sometimes been violently interventionist. In the case of football hooliganism, the authors of research funded by the Department of the Environment conclude that heavier policing and greater control have led to the rise of 'super-hooligans' (Hope and Shaw, 1988). The short, sharp shock given to young male prisoners in detention centres failed: 63 per cent of young offenders discharged in 1983 were reconvicted within two years.

A central item in the law and order debate is the ethos and ethics of the police and judiciary and the controls over them. The police are not a unitary body. Corruption, bribery and violence have sometimes been rife, with internal inquiries thwarted by silence and non-cooperation. Senior police officers seem unable to do much to stamp out racism and sexism within the police, although more recently a new and sympathetic approach to rape victims has emerged in some police authorities. Some judges continue to make racist and sexist statements and judgements. The problem can be seen as one of individual and small group prejudice; more pessimistically, racism and sexism may be deeply embedded at an institutional level.

External control of the police and the judiciary is contentious. A number of Labour local authorities have urged local democratic control, either through the existing police committees or by setting up new 'police support units'. Such approaches are rejected by the police and by central government. But the ability of central government to control some aspects of the operation of law and order agencies is weak. On the issue of custodial sentences, for instance, during 1988 the Home Secretary Douglas Hurd (faced with a growing prison crisis and evidence that prisons were 'schools of crime') made a number of statements arguing that prison should be used only for violent offenders or as a last resort. Yet the judiciary maintained their established position that sentencing of convicted criminals in courts of law should have nothing to do with politicians.

Law and order has grown in importance in maintaining social control. To some extent the growth has paralleled the declining success of the agencies of 'soft control', such as the education system and welfare services, and a move away from political legitimation achieved through consensus towards consent secured by coercion and repression. The agencies of law and order are, however, in an ambiguous position. Much of the work of the judiciary and police continues, as it has for a long time, to be about protection of the individual in society and maintaining social order. But recent developments question the notions of the law as a neutral instrument devised and implemented in the public good and the police as the servants of the community. There may indeed be, as some on the Left have argued, a 'populist groundswell' of disquiet over crime and violence in society, but at the same time the increasingly authoritarian nature of police and judiciary has undermined many people's belief in the agencies of law and order.

A NEW BRITAIN?

At the end of the chapter, what general assessment can be made of Thatcherism's impact on Britain and British society? Despite over a decade of government and persistent rhetoric claiming that fundamental change has been achieved, it is surprisingly difficult to pinpoint the exact result.

Two conclusions stand out. First, too often Thatcherism is blamed or congratulated for change when fundamental causes rest elsewhere, or where Thatcherism is part of wider contributory factors. It is difficult to separate Thatcherism from other causes of social change in Britain. Second, in all of the areas covered in this chapter it is important to distinguish policy statements and political rhetoric from actual policies and their consequences. There is often a gap between words and events and between intent and reality. What are presented as radical and mould-breaking policies sometimes are nothing of the sort. Across a number of areas, including, for example, public expenditure and some of the welfare services, the Thatcher governments' impact has been mixed. Even the 'successes' of Thatcherism, such as privatisation, are not as clear-cut as first appears. In other cases, including law and order, there is evidence pointing to the failure of Mrs Thatcher's governments, with policies having the opposite effect from that intended – for example, appearing to contribute to a deterioration rather than an improvement in crime rates.

One of the problems in assessing Thatcherism's role in change is that certain answers cannot be provided to the 'what if?' questions. What if Labour had won the 1979 election? What if Mrs Thatcher had not become Prime Minister? What if North Sea oil had remained undiscovered? What if the Falklands War had not taken place? What if proportional representation existed? What if there is a new world slump? Our own view is that the politics of Britain would not have been so different without Mrs Thatcher. A glance across the Channel or the Atlantic seems to reveal very similar processes at work through much of the Western world.

These conclusions do not suggest that Thatcherism has

been unimportant. Although in a very pragmatic and uneven manner, Thatcherism has sought to push and pull social change in Britain in particular directions. Typically, the Thatcher governments have had most obvious success where policies have helped along processes already at work. It has proved a far more difficult task to stop and turn countervailing tendencies. Denationalising industries already run on market lines is relatively easy. Transforming the largely socialised NHS has been difficult. Perhaps because of these sorts of institutional and political barriers. Thatcherism has sometimes been a cumulative programme of often small-scale changes.

With regard to the impact of Thatcherism on people in their everyday lives, it is important again not to see Mrs Thatcher as the cause of all change. Yet it is also the case that many people's lives have changed because of the activities of the Thatcher governments. Much depends on who you are, what you do and where you live. Some people have more affluence and more freedom because of Thatcherism. Others have become poorer and subject to ever more rigorous control. Britain has become a more unequal society under Mrs Thatcher.

FURTHER READING

Two of the many fulsome biographies of Mrs Thatcher are Cosgrave (1985) and Harris (1988). Critical assessments of Thatcherism from a variety of perspectives are provided by Gamble (1988); Green (1987); Hall (1988); Jessop *et al.* (1984); Kavanagh (1987); King (1987); Krieger (1986); Miliband *et al.* (1987); and Skidelsky (1988). It is also worth looking at the publications of right-wing pressure groups such as the Institute of Economic Affairs, the Centre for Policy Studies and the Adam Smith Institute.

An excellent source of information on the evolution of

'public opinion' is the *British Social Attitudes* surveys (e.g. Jowell *et al.*, 1987).

For discussions of the failure of monetarist policy, see Green (1987); Hillard (1986); King (1987); and Smith (1987). The key episode in 1980s industrial relations was the miners' strike of 1984–5. Two contrasting perspectives are given by Beynon (1985) and MacGregor (1986). MacInnes (1987) is a useful account of the impact of Thatcherism in the workplace and on trades unions.

The annual public expenditure white papers are readable insights into government thinking, as well as providing a mass of useful information. See, for example, HMSO (1988a and 1988b).

A good if by now somewhat dated introduction to privatisation is Le Grand and Robinson (1984). A comprehensive and critical account of the 1980s reform of local government is Duncan and Goodwin (1988). For the story of how the planning system has changed and a case study of the transformation of London's docklands, see Ambrose (1986). Local socialism is discussed in Boddy and Fudge (1984). The reform and sale of council housing are covered by Murie and Malpass (1987) and Forrest and Murie (1988). *London Industrial Strategy* (GLC, 1985) explains the ideals and plans behind the Greater London Council's policies for local economic intervention.

The now classic 'wet' official interpretation of the 1980s inner-city disturbances is Lord Scarman's report on the 1981 Brixton riot (HMSO, 1981). See also Kettle and Hodges (1982). Other dimensions of the law and order debate are covered by Belsey (1986), Wallington (1984), Taylor (1987), Hillyard and Percy-Smith (1988).

PART 5

Divided Britain

13

Income, Wealth and Poverty
Michael Ball

The US economist Robert Solow suggested in 1987 that conservative economics in the 1980s was fundamentally concerned with the distribution of wealth and power. Rather than being uncaring, as is often claimed, right-wing governments, such as those of Reagan and Thatcher, passionately care about redistributing wealth in favour of the wealthy and power in favour of the powerful (Solow, 1987b). This chapter assesses how far distribution in contemporary Britain corresponds to this dictum.

Wealth and power can be seen in straightforward economic terms as the incomes and wealth people have, both absolutely and in terms of their changing distribution. Both are outcomes of a complex web of contemporary economic and social processes, some of which were considered in earlier chapters. But what the previous chapters did not explicitly consider are the ways in which economic and social divisions fundamentally structure society and lead to the current distribution of wealth and power.

The issue is the class structure of British society. Class can be seen in many ways, from the convenient divisions of a market researcher to a Marxist view of class as the prime determinant of the history of all hitherto existing societies. So it is not a simple task to map out Britain's class structure or to assess changes within it. The debate about the role, if any, of class is not solely an abstract exercise, but is rooted in the transformations occurring

in contemporary advanced societies. Class analysis
relates directly to politics and to attempts at understanding why so many people in what ostensibly are democra-
cies have acquiesced to or enthused about governments'
proud of highly inegalitarian policies. The question of
class is only raised in specific contexts in this chapter,
but it forms the principal theme of the next and final
chapter.

The next section looks at the distribution of income
and examines whether there has been a shift from the
poorest to the richest. The answer is clear, although its
causes are not. Average living standards rose substantially in the 1980s in contrast to the 1970s. But the
average hides a wide diversity of experience at all income
levels. The following section considers the distribution of
wealth, which is even more unequally distributed than
income. A long-term redistribution of the share of wealth
away from the very rich to the middle class was halted in
the 1980s, while the bottom half of the population owned
a very small part of total wealth. The final section
considers the poor. While the rich have got richer, the
poor have grown considerably in number. Millions of
people in the 1980s either experienced considerable
reductions in their standard of living, frequently through
unemployment, or did not enjoy the levels of income they
previously could have reasonably expected – many young
people and those at the margins of regular, full-time
employment.

In a number of respects the object of this chapter is to
be descriptive. But interpretation requires some underlying conception of wider processes at work. Definition
of data categories themselves sometimes has to be based
on concepts that are highly controversial. So even
description will not be able to avoid dealing with some
of the controversies. Dispute is particularly marked in
definitions of wealth and poverty, and so this chapter has
to consider some of the issues surrounding those debates.
Wealth is usually described in the official statistics as a

command over resources, be they for consumption or for investment, whereas critics of this formulation would argue that a key benefit of great wealth is economic power. In the poverty debate, the definition of poverty is again a controversial topic. Should an absolute standard be used or is a measure related to the current overall level of incomes better? A related issue is the link between low incomes and severe deprivation. One of the objects of the welfare state, after all, was to break that link but it seems to have met with only limited success.

INCOME

Living standards and the distribution of income

It is only in the past fifty years that the spectre of poverty has been banished from the lives of the majority of the British population. Significant rises in wages in the years after the First World War and falling family sizes finally enabled many working-class households to live above the margins of subsistence, unless hit by unemployment (Rubinstein, 1986). The age of mass affluence is an even more recent phenomenon barely more than a generation old. Expressed in 1980 prices, the weekly earnings of a male manual worker in 1951 were only £60; by 1976, they had risen to £109 (Halsey, 1987) and further increased to £122 by 1987 – so they doubled over the thirty-six-year period. Long-term data for women or other occupations are less easy to find.

Britain has always been an unequal society. The advent of industrial capitalism greatly increased the proportion of income and wealth going to the rich. Economic historians estimate that inequality increased markedly in the nineteenth century up to the 1870s, after which point it stabilised or improved slightly until 1914 (Williamson, 1985; Rubinstein, 1986). The inter-war years saw further erosion of landed wealth and some redistribution of income towards those in skilled and middle-class jobs. Economic conditions in the Second World War again improved the position of wage- and salary-earners (see Table 2.3).

Since 1945, the top half of all households have always received more than three-quarters of total incomes. The income share of the bottom 50 per cent has been virtually constant throughout the post-war years, despite the appearances engendered by the welfare state and progressive taxation. They have consistently received between 23 and 24 per cent of all pre-tax income ever since 1949. The position is altered only slightly by using post-tax data.

At the other end of the scale, the income share going to the top 1 per cent fell steadily from 11.2 per cent in 1949 to 5.3 per cent in 1978/9, but during the 1980s it began to rise again, reaching 6.3 per cent by 1984/5. The redistribution away from the rich in the three decades to 1980 was towards the 'middle class', the next 40 per cent of the distribution, although both they and the lower 50 per cent lost out to the top 10 per cent in the 1980s (*Economic Trends*, November 1987). All groups, of course, have become better-off during the past forty years or so, the changing shares indicate which part of the income profile is doing relatively better at a particular time.

The data considered above were derived from income tax returns and the Family Expenditure Survey for those not paying tax. Much income slips through this statistical net (such as that earned in the informal economy). The better-off generally tend to be more adept at avoiding taxation and get greater rewards for doing so. The degree of inequality could consequently be understated by using income tax returns, so it is perhaps not surprising that a slightly different picture emerges from expenditure surveys. A study of Family Expenditure Survey data for the three years 1967, 1977 and 1983 by Morris and Preston (1986) showed that inequality persistently increased between each of those years, although from 1966 to 1977 the richest lost a small part of their share.

From the information presented so far, a number of themes emerge. First, Britain is a country in which the distribution of incomes is, and always has been, highly unequal. As Chapter 3 noted, wartime has been the major impetus in the twentieth century towards establishing a radical shift of incomes towards those in the lower half of the spectrum. Second, there is some evidence that the earlier gains achieved by the lower half of the population have been eroding for many years, starting well before the Conservative administrations of the 1980s. In order to begin to piece together an explanation of why this has happened it is necessary to look at the source of households' incomes.

Income and earnings

Sources of income have altered considerably over the past fifteen years, as the data in Table 13.1 show. The contribution of wages and salaries to total household income fell substantially between 1975 and 1986 from 69 per cent to 60 per cent reflecting the growth of mass unemployment and the increased size of the dependent population (see Chapters 6 and 7). The fall in the share would have been greater but for the substantial rise in the earnings of many in full-time employment. The lost waged share has been taken up by increases in both unearned income and private-sector pensions (together up 4 per cent) and in social security benefits (up 3 per cent).

It is interesting to note the timing of the shifts in sources of income. The decline in the proportion of income from waged work occurred throughout the period, 1975–85; social security rose commensurately, but the shares of unearned income, derived from sources such as rents and dividends, and private pensions only increased after 1979. Part of the increased role of social security

TABLE 13.1 *Sources of Household Income and Direct Taxation, 1975–86*

| | Percentage of total household income | | |
	1975	1979	1986
SOURCE			
Wages and salaries	69	66	60
Self-employed income	8	8	9
Rent, dividends and interest	6	6	9
Private pensions, annuities, etc.	5	5	8
Social security benefits	10	12	13
Other current transfers	2	2	3
DIRECT TAXES			
Income taxes	17	14	15
National insurance	3	3	4
Pension schemes	2	2	2
Total direct taxes	22	19	21

Source: *Social Trends.*

payments is a direct consequence of deindustrialisation and the inability of the economy to generate sufficient well-paid alternative sources of employment. Overall, the rise in the significance of social security would have been higher but for cutbacks and greater selectivity in social security benefits (see Chapter 11). The growth in the role of unearned income conversely is indicative of the response of the three Thatcher administrations to economic crisis and transformation – the export of capital, a boom in property markets and an increase in company profits and dividends.

The changes in sources of income contribute to an explanation of the strengthening of the shares of the upper income groups. It can be surmised that the growth of dependence on social security has helped increase inequality. Divisions have also grown within the dependent population particularly between the elderly relying on social security and those relying on private-sector pensions and unearned income in the form of rent, interest and dividends. But within that declining source of income, waged employment, the structure of earnings has been changing as well, although there has not simply been a redistribution away from the lowest wage-earners.

Although income from waged work has been a declining proportion of total household income, it is still the most important source. Much publicity has been given to the fact that the highest income-earners received the greatest rises during the 1980s. This fact, however, needs to be put into the comparative context of what has been happening to other earnings.

The most common way to compare relative trends in earnings is to examine rates of change over time at particular points on the earnings spectrum, such as at the median and at the lowest and highest deciles, with the situation of men and women presented separately. Deciles refer to points on the income distribution, in this case the income of those at the tenth percentage point above the lowest income and the tenth percentage point below the highest. (They are not the respective averages for all those in the bottom or top 10 per cent of the income distribution as is sometimes mistakenly believed.)

Table 13.2 shows the median wage for men and women and the proportions of it earned at the lowest and highest deciles for 1970, 1981 and 1986. This enables a rough picture to be drawn of the changing fortunes of those in different parts of the incomes spectrum over that time period. It can be seen that the highest-earning men consistently increased their position relative to other male employees throughout the period. The lowest earning decile of men conversely maintained their relative position during the 1970s, but then saw it decline in the 1980s. For women, the picture is different. The

TABLE 13.2 *The Dispersion of Earnings, 1970–86*

| | Males | | | Females | | |
	1970	1981	1986	1970	1981	1986
ALL EMPLOYEES						
Highest decile as % of median	162	168	173	169	172	170
Lowest decile as as % of median	64	64	60	67	68	65
Median (£s)	26.8	124.6	185.1	14.7	82.8	123.4
Female median as % male median	55	66	66			

Source: *Social Trends.*

highest earners did better than their male equivalents relative to the female median during the 1970s and early 1980s, but not later. The relative loss for the lowest female decile was also less than for men in the 1980s. In part, the difference reflects the growth of low-wage female employment in the 1980s. Proportionately more women's jobs are at the bottom end of the earnings spectrum, so the distribution of women's earnings has a different skew from that of men. Both distributions are left-skewed, however, which means that most men and women earn less than average earnings (i.e. the median is less than the mean). Overall, women working full-time earn far less than their male equivalents, so even women at the highest decile are earning far less than their male counterparts. Equal pay legislation improved the situation somewhat in the 1970s, with women's median earnings up from 55 to 66 per cent of men's – but no further equalisation occurred in the 1980s and some evidence suggests a slight widening of the gap.

Real earnings show an even more favourable situation for those on the highest incomes. Real earnings take account of taxes and benefits plus an adjustment over time for inflation. As a result a 'representative' household structure has to be used when calculating the effects of taxes and benefits. The experience of other household types, of course, will generally not be the same owing to distinct tax and benefit incidences. A common category used in the presentation of government statisticians is a married man with a wife who has no earnings and two children aged under eleven. So such men's real earnings – that is, deflated weekly earnings after income tax, national insurance contributions and child benefit – provide an easily available rough guide to relative changes in real incomes. Real earnings data for them show that the highest earners started to do differentially better in 1977 and consistently did so into the late 1980s. Real earnings at the highest decile rose by a third between 1977 and 1986, whereas the median improved by only a quarter and the lowest decile by 17 per cent (calculated from *Social Trends*).

Real earnings data crudely suggest, in other words, that from 1977 to 1986 earnings at the highest decile increased by twice as much at the lowest. There is also no reason to expect that the late-1980s boom subsequently narrowed the divergence. In part, the differential grew because income tax cuts favoured the better-off, a trend exacerbated by the reduction of the highest income tax rate to 40 per cent in the 1988 Budget. The inequitable nature of the reduction in income tax from 1978–9 to 1988 meant that the average tax liability of highest-decile earners fell from 31 to 26 per cent, while for lowest-decile direct taxation only fell 12 to 9 per cent. Percentages, of course, do not represent the true differential shift of the tax burden away from the rich, as the fall for the rich is a percentage of a much larger sum.

The information on incomes considered so far refers only to parts of the income spectrum (such as medians and deciles). Many people assume that it is possible to interpret such an analysis immediately into the experience of individuals. This unfortunately is not true, because the population from which the earnings data are derived is continually changing. Looking at the income spectrum alone consequently can give misleading impressions of what is happening to particular groups, especially when there is much occupational change as has happened in Britain over the past twenty years. As this point is often ignored or misunderstood, it is useful to present a simple arithmetical example of the potential effects, taken from Adams *et al.* (1988).

Suppose there are 100 individuals ranked so that the lowest earns £1, the next £2 up to the highest with £100. The lowest decile point is £10 and the highest £90. If all people earning between £41 and £60 are taken out of the population, new decile points have to be calculated. The lowest is now £8 and the highest £92, giving the impression that the rich have gained and the poor have lost despite the fact that they all still have the same earnings. The problem is a variation on the old theme of relative versus absolute change. Economic change in Britain since the early 1970s has created a similar effect of removing large numbers from the middle of the earnings spread – especially men, many of them skilled, from manufacturing. So some of the relative improvement of the highest earners may derive from such a statistical artifact.

Evidence on occupational groups from the New Earnings Survey does exist to help overcome these compositional problems. Again the data present problems as isolating relative changes for occupations between specific points in time can give misleading impressions, as pay awards are not all granted at the same time and occupational groups might temporarily fall behind only to catch up in the next pay-round. There is also considerable variation in levels of pay in each occupation; statistically the variation in pay within occupations is virtually as great as between occupations (Atkinson, 1983). Despite these caveats, however, some strong trends stand out when occupational pay data are compared for the 1970s and the 1980s.

Although occupational data show a messy picture of great variation within income bands, the broad features are still the same as that shown by the income distribution data. The better-off still did the best in the 1980s and, on average, the lowest-paid fared among the worst. Furthermore, they show a dramatic shift in the fortunes of the high-earners before and after 1979. A study by Adams *et al.* (1988) provides the best available information; although one of their interpretations of the data, that there was no systematic variation in earnings between lower- and better-paid occupations, is highly questionable. Using occupational data from 1973 to 1986, with 1979 as a benchmark, they show that the variation in earnings between occupations widened considerably after 1979. The widening of the earnings-spread occurred at all income levels. Some lower-paid occupations experienced considerable earnings improvement, others very little; a number of middle-income occupations even faced real income falls.

Part of the reason for the greater dispersion of earnings in the 1980s arose from the earlier effectiveness of incomes policies in the mid-1970s, which put emphasis either on flat-rate increments or on rises that favoured the lower-paid. In the subsequent period there was likely to have been a readjustment of differentials; in the public sector some of them occurred under the aegis of the 'Clegg' awards drawn up under the pay policies of the last Labour government. Adams *et al.*'s data show that the highest-earning occupations fared the worst from 1973 to 1979; the real income of some groups even fell (by around 5 per cent for the worst-affected groups, those classified under professional, management and administration and professional in education and health). Most lower-earning occupations, conversely, experienced real income rises. In the 1980s the picture is completely different. Professional categories have done far better than the others, with some achieving percentage rises in real earnings almost ten times those of the worst manual ones. For example, the occupational group, professional, management and administration had real earnings increases of almost 29 per cent between 1979 and 1986, whereas those in construction and mining achieved just over 3 per cent.

One group not covered by the occupational data considered above are part-time workers. As Chapter 6 showed, there has been a large growth in the number of part-time workers over the past decade or so. The majority of part-timers are women (83 per cent in 1986), so their pay rates already start off with the handicap of the relatively low pay offered to full-time women workers. In addition part-time workers are generally paid less on an hourly basis than full-timers. A survey by the union NUPE in 1986, for instance, found that in the health service women administrative and clerical part-timers were paid 86 per cent of the full-time rate; in local government, similar part-time grades were paid 82 per cent of the full-time rate, while manual grades were paid 89 per cent. The lower hourly part-time pay exists despite loss of the chance of overtime pay, bonuses and various employee benefits (NUPE, n.d.). The growth of part-time work has been concentrated in the service sector: 80 per cent of part-timers work there – around 20 per cent as child minders, home helps and in catering; a further 17 per cent work in such jobs as cleaning and kitchen assistants (NUPE, n.d.).

Interpreting the general pattern of change of earnings in the 1980s is hazardous, as individual experiences have been so varied and interpretation itself depends on the underlying theory used. Nevertheless, some tentative conclusions can be drawn.

First, it would seem that occupational labour markets in Britain are fairly flexible in terms of rates of pay, and that rates of change in earnings in particular labour markets are influenced by the contemporary balance of demand and supply. This is indicated by the wide dispersion of real earnings growth at all levels of income and the much faster growth in the earnings of occupational groups where strong demand has outstripped supply, such as professionals and others with specific technical skills. Over the period 1979–86, Adams *et al.* (1988) conclude, the occupations doing least well in the pay stakes were concentrated in the middle of the income distribution, precisely the area where labour demand has plummeted with deindustrialisation. Such evidence casts doubt on theories which emphasise the rigidity of labour markets and wages in Britain, whether they are the natural-rate-theory explanation of continuing high unemployment or insider/outsider explanations of workers being able to keep up the price of their jobs by excluding others (see Chapters 3 and 5).

Second, the overall pattern of changes in pay fits in with the way in which the British economy has been altering since the early 1970s. It corresponds to the decline of manufacturing and the growth of services, and within the service sector to a strong expansion of high-value professional skills and the existence of large numbers of fairly simple clerical and manual jobs – more often than not given to low-paid, part-time women. (Chapter 14 includes an analysis of changes in occupational class.)

Another feature of the pattern of earnings may strike some as odd. The sectors of the economy with the greatest employment growth have not generally experienced the largest growth in average earnings. Average earnings refer to the remuneration paid on average to all employees in an industry from the managing directors to the caretakers. How they change is affected by a combination of how the earnings of individual occupations change and shifts in the occupation composition of employees in an industry.

Table 13.3 shows average earnings (called remuneration in the table) in each industry relative to national

TABLE 13.3 *Labour Remuneration and Employment Shares (percentages)*

	Average remuneration relative to national average[1]		Share of total employees	
	1970–4	1980–4	1980–4 average	Change 1970–4 to 1980–4
Agriculture, forestry & fisheries	65.5	56.4	1.6	–0.4
Mining & quarrying	115.4	134.4	1.5	–0.2
Manufacturing	100.5	108.0	27.1	–7.9
Electricity, gas and water	121.1	151.3	1.5	–0.1
Construction	105.0	103.9	5.0	–0.6
Wholesale, retail, restaurants & hotels	77.9	74.3	18.2	2.3
Transport, storage & communication	121.4	120.1	6.3	–0.4
Finance, insurance, real estate & business services	133.3	129.0	8.1	2.3
Community, social & personal services	94.4	62.6	6.5	1.6
Producers of government services	91.0	93.3	24.1	3.3

1. Remuneration per employee is calculated by dividing total employee earnings by number of employees.
Source: OECD (1988).

average earnings for 1970–4 and 1980–4, and it compares them to the share of total employment and the rate of growth of employment in each industry. What is most surprising about changes in average earnings is that only one of the four sectors registering employment growth saw average earnings in the industry rise relative to the national average – producers of government services. Even then the increase was slight, leaving average pay there still below the national average. Remuneration in the welfare state (encompassing most of the community, social and personal services row of Table 13.3) fell dramatically to 62 per cent of the national average. Even the 'Yuppie' sector of finance, insurance, property and business services saw average earnings decline relatively. As some well-paid jobs in all those service sectors did well in the pay stakes in the 1980s, the most likely explanation of the remuneration changes is that many new jobs created have been low-paid in those sectors, and perhaps that some existing jobs have not kept up their previous relative position. This could have arisen through switches to part-time working, or because of less than average pay increases, or probably through a combination of both factors.

The role of government

It is not possible to put a firm line around to 'free' market or to delimit a sphere called 'the effects of government policy'. Governments affect the framework within which markets operate structurally and in terms of contemporary macroeconomic policy; while any claimed result of government action could actually be the consequence of something else. Only informed guesses can be made about likely influences of government on the growth of income disparity.

In the previous section it was suggested that changes in relative earnings in the economy have broadly corresponded to prevailing economic forces. The growth of professional earnings (from amongst whom many of the top fifth of earners will be found) corresponds to the changing structure of the economy elaborated in previous chapters. The low-paid have faced a different economic environment of an excess of people looking for such work and altered employment practices with firms prepared to take advantage of both. The middle of the earnings spectrum itself has been altered with the loss of thousands of skilled jobs to mechanisation and deindust-rialisation. All of these trends, it should be noted, predate the 1980s. Again, the growth in earnings disparities corresponds to the shifts which started in the 1970s. The changes cannot be attributed solely to the efforts of the 1980s Conservative administrations.

Government in the 1980s did have an influence, nevertheless, through its taxation and benefit policies, trade union legislation, and through the jettisoning of previous (weak) barriers against low pay, such as the wages councils. In addition, it has encouraged low pay in the public sector and in firms reliant on public-sector work (areas where low pay is concentrated) through public expenditure constraints, forms of privatisation and implicit public-sector incomes policies.

In contrast, the pattern of pay in the 1970s and the extent of wage conflicts show a different picture of governments trying to grapple with inflation by the use of incomes policies, amongst other measures, while failing to recognise underlying structural changes in the economy. Overall real earnings growth was sluggish in line with poor overall economic growth (see Chapter 2). The incomes policies were already breaking down by 1978, so the constraints which benefited the lower-paid relatively were concentrated into a few years, after which the disparities increasingly favoured higher-earners. The Labour government with its incomes policies from 1974 to 1979 was trying in effect to control the price of one commodity (labour) without attempting to interfere with the underlying economic structure and the processes associated with it. Structural change was mistakenly regarded as temporary effects of short-term economic crisis. Labour failed to address the trajectory in which the British economy was moving, and did not try to alter it in ways which might have made some of its social aims more feasible.

Paradoxically, one of the few structural changes Labour attempted – with some prodding from the IMF – was a Thatcher-like one of rolling back public expenditure, meeting with far more success than the Conservatives did for much of the 1980s (see Chapter 12). Meanwhile the benefits offered by the Social Contract to the lower-paid were small, particularly in light of the public expenditure cutbacks in operation, and at the same time middle-to-higher-income-earners found their incomes squeezed. Here was the economic recipe that led to substantial political disenchantment, as shown during the 1979 'Winter of Discontent', when the low-paid went on strike for higher pay and greater public expenditure and many middle-to-high-income-earners transferred their political allegiance to the Conservatives.

Conservative administrations in the 1980s did not ignore structural parameters. To an extent, their practice did not follow their rhetoric, as with denunciation of price intervention while using it extensively with regard to interest rates, the value of sterling, and public-sector pay. Intervention, none the less, was still directed at what they regarded as the underlying weaknesses of economic structures – in the form of privatisation, trade union legislation and other measures. Tory success in altering the structure of the economy has met with mixed and rather limited success, as Chapter 12 argued. Yet in many respects the strategies of the Tories have flowed along with developments in the economy. The favouring of upper income groups, for instance, has broadly corresponded to contemporary economic change and the pressures it has induced in the labour market. In this way, the Conservatives have been able to claim the success and inevitability of their fundamental philosophy of favouring the better-off and punishing the poor, a success which was not economically necessary but, rather, politically inspired.

One conclusion, for those who find the current distribution of income and the extent of poverty distasteful, is that trying to deal with the consequences of economic outcomes in terms of income distribution has only a chance of working if intervention is simultaneously embarked upon to shift the trajectory of the economy. Trying to alter prices (or incomes) without tackling the causes of those prices can only be a short-lived remedy.

The final conclusion relates to Solow's statement at the beginning of the chapter. The broad trend of income change has been to the better-off. In this context, his dictum is true. But it has not simply been the result of Mrs Thatcher's administrations. Any feasible alternative government to hers is unlikely to have tried to push through a programme that would have sent the British economy along a different path to a successful conclusion. Without that as the alternative scenario for comparison, 'economic forces' rather than governments have to be said to have ruled the day.

WEALTH

The top fifth of British households receive 40 per cent of all final income; the distribution of wealth is even more unequal. On official calculations, in 1985, 40 per cent of all marketable wealth was owned by the 5 per cent wealthiest households (*Social Trends*).

Estimating wealth is fraught with problems as there is no annual wealth census equivalent to income tax returns. To an extent, it is also difficult to know whether to classify some things as income or as wealth. Crude estimates are made of personal wealth, relying on such information as estate returns at death. Many people obviously have a strong incentive to hide all or part of their wealth from the official gaze, so it could easily be the case that wealth statistics understate certain forms of wealth, especially those held by the rich (Hird and Irvine, 1979).

Empirical problems are compounded by the difficulties of understanding what is meant by wealth. Two basic views can be taken on the meaning of wealth and, although interrelated, they have very different meanings. One definition of wealth, used in the official statistics, is concerned with command over future economic resources. The other is concerned with economic power, discerning who has ultimate control over the major economic decisions taken in the private sector of the economy. The conclusions reached are very different.

In the command-over-future-economic-resources definition, income is a flow concept – say, resources received in a given year; while wealth is a stock concept – resources or promises of resources (like a pension scheme or share certificate) held for future years. Wealth in this formulation consists of a variety of marketable goods and certificates plus unmarketable occupational and state pension rights and tenancy rights. Table 13.4

TABLE 13.4 *Components of Personal-Sector Net Wealth, 1971 and 1986*

| | Percent of total | |
	1971	1986
Dwellings (net of mortgage debt)	22.1	31.6
Other fixed assets	8.9	7.6
Non-marketable tenancy rights	9.9	8.1
Consumer durables	8.3	8.1
Building society shares	6.0	7.9
National Savings, bank deposits, etc.	11.9	8.0
Stocks and shares	21.7	9.3
Other financial assets (net of liabilities)	11.1	19.4
TOTAL WEALTH (£s billion)	199.3	1468.1

Source: *Social Trends*, 1988.

shows the broad categories and their relative importance in 1971 and 1986.

The value of wealth changes over time. The value of total wealth holdings in 1986 was approximately 75 per cent higher in real terms than in 1971. So a declining proportion of wealth held in a particular form does not necessarily imply an absolute fall in the real value of wealth held in that way. The value of individual wealth items can also vary. Stock exchange share-price crashes can knock billions off the value of shares, as happened in 1987 and earlier in 1974; while rising markets will increase their value and the estimated share of wealth held in that form. Price variations in the housing market play a similar role. So when looking at proportions of wealth held in particular assets it should be remembered that price movements might change the proportions from year to year – although, in general, clear trends are still discernible.

It can be seen from Table 13.4 that the shares of different types of wealth in the total changed substantially between 1971 and 1986. Dwellings grew considerably from 22 per cent of all wealth to 32 per cent, reflecting the growth of owner-occupation and house-price increases. The other major shifts have been the sharp fall for stocks and shares from 22 per cent to 9 per cent, and the growth of other financial assets from 11 per cent to 19 per cent. The fall in stocks and shares dates from the early 1970s. It was partially caused by the collapse of share prices in 1973/4, when they fell by about 40 per cent. As most shares are held by the wealthiest individuals, that share-price collapse was estimated to have reduced the proportion of wealth owned by the top 1 per cent by a little over 3 per cent (Atkinson and Harrison, 1978). Since the mid-1970s shares have not regained their previous popularity, although there was a slight increase in the 1980s, which may be attributable to the privatisation programme. The growth of other financial assets, shown in Table 13.4, probably reflects the greater range of potential investment media now available, and growing investor sensitivity to asset risk and taxation.

What is included and excluded from the wealth data is to a certain extent arbitrary and open to question. Each item influences the final calculated distribution of wealth. Housing wealth is included, but, as Chapter 8 argued, the benefits to home-owners of housing wealth are mixed. The benefits of long tenancies on rental housing are also included, although their benefits could easily be outweighed by a combination of probable lower maintenance by the landlord and enforced immobility. Similarly, consumer durables are included, but not the benefits conferred by public-sector wealth on private individuals through the provision, for instance, of communal facilities. People's qualifications and skills training similarly are excluded despite their crucial effect on future earning power.

The inclusion of 'popular' forms of wealth, like housing, pensions, consumer durables and tenancy rights, of course, considerably reduces the share of total wealth held by the rich. A steady redistribution of the share of wealth away from the very rich has taken place since the mid-1920s, as Tables 13.5 and 13.6 show. The share of the top 1 per cent of wealth-holders fell from an estimated 58 per cent in 1924–30 to 20 per cent in 1985; although, as Table 13.6 shows, wealth is still highly concentrated. The total value of wealth has also increased considerably since the 1920s, so a reduction in the proportion of wealth

TABLE 13.5 *Share of Wealth Held by Top 1 Per Cent, 1924–71 (percentages)*

1924–30	1936	1951–4	1960	1965	1971
58	54	44	34	33	30

Source: Atkinson and Harrison (1978).

TABLE 13.6 *Distribution of Wealth, 1971–85 (percentages of population over age 18)*

	1971	1976	1981	1985
Marketable wealth				
Most wealthy 1%	31	24	21	20
Most wealthy 10%	52	45	40	40
Most wealthy 25%	86	84	77	76
Most wealthy 50%	97	95	94	93
Marketable wealth plus occupational and state pension rights[1]				
Most wealthy 1%	21	14	12	11
Most wealthy 10%	37	27	24	25
Most wealthy 25%	69–72	58–61	55–58	57–60
Most wealthy 50%	85–89	80–85	78–82	81–85

1. Estimates of effect of pensions vary with assumptions made.
Source: *Social Trends*, 18 (1988).

held by the richest does not necessarily mean an absolute reduction in the value of their wealth-holdings.

The decline of the wealth shares of the highest groups until the 1980s was not the consequence of a redistribution to the poor. Wealth instead has trickled down a rung or two, predominantly to the upper-middle tier (those lying between 25 and 50 per cent of the most wealthy). The bottom 50 per cent of the population still have virtually no wealth at all – 7 per cent of total wealth to share between all of them in 1985.

The increased share of the upper-middle group is likely to have been the result of the growth of new popular 'middle-class' assets rather than of a redistribution of the traditional sources of wealth and privilege. The effect of the new middle-class forms of wealth can be seen in the separate estimates presented in Table 13.6 that include occupational and state pension rights. The share of the highest wealth-holders is considerably reduced; whereas the share of the 25 to 50 per cent highest wealth-holders experiences the greatest increase, rising from 17 per cent to 25 per cent of all wealth.

Another factor which might have reduced the share of the rich is tax avoidance by wealthy families; achieved, for example, by spreading the wealth around the family to avoid inheritance taxes. As the wealth statistics described above are based on individual rather than families and dynasties, such avoidance strategies give a false impression of a redistribution of wealth away from very rich families. It is difficult to be precise about the effects of such strategies. Atkinson and Harrison (1978) argue that the effect is not great. Their statistical analysis found only a slight increase in the share of wealth held by the very rich if families rather than individuals are used as the basis of calculation. Other commentators have put great emphasis on the ability of wealthy families to continue to reproduce themselves and their wealth from generation to generation despite the apparent existence of draconian estate taxes (Scott, 1982). The failure of any post-war government to implement an effective wealth tax contributes to such dynastic longevity.

Between 1980 and 1985 the share of total wealth of the very rich stabilised, in contrast to the sharp falls of the 1970s. If pension rights are included, the shares of all but the richest in the upper half of the distribution actually increased during the 1980s.

Wealth and power

Official statistics on the shares of total wealth held by particular groups only distinguish marketable and non-marketable wealth and do not consider the qualitatively different attributes particular forms of wealth bring to their owners. They, for instance, treat the value of wealth held in the form of consumer durables as equivalent to that held in stocks and shares. Yet, shares may enable their owners to influence the production of wealth itself; consumer durables generally do not. Wealth in particular forms, in other words, confers power. Most of the wealth held by the lower 75 per cent of the population ranked by wealth does not give them direct economic power, whereas that of the rich may well do.

One way of examining the issue of economic power is to look at the distribution of share-ownership. At the end of 1986, the personal sector held 25 per cent of company shares outstanding; while financial institutions, other than banks, held 50 per cent.

Some individuals have large shareholdings that give them influence over companies. In 1970, the wealthiest 5 per cent of individuals held over 96 per cent of all personally owned shares (Scott, 1982); popular capitalism and the declining role of shares in personal wealth may have since diminished the percentage somewhat, but the concentration remains marked.

Shareholdings by financial institutions primarily represent the holdings of pension funds and insurance companies. Although many pension funds are non-profit, they invariably have an obligation to maximise the return on their investments. This means that those paying into the scheme and receiving pensions have no influence over the investment decisions taken. Many pension funds and insurance companies rely for advice (and sometimes day-to-day management) on an exclusive circle of merchant banks in the City. There is consequently a massive concentration of power in the decisions of a handful of pension fund managers and their advisers. The composition of boards of companies is influenced by them; the fate of takeovers depends on their actions; and major flows of capital into and out of the country are affected by their judgements. These financial institutions are major investors overseas. In 1986, for example, the non-monetary financial institutions held foreign shares and government bonds equivalent to half of all their UK shareholdings.

The concentration of economic power in the hands of the pension funds and insurance companies has been widely criticised (Minns, 1980; Plender, 1984). The managers of institutions such as pension funds, however, are constrained by the need to maximise the returns on their investments, so their power is not as absolute as it seems. Critics are not impressed by the strength of the constraints, pointing to the importance of 'sentiment' and other expectation-forming factors in investment decisions, to the ability of the funds to hide bad investment mistakes from effective public scrutiny, and the rarity of fund managers being sacked.

Shareholders' power has limits. Companies' investment and operational decisions are generally made by senior management, especially executive directors, rather than directly by major shareholders. But shareholders still have considerable power, particularly if they hold significant minority stakes. They may be able to influence the appointment of boards of directors and the overall management structure of a firm. So major shareholders can express indirect disapproval of management decisions and possibly remove specific senior managers or directors. If a company performs badly, shareholders can sell their shares, pushing down the share price. Other companies may search for such badly performing companies with an eye to acquisition and improving performance. Thus shareholders can also influence management through the threat of takeover. Yet senior managers can still try to insure themselves against the consequences of wrong decisions. A substantial number protected themselves in the 1980s against the financial loss of dismissal by demanding contracts with highly attractive termination clauses. So, ironically, some of the prime champions of the coercive effect of market forces protected themselves against the consequences of medicine they claimed was so beneficial!

Large modern companies are characterised by a separation of ownership and control. Shareholders legally own companies but have only limited control over their actions. Decision-making lies primarily in the hands of executive managers who generally have small shareholdings, if any. In pension funds and mutual life insurance companies, the effect is greater as individual members have no influence on the investment decisions and shareholdings undertaken nominally on their behalf. So ownership of wealth, even in the tangible form of ownership of shares in a company, does not necessarily confer economic power. Popular capitalism in the form of extending share-ownership to wider sections of the population in the 1980s (see Chapter 10) has enabled more people to savour the delights of the rentier, albeit in a small way, rather than extended to more people the experience and rewards of entrepreneurship.

The separation of ownership and control in the modern large corporation has led some commentators to suggest the existence of a very small, but highly influential, 'business class'. Scott (1982) suggests that it can be delimited by looking at the top thousand companies. In the late 1970s the number of directors, senior executives, principal shareholders and their families, he estimates, were between 25,000 and 50,000 people; a much smaller number than the top 1 per cent in income or wealth distribution terms. Associated with the core of the business class are those with strong links to it, drawn from amongst the large landowners and other members of the 'Establishment' who are found at senior levels within the Civil Service, the Law, the Church and the Army, and from within the learned professions in universities, medicine and the arts. Such people are likely to have considerable wealth, experience strong cultural, educational and kinship links with the core of the business class and have children who may easily follow business careers. Altogether Scott reckoned that about 0.2 per cent of the British population belonged to the business class and its fringes.

Others have looked at the social composition of the business leaders to draw out trends in the reproduction of the upper social strata. They have identified a myriad of interlocking directorships; a preponderance of public-school and Oxbridge educations; and extensive links between the nobility and the leaders of industry and politics. Britain exhibits a resilient longevity of its upper class according to such investigations. It is a class which is capable of absorbing to a limited extent successful individuals from other backgrounds who if excluded might combine to form a potential threat to its power and influence. The absorption and adaptation, however, never undermine the continuing cohesion of the class and its social mores (cf. Miliband, 1969). Other studies have concentrated on examining the directorship of manufacturing companies and financial groups to find out the extent of interlocking directorships with individuals sitting on the boards of a number of companies. Interlinkages are substantial with individuals often on the boards of both industrial and financial firms. This evidence has been used to argue against the notion of a division between the City and manufacturing industry (Barratt Brown, 1988).

Identification of a small group that seems to have considerable economic power and political influence places emphasis on the behaviour of individuals in an elite, and the means by which it is formed and constrained by the education and culture of that elite. The activities of the British upper class, the 'Establishment' or the 'business class' may be highly distinctive from that of other social groups, and to an extent from the behaviour of elites in other societies. It has certainly led to a mass of novels, films, plays and TV programmes that highlight the distinctiveness. But the significance of individual behaviour can easily be exaggerated in understanding the processes that form and structure the development of British society. Even when power is viewed in terms of a business class, many economic decisions are taken well beyond British shores in, for example, the headquarters offices of US and Japanese multinationals. Neither does the fact that one person holds directorships to two companies with conflicting interests necessarily make the conflicts go away. Rather than being able to smooth over differences of interest, it could be just as easily argued, such individuals are hedging their bets by backing both contestants. It is too easy within a behavioural class theory, in other words, to give excessive autonomy to individuals and their class interests, at the expense of recognising the economic and social constraints within which they are forced to operate. After all, despite its power, the upper class has never been able to mould British society entirely in the fashion many believe it would desire.

THE NEW POOR

What is poverty?

The increasing disparity of incomes in contemporary Britain reflects growing poverty as well as wealth. Yet, finding out who constitute the poor, their absolute number and the ways they survive is difficult both conceptually and empirically.

There is a considerable debate about the definition of poverty. Two fundamental issues are the subject of controversy: the *scale* of poverty at a particular place and point in time, and the *causes* of that poverty. Discovery of widespread poverty may lead to a search for the causes of it and hence to a questioning of the operation of key social and distributional mechanisms. Such an impetus from measurement to explanation was associated with the pioneering statistical investigations of

Booth and Rowntree in the late nineteenth and early twentieth centuries. The search for causes was again put on the agenda in the 1960s with the rediscovery of poverty in Britain when many people thought it had been banished by the welfare state.

Definition, scale and cause are never far apart in the poverty debate, as the notion of poverty itself depends on theories of society and social justice. Many people find poverty morally unacceptable. Yet there is considerable variation in the extent to which people are prepared to accept redistributions of wealth and income and the reordering of the economy necessary to banish poverty. The existence of poverty is sometimes regarded as natural and inevitable. Some theories see poverty as a good thing: a threat to encourage people to strive, work hard and accept realistic wage rates. Controversy surrounds the means necessary to eradicate poverty, because the types of change required to alleviate it depend on views of its cause.

Measuring poverty faces the initial difficulty of finding a widely acceptable definition of poverty. A common complaint in the poverty debate is that investigation operates in a system where the goalposts keep on moving. At one extreme is the view that there is an absolute definition of poverty associated with a minimum subsistence level of consumption. Rowntree talked in terms of consumption necessary for physical efficiency. In practice, his bundle of necessities was not an absolute minimum standard but determined by contemporary views of the acceptable minimum consumption standards for working-class families. Some recent writers have tried to restrict the idea of poverty to a low absolute physical standard. Joseph and Sumption (1979), for example, suggest that poverty exists at income levels below which a family cannot afford to eat. Absolute poverty, however, is a contradiction in terms as poverty is always a relational concept. The idea of trying to find a universally applicable fixed basket of consumption goods

407

is simplistic, and rarely attempted in systematic investigations. Perceptions of minimum standards change with time and place. 'Afford to eat', for instance, would not in modern Britain be associated with bread and water alone. Necessities are similarly created and defined within societies rather than constituting universal physical criteria. A car may be a necessity for anything beyond a restricted life in a dispersed rural community lacking public transport. Fridges are essential to store food when houses are centrally heated and local shops a thing of the past, as Donnison (1988) argues. Yesterday's luxuries, in other words, turn into tomorrow's necessities not only because of rising expectations. Different social groups also have distinct ideas of what is necessary. Vegetarians, for example, would object to the inclusion of meat.

The notion of relative poverty can easily be made to seem the absurd provenance of do-gooders. Ridicule may be directed at the idea by pointing out that in a society of multi-millionaires with an unequal distribution of income and wealth the lowest categories of millionaire could be claimed to be in poverty – the Beverly Hills syndrome. In most contemporary societies, however, deprivation has a stark meaning, in which exclusion from the ordinary way of life and activities of the community leads to a pinched existence. Associated with such isolation may be physical discomfort and poor health. Concern is often focused on children in families suffering severe deprivation, as the possibilities they face in terms of their whole future from their earliest days are severely constrained relative to those in better-off families. Deprivation is multi-faceted, occurring whenever someone does not possess, consume, achieve or experience specified items and events regarded as necessaries. Food, housing, health, education are all part of those items and events, but so are the usual social activities of entertainment and present-giving. Poverty in the deprivation formulation occurs when an individual or household suffers systematic deprivation across a range of activities;

they are, in other words, denied a reasonable quality of life.

On occasions, the degree of deprivation classified as 'poverty' has been assessed by the investigator based on his or her own (and frequently controversial) estimation of what is necessary (e.g. Townsend, 1979). An alternative approach has been tried through the use of opinion-poll techniques to construct a view of what most people in Britain think constitutes deprivation (Mack and Lansley, 1985). Problems arise with the consensual approach in that people may have only limited and biased information on which to base their views. Few people, apart from the poor themselves, are likely to be fully aware of what the experience of severe deprivation means for someone. One study found that almost 50 per cent of its middle-class sample changed their minds and were prepared to be worse off to alleviate poverty after receiving information about benefit levels in Britain (Walker, 1987). Another problem is that people's views are socially conditioned and so the majority view of the poor may contain implicit social prejudices, like the frequently held one that people are poor only through laziness or some mental or physical inadequacy.

Practical as well as conceptual problems arise with the measurement of poverty. Poverty refers to an outcome – a physical lack of goods and services classified as necessary for a reasonable standard of living in a particular society. Periodic surveys may be able to investigate who lacks necessities, but such surveys are expensive. In addition, they may underestimate poverty through low response rates amongst the poor, whose experience of officialdom may make them reluctant to answer surveys. In the absence of detailed, continuous information on the acquisition of necessities, low income is used as a proxy for deprivation. Income data are much easier to acquire. A prime source is the Government's Family Expenditure Survey (FES), initiated in 1953, and now annual. This survey of expenditure patterns is primarily designed to provide weights for calculating the retail price index, but has been used extensively to investigate consumption behaviour and low incomes. Again, there is likely to be an underenumeration of the poor. The Government ceased to publish detailed poverty statistics on a continuous basis in the early 1980s; now instead it provides infrequent low-income surveys.

The supplementary benefit (SB) level has become the usual benchmark for measuring poverty, although it and other income measures face the conceptual problems discussed below. By convention, three supplementary-benefit-related poverty criteria are generally used: all those with incomes up to 140 per cent of SB, at SB or less, and below SB. SB was renamed Income Supplement in the 1988 Social Security Act (see Chapter 12), but the traditional phrase will be used here for consistency. An alternative formulation is to look at families below a fixed point in the overall distribution of income. One common measure is the lowest quintile group: the 20 per cent of families with the lowest net incomes once adjustments are made for differences in the size and composition of families.

Problems arise with the use of income data and supplementary benefit in particular. Income data do not necessarily correspond to deprivation as goods and services may be provided on non-market criteria, either by the state or by some other formal institution or informally. In fact, one of the founding principles of the welfare state was to take certain key goods out of the market nexus in order to break the link between low income and poverty. Minimum housing and health standards have increased for many poor people, although relative to the rest of the population their lot may not have improved much (see Chapters 8 and 9). Households may also be able to supplement their formal income from wealth (important for some of the low-income elderly), from domestic labour, cash from the informal economy and other means. However, the available evidence, as

Donnison (1988) concludes, is that the poor do not gain relatively from such sources; rather, they reinforce the original distribution of income.

The link between low income and deprivation is essentially an empirical one. In some societies many aspects of existence will be derived outside the formal cash economy, in others the opposite will be true. In Britain, a series of empirical studies undertaken in the late 1970s and early 1980s indicate that the low income/deprivation relationship is a close one. A sharp increase in deprivation seems to occur at a level of income 150 per cent above supplementary benefit level, below which people have to withdraw from a whole range of activities and can no longer afford many goods (Mack and Lansley, 1985). The rundown of the welfare state and the increasing use of market-inspired pricing in areas like rental housing during the Thatcher years is likely to have further increased the close relationship between low income and deprivation.

Using benefit rates as a measure of poverty presents problems. There are many different rates depending on the type of household and the benefits for which they are eligible. Benefit levels also vary, with the rate for certain individuals being worse than for others; the rate for children is frequently claimed to be especially meagre. As a measure of relative poverty, use of supplementary benefit levels depends additionally on assuming a constant ratio of benefit to average incomes which in practice does not exist. An unscrupulous government could cut the supplementary benefit level dramatically, and by using one of the SB-related criteria actually claim that poverty had fallen! With these problems in mind, it is now possible to quantify the extent of poverty in Britain and some characteristics of the poor.

The scale of poverty

On all criteria poverty is a major feature of contemporary

411

Britain. Its incidence increased markedly after the mid-1970s, and with the increase the characteristics of the poor altered, away from the elderly towards those of working age.

There has been a number of poverty surveys based on criteria of deprivation. One of the best-known is Mack and Lansley's (1985) study, based on a 1983 survey. In it poverty was defined as the point below which people could not afford at least three out of twenty-six items classified as necessities by a survey of public opinion. They calculated that 5 million adults and 2.5 million children were living in poverty, and that 12.1 million adults and children were in or on the margins of poverty – a staggering 22.2 per cent of the population.

Poverty can lead to severe deprivation, as can be seen in the accounts given of their lives by the poor in Mack and Lansley's survey, and many other indicators of deprivation exist. Much deprivation arises from the low level of supplementary benefits. A study, for instance, of families living on SB in 1986 concluded that a family with two children could expect to have a diet 6500 calories short of nutritional adequacy (Bradshaw, 1987). The Child Poverty Action Group have listed a series of depressing statistics about the millions of people who have to 'make do' in affluent Britain (CPAG, n.d.). With regard to food, for instance, the fact is cited that in 1984 a family with two children on an income of £270 or more a week spent 43 per cent more per person on food than a similar family on an income of £83 or less. Another survey found that 51 per cent of one-parent mothers cut down on food to save money. The DHSS found in 1982 that couples with children living on SB ran out of money most weeks, 70 per cent experienced acute anxiety about money problems and 63 per cent lacked a complete standard set of clothing. With regard to health, poverty leads to death and sickness. In 1985, for example, babies born in the lowest social class (class V) were 59 per cent more likely to be stillborn or die than babies born in the highest official social class (class I) (CPAG, n.d.) (see Chapter 9 also).

Social security payments are low in Britain and contribute to the high measured incidence of deprivation. Table 13.7 contrasts SB rates with the average expenditure of British families, where it can be seen that the benefit levels expect claimants to live on around a third to a fifth

TABLE 13.7 *Social Security Benefits Compared with Average Household Expenditure*

	Weekly rates of SB (excluding housing benefit)[1] £	Average non-housing weekly expenditure of all households[2] £	SB rate as % of average weekly expenditure	Income support as % of average earnings, April 1988
Single person	30.40	82.78	37	19
Married couple	49.35	151.40	33	28
Married couple + 2 children under 11	70.15	166.60	42	37

1. SB levels at March 1987.
2. Average expenditure data for 1985.
Source: CPAG (n.d.), Department of Social Security.

of what equivalent average families spend. Low pay, however, is also a major factor. In 1983, of families with children in or on the margins of poverty (encompassing 7.1 million people in all), 49 per cent were there through low pay, while 25 per cent were poor through unemployment (*Hansard*, 9 December 1986).

Poverty increased significantly in the 1980s. The Government ceased to publish the FES estimates of those in poverty after 1983. Between 1979 and 1983 the number of persons in families at or below SB level rose from just under 6 million to over 8 million; by 1987 the number had grown further to an estimated 9 million – a 50 per cent increase since 1979. In 1983, the latest available data, 2.8 million people were actually living on incomes below the SB level. In 1983, 16.4 million people, almost a third of the population, were living on incomes equivalent to 140 per cent of SB level or less. Between 1978 and 1987, the real value of SB increased by 5 per cent, whereas real disposable income per capita (a measure of average incomes after taxes and benefits) rose by 14 per cent, so the poor not only increased in number but were also becoming relatively worse off. (All data from Piachaud, 1987.)

In another study, Piachaud (1988) compared patterns of poverty throughout the twentieth century. The absolute standard of living of the poor has undoubtedly improved. The real value of supplementary benefit, for example, approximately doubled between 1948 and 1987. Yet, in terms of the total numbers of poor, and their standards of living relative to the rest of the population, the picture looks bleak. To avoid the problem of changing SB rates, Piachaud used the results of earlier surveys to calculate constant relative poverty levels based on fixed proportions for different family types of personal disposable income per capita between given dates. For the first half of the century there is a marked decline in the incidence of poverty, down from 9.9 per cent in 1899 to 1.2 per cent in 1953. Yet poverty rose again during the 1950s, and the 1960s saw the 'rediscovery' of its existence.

Data are better after 1973. Table 13.8 reproduces Piachaud's results for the period 1973–83. Looking at the overall incidence of poverty first, it can be seen in Table 13.8 that there was a marked rise in poverty from 1975 onwards and the 1983 figure is not dissimilar from that of Mack and Lansley (1985) discussed above. The rise in poverty predates the advent of the 1980s Conservative administrations. The table also indicates that there has

TABLE 13.8 *The Growth and Incidence of Poverty, 1973–83*

	Percentage of families at constant relative poverty levels		
	Over pension age	Under pension age	All
1973	59.3	6.7	19.4
1975	36.3	5.4	14.2
1979	52.1	9.9	20.3
1983	43.0	17.2	23.3

Source: Piachaud (1988).

been a major shift in the composition of the poor away from the elderly towards those under pensionable age. According to Piachaud's data, the majority of pensioners were poor in 1973 (59 per cent); by 1983 increases in the real value of state pensions and the growth of private occupational pensions amongst the elderly meant that the situation had improved, with only 43 per cent (still a large proportion) in poverty. The situation of the elderly could also have worsened subsequently with the overall reform of the supplementary benefits system and the cutbacks in specific benefits associated with it. In contrast, while only 7 per cent of those families with a head under pensionable age were in poverty in 1973, the number had escalated to 17 per cent by 1983.

More information can be obtained on the changing characteristics of people in poverty by looking at the lowest quintile group in the overall distribution of income. Table 13.9 compares the types of family in the lowest quintile of the income distribution in 1971 and 1985. Again the decline in pensioners as a proportion of the poor can be seen. The big increases were for single people of working age (up by 15 per cent) and families with children (up by 8 per cent). The shift reflects the growth in unemployment and single-parent families.

TABLE 13.9 *The Changing Characteristics of the Poor, 1971 and 1985*

| | Percentage of lowest quintile group | |
	1971	1985
FAMILY TYPE		
Pensioners	52	27
Single people of working age	19	34
One-parent families	5	8
Working-age couple without children	7	9
Working-age couple with children	17	22

Source: *Social Trends*, 18 (1988).

In the early 1970s it could be argued that much poverty arose from the meagreness of state retirement pensions. Low wages formed another but much smaller cause, as did single-parent families, in which the parent – usually the mother – either could not enter waged work or only low-paid employment. In the 1980s chronic unemployment and the extension of low pay added new dimensions to poverty, transforming the composition of the poor. The unemployment effect can be seen in the increased number of those claiming benefit because of unemployment, which more than doubled from 1,456,000 in 1976 to 3,023,000 in 1986. These numbers, and the proportions given previously, are stock terms – numbers at a particular point in time. The flow of people into and out of poverty and its margins will be far greater; as, for example, with people who experience several months of unemployment, and run down any savings they might have had, or those who take a low-paid job in the hope that it will be only temporary but find they are stuck in it for longer than expected. Put another way, millions more people than shown by figures for a particular point in time experience at least a period of poverty during their lives, although no data exist to quantify the effect accurately. The threat of poverty is a major feature of existence in modern Britain for large numbers of ordinary people.

The causes of poverty

Given the enormous growth in poverty during the 1980s, it is easy to blame the Government for its existence, although the changing structure of the economy and of Britain's population are prime causes of the increase in poverty. Government strategies in the 1980s were not directed toward eradicating poverty. In this sense the Government must bear responsibility. Despite claims that governments can do little, a wide variety of economic prescriptions and their underlying theories from across a broad political spectrum would argue that programmes could be devised to improve the lot of the poor. All such programmes would require a degree of income distribution, which makes implementation of them a sensitive political matter.

Non-political explanations of poverty exist. One would suggest it is part of the structure of contemporary British society, and can only be understood in relation to the broad social organisation of society, particularly the complex network of class, and is considered in the following chapter. Another line of reasoning places the blame for the existence of poverty on the poor themselves by positing theories of how the poor are created.

In the late 1980s there is much media discussion of a new culture of poverty; even Mrs Thatcher talks of the people her 'revolution' has passed by. Within the vague use of the term is a theory about why people are poor. The standard poverty data examine the number in poverty, and only give information on certain general characteristics of the poor. The data do not identify individuals, how long they had been poor, their social origins or other characteristics such as educational attainment and place of residence. The concept of an underclass implants a wider and invalid deductive leap on to the basic data. The implication is that specific social characteristics identify the underclass, and ensure that people with those characteristics and their offspring remain in it for all their lives. It is only isolated individuals with atypical strength of character who climb their way up the social ladder out of the underclass. This explanation of poverty places blame on the social inadequacies of the poor, or in the specific case of the unemployed poor on their unwillingness to price themselves back into work through accepting sufficiently low wages. The rest of the population is not afflicted with those inadequacies, and so can successfully exist within the contemporary structure of society. The existence of poverty, therefore, is reduced to one of 'problem case' people and their offspring who for one reason or another cannot cope with modern life. Mass poverty does not justify criticism of the fundamental structure of society. The existence of widespread poverty may affect the charitableness of the 'haves' but it does not, within this formulation, lead them to question the causes of inequality.

Such theories have a long, inglorious existence. Because of difficulties of definition it has always proved difficult, empirically, to identify the individuals caught in the culture of poverty. Studies looking at the poor over time also disprove the rigid social immobility hypothesis. Many benefit claimants, for instance, do not remain benefit claimants for ever; nor do their children necessarily grow up to be the next generation of claimants (Macnicol, 1987). As noted above, what is more likely is that large numbers of people move into and out of poverty, especially given that much modern poverty is associated with low pay and unemployment. Such a statement, of course, does not deny that there are many people who are systematically disadvantaged. The long-term unemployed, for instance, find it increasingly difficult to find work (see Chapter 7). The children of low-income families are unlikely to have the educational advantages of those in better-off families. Such people and families, however, are an integral part of society, rather than a semi-autonomous, problematic residuum.

The growth of poverty has been a structural feature of contemporary Britain. governments in the 1970s and 1980s have been in power during an economic transformation one result of which has been a major growth of poverty. Conservative Governments in the 1980s have talked in terms reminiscent of the theory of a culture of poverty when discussing the debilitating and depressing effects on individuals of state dependency. So it may seem paradoxical to many that those same governments have presided over the greatest post-war growth in the number of individuals who through no fault of their own have been forced to depend on state benefits.

In this sense, Solow's statement at the beginning of the chapter holds true. It is not that the Conservatives do not care about the poor; it is just that they care far more about the wealthy and about creating an economy in which the wealthy get richer. To an extent, the low level of benefits paid to the poor is deliberate. It is said to free up the labour market – a view supported by many economists as Chapter 3 showed. The OECD review of the British economy in 1988 spoke in congratulatory terms of the reduction of short-term unemployment benefits from an estimated 79 per cent of income in work in 1978 to only 60 per cent in 1983. The poor, and many others, might not feel the same.

One of the features of the market-orientated economics of the 1980s, particularly in its more popularised forms, is that the 'market' outcome is always superior and that there is only one conceivable set of outcomes from a market. The distribution of income is what it is and can never be changed without causing widespread economic chaos. Such a view is theoretical nonsense. But exposure of inadequate theories of itself does not change much. Eradication of poverty requires a fundamental shift of economic and social power, if any realistic programme is to succeed.

FURTHER READING

Atkinson (1983) is an excellent introduction to the economics of inequality. *Economic Trends* provides periodic assessment of the distributional implications of the tax and benefit systems, while *Social Trends*, the annual survey, is a good data source. The *Journal of Social Policy* during 1987 and 1988 provided a good series of articles around the issue of poverty, a number of which are cited in the text. Townsend (1979) and Mack and Lansley (1985) are excellent surveys of the state of being poor in modern Britain. The Child Poverty Action Group's publications (like CPAG, n.d.) are always worth consulting.

APPENDIX

Data on Income and Wealth

The validity of statements on changes in wealth and income distribution obviously depend on the accuracy of the underlying data. Unfortunately income and wealth data are not particularly accurate owing to problems of measurement and controversy over what should be included or excluded.

With regard to income, the prime source is Inland Revenue tax returns, supplemented by evidence from the

Family Expenditure Survey for those whose incomes are too low to qualify for tax. To original incomes are added the net effect of government direct and indirect taxes, cash transfers (like income supplement) and transfer in kind to give final income. The major data problem here, of course, is the accuracy of tax returns as a true reflection of final incomes. People have an incentive not to declare items of income, while the 'informal' economy is defined precisely on the absence of tax. It is difficult to know how undeclared incomes would affect the distribution of income rather than the overall sum.

Income as defined above has excluded a number of elements of what most people regard as income, and it excludes factors which a large number of economists would like included plus other elements of unpaid labour which contribute to the well-being of a household as much as goods and services bought with earned income.

Most people regard the perks of some jobs as income, such as cars, free lunches, cheap credit and holidays. Yet British income statistics take little account of fringe benefits – and often they are greater for those on higher incomes. More controversial would be to include the benefits of home production (like do-it-yourself and housework) or of extra leisure time. Another factor that most would regard as obviously important is the effect of inflation when comparing incomes over time. Income distribution statistics usually take no account of inflation, yet the impact of inflation can vary between different types of household and income band and so alter the real distribution of income.

Some economists argue that the definition of income used is inadequate for an accurate picture of issues associated with equality. Incomes vary according to age, and can fluctuate even on a month-to-month basis for some, depending on bonuses and periods of unemployment. To overcome these variations a longer perspective on a person's lifetime earnings should be taken. A student about to embark upon a successful career in the City might currently be very poor, but does that matter? Questions arise here over minimum acceptable current levels of income. At the extreme, should a person who is likely to be rich in the future, but cannot borrow on the prospect, be allowed virtually to starve today? The moral aspects of distributional issues, in other words, come into the definition of income itself.

Another point noted by economists concerned with distribution is that income should include income implicitly derived from certain forms of property and the net capital gains made by a person as well as his or her monetary income. Some of the benefits derived from capital are already included in the income statistics, such as interest payments. But others are excluded, notably the implicit rental income home-owners are said to derive from their homes. Capital gains and losses are another matter. It is argued that they should be included as the most satisfactory definition of income is one based on measuring all the factors affecting a person's well-being in a given time period on the assumption that the real value of the person's wealth remains constant. On this definition losses and gains made on the stock exchange should be included in income. Others might feel that this would generate wide fluctuations in some people's income and fail to give an accurate picture of what is generally meant by income. This argument in effect is saying that the assumption of a constant value of wealth is too rigid.

If including all these various elements alters the calculated distribution of income at one point in time, it makes estimation of changes in distribution over time especially hazardous as so many unknowns are changing possibly in distinct ways. Official statistics limit themselves to original and final income without these adjustments. Some would argue consequently they miss so much as to be worthless. Yet the official inclusions do conform to popular conceptions of income reasonably

422

well, so perhaps provide some acceptable but limited indicator of distributional change.

Wealth data are calculated using the estate multiplier approach. It is based on the tax returns of the estates of people who die each year. Average death rates for specific social groups are then used to multiply estates into estimates of total wealth and the number of wealth-holders. Strong assumptions are required to derive the estimates. Those who die have to be assumed to be representative of those still living in their group. The estate returns themselves have to be assumed to be accurate, whereas there are obvious omissions. Very small estates (the domain of many people) are excluded from taxation, while those who are liable to tax have incentives to avoid paying it on the inheritance they bestow. Some assets may be under- or over-valued. One example is the true long-term value of shares (which may currently under-value the assets of a company – though the takeover practices of the 1980s are likely to have reduced this effect). Another is the valuation of life insurance and pension policies. Should they be valued at their current redemption value, which is usually small, or at their estimated value at maturity, as the calculations assume? Maturity values give a much more equal picture of wealth distribution. Similar problems arise with the value of consumer durables including housing and rights to tenancies.

For further details, see *Economic Trends*, November 1978, and Atkinson (1983).

14

Class and Stratification
Fred Gray

Underlying the notion of social class is belief in the existence of systematic inequality and stratification in society. Social classes are groups of people with common characteristics and interests which tend to lead to similar social and political activities and practices. Social classes have differential access to resources and power. How power is used and resources are distributed are important components of social change. The determinants of class structures are located in the social and economic organisation of society. Classes, in turn, are instrumental in producing and shaping social change.

A major objective of this chapter is to explore the relationships between class, the organisation of society and social change. There is no universally agreed definition of class. Class is a central but difficult concept over which, like the state, there is intense argument and debate. Different perspectives suggest different relationships between class, society and change. Looking at the changing class structure of Britain involves assessing the validity of different theories of class with which empirical data about stratification are interpreted.

In much class analysis occupation is stressed as a prime component of an individual's social class position. Changes in Britain's occupational structure, in turn, are seen to have consequences for the overall class structure. While there is a paucity of empirical information about social class proper, there is a considerable amount of data available about Britain's occupational structure and how it has changed during the twentieth century. This information is discussed in the first section.

The most widely used and popular view of social class is that provided by the Government's Registrar-General. It is examined in the second section. This official and essentially descriptive picture of social class is rejected as an inadequate conceptualisation of social stratification in Britain.

All discussion of class is bound up with explicit or implicit views about the role of class in the structure of the economy and society. While there are a great variety of perspectives on this relationship, they may be broadly categorised as falling under one of two headings. Under one heading are those approaches stressing that class is the primary source of social stratification in Britain. Work of this kind is explored in the third section. Attention is focused on the contribution of Marxist and Weberian approaches to the analysis of class in Britain. Another broad category of work, discussed in the fourth section, emphasises the erosion of class-based stratification. According to many authors, social change has resulted in the radical restructuring of social divisions and inequality in modern Britain. A common view is that class has declined in importance, or even that it has been replaced by alternative forms of stratification. The evidence supporting such propositions is critically assessed.

OCCUPATION AND CLASS

The starting-point of most accounts of class is paid employment. At an individual level occupation is of immense importance in determining the quality and nature of most people's lives both in and out of work (see Part 2). Within work, a person's job determines his income, how he spends his working life and what he does, workplace status and prestige, and conditions of employment. An individual's occupation and that of other present (and past) members of his household or family are of considerable significance outside the workplace, providing or denying a range of opportunities and resources in areas as diverse as housing, education, health, recreation and politics. Occupation is a powerful factor in the creation of different life-styles and, in turn, is bound up with the social relations experienced by people both as individuals and as members of social groups. It has major consequences for social structure – the overall patterning of social groups in society.

The difficult task of analysing the relationships between occupation and social class is a theme taken up later in the chapter. The objective of this section is to describe what a number of commentators have termed Britain's 'occupational class' structure and explore how it has changed over time. This objective is best-achieved by using the occupational information collected by the Government's Registrar-General as part of the ten-yearly population census. Indeed, this is the only source available which allows comparisons over a long period of time, specifically the period from 1911 to 1981.

Occupational stratification 1911–81

Raw census data on occupational change contain various methodological and measurement problems. Significant coding errors sometimes arise through inadequate information provided by census respondents, imprecise occupational categories, and the method of allocating individuals to particular occupational groups. Some 1911 occupations no longer exist. New occupations have emerged. In other cases, although individual occupations may retain the same title, what they entail and their pay and conditions may have radically altered. A number of occupations have been moved over time from one OPCS

(Office of Population Censuses and Surveys) occupational class to another.

Despite all these difficulties, Routh's (1980, 1987) reworking of census data, to construct as consistent a time series as possible, reveals a great deal about changes in Britain's occupational class structure over the period 1911–81 (Tables 14.1 and 14.2). Table 14.1 shows each of Routh's seven classes increasing or decreasing in relative size throughout the whole period. Much the same picture of flexible, changing, occupational structure and classes applies for the nineteenth century. There appears to have

TABLE 14.1 *The Changing Pattern of Occupational Class, 1911–81 (percentages)*

	1911	1921	1931	1951	1961	1971	1981
1. Professional	4.1	4.5	4.6	6.6	9.0	11.1	14.7
2. Employers, proprietors, managers, administrators	10.1	10.5	10.4	10.5	10.1	12.4	14.0
3. Clerical	4.8	6.7	7.0	10.7	12.7	13.9	14.8
ALL NON-MANUAL	19.0	21.7	21.9	27.8	31.8	37.4	42.4
4. Foremen, inspectors, supervisors	1.3	1.4	1.5	2.6	2.9	3.9	4.2
5. Skilled manual	30.6	28.8	26.7	25.0	n.a.	21.6	17.6
6. Semi-skilled manual	39.5	33.9	35.0	32.6	n.a.	24.6	24.1
7. Unskilled manual	9.6	14.2	14.8	12.0	n.a.	12.5	10.7
ALL MANUAL	81.0	78.3	78.1	72.2	68.2	62.6	56.6
TOTAL	100.0	100.0	100.0	100.0	100.0	100.0	100.0

Source: Tables 3.1 and 4.2, Routh (1987).

been no 'golden age' characterised by a static, unchanging occupational class structure.

Over the long period since 1911 the dominance of manual occupational classes (which in 1911 accounted for four out of five occupations) has considerably lessened, particularly in the post-1945 decades, with non-manual classes correspondingly gaining importance. During the late 1980s non-manual groups probably became a majority of the economically active population.

The greatest rate of increase was for professional and clerical non-manual groups and for the 'foremen, inspectors supervisors' class. Each more than trebled its percentage share. The expansion of the professional class arises from the growth of 'middle-class' occupations as diverse as engineers, architects, teachers and nurses. The figures for the clerical class reveal the growing significance of non-manual but 'working-class' occupations. Only 4 per cent of occupations in 1981 were foremen, inspectors and supervisors, but the relatively large growth of this class over the century perhaps implies that such occupations have become more important as productivity has increased and production methods have become more complex.

Although manual work dominated over non-manual work in 1981 as it did in 1911, it has drastically declined in its relative importance. The fall is especially clear-cut for both skilled and semi-skilled groups. According to Routh's figures, the unskilled manual class grew in importance up to at least 1931. Their percentage share fell subsequently, but was still greater in 1981 than in 1911. Classification difficulties may account for this pattern. Routh assumes that the growing number of 'inadequately described' occupations – increasing from 80,000 in 1951 to 645,000 in 1971 to over 950,000 in 1981 – are best allocated to the unskilled manual class. This may be the best procedure, but it raises doubts over the precise size of the class.

Information on absolute changes in the number of

TABLE 14.2 *Absolute Changes in Occupational Class, 1911–81 (thousands)*

	1911	1921	1931	1951	1961	1971	1981
1. Professional	744	875	968	1493	2128	2770	3724
2. Employers, proprietors, managers, administrators	1861	2022	2179	2364	2388	3110	3552
3. Clerical	887	1300	1465	2404	3002	3479	3761
ALL NON-MANUAL	3492	4197	4612	6261	7518	9859	11037
4. Foremen, inspectors, supervisors	236	279	323	590	n.a.	968	1072
5. Skilled manual	5608	5573	5619	5616	n.a.	5410	4470
6. Semi-skilled manual	7244	6544	7360	7338	n.a.	6162	6121
7. Unskilled manual	1767	2740	3115	2709	n.a.	3125	2706
ALL MANUAL	14855	15136	16417	16253	16121	15665	14369
TOTAL	18347	19333	21029	22514	23639	25024	25406

Source: Tables 3.1, 4.1 and 4.2, Routh (1987).

people in each occupational class (Table 14.2) provides additional insights into Britain's changing occupational class structure. The total number of 'occupied' people increased by over 7 million between 1911 and 1981. Over the period the professional class rose steeply, by 3 million people, with the greatest single increase taking place in the decade to 1981. The clerical class rose by almost as much, with the ten years after 1951 witnessing the biggest increase. The skilled and semi-skilled classes have fallen absolutely since 1931, by well over a million in each case.

Occupational class and gender

Table 14.3 explores the relationship of occupational class to gender between 1951 and 1981, using Routh's extended class categories. The number of economically active men rose by 2.3 million between 1951 and 1971 and then declined by 0.4 million. The number of economically active women rose throughout the period: by 2.2 million between 1951 and 1971, and by a further 0.7 million between 1971 and 1981. The figures show what has been called the 'feminisation' of the labour force.

TABLE 14.3 *Occupational Classes by Gender, 1951, 1971, 1981 (percentages)*

	1951 Male	1951 Female	1971 Male	1971 Female	1981 Male	1981 Female
1A. Professional – higher	2.6	0.5	4.9	0.6	4.9	1.0
1B. Professional – lower	3.2	8.2	6.0	10.9	7.5	15.7
2A. Employers, proprietors	5.7	3.2	5.1	2.8	4.4	2.3
2B. Managers, administrators	6.8	2.7	10.9	3.5	13.8	5.2
3. Clerical	6.4	20.4	6.4	27.0	5.7	29.1
4. Foremen, inspectors, supervisors	3.3	1.1	5.0	1.8	5.2	2.7
5. Skilled manual	30.4	12.8	29.3	8.4	25.5	5.2
6. Semi-skilled manual	27.6	40.5	20.7	31.5	21.9	27.6
7. Unskilled manual	14.2	10.6	11.9	13.6	10.2	11.3
TOTAL (thousands)	13584	6930	15884	9138	15527	9879
TOTAL (percentages)	100.2	100.0	100.2	100.1	100.1	100.1

Source: Table 4.2, Routh (1987).

Women are in a minority in some occupational classes, most noticeably in the higher professional; employers, proprietors; managers and administrators; foremen; and skilled manual worker classes. Conversely, women are much overrepresented in a small number of occupational classes. They dominate in clerical and lower professional occupations, and also constitute much of the unskilled manual and semi-skilled manual classes. Table 14.3 suggests that the distribution of women between occupational classes is in a state of flux, but also that women are little nearer to achieving occupational equality with men. Rather than narrowing, the pattern of gender occupational segregation has simply changed over time.

Perhaps against such conclusions, the point should be made that occupational classifications tend to be gender-biased. While relatively fine distinctions are used to distinguish male-dominated occupations, the paid employment likely to be done by women tends to be lumped into a few amorphous and undifferentiated groups. The clerical class, for example, covers a considerable range of occupations with wide variations in skill. There is, most graphically, seemingly no female equivalent of 'foreman'.

A number of conclusions stand out about how the occupational class structure evolved over the seventy years from 1911. The 'occupied population' increased by over 7 million people. At the start of the period the manual occupational classes dominated absolutely and relatively. By 1981 this was still the case, but only just. Non-manual classes have increased greatly, especially since 1951. The reverse is true for the manual classes. The pattern for specific classes is more complicated. The professional class grew most strongly in the decade to 1981. This was also the period when the number of skilled manual workers fell most steeply. In contrast, the fastest growth of clerical workers and the sharpest fall for the semi-skilled was a decade or two earlier. The relative position of men and women in the occupational class structure evolved over the post-war period. Although women have become an increasingly important part of the non-manual workforce, they remain much under-represented in what most people view as the most powerful and prestigious occupations.

Occupational stratification since 1981

All these comments relate to the period up to 1981. Another set of official statistics, the *Labour Force Survey*, suggests that there were further and rapid changes in occupational class structure during the years from 1979 to 1985 (Table 14.4). In the 1980s managerial and

TABLE 14.4 *Occupational Class Change, 1979–85 (percentages)[1]*

	1979	1981	1983	1985
Managerial and professional	24	27	29	31
Clerical and related	16	16	16	16
Other non-manual	7	7	8	8
Craft and foremen	19	18	17	17
General labourers	2	2	1	1
Other manual	32	29	29	28

1. Percentages contain rounding errors.
Source: *Labour Force Survey.*

professional occupations continued to expand rapidly in percentage terms – from less than one in four jobs in 1979 to more than three out of ten in 1985. 'Other non-manual' occupations rose slightly, but the other four occupational classes used in the survey either fell or remained static. Even the previously fast-growing clerical group failed to increase in proportionate terms.

Manual occupations appear to have continued on a long-term downward trend throughout the century. However, the continuation of this pattern during the 1980s is partly a product of the survey methods used. The historically high rates of unemployment experienced during the 1980s hit hardest at people in manual occupations. It is these groups most likely to be under-represented in the *Labour Force Survey*, being excluded because they are unemployed or 'inadequately described'. The issue here is partly that of whether people of working age but without paid employment should be included in the occupational class structure of Britain. To take an obvious example, does an office cleaner or shipbuilder who is made redundant retain his occupational class as a unskilled and skilled manual worker respectively, or does he leave the occupational class structure and become effectively classless until and unless he finds paid work again? Much the same question needs to be asked for women who cease waged labour to work in the home.

Many of the debates about social class, discussed in the remainder of the chapter, revolve around interpreting and explaining the various trends in occupational stratification examined in this section. Although occupational class and social class are related, social class is much more than occupational class. The two should not be conflated or equated with one another. This, however, is precisely what the dominant official account of class in Britain does. The official view of class is critically assessed in the following section.

THE OFFICIAL VIEW OF CLASS

The most commonly used definition and description of social class in Britain is that used in the decennial population census, organised by the Registrar-General and carried out by the OPCS. The Registrar-General uses a five-fold social-class categorisation. What is termed social class I is made up of professional occupations. Social class II consists of 'intermediate' occupations. Social class III comprises skilled occupations, and is subdivided into non-manual and manual categories. Social class IV is equated with partly skilled manual occupations. Social class V contains unskilled manual occupations.

The Registrar-General's schema is the most popular description of social class. It is the 'official view', widely used in government publications. Commentators often treat it as an accurate and appropriate description of social class in Britain.

There are, however, a number of major weaknesses in the OPCS categorisation, limiting its usefulness as a tool in social-class analysis. The schema has no rigorous theoretical basis. At a surface level the OPCS social classes are produced by grouping occupations into different categories. The Registrar-General's social classes are simply one variety of the occupational classes discussed in the last section, but with social-class name-tags added. Occupational classes are essentially descriptive categories. It is for this reason that social researchers are able to rearrange them and invent new groupings as they wish, and why occupational classifications have changed over time and appear in a number of different guises. Occupational classes are incoherent groupings lacking the shared common objective interests necessary to make them social classes. A person's occupational description at best hints at the determining characteristics of their social class position.

There are other reasons for dissatisfaction with the official schema. Beneath the surface it is laden with values about how society is stratified. Before 1980 the OPCS social classes were a classification of occupations on the basis of their reputed 'standing within the community'. Since then occupational skill has been used instead, although the change in practice is only minor.

No justification, for example, is given for why a skilled craftsman is deemed to have lower standing or less occupational skill than a clerical worker or a junior professional employee. There is a problem, in other words, in the way in which particular occupations are placed in the five class categories.

Lying behind phrases such as 'social standing' and 'occupational skill' are value judgements about particular groups of workers. To categorise classes on the basis of a numerical ordering (I to V in the case of the OPCS classification) or to use words such as 'upper', 'higher', 'top', 'middle', 'lower' or 'bottom' is to assess their presumed social worth. This sort of social class arithmetic uses much the same accounting method as beauty contests, academic exams and horse races, with the first or upper being 'better' than fifth or lower.

The origins of the Registrar-General's classification date back to turn-of-the-century debates about social stratification. Occupational classes were devised to assess the distribution of infant mortality and refute the widely believed argument that Britain's population was stratified on the basis of biologically inherited abilities. Although disproved, the idea of social stratification being bound up with the 'survival of the fittest' remains rooted in the contemporary OPCS class schema (Marshall *et al.*, 1988). Who gets what job and who ends up in which social class, in this view, has nothing to do with the distribution of power and resources in society.

Assessments of social and occupational class were somewhat different in the middle of the last century. The 1851 census, for example, used a seventeen-fold classification of occupations. 'Persons of rank, property or independent means' (class 16) were sandwiched between 'unskilled or unspecified labour' (class 15) and 'useless or disabled members of society, criminals, paupers, pensioners and others supported by the community' (class 17). The mid-nineteenth-century classification echoed an earlier view of class in which the 'privileged' and 'idle' classes were lumped together and contrasted with 'useful' or 'productive' classes (Williams, 1983).

Official classifications of social and occupational classes are not objective or independent measures, but are rooted in the dominant values of the society in which they are constructed and used. Seen in this way, the OPCS classification is itself a reflection and product of social stratification in Britain.

The problem of using official occupational categories and statistics to analyse social class is compounded when the usual labels are removed and replaced with new ones of supposedly greater sociological or political significance. Some authors, for example, have identified a professional and managerial 'service class' (discussed in the next section) by simply equating it with the Registrar-General's first two social classes. If it is theoretically justified to talk about a service class, its empirical extent and character are unlikely to be gauged by using a preexisting categorisation, particularly one so value-laden as that provided by the Registrar-General.

SOCIAL CLASS AND SOCIAL CHANGE

There are two contrasting approaches to the role and importance of social class in contemporary Britain. In one view class is seen as the basic source of stratification in society, though related in a variety of ways to social change. This section explores a range of work adopting this approach. In a second view, examined in the last section of the chapter, class is argued to have lost its significance as a primary social divide.

Most analysis championing the cause of class falls into one of two theoretical camps, following perspectives originally developed by Karl Marx and Max Weber. Marx and Weber, two 'founding fathers' of the social sciences, developed distinct views of the basis of social stratification, leading to separate, alternative perspectives, definitions and explanations of social class, though on some counts they overlap.

Marxist class analysis

Marxist analysis of class focuses on economic divisions. In the pure capitalist mode of production, there are two opposing classes: capitalists who own the means of production and the working class who sell their labour to capitalists and are exploited by them. Marx never regarded any real society as corresponding perfectly to this abstract model. A wide variety of other classes were possible but, in societies dominated by capitalism, the capital/labour divide was the key one. In this view class and class struggle are the mechanisms providing the central structures and dynamics of society. Many authors argue that the schism between capital and labour still represents the major economic and social divide in modern Britain.

Other Marxist commentators argue against a crude reduction of the British class structure into two classes. They refute the 'bosses versus workers' slogans of some left-wing groups, and more complex class structures are advocated. Evidence is used to demonstrate that Britain's class structure was not a simple dichotomy in the past, and is even more complex today. During the nineteenth century, for example, there were major divides within the working class. The existence of a traditional self-employed petty bourgeoisie, both owning some of the means of production and using its own labour, has also sat rather uneasily in cruder Marxist class analyses.

Today's class structure presents additional problems of interpretation. In the last chapter it was pointed out that there are important distinctions to be made between the ownership and control of wealth and capital; distinctions which cast doubt on the existence of a self-contained capitalist class. The 'middle class' (or classes) is now a long-established feature of British society. While not being strictly capitalist, lacking ownership of the means of production, sections of the middle class hold organisational positions that involve directing and managing investment and the labour process. One line of reasoning from within Marxism argues that they are, in effect, in a contradictory class location: at one and the same time they are exploited by capital and exploit for capital. The existence of affluent workers suggests to some an even greater fragmentation amongst the British working class. Though Marx never claimed they would be, it is clearly the case that workers are not made increasingly poor by capitalism: living standards have risen for manual occupations.

Other authors point to the growing international character of the class system, and the inadequacy of isolating class in Britain alone. This is a point which has been made by non-Marxists as well on many occasions since the nineteenth century. In the 1940s, for instance, George Orwell argued that most of the British working class lived overseas in one or other of the components of the British Empire. The British Empire may have gone, but the argument that British capital exploits working-class people overseas remains as strong as ever.

Another complexity is the role of the state in the class arena. For Marxists the state is constituted out of class struggle, but it also influences the class structure as well. There is considerable disagreement among Marxists over how far state intervention can amend class experiences and class itself, and to what extent the state can be controlled or shaped by the working class. At another level, the state has emerged as a major employer. State employees are removed from the exploitative relations between capital and labour, and instead more often confront the state itself. Similarly, the state has a central role in providing for and managing the increasing proportion of the population who, in its broadest sense, are out of work. Where and how do welfare recipients fit into the class structure?

Weberian class analysis

Weberians see class as the result of differential 'life chances' distributed by 'the market'. In this view Britain's class structure is multi-faceted. Different markets – for jobs, housing, education, and so on – lead to distinct although overlapping hierarchies, with individuals sorted into social groups according to their success in the unequal competition for scarce resources and power. However, just as there are wildly different Marxist approaches to class, so Weberian views vary. Some emphasise the primary role in stratification of 'the social relations of production', examining a variety of factors in an individual's work situation which put them in a particular social class. At another extreme Weberians simply take for granted readily available information about income or occupation, as a measure, for example, of 'life chances' and class stratification. In such views, class is crudely defined as market capacity and material life chances. Another Weberian tendency is to isolate one particular dimension of market situation. A good example is much of the work on housing classes and consumption cleavages asserting that the life chances distributed in consumption markets are independent of inequalities produced in the labour market. In this view whether someone is a council tenant or home-owner, for example, may be more important for social stratification than the workplace.

There is, of course, a debate among Weberians about what Weber actually said. Reading Weber suggests to some commentators that on a number of crucial issues – for instance, on the underlying importance of property ownership or the lack of it – the differences between Marx and Weber were minimal. In contrast to most Marxists, however, Weberians tend not to be concerned with the economic foundations of class. At its most interesting, Weberian analysis emphasises that market situation, status, skills and political influence are crucial components of social stratification bound together, with property ownership and control, in complex reciprocal relationships.

There is, then, an unresolved theoretical debate or series of debates about social class amongst and between Marxists and Weberians. At times this has extended to Marxists accusing other Marxists, whose position they disagree with, of being Weberian, and Weberians claiming that the work of a self-confessed Marxist in fact has more akin to Weber than to Marx. The further one moves into the complexities of theoretical argument and counter-argument, the more intractable becomes the debate. Most studies of class in Britain are about what class is and how to define it, and why a particular theory is right and another wrong, rather than offering insights into what is going on in the real world.

Despite this theoretical *impasse*, there is, however, a growing acceptance of the complexity of class structure. Rather than a simple dichotomy or trichotomy of social class (into, say, capitalist class and working class; non-manual class and manual class; or, upper, middle and lower classes), it is often said to be more appropriate to look at a much larger number of different class locations. Classes may be distinguished, for example, on the basis of the extent of their ownership and control of property or the means of production. An individual's class position will be determined by characteristics such as his position in an organisational structure (whether he is a manager or a supervisor, for instance), the skills and credentials he has, and whether he is located in the public or the private sector (or a particular segment of these two sectors).

One difficulty with this approach is that of putting empirical flesh on to what becomes an even more complex theoretical skeleton. It is one thing to identify a dozen class locations, but far more problematic to examine such a complex class structure in the real world. Perhaps for this reason, most researchers attempting to map Britain's evolving class structure sooner or later are led back to a two- or three-fold class analysis, albeit still discussing internal differentiation within each broad class.

Some of the complexities and confusions of class analysis may arise from a lack of clarity in objectives. Class for many seems to have to perform two conceptually related but fundamentally incompatible roles. In one role, it is supposed to measure and encapsulate the multi-faceted characteristics of social inequality, be they defined in terms of access to and use of economic resources, social status or political power. In the other, it is supposed to highlight the prime motors of social change. The two roles, though interrelated, are not the same. Marxists, in particular, would argue that development and reproduction of most inequalities can only be understood in relation to the evolving framework of the capital–labour class relation.

Class and inequality in contemporary Britain

The most detailed and comprehensive examination of social class in contemporary Britain has been made by researchers adopting a Weberian perspective. Relatively specific concerns with social mobility and class structure provide the focus for the massive Nuffield College, Oxford, projects (Goldthorpe, 1980 and 1987) largely carried out in the 1970s. During the mid-1980s a team of researchers at the University of Essex looked more generally at the importance of social class in contemporary Britain, basing their analysis on a nationwide survey of 1770 employed people (Marshall et al., 1988).

The Nuffield and Essex projects both argue that throughout the post-war period class has been a key source of stratification in British society, with 'distributional inequalities' largely springing from social class.

441

Class is of crucial importance, shaping the sociopolitical characteristics of both households and individuals. The panorama where class is central ranges from the obvious area of employment, through the opportunities for class and occupational mobility, to individual voting intentions, and beliefs and perceptions about social stratification in society.

Both projects used the same schema, defining class in terms of work and market situation. Individuals and households were allocated to particular classes on the basis of sources and levels of income, their economic security and chances of economic advancement, and their degree of authority, control and autonomy within work. The three basic classes derived were termed 'service', 'intermediate' and 'working', and were further divided into eleven sub-classes.

The phrase 'service class' is used to describe those who run a modern mixed economy. It is made up of professionals, administrators and officials, managers and supervisors of non-manual workers. The intermediate class is formed by routine non-manual workers, lower-grade technicians, supervisors of manual workers and the self-employed. The working class comprises skilled and unskilled manual workers.

Over the post-war period the overall shape of Britain's class structure has altered in important respects, in part reflecting the occupational changes discussed earlier in the chapter. In particular, the working class has shrunk in size, while the service class has rapidly expanded.

Although shrinking in size, both Essex and Nuffield researchers argue that the working class remains a cohesive group. A number of commentators disagree, however, suggesting that the working class has been fundamentally split by the formation of a distinct underclass. The underclass, or what some Marxists term 'the surplus population' or 'stagnant reserve army', was a notable feature of Victorian Britain. In one line of thinking, its current re-emergence is largely an issue of race and class, the underclass being largely made up of black people. Others suggest the underclass consists of the long-term unemployed or underemployed and their families, and that a white underclass is increasingly isolated in council-estate and new-town 'ghettos' in declining regions such as the North East.

The service-class concept has been used by both Marxist and Weberian writers on class, often in surprisingly similar ways. Proponents of the service class thesis link the development of the class with recent social and economic change – particularly the growth of 'unproductive labour' in service employment and the state and increasing specialisation in the social division of labour. Most see the class as a cohesive, powerful and advantaged social grouping. Other researchers argue the service class is simply the middle class under a different name, and that like the middle class it is fragmented, covering a range of disparate groups often lacking common interests.

The service class concept is used by Nuffield and Essex researchers to illuminate patterns of social mobility – the movement of people from one class to another. The initial post-war expansion of the service class depended on the recruitment to it of people from other class locations or backgrounds. There were opportunities for the children of working-class parents to be socially mobile. Indeed, the service class could not have increased in size so rapidly without recruiting from other classes. Absolute mobility therefore increased during the post-war period because of the fast-changing occupational structure. This, however, appears to have been most true of the early post-war period. Over time the growth of the service class has been increasingly fuelled from within. As the class has expanded, so there have been more children of service-class workers recruited directly into it. In contrast, the shrinking working class has been self-recruiting since the Second World War. An increasingly polarised class structure is the consequence.

Despite sometimes high absolute mobility, relative

mobility rates for different classes have remained unchanged. The Essex team found that the sons of service-class parents are seven times more likely to obtain service-class jobs than the sons of working-class parents. The Nuffield researchers put the odds higher: thirty to one. The situation is more extreme in the case of women. Men from working-class origins find it difficult to enter the service class, but the odds are stacked even higher against women. Evidence suggests that the barriers to greater mobility remain essentially the same today as they were in the inter-war years and even at the start of the twentieth century.

Such conclusions are notable on a number of counts. The dream of many liberals of an open, fluid and classless social structure is as far from being realised as ever. Post-war programmes of social reform, much of it initiated by the Labour Party, appear to have had little, if any, impact. The educational restructuring (discussed in Chapter 10) centred on the objective of encouraging social mobility, for example, appears to have foundered on the permanence of Britain's class structure. Nor have the considerable economic and occupational changes of the last forty years reduced class inequalities. Put another way, the class structure appears to perpetuate social inequalities. Goldthorpe (1987), for example, writes of 'the flexibility and effectiveness with which the more powerful and advantaged groups in society can use the resources at their disposal to preserve their privileged positions'. The dominant classes have successfully resisted the effective implementation of egalitarian measures, while economic growth favours powerful classes and further disadvantages weak classes.

The pattern of social mobility in post-war Britain pinpoints some of the interrelationships between class and social change. In both the immediate past and the longer term, society has been reshaped in a variety of ways. This reshaping has had a considerable impact on social class in Britain. But social change has also been a product of Britain's class structure. Power to affect and determine change is unequally distributed between social classes. At this level the transformation of Britain has been a conservative and status-quo affair, tending to confirm and reinforce social inequalities between the powerful and the powerless.

There are, apart from class, two other key sources of stratification: race and gender. Urry's (1985) view that social inequalities in Britain 'cannot be simply reduced to the class relations between capital and wage-labour' is nowadays a widely accepted position. In the case of gender, a major issue is whether the household, or the individual, or both, is the proper unit of class analysis. Do women living with a male partner adopt the class position of the man? The information on occupational class, discussed above, suggests not, and that at least for working women both individual and household class positions are important.

Both the Nuffield and the Essex researchers suggest that gender inequalities cut through class in important ways. For example, women are underrepresented in privileged class locations and overrepresented in those with fewer advantages. But comparing men and women within the same class reveals another level of inequality. Although proportionately just as well if not better qualified than men, women have poorer work experiences and fewer opportunities than men of the same class. In focusing on class, however, both studies tend to push gender inequalities to one side, seeing them as important but subsidiary issues.

THE END OF CLASS?

'Class has lost or is losing its role as the major social divide in society.' During the 1970s and 1980s this view was expressed by writers across a wide range of political opinions. All are united, however, by the contention that radical social change has occurred which has so altered the sources of inequality that the significance of class-based stratification has been irrevocably lessened.

The clearest statements about the erosion of class-based stratification come from those authors who argue *the end of class*. Britain and other Western nations, the argument goes, have experienced radical – even epochal – economic changes. In turn, society, culture and politics have been transformed. For some writers the changes are equal to those wrought in the industrial revolution and during the transition from feudalism to capitalism. They are captured by phrases such as 'post-industrial', 'post-Fordist', 'post-modernism', and the transition from 'organised' to 'disorganised capitalism'. Although the details of the argument vary, for many writers the result is that class itself has disappeared, or will soon do so.

In one view, perhaps best-represented by André Gorz (1982), capitalism has moved into a post-industrial era in which the working class has become superfluous. While the traditional working class has become a privileged minority, a new 'non-class' of the unemployed and underemployed has emerged, made up of those excluded from industrial production by automation. The new proletariat, it is argued, does not identify itself with work or the work ethic, and instead seeks individual autonomy in a variety of non-work spheres.

An alternative vision of post-industrial society is held by liberals such as Daniel Bell (1976) (see Chapter 5). Ever more jobs involve responsibility, control and technical expertise. Workers are more middle-class, individualistic and consumer-orientated in their life-styles and beliefs. Class consciousness and conflict have declined as society has become more egalitarian and open. For some authors a liberal classless society is the anticipated result. To some extent this is the vision of Britain held by Mrs Thatcher and her followers, with society made up of individuals not of social groups.

Other authors argue that class will disappear for

different reasons. In one widely quoted Marxist account provided by Henry Braverman (1974), the working class has become increasingly alienated, having less expertise, responsibility and control in work. The consequence is heightened class consciousness and conflict, so leading to the replacement of capitalism with a classless socialism.

A contrasting perspective emphasises the *fragmentation of class* rather than its disappearance. A persistent theme is that the working class has become less coherent and homogeneous. Leadbeater (1988), for example, argues that the economic restructuring of the 1980s has dissolved long-established sources of solidarity and common identification, producing deep divisions within the working class. Previous contrasts between blue- and white-collar workers and the skilled and unskilled are being superseded by 'much more fundamental' divides. The employed, full-timers, those skilled in new technologies and people in the South East are set against the long-term unemployed, part-time and temporary workers, those without skills in new technologies, and people living in the rest of Britain.

A further argument is that work itself has become less important for the working class. Traditional forms of class identity, based on locality and community, shared political objectives including unionism, have given way to new sectional interests centred on individualism, consumerism and the home. Beliefs and attitudes have adjusted with the assumed re-alignment in social stratification. For Lukes (1984), there has been a growth 'of instrumental, pecuniary, egoistic, in short capitalist values and attitudes'. The Marxist historian Hobsbawm (1981) agrees, stressing the increasing domination of 'the values of consumer-society individualism and the search for private and personal satisfactions above all else'.

Another approach to contemporary social divides concentrates not so much on what is happening to class but more on the increasing importance of *non-class stratification*. Proponents of this view all abandon or ignore class, but disagree about which sectional divides are most important. Attention is focused on public and private consumption; the ownership or lack of ownership of property; those in or out of work; age and household-type differentials; and inequalities springing from differences between geographical localities.

When the various stratifying factors are drawn together, it is possible to build up a picture of society divided into privileged and powerful groups and under-privileged and powerless groups. Successful groups include middle-aged, two-earner households in well-paid (typically private-sector) employment; those owning private property, especially home-owners; and people living in suburbs and rural areas, particularly in the South – what has been termed 'deep' or 'middle' England. Such groups are contrasted with the young and the old; single parents; the unemployed and the underemployed dependent on state benefits; those working in the public sector; people without private property, especially council house tenants; inner-city residents; and people in the North.

One strongly developed perspective on the replacement of class argues that sectoral *consumption cleavages* have emerged as the new social divide in Britain. Consumption cleavages are defined as lines of vertical division in society. They cut through the horizontal divisions of social class. The resulting social groupings, of people united by shared common interests, are independent of class location. In this view consumption cleavages exist around the public-versus-private provision of housing, transport, education and health care, although housing is generally singled out as the most important divide. At its simplest the consumption cleavage thesis asserts that a home-owner and council tenant will have conflicting interests, attitudes and political beliefs, even though they may have identical jobs in the same workplace. A number of commentators echo Saunders's (1985) view that social and political consumption cleavages are as important as, if not more important than, class divisions arising from the social organisation of production.

The concern with housing consumption cleavages is part of a well-established Weberian tradition in which 'housing class' can be as central as social class in determining social divides and inequality. A number of Marxists have made similar arguments, suggesting that particular tenures (both council renting and owner-occupation) may tie people into status-quo social relationships. Leadbeater (1988), for example, asserts that the protection of the private space for the home-owning consumer incorporates people within a general defence of private property which, in turn, strengthens support for private ownership and control in the economy.

Many decline-of-class writers draw on information about *class and voting* to support their assertions. Over a long period of time, and particularly during the post-war period, the percentage of the vote cast for the Labour Party has tended to fall. In the 1983 general election, for example, Labour received its smallest share of the vote since 1918. Many observers interpret this trend as strong evidence of 'class disalignment' – the separation of class from voting, and particularly the decline of working-class support for the Labour Party. Sarlvik and Crewe (1983), for instance, argue that class voting has fitfully but gradually declined over a long series of elections.

The contention here is not simply that the Labour vote has fallen because the working class has decreased in size, but that class itself has become less important in determining how people cast their vote and in politics generally. Consumption cleavage advocates assert that consumption patterns, and housing tenure in particular, have increasingly replaced class as explanations of voting and political activity. People are said to be more likely to vote Conservative because they are home-owners. Other authors point to the changing geographical pattern of voting, and the increasing contrasts between

Conservative-dominated suburbs, rural areas and the South, and the remaining Labour heartlands in inner urban areas, especially in Scotland, Wales and the North of England.

In summary, a large and mounting body of literature from a diverse range of standpoints asserts that class in modern Britain has become less important or even irrelevant. If just a few of these arguments were correct, contemporary Britain would indeed be undergoing revolutionary change. For the first time in the better part of two centuries, the generally accepted basis of stratification in society would have been banished.

There are, however, a number of reasons to be sceptical of the decline-of-class thesis in its variety of guises. First, the present day is typically contrasted with an unsubstantiated picture of class in the past. Second, there is limited evidence to support the view that current changes in the economic base and social and political organisation of society are as epochal as assumed. Third, alterations in the contemporary class structure are asserted rather than demonstrated. Decline-of-class theorists either draw upon surprisingly little empirical data to support their views, or, if empirical evidence is used, ignore rival interpretations of the same information.

Class and history

A major criticism of the decline-of-class thesis is that it adopts an ahistorical view of the past. On both the left and the right, sweeping assumptions tend to be made that class in the past was radically different from what it is today. For writers on the left, the present is contrasted with a supposed golden age in which the class structure was clear-cut and unchanging. In this 'traditional' view, an undifferentiated and united working class shared common interests, beliefs and actions based on work, locality and community. Pit villages, steel towns and docklands provide the archetype localities for such a working class.

On close inspection the golden-past image of class is skin-deep and tarnished. Supposedly 'traditional' communities and class patterns often appear surprisingly modern and in a constant state of flux. Industrial communities were movable feasts, developing, evolving and sometimes withering according to the dictates of industrial change. Commentators, in harking back to a golden past, usually seem to have in mind just one of a range of different working-class localities. In so far as the working class was based in locality and community, there is little reason to suppose that inter-locality and inter-community relationships were strong other than in the most exceptional circumstances. There has never been, as such, a single and united national working class. Even national organisations, such as trade unions and political parties, have tended to represent not the whole class but dominant sections of it. Trade union membership peaked, after all, in the 1970s and it is still higher than it was prior to the late 1930s (see Chapter 5).

The available evidence suggests a changing variety of working-class life-styles and cultures. Young and Willmott's classic study (1962) shows that in places family and kinship were all-important working-class concerns. Elsewhere competition and individualism were rife. This is a point driven home by authors as diverse as Engels (1969) writing about the 'narrow self-seeking' of the working class in mid-nineteenth-century Northern cities; the socialist Tressell (1955) despising the working class in Edwardian 'Mugsborough' (Hastings); and Roberts (1971) describing turn-of-the-century Salford. Sexism and an imperialism heavily tinged with racism were prevalent in most male- and white-dominated communities, although occasionally women and migrants did have considerable power and status both in and out of work.

Within particular localities there were clear differences and sometimes conflicts between working-class groups.

Throughout the nineteenth and twentieth centuries the working class has been segmented in a number of ways on the basis of work, skill, gender, status, origin, degree of respectability, and locality. For example, during the nineteenth century a high-status, respectable, relatively high-income, and home- and family-centred 'aristocracy of labour' was made up of craftsmen and skilled manual workers. In the same period a contrasting 'underclass' or 'reserve army of labour' can be identified of extremely poor, unskilled, scapegoated, 'undeserving' and often unemployed groups. But neither of these groups was homogeneous nor necessarily united and self-contained.

In some places – as diverse as Bristol, South Wales and Cornwall – working-class home-ownership has been important for a long period. Sometimes the home was related to a private individualism focused on self and family. On other occasions it provided a platform for collective action in the community and workplace. (Much the same point was made by some commentators on the 1984 miners' strike.)

Working-class lifestyles and cultures have always covered a diversity of forms. The past dominance of 'traditional' working-class occupations and communities appears more as wishful thinking than fact. Work, community and locality, and characteristics such as unity and solidarity, were not always important in the working class – at least not in the way many present-day commentators suggest. Similarly, what for some writers on the left are the recently discovered sins of working-class privatism and home- and family-centred life have, in fact, been characteristic of much of the working class for a century or more. Writers on class today are usually very selective in which aspects of the past they highlight and compare with the present.

The historical weakness of many decline-of-class theories has another dimension. Throughout the history of post-war class analysis there has been a persistent tendency to assume that social stratification has been undergoing radical change of a kind not previously experienced.

Writing in the mid-1950s and describing what he saw as the erosion of northern working-class culture, Richard Hoggart in an influential book (1957) accepted that a 'bloodless revolution' was taking place. The great majority of people were 'being merged into one class' and becoming culturally classless. Hoggart focused on the penetration of a mass culture into specific local, class-based cultures. Other commentators in the 1950s and 1960s were more concerned with the impact of affluence on the working class, although this work, too, had its cultural dimension. The general contention was that the divide between the middle class and the working class was declining, with affluent workers being subjected to 'embourgeoisement'. As living standards rose during this 'you've never had it so good' era, the working class had become less cohesive and less important, with some groups of manual workers even becoming 'middle class'. This theme was examined by Goldthorpe et al. (1969) in a widely quoted study of Luton car workers. While dismissing the idea of embourgeoisement, and concluding that affluent car workers were still working-class, the authors of the Luton study were faced with the conundrum that the lifestyles of most workers were family-centred and privatised, with work a source of money rather than of life satisfaction. The answer to this riddle provided by the *Affluent Worker* authors was that such workers were 'prototypical' – an advance guard whose lifestyles and attitudes would eventually be assumed by all workers in advanced capitalist societies. An alternative answer, suggested above, is that it is nothing new, having long been in evidence along with other working-class ways of life and cultures.

Class, then, has been on its deathbed for at least four decades. It has been buried, supposedly for good, on a number of occasions, resurrected from its grave a year or two later, only to be placed in its coffin once more. Yet the working class appears to be pushed into non-work concerns and home- and family-centred preoccupations because of both economic prosperity and rising affluence *and* economic recession. Economic change may be the root cause for class to lose its salience, but it seems unlikely that such different economic circumstances can lead to the same result.

Most varieties of the decline-of-class argument make claims about the relationships between economic change and social change. Such theories often have a strong predetermined and functionalist tint. Long-term economic processes, it is assumed, lead to changes in the class structure which then alter the social and political structure of society. A key issue is whether or not economic change is occurring on the lines suggested.

While accepting that Britain's economy and society are in a constant state of flux, we have argued against perspectives suggesting that there has been a revolution in British society. There is little solid empirical evidence to support either the broad outline or specific details of such contentions. And yet most contemporary end-of-class and fragmentation-of-class authors accept one or other of the 'post' this or that theories. There have recently been important changes in economic processes generally and work in Britain in particular. But, then, in both respects Britain has constantly been adjusting over the last two centuries. It is difficult to support the argument that the current shifts are more fundamental than any before as far as class is concerned. Particular types of work and the institutions associated with them evolve over time, and indeed come and go. A long historical perspective suggests the enduring, if transforming, character of class in Britain.

Similar criticisms can be applied to the non-class and consumption cleavage varieties of the decline-of-class thesis. One difficulty is the tendency to overgeneralisation. It is assumed that people within non-class sectoral divides are united by cohesive common interests. But not all home-owners derive capital gains, greater freedom and a wider housing choice. The same point applies to most of the non-class stratification characteristics that have been suggested. It is not possible to regard as in any sense socially privileged many people living in suburbs, or in rural areas or southern England. Equally, some of the young and old, inner-city dwellers, and people in the North are powerful and privileged.

Many supposed non-class sources of stratification lack theoretical or conceptual clarity. Proponents of consumption cleavages generally fail to provide a coherent explanation of the underlying basis of such divisions. Some authors have resorted to the unsupportable theory of a dominant ideology (see Chapter 11). This suggests that people are somehow duped into accepting owner-occupation and other privatised forms of consumption against their better (and unrecognised) class interests. Others have sought explanation for housing divides in the equally vague notion of 'ontological security', suggesting there are deep psychological reasons why owners may conflict with tenants. A further attempted solution is to argue that the basis of housing cleavages lies in the inherently different 'rights' attached to each form of property-ownership. In this view, home-owners necessarily have more rights over their property than do council tenants, and there is, consequently, an underlying conflict between the two groups.

In many cases what are presented as new non-class divides appear on closer examination to have strong class connotations. This applies particularly to much of the work on housing cleavages and the differences and conflicts between and within home-ownership and council renting. Some authors push this perspective further, agreeing that seemingly non-class consumption cleavages are class-related, but also arguing that class needs to be defined to take account of consumption and cultural issues. Seeing the construction of social classes as a consumption and cultural question, as well as springing from the economic organisation of society, also has some relevance to the debate about class and voting. It suggests that within-class voting may be influenced by consumption issues: working-class home-owners may vote Conservative rather than Labour because it is in their immediate class interests to do so.

There are other reasons for being cautious about the class and voting dealignment thesis. For example, some supposed non-class variables (such as housing tenure) may actually be no more than surrogates for class. Another argument is that, once the decline in the absolute size of the working class has been taken into account, the remaining fall in the Labour vote says more about the unpopularity of the Labour Party than the fragmentation or changing values of the working class. Labour support appears to have declined not only amongst manual workers but also across all classes.

The issue is partly one of whether British party politics has ever been class-based. Ideas about class dealignment appear of little value if the Labour Party is neither a socialist nor a working-class party. Similar questions can be raised about the class character of the Conservative Party. How people vote in Britain may be at best tangentialy related to class but, then, there would be little reason for expecting otherwise. More often than not the patterns of cause and effect are asserted rather than demonstrated. The importance of class is simply read off changing voting patterns. This is an inadequate procedure, dismissing the complexities of contemporary class and politics.

FURTHER READING

The most accessible account of long-term change in Britain's occupational structure is Routh (1987), although it is marred by unsubstantiated assertions about the superiority of professional and clerical work over manual work. His earlier book (Routh, 1980) is a more detailed analysis of occupations and pay in the period 1906–79.

A brief but fascinating account of the origins and evolution of the use of the word 'class' in the English language is provided by Williams (1983).

There are an immense number of books and articles about social class. Abercrombie and Warde (1988) provide a concise account of some of the main themes. Giddens (1980) is a much-quoted account of the class structure of capitalist societies in general. A particularly influential 1980s writer is the American E. O. Wright (1985).

The working class is reviewed by Roberts *et al.* (1977) and Roberts (1978). Discussion of the contemporary underclass is in Byrne and Parson (1983) and Gilroy (1987). Assessments of differing perspectives on the middle class are given by King and Raynor (1981) and Abercrombie and Urry (1983). Thrift (1987) is a review of the service-class concept and local case studies with a strong geographical tint. The special issue of *Marxism Today* (1988) explores the radically 'New Times' assumed by a number of authors on the left to have major consequences for class.

An early influential study of housing class is Rex and Moore (1967). Dunleavy (1980) and Saunders (1979 and 1984) are among the strongest proponents of consumption cleavages. The consumption cleavage debate, in both its Weberian and Marxist forms, is assessed by Gray (1982). Forrest and Murie (1987) emphasise the relationships between housing and class. The declining associations between class and voting are clearly argued by Franklin (1985) and Crewe (1988). Counter-interpretations of voting patterns are in Ball (1985) and Heath *et al.* (1985).

Apart from the Nuffield projects (see below), the only nationwide study adequately to combine theory with empirical research is that by researchers at the University of Essex. The main published account of this work

(Marshall *et al.*, 1988) is also an excellent guide to contemporary debates about class in Britain. None the less, the book is detailed and specialist. It can be sampled by reading Chapters 1, 8 and 10, and the concluding sections of the remaining chapters.

The Nuffield projects provide the best analysis of social mobility. The results are detailed in Goldthorpe (1980). It is also worthwhile looking at the second edition of the book (Goldthorpe, 1987) to see how debate about mobility – over gender differences and the impact of 1980s social change – has moved in a relatively short period. A more accessible if somewhat dated account of social mobility is Heath (1981).

Some of the best of the mounting body of work on the British class structure in history is Crossick (1978), Daunton (1983), Gray (1981), Kirk (1985), Mann (1986) and Stedman Jones (1983). An alternative source of valuable evidence is the work of writers alive during the nineteenth and early twentieth centuries, including Engels (1969), Tressell (1955) and Roberts (1971). Information about and case studies of working-class home-ownership in the past are given by Ball (1983), Franklin (1986 and 1987) and Rose (1987).

REFERENCES

Abercrombie, N., Hill, S. and Turner, B. S. (1980) *The Dominant Ideology Thesis*, Allen and Unwin, London.

Abercrombie, N. and Urry, J. (1983) *Capital, Labour and the Middle Classes*, Allen and Unwin, London.

Abercrombie, N. and Warde, A. (1988) *Contemporary British Society*, Polity Press, Cambridge.

Adams, M., Maybury, R. and Smith, W. (1988) 'Trends in the distribution of earnings, 1973 to 1986', *Employment Gazette*, February.

Aglietta, M. (1979) *A Theory of Capitalist Regulation*, Verso, London.

ALA (1988) *Tenants in Power*, Association of London Authorities, London.

Alford, B. (1981) 'New industries for old? British industry between the wars', in Floud and McCloskey (1981).

Allatt, P., Keil, T., Bryman, A. and Bytheway, B. (1987) *Women and the Life Cycle*, Macmillan, London.

Allat, P. and Yeandle, A. (1986) 'It's not fair, is it? Youth unemployment, family relations and the social contract', in Allen, S. *et al.* (1986).

Allen, S. and Walkowitz, C. (1987) *Homeworking: Myths and Realities*, Macmillan, London.

Allen, S., Waton, A., Purcell, K. and Wood, S., eds (1986) *The Experience of Unemployment*, Macmillan, London.

Ambrose, P. (1986) *Whatever Happened to Planning?*, Methuen, London.

Anderson, P. (1987) 'The figures of descent', *New Left Review*, 161, 20–77.

Armstrong, P., Glyn, A. and Harrison, J. (1984) *Capitalism since World War II*, Fontana Paperbacks, London.

Atkins, F. (1986) 'Thatcherism, populist authoritarianism and the search for a New Left strategy', *Capital and Class*, 28, 25–48.

Atkinson, A. (1983) *The Economics of Inequality*, Oxford University Press, Oxford.

Atkinson, A. and Harrison, A. (1978) *Distribution of Personal Wealth in Britain*, Cambridge University Press, Cambridge.

Atkinson, A., Hills, J. and Le Grand, J. (1987) 'The Welfare State', in Dornbusch and Layard (1987).

Atkinson, J. (1984) 'Manpower strategies for flexible organisations', *Personnel Management*, August.

Bacon, R. and Eltis, W. (1976) *Britain's Economic Problem: Too Few Producers*, Macmillan, London.

Ball, M. (1983) *Housing Policy and Economic Power*, Methuen, London.

Ball, M. (1985) 'Coming to terms with owner occupation', *Capital and Class*, 24, 42–57.

Ball, M. (1986) 'Housing analysis: time for a theoretical refocus?', *Housing Studies*, 1, 147–65.

Ball, M. (1988) *Rebuilding Construction. Economic Change and the British Construction Industry*, Routledge, London.

Ball, M., Harloe, M. and Martens, M. (1988) *Housing and Social Change in Europe and the USA*, Routledge, London.

Barnett, C. (1987) *The Audit of War*, Macmillan, Basingstoke.

Barr, N. (1987) *The Economics of the Welfare State*, Weidenfeld and Nicolson, London.

Barratt Brown, M. (1988) 'Away with the great arches: Anderson's history of British capitalism', *New Left Review*, 167, 22–52.

Bean, C. (1987) 'The impact of North Sea oil' in Dornbusch and Layard (1987).

Bean, C., Layard, R. and Nickell, S., eds (1987) *The Rise of Unemployment*, Basil Blackwell, Oxford.

Beckerman, W. (1985) 'How the battle against inflation was really won', *Lloyds Bank Review*, January, 1–13.

Beckerman, W. and Jenkinson, T. (1986) 'What stopped the inflation? Unemployment or commodity prices', *Economic Journal*, 96, 39–54.

Begg, D., Dornbusch, R. and Fischer, S. (1987) *Economics*, 2nd edition, McGraw Hill, Maidenhead.

Bell, D. (1976) *The Coming of Post-Industrial Society*, Penguin, Harmondsworth.

Belsey, A. (1986) 'The New Right, social order and civil liberties', in Levitas, R., ed., *The Ideology of the New Right*, Polity, Cambridge.

Bernstein, B. (1977) 'Social class, language and socialisation', in Karabel, J. and Halsey, A. H., eds., *Power and Ideology in Education*, Oxford University Press, New York.

Beurat, K. and Makings, L. (1987) 'I've got used to being independent now: women and courtship in a recession' in Allatt, P. *et al.*, eds, *Women and the Life Cycle*, Macmillan, London.

Beynon, H. (1973) *Working for Ford*, Allen and Unwin, London.

Beynon, H., ed. (1985) *Digging Deeper: Issues in the Miners' Strike*, Verso, London.

Black, J. and Stafford, D. (1988) *Housing Policy and Finance*, Routledge, London.

Blaug, M. (1984) 'Privatisation of education', in Le Grand, J. and Robinson, R., eds (1984), *Privatisation and the Welfare State*, Allen and Unwin, London.

Boddy, M. and Fudge, C. (1984) *Local Socialism?*, Macmillan, London.

Bourdieu, P. (1974) 'The school as a conservative force', in Eggleston, J., ed., *Contemporary Research in the Sociology of Education*, Methuen, London.

Bradshaw, J. (1987) 'Evaluating adequacy: the potential of budget standards', *Journal of Social Policy*, 322–431

Bowley, M. (1945) *Housing and the State*, Allen and Unwin, London.

Brah, A. (1986) 'Unemployment and racism: Asian youth on the dole', in Allan, S. *et al.*, eds, *The Experience of Unemployment*, Macmillan, London.

Braverman, H. (1974) *Labour and Monopoly Capital: the Degradation of Work in the Twentieth Century*, Monthly Review Press, New York.

Brown, M. (1983) *The Structure of Disadvantage*, Heinemann, London.

Bryman, B., Bytheway, B., Allatt, P. and Keil, T. (1987) *Rethinking the Life Cycle*, Macmillan, London.

Buiter, W. and Miller, M. (1983) 'The economic consequences of Mrs Thatcher', *Brookings Papers in Economic Activity*, 305–79.

Burgess, R. (1986) *Sociology, Education and Schools*, Batsford, London.

Burnett, J. (1986) *The Context of British Politics*, Hutchinson, London.

Byrne, D. and Parson, D. (1983) 'The state and the reserve army: the management of class relations in space', in Anderson, J., Duncan, S., and Hudson, R. eds, *Redundant Spaces in Cities and Regions*, Academic Press, London.

Caincross, A. (1987) *Years of Recovery: British Economic Policy 1945–51*, Methuen, London.

Calnan, M. (1987) *Health and Illness: the Long Perspective*, Tavistock, London.

Calnan, M. (1988) 'Towards a conceptual framework of lay evaluation of health care', *Social Science and Medicine*, 27, 927–33.

Campbell, B. (1984) *Wigan Pier Revisited*, Virago, London.

Carr-Hill, R. (1987) 'The inequalities in health debate: a critical review of the issues', *Journal of Social Policy*, 16, 509–42.

Carruth, A. and Oswald, A. (1987) 'Wage flexibility in Britain', *Oxford Economic Papers*, 49, 59–78.

Cavendish, R. (1982) *Women on the Line*, Routledge and Kegan Paul, London.

Coates, D. (1984) *The Context of British Politics*, Hutchinson, London.

Coates, D. and Hillard, J., eds (1987) *The Economic Revival of Modern Britain: the Debate between Left and Right*, Gower, Aldershot.

Cooke, K. (1987) 'The withdrawal from paid work of the wives of unemployed men: a review of research', *Journal of Social Policy*, 16, 371-82.

Connell, D. (1979) *The UK's Performance in Export Markets – Some Evidence from International Trade Data*, Discussion Paper 6, National Economic Development Office, London.

Cosgrave, P. (1985) *Thatcher: the First Term*, Bodley Head, London.

Cotterell, P. (1983) *Industrial Finance, 1830–1914*, Methuen, London.

Cox, A., Furlong, P. and Page, E. (1985) *Power in Capitalist Societies: Theory, Explanation and Cases*, Wheatsheaf Books, Brighton.

Cox, C. B. and Boyson, R., eds (1975) *Black Papers 1975*, J. M. Dent, London.

Coyle, A. (1984) *Redundant Women*, The Women's Press, London.

CPAG (n.d.) *Poverty, the Facts*, Child Poverty Action Group, London.

Crewe, I. (1988) 'The grim challenge of the ballot box', *Guardian*, 1 October.

Crossick, G. (1978) *An Artisan Elite in Victorian Society*, Croom Helm, London.

Crouzet, F. (1982) *The Victorian Economy*, Methuen, London.

Culyer, A. and Jonsson, B. (1986) *Public and Private Health Services*, Basil Blackwell, Oxford.

Cutler, T., Williams, K. and Williams, J. (1986) *Keynes, Beveridge and Beyond*, Routledge and Kegan Paul, London.

Daunton, M. (1983) *House and Home in the Victorian City*, Edward Arnold, London.

Davies, S. and Caves, R. (1987) *Britain's Productivity Gap*, Cambridge University Press, Cambridge.

Dearden, S. (1986) 'EEC membership and the United Kingdom's trade in manufactured goods', *National Westminster Bank Review*, February, 15–25.

Dearlove, J. and Saunders, P. (1984) *Introduction to British Politics*, Polity, Cambridge.

Department of Education and Science (1972) *Education: A Framework for Expansion*, Cmnd 2174, HMSO, London.

Department of Education and Science (1988) *Top-up Loans for Students*, Cmnd   , HMSO, London.

DHSS (1976) *Sharing Resources for Health in England: Report of the Resource Allocation Working Party*, HMSO, London.

DoE (1985) *An Inquiry into the Condition of the Local Authority Housing Stock in England*, Department of the Environment, London.

Dex, S. (1985) *The Sexual Division of Work*, Wheatsheaf, Brighton.

Donnison, D. (1988) 'Defining and measuring poverty: a reply to Stein Ringen', *Journal of Social Policy*, 17, 367–74.

Dornbusch, R. and Layard, R., eds (1987) *The Performance of the British Economy*, Clarendon Press, Oxford.

Douglas, J. W. B. (1964) *The Home and the School*, McGibbon and Kee, London.

Douglas, J. W. B. (1968) *All Our Future*, Peter Davies, London.

Dow, C. (1987) 'A critique of monetary policy', *Lloyds Bank Review*, October, 20–32.

Doyal, L. (1979) *The Political Economy of Health*, Pluto, London.

Duncan, S. and Goodwin, M. (1988) *The Local State and Uneven Development*, Polity Press, Cambridge.

Dunleavy, P. (1980) *Urban Political Analysis*, Macmillan, London.

Dunleavy, P. and Husbands, C. (1985) *British Democracy at the Crossroads*, Allen and Unwin, London.

Dunleavy, P. and O'Leary, B. (1987) *Theories of the State: the Politics of Liberal Democracy*, Macmillan, London.

Dunning, J. (1985) 'Multinational enterprises and industrial restructuring in the UK', *Lloyds Bank Review*, October, 1–19.

Ehrenreich, B. and English, D. (1979) *For Her Own Good*, Pluto, London.

Elbaum, B. and Lazonick, W., eds (1987) *The Decline of the British Economy*, Oxford University Press, Oxford.

Engels, F. (1969) *The Condition of the Working Class in England*, Panther, London.

Equal Opportunities Commission, (1987) *Women and Men in Britain: a Statistical Profile*, HMSO, London.

Eysenck, H. (1971) *Race, Intelligence and Education*, Temple Smith, London.

Feminist Review (1986) *Waged Work: a Reader*, Virago, London.

Fieldhouse, D. (1973) *Economics and Empire 1830-1914*, Macmillan, London.

Fine, B. (1988) *Marx's Capital*, Macmillan, London.

Fine, B. and Harris, L. (1985) *The Peculiarities of the British Economy*, Lawrence and Wishart, London.

Floud, R. and McCloskey, D., eds (1981) *The Economic History of Britain since 1700*, Volume 2: *1860 to the 1970s*, Cambridge University Press, Cambridge.

Foreman-Peck, J. (1983) *A History of the World Economy*, Wheatsheaf, Brighton.

Forrest, R. and Murie, A. (1987) 'The affluent home-owner: labour market position and the shaping of housing histories', in Thrift, N. and Williams, P., eds,

Class and Space: the Making of Urban Society, Routledge and Kegan Paul, London.

Forrest, R. and Murie, A. (1988) *Selling the Welfare State*, Routledge, London.

Franklin, A. (1986) 'Owner occupation, privatism and ontological security: a critical reformulation', School for Advanced Urban Studies Working Paper, University of Bristol.

Franklin, A. (1987) 'Working-class privatism: an historical case study of Bedminster, Bristol', School for Advanced Urban Studies Working Paper, University of Bristol.

Franklin, M. (1985) *The Decline of Working-Class Voting in Britain*, Clarendon Press, Oxford.

Fraser, D. (1973) *The Evolution of the British Welfare State*, Macmillan, London.

Freeman, R. (1988) 'Labour market institutions and economic performance', *Economic Policy*, 6, 64–78.

Fryer, D. and Warr, P. B. (1984) 'Unemployment and cognitive difficulties', *British Journal of Clinical Psychology*, 23, 67–8.

Gamble, A. (1981) *Britain in Decline*, Macmillan, London.

Gamble, A. (1988) *The Free Economy and the Strong State*, Macmillan, London.

General Medical Services Committee (1979) *Report of the New Charter Working Group*, British Medical Association, London.

Gershuny, J. (1978) *After Industrial Society? The Emerging Service Economy*, Macmillan, London.

Gershuny, J. and Miles, I. (1983) *The New Service Economy*, Frances Pinter, Brighton.

Giddens, A. (1980) *The Class Structure of Advanced Societies*, Hutchinson, London.

Gillies, D. *et al.* (1984) 'Analysis of ethnic differences on still births', *Journal of Epidemiology and Community Health*, 38, 214–17.

Gilroy, P. (1987) *There Ain't No Black in the Union Jack*, Hutchinson, London.

Goldthorpe, J. (1980) *Social Mobility and Class Structure in Modern Britain*, Oxford University Press, Oxford (1st edition).

Goldthorpe, J. (1987) *Social Mobility and Class Structure in Modern Britain*, Oxford University Press, Oxford (2nd edition).

Goldthorpe, J., Lockwood, D., Bechhofer, F. and Platt, J. (1969) *The Affluent Worker in the Class Structure*, Cambridge University Press, Cambridge.

Gordon, D. (1988) 'The global economy: new edifice or crumbling foundations?', *New Left Review*, 168, 24–64

Gorz, A. (1982) *Farewell to the Working Class: an Essay on Post-Industrial Society*, Pluto Press, London.

Gray, F. (1982) 'Owner occupation and social relations', in Merrett, S. with Gray, F., *Owner Occupation in Britain*, Routledge and Kegan Paul, London.

Gray, R. (1981) *The Aristocracy of Labour in Nineteenth Century Britain*, Macmillan, London.

Greater London Council (1985) *London Industrial Strategy*, GLC, London.

Green, D. R. (1987) *The New Right: the Counter-Revolution in Political, Economic and Social Thought*, Wheatsheaf, Brighton.

Hall, S. (1979) 'The Great Moving Right Show', *Marxism Today*, 23, 1.

Hall, S. (1984) 'The rise of the representative/interventionist state, 1880s–1920s', in McLennan, G., Held, D. and Hall, S., eds, *State and Society in Contemporary Britain: a Critical Introduction*, Polity Press, Cambridge.

Hall, S. (1985) 'Authoritarian populism: a reply', *New Left Review*, 151, 115–24.

Hall, S. (1988) *The Hard Road to Renewal: Thatcherism and the Crisis of the Left*, Verso, London.

Halpern, S. (1985) 'What the public thinks of the NHS', *Health and Social Services Journal*, 702–4.

Halsey, A. (1987) 'Social trends since World War II', *Social Trends*, 17, HMSO.

Halsey, A., Heath, A. and Ridge, J. (1980) *Origins and Destinations*, Clarendon Press, Oxford.

Ham, C. and Hill, M. (1984) *The Policy Process in the Modern Capitalist State*, Wheatsheaf, Brighton.

Hardach, G. (1987) *The First World War*, Penguin Books, Harmondsworth.

Harley, C. and McCloskey, D. (1981) 'Foreign trade: competition and the expanding international economy', in Floud, R. and McCloskey, D., eds., *The Economic History of Britain since 1700*, Vol. 2: *1860 to the 1970s*, Cambridge University Press, Cambridge.

Harris, C. C. (1987) *Redundancy and Recession in South Wales*, Basil Blackwell, Oxford.

Harris, K. (1988) *Thatcher*, Weidenfeld and Nicolson, London.

Harris, L. and Coakley, J. (1984) *The City of Capital*, Basil Blackwell, Oxford.

Harris, L., Coakley, J., Croasdale, M. and Evans, T., eds (1988) *New Perspectives on the Financial System*, Croom Helm, London.

Hayek, F. A. (1980) *1980s Unemployment and the Unions*, IEA, London.

Heath, A. (1981) *Social Mobility*, Fontana Paperbacks, London.

Heath, A., Jowell, R. and Curtice, J. (1985) *How Britain Votes*, Pergamon Press, Oxford.

Hedstron, P. and Ringen, S. (1987) 'Age and income in contemporary society: a research note', *Journal of Social Policy*, 16, 227–39.

Held, D. (1984a) 'Power and legitimacy in contemporary Britain', in McLennan *et al.* (1984).

Held, D., ed. (1984b) *States and Societies*, Martin Robertson, London.

Hewison, R. (1987) *The Heritage Industry*, Methuen, London.

Higgins, J. (1988) *The Business of Medicine: the Private Market in Health Care in Britain*, Macmillan, London.

Higgins, J. (1988a) 'The private market in health care', *ESRC Newslatter*, 62, June, 8–10.

Hillard, J. (1986) 'Thatcherism and decline' in Coates, D. and Hillard, J., eds, *The Economic Decline of Modern Britain*, Wheatsheaf Books, Brighton.

Hillyard, P. and Percy-Smith, J. (1988) *The Coercive State*, Fontana, London.

Hindess, B. (1987) *Freedom, Equality, and the Market: arguments on Social Policy*, Tavistock Publications, London.

Hinton, J. (1983) *Labour and Socialism: a History of the British Labour Movement 1867–1974*, Wheatsheaf Books, Brighton.

Hird, C. and Irvine, J. (1979) 'A critique of wealth statistics', in Irvine, J. and Miles, J., eds, *Demystifying Social Statistics*, Pluto Press, London.

HMSO (1980) *The Government's Expenditure Plans 1980–81 to 1983–84*, Cmnd 7841.

HMSO (1981) *The Brixton Disorders, 10–12 April 1981: Report of an Inquiry by Lord Scarman*, Cmnd 8427.

HMSO (1986) *The Government's Expenditure Plans, 1986 to 1989*, Vol. II, Cmnd 9202–11.

HMSO (1987) 'The distribution of income in the United Kingdom, 1984–85', *Economic Trends*, 409, 94–104.

HMSO (1988a) *The Government's Expenditure Plans 1988–89 to 1990–91*, Vol. I, Cm 288–11.

HMSO (1988b) *The Government's Expenditure Plans 1988–89 to 1990–91*, Vol. II, Cm 288–11.

HMSO (1989) *Working for Patients*, Cm 555.

Hobsbawm, E. (1969) *Industry and Empire*, Penguin, Harmondsworth.

Hobsbawm, E. (1981) 'The forward march of labour halted', in Jacques, M. and Mulhern, F., eds, *The*

Forward March of Labour Halted?, New Left Books, London.

Hoggart, R. (1957) *The Uses of Literacy*, Chatto and Windus, London.

Hope, T. and Shaw, M., eds (1988) *Communities and Crime Reduction*, Home Office Research and Planning Unit, HMSO, London.

House of Lords Committee (1985) *Report from the Select Committee on Overseas Trade*, HMSO, London.

HPR (1977) *Housing Policy Review*, Technical Volume 1, HMSO, London.

Hunt, M. (1987) *Cleaning and Catering*, West Yorkshire Low Pay Unit, Batley, Yorkshire.

Ingham, G. (1984) *Capitalism Divided? The City and Industry in British Social Development*, Macmillan, London.

Jarvis, V. and Prais, S. (1988) *Two Nations of Shopkeepers: Training for Retailing in France and Britain*, Discussion Paper 140, NIESR, London.

Jencks, C. et al. (1972) *Inequality: A Reassessment of the Effect of Family and Schooling in America*, Basic Books, New York.

Jenkins, R. (1987) *Transnational Corporations and Uneven Development*, Methuen, London.

Jenkinson, T. (1987) 'The natural rate of unemployment: does it exist?', *Oxford Review of Economic Policy*, 3, 3, 20–6.

Jensen, A. (1973) *Educability and Group Differences*, Methuen, London.

Jessop, B. (1982) *The Capitalist State*, Martin Robertson, Oxford.

Jessop, B., Bonnett, K., Bromley, S. and Ling, T. (1984) 'Authoritarian populism, two nations and Thatcherism', *New Left Review*, 147, 32–60.

Jessop, B., Bonnett, K., Bromley, S. and Ling, T. (1987)

'Popular capitalism, flexible accumulation and left strategy', *New Left Review*, 165, 104–22.

Jones, D. (1985) *The Import Threat to the UK Car Industry*, Science Policy Research Unit, University of Sussex, Brighton.

Jordan, A. G. and Richardson, J. J. (1987) *British Politics and the Policy Process*, Allen and Unwin, London.

Jordan, B. (1985) *The State: Authority and Autonomy*, Basil Blackwell, Oxford.

Joseph, K. and Sumption, J. (1979) *Equality*, John Murray, London.

Jowell, R., Witherspoon, S. and Brook, L., eds (1987) *British Social Attitudes, 1987 Report*, Gower, Aldershot.

Kahn, A. (1946) *Great Britain in the World Economy*, New York.

Kaldor, N. (1982) *The Scourge of Monetarism*, Oxford University Press, Oxford.

Kaldor, N., Sharp, M. and Walker, W. (1986) 'Industrial competitiveness and Britain's defence', *Lloyds Bank Review*, 162, 31–49.

Katrak, H. (1973) 'Human skills, research and development, and scale economies in exports of the UK and USA', *Oxford Economic Papers*, 25, 337–60.

Kavanagh, D. (1985) *British Politics, Continuities and Change*, Oxford University Press, Oxford.

Kavanagh, D. (1987) *Thatcherism and British Politics: the End of Consensus?*, Oxford University Press, Oxford.

Kay, J. and Thompson, D. (1986) 'Privatisation: a policy in search of a rationale', *Economic Journal*, 96, 18–32.

Kay, J. and Thompson, D. (1987) 'Policy for industry', in Dornbusch, R. and Layard, R., eds, *The Performance of the British Economy*, Clarendon Press, Oxford.

Kettle, M., and Hodges, L. (1982) *Uprising! The Police, the People and the Riots in Britain's Cities*, Pan, London.

Keynes, J. (1936) *The General Theory of Employment, Interest and Money*, Macmillan, London.

Kilpatrick, A. and Lawson, A. (1980) 'On the nature of industrial decline', *Cambridge Journal of Economics*, 4, 85–102.

King, M. and Atkinson, A. (1980) 'Housing policy, taxation and reform', *Midland Bank Review*, Spring, 7–15.

King, D. (1987) *The New Right: Politics, Markets and Citizenship*, Macmillan, London.

King, R. and Raynor, J. (1981) *The Middle Class*, Longman, London.

King, S. (1988) 'Temporary workers in Britain', *Employment Gazette*, Vol. 96, 238–47.

Kirk, N. (1985) *The Growth of Working Class Reformism in Mid-Victorian England*, Croom Helm, London.

Krieger, J. (1986) *Reagan, Thatcher and the Politics of Decline*, Polity, Cambridge.

Lash, S. and Urry, J. (1987) *The End of Organised Capital*, Polity, Cambridge.

Lawson, J. and Silver, H. (1973) *A Social History of Education in England*, Methuen, London.

Layard, R. and Nickell, S. (1987) 'The labour market', in Dornbusch, R. and Layard, R., eds, *The Performance of the British Economy*, Clarendon Press, Oxford.

Leadbeater, C. (1988) 'Power to the person', *Marxism Today*, October, 14–19.

Leadbeater, C. and Lloyd, J. (1987) *In Search of Work*, Penguin, Harmondsworth.

Le Grand, J. (1982) *The Strategy of Equality: Redistribution and the Social Services*, Allen and Unwin, London.

Le Grand, J. and Robinson, R., eds (1984) *Privatisation and the Welfare State*, Allen and Unwin, London.

Lee, C. (1986) *The British Economy since 1700*, Cambridge University Press, Cambridge.

Levitas, R., ed. (1986) *The Ideology of the New Right*, Polity, Cambridge.

Lipietz, A. (1987) *Mirages and Miracles*, Verso Books, London.

Lovering, J. (1985) 'Regional intervention, defence industries and the structuring of space in Britain: the case of Bristol and South Wales', *Environment and Planning: Society and Space*, 3, 85–107.

Lovering, J. and Boddy, M. (1988) 'The geography of military industry', *Area*, 20, 1, 41–51.

Lukes, S. (1984) 'The future of British socialism?' in Pimlott, B., ed., *Fabian Essays in Socialist Thought*, Heinemann, London.

McBride, T. (1976) *The Domestic Revolution*, Oxford University Press, Oxford.

MacGregor, I. with Tyler, R. (1986) *The Enemies Within: the Story of the Miners' Strike, 1984–5*, Collins, London.

MacInnes, J. (1987) *Thatcherism at Work*, Open University Press, Milton Keynes.

McIntosh, M. (1984) 'The family regulation and the public sphere', in McLennan, G. *et al.*, eds, *State and Society in Contemporary Britain: A Critical Introduction*, Polity, Cambridge.

Mackintosh, J. P. (1982) *The Government and Politics of Britain*, Hutchinson, London (5th edition, revised by P. Richard).

McLennan, G. (1984) 'The contours of British politics: representative democracy and social class', in McLennan *et al.* (1984).

McLennan, G., Held, D. and Hall, S., eds (1984) *State and Society in Contemporary Britain: a Critical Introduction*, Polity, Cambridge.

Macnicol, J. (1987) 'In pursuit of the Underclass', *Journal of Social Policy*, 293–318.

Mack, J. and Lansley, S. (1985) *Poor Britain*, Allen and Unwin, London.

Malpass, P., ed. (1986) *The Housing Crisis*, Croom Helm, London.

Mann, K. (1986) 'The making of a claiming class', *Critical Social Policy*, 15.

Marmot, M., Adelstein, A. and Bulusu, L. (1984) 'Immigrant mortality in England and Wales, 1970–78', *OPCS Studies on Medical and Population Subjects*, No. 47, HMSO, London.

Marshall, G., Newby, H., Rose, D. and Vogler, C. (1988) *Social Class in Modern Britain*, Hutchinson, London.

Martin, J. and Roberts, C. (1984) 'Women and employment: a lifetime perspective' *Social Survey*, SS 1143, OPCS, London.

Martin, R. and Rowthorn, B., eds (1986) *The Geography of Deindustrialisation*, Macmillan, London.

Marxism Today (1988) 'New Times', 22, 10 October.

Massey, D. (1984) *Spatial Divisions of Labour*, Macmillan, London.

Matthews, R., Feinstein, C. and Odling-Smee, J. (1982) *British Economic Growth, 1856–1973*, Clarendon Press, Oxford.

Mayer, C. (1987) 'The assessment: financial systems and corporate investment', *Oxford Review of Economic Policy*, 3, 4, i-xvi.

Merrett, S., with Gray, F. (1982) *Owner Occupation in Britain*, Routledge and Kegan Paul, London.

Middlemas, K. (1979) *Politics in Industrial Society: the Experience of the British System since 1911*, André Deutsch, London.

Miliband, R. (1969) *The State of Capitalist Society*, Weidenfeld, London.

Miliband, R. (1982) *Capitalist Democracy in Britain*, Oxford University Press, Oxford.

Miliband, R., Panitch, L. and Saville, J., eds (1987) *Socialist Register*, Merlin, London.

Minford, P. and Matthews, K. (1987) 'Mrs Thatcher's economic policies', *Economic Policy*, 5, 57–102.

Minford, P., Peel, M. and Ashton, P. (1987) *The Housing Morass: Regulation, Immobility and Unemployment*, Institute of Economic Affairs, London.

Minns, R. (1980) *Pension Funds and British Capitalism*, Heinemann, London.

Moran, M. (1985) *Politics and Society in Britain: and Introduction*, Macmillan, London.

Morris, C. and Preston, I. (1986) 'Taxes, benefits and the distribution of income, 1968–83', *Fiscal Studies*, 7, 4, 18–27.

Morris, L. (1987) 'The life cycle and the labour market in Hartlepool', in Bryman *et al.* (1987).

Mowat, C. L. (1968) *Britain between the Wars*, Methuen, London.

Muellbauer, J. (1986) 'The assessment: productivity and competitiveness in British manufacturing', *Oxford Review of Economic Policy*, 2.

Murie, A. and Malpass, P. (1987) *Housing Policy and Practice*, Macmillan, London.

Murray, R. (1981) *Multinationals beyond the Market*, Harvester Press, Brighton.

Murray, R. (1988) 'Life after Henry (Ford)', *Marxism Today*, October.

Nichols, T. (1986) *The British Worker Question: A New Look at Workers and Productivity in Manufacturing*, Routledge and Kegan Paul, London.

NIESR (1982) *The British Economy*, Heinemann Educational Books, London.

NUPE (n.d.) *A Fair Deal for Part-Time Workers*, National Union of Public Employees, London.

OECD (1988) *OECD Economic Surveys: United Kingdom, 1987/88*, Organisation for Economic Co-operation and Development, Paris.

Offer, A. (1980) 'Ricardo's paradox and the movement of rents in England, *c*.1870–1910', *Economic History Review*, 2nd series, 33, 236–52.

OPCS (1986) 'Mortality statistics, perinatal and infant: social and biological factors for 1984', Series DH3, No. 17, HMSO, London.

Oulton, N. (1987) 'Plant closures and the productivity "miracle" in manufacturing', *National Institute Economic Review*, August, 53–9.

Pahl, R. (1984) *Divisions of Labour*, Basil Blackwell, Oxford.

Pahl, R. (1988) *On Work*, Basil Blackwell, Oxford.

Peacock, A. and Wiseman, J. (1968) *The Growth of Public Expenditure in the UK*, Allen and Unwin, London.

Phillips, D. R. and Vincent, J. A. (1986) 'Petit bourgeois care: private residential care for the elderly', *Policy and Politics*, 14, 189–208.

Piachaud, D. (1987) 'The growth of poverty', in Walker, A. and Walker, C., eds, *The Growing Divide*, Child Poverty Action Group, London.

Piachaud, D. (1988) 'Poverty in Britain, 1899 to 1983', *Journal of Social Policy*, 17, 335–50.

Piore, M. J. and Sabel, C. F. (1984) *The Second Industrial Divide: Possibilities for Prosperity*, Basic Books, New York.

Plender, J. (1984) *That's the Way the Money Goes*, Weidenfeld and Nicolson, London.

Plowden Report (1967) *Children and Their Primary Schools: a Report of the Central Advisory Council for Education*, HMSO, London.

Policing London (1987) 30, December.

Pollard, S. (1983) *The Development of the British Economy: 1914–1980*, Edward Arnold, London (3rd edition).

Pollert, A. (1988a) 'Dismantling flexibility', *Capital and Class*, 34, 42–75.

Pollert, A. (1988b) 'The "flexible firm": fixation or fact?' *Work, Employment and Society*, 2, 281–316.

Pollitt, C. (1984) 'The state and health care', in McLennan *et al.* (1984).

Posner, M. and Sargent, J. (1987) 'A case of Eurosclerosis?', *Midland Bank Review*, 9–17.

Prais, S. (1981) *Productivity and Industrial Structure: a*

Statistical Study of Manufacturing Industry in Britain, Germany and the United States, Cambridge University Press, Cambridge.

Pratten, C. (1976) *Labour Productivity Differentials within International Companies*, Cambridge University Press, Cambridge.

Pratten, C. (1986) 'The importance of giant companies', *Lloyds Bank Review*, 159, 33–48.

Purcell, K., Wood, S., Waton, A and Allen, S., eds (1986) *The Changing Experience of Employment: Restructuring and Recession*, Macmillan, London.

Ray, G. (1987) 'Labour costs in manufacturing', *National Institute Economic Review*, May, 71–4.

Rex, J. and Moore, R. (1967) *Race, Community and Conflict: a Study of Sparkbrook*, Oxford University Press, Oxford.

Roberts, K. (1978) *The Working Class*, Longman, London.

Roberts, K., Cook, F., Clark, S. and Semeonoff, E. (1977) *The Fragmentary Class Structure*, Heinemann, London.

Roberts, R. (1971) *The Classic Slum*, Penguin, Harmondsworth.

Robinson, E. (1968) *The New Polytechnics*, Penguin, Harmondsworth.

Rose, D. (1987) 'Home ownership, subsistence and historical change: the mining district of West Cornwall in the late nineteenth century', in Thrift, N. and Williams, P., eds, *Class and Space: the Making of Urban Society*, Routledge and Kegan Paul, London.

Rose, M. (1988) *Industrial Behaviour: Research and Control*, Penguin, Harmondsworth.

Routh, G. (1980) *Occupation and Pay in Great Britain 1906–79*, Macmillan, London.

Routh, G. (1987) *Occupations of the People of Great Britain, 1801–1981*, Macmillan, London.

Rowthorn, R. (1980) *Capitalism, Conflict and Inflation*, Lawrence and Wishart, London.

Rowthorn, R. and Wells, J. (1987) *Deindustrialisation and*

Foreign Trade, Cambridge University Press, Cambridge.

Rubery, J. ed. (1988) *Women and Recession*, Routledge and Kegan Paul, London.

Rubinstein, W. (1986) *Wealth and Inequality in Britain*, Faber and Faber, London.

Rustin, M. (1986) 'Lessons from the London Industrial Strategy', *New Left Review*, 155, 75–85.

Rutter, M. and Madge, N. (1976) *Cycles of Disadvantage*, Heinemann, London.

Rutter, M., Maughan, B., Mortimore, P. and Ouston, J. with Smith, A. (1979) *Fifteen Thousand Hours*, Open Books, London.

Sarlvik, B. and Crewe, I. (1983) *Decade of Dealignment*, Cambridge University Press, Cambridge.

Saunders, P. (1979) *Urban Politics: a Sociological Investigation*, Hutchinson, London.

Saunders, P. (1984) 'Beyond housing classes: the sociological significance of property rights and means of consumption', *International Journal of Urban and Regional Research*, 8, 202–27.

Saunders, P. (1985) 'Space, the city and urban sociology', in Gregory, D. and Urry, J., eds, *Social Relations and Spatial Structures*, Macmillan, London.

Savage, D. and Biswas, R. (1986) 'An analysis of post-war growth rates and an illustrative long-term projection', *National Institute Economic Review*, November, 59–69.

Scott, A. (1988) 'Flexible production systems and regional development', *International Journal of Urban and Regional Research*, 12, 171–85.

Scott, A. and Storper, M., eds (1986) *Production, Work and Territory*, Allen and Unwin, London.

Scott, J. (1982) *The Upper Classes*, Macmillan, London.

Simmie, J. and James, N. (1986) 'The money map of defence', *New Society*, 31, January, 179–80.

Singh, A. (1977) 'UK industry and the world economy: a case of deindustrialisation', *Cambridge Journal of Economics*, 1, 113–36.

Skidelsky, R., ed. (1988) *Thatcherism*, Chatto and Windus, London.

Smith, A. (1776) *The Wealth of Nations*, abridged 1970 version, ed. Skinner, A., Penguin, Harmondsworth.

Smith, D. (1987) *The Rise and Fall of Monetarism*, Penguin, Harmondsworth.

Solow, R. (1987a) 'Unemployment: getting the questions right', in Bean, C., Layard, R. and Nickell, S., eds, *The Rise in Unemployment*, Basil Blackwell, Oxford.

Solow, R. (1987b) 'The Conservative revolution: a round-table discussion', *Economic Policy*, 181–5.

Spender, D. and Sarah, E., eds (1980) *Learning to Lose*, The Women's Press, London.

Spring-Rice, M. (1939) *Working-Class Wives*, Penguin Books, Harmondsworth (second edition Virago, 1981).

Stanworth, M. (1983) *Gender and Schooling*, Hutchinson, London.

Stedman Jones, G. (1974) *Outcast London*, Oxford University Press, Oxford.

Stedman Jones, G. (1983) *The Language of Class*, Cambridge University Press, Cambridge.

Stopford, J. and Turner, L. (1985) *Britain and the Multinationals*, John Wiley, Chichester.

Taylor, I. (1987) 'Law and order, moral disorder: the changing rhetorics of the Thatcher', in Miliband, R. *et al.*, eds, *Socialist Register*, Merlin, London.

Taylor-Gooby, P. (1986) 'Privatisation, power and the welfare state', *Sociology*, 20, 228–46.

Tebbit, N. (1985) in the *Guardian*, 15 November.

Thane, P. (1982) *The Foundations of the Welfare State*, Longman, London.

Therborn, G. (1984) 'The prospects of labour and the transformation of advanced capitalism', *New Left Review*, 145, 5–38.

Thirwall, A. (1982a) *Balance of Payments Theory and the United Kingdom Experience*, Macmillan, London.

Thirwall, A. (1982b) 'Deindustrialisation in the United Kingdom', *Lloyds Bank Review*, April, 22–37.

Thompson, E. P. (1980) 'The secret state' in Thompson, E. P., ed., *Writing by Candlelight*, Merlin, London.

Thompson, G. (1984) 'Economic intervention in the post-war economy', in McLennan, G. *et al.*, eds, *State and Society in Contemporary Britain: a Critical Introduction*, Polity, Cambridge.

Thrift, N. (1987) 'Introduction: the geography of late twentieth-century class formation', in Thrift, N. and Williams, P., eds, *Class and Space: the Making or Urban Society*, Routledge and Kegan Paul, London.

Townsend, P. (1979) *Poverty in the United Kingdom*, Penguin Books, Harmondsworth.

Townsend, P. and Davidson, N., eds (1982) *The Black Report*, Penguin, London.

Townsend, P., Davidson, N. and Whitehead, M. (1988) *Inequalities in Health*, Penguin, London.

Tressell, R. (1955) *The Ragged Trousered Philanthropists*, Lawrence and Wishart, London.

Tunstall, J., ed. (1974) *The Open University Opens*, Routledge and Kegan Paul, London.

UNCTC (1983) *Transnational Corporations in World Development: Third Survey*, United Nations Centre on Transnational Corporations, New York.

Urry, J. (1985) 'The Class Structure', in Coates, D., Johnston, G. and Bush, R., eds, *A Socialist Anatomy of Britain*, Polity, Cambridge.

Vane, H. R. and Caslin, T. (1987) *Current Controversies in Economics*, Basil Blackwell, Oxford.

de Vroey, M. (1984) 'A regulation approach interpretation

of the contemporary crisis', *Capital and Class*, 23, 45–66.

Wainwright, H. (1988) *Labour: a Tale of Two Parties*, Hogarth Press, London.

Walby, S. (1986) *Patriarchy at Work*, Polity Press, Oxford.

Wallington, P., ed. (1984) *Civil Liberties 1984*, Martin Robertson, Oxford.

Walker, R. (1987) 'Consensual approaches to poverty: towards a methodological alternative', *Journal of Social Policy*, 213–26.

Warde, A. (1985) 'The homogenisation of space? Trends in the spatial division of labour in twentieth-century Britain', in Newby, H. *et al.*, eds, *Restructuring Capital*, Macmillan, London.

Warr, P. B. and Jackson, P. R. (1984) 'Men without jobs: some correlates of age and length of employment', *Journal of Occupational Psychology*, 57, 77–85.

Warren, B. (1980) *Imperialism: Pioneer of Capitalism*, Verso Books, London.

Webster, J. (1986) 'Word processing and the secretarial labour process', in Purcell, K. *et al.*, eds, *The Changing Experience of Employment*, Macmillan, London.

West, P. (1976) 'The physician and treatment of childhood epilepsy', in Wadsworth, M. and Robinson, D., eds, *Studies in Everyday Medical Life*, Martin Robertson, London.

Westwood, S. (1984) *All Day, Every Day*, Pluto, London.

Whitehead, M. (1988) *The Health Divide: Inequalities in Health in the 1980s*, Health Education Council, London.

Wiener, M. (1981) *English Culture and the Decline of the Industrial Spirit*, Cambridge University Press, Cambridge.

Wilkinson, R. (1986) *Class and Health*, Tavistock, London.

Williams, A., ed. (1987) *Health and Economics*, Macmillan, London.

Williams, K., Williams, J. and Thomas, D. (1983) *Why Are the British Bad at Manufacturing?*, Routledge and Kegan Paul, London.

Williams, K., Williams, J. and Haslam, C. (1987) *The Breakdown of Austin Rover*, Berg, Leamington Spa.

Williams, R. (1983) *Keywords*, Fontana, London.

Williamson, J. (1985) *Did British Capitalism Breed Inequality?*, Allen and Unwin, Boston.

Willis, P. (1984) 'Youth unemployment', *New Society*, 67, 475–7.

Wilson Committee (1980) *Report of the Committee Reviewing the Functioning of the Financial Institutions*, Cmnd 7937, HMSO, London.

Wolch, J. and Dear, M., eds (1988) *The Power of Geography: How Territory Shapes Social Life*, Unwin Hyman, London.

Wood, S., ed. (1982) *The Degradation of Work?*, Hutchinson, London.

World Bank (1987) *World Development Report*, Oxford University Press, Oxford.

Wright, E. (1985) *Classes*, Verso, London.

Wright, P. (1987) *On Living in an Old Country*, Verso, London.

Young, M. (1958) *The Rise of the Meritocracy*, Thames and Hudson, London.

Young, M. and Willmott, P. (1962) *Family and Kinship in East London*, Penguin, Harmondsworth.

AUTHOR INDEX

AUTHOR INDEX

SUBJECT INDEX